Achieving Business Excellence Through Triple Transformation

Meltem Okur Dinçsoy
Trakya University, Turkey

Hamit Can
Trakya University, Turkey

IGI Global
Scientific Publishing
Publishing Tomorrow's Research Today

Vice President of Editorial	Melissa Wagner
Managing Editor of Acquisitions	Mikaela Felty
Managing Editor of Book Development	Jocelynn Hessler
Production Manager	Mike Brehm
Cover Design	Phillip Shickler

Published in the United States of America by
IGI Global Scientific Publishing
701 East Chocolate Avenue
Hershey, PA, 17033, USA
Tel: 717-533-8845
Fax: 717-533-8661
Website: https://www.igi-global.com E-mail: cust@igi-global.com

Library of Congress Cataloging-in-Publication Data

Names: Okur Dinçsoy, Meltem, 1974- editor. | Can, Hamit, 1988- editor.
Title: Achieving business excellence through triple transformation / edited by Meltem Okur Dinçsoy, Hamit Can.
Description: Hershey, PA : IGI Global Scientific Publishing, [2025] | Includes bibliographical references and index. | Summary: "The primary objective of the book is to provide business leaders, entrepreneurs, and scholars with a structured and actionable framework that integrates digital, cultural, and strategic transformations as a pathway to sustained business excellence"-- Provided by publisher.
Identifiers: LCCN 2024055456 (print) | LCCN 2024055457 (ebook) | ISBN 9798369394359 (hardcover) | ISBN 9798369394366 (paperback) | ISBN 9798369394373 (ebook)
Subjects: LCSH: Organizational change. | Success in business.
Classification: LCC HD58.8 .A286 2025 (print) | LCC HD58.8 (ebook) | DDC 658.4/06--dc23/eng/20250130
LC record available at https://lccn.loc.gov/2024055456
LC ebook record available at https://lccn.loc.gov/2024055457

British Cataloguing in Publication Data
A Cataloguing in Publication record for this book is available from the British Library.

Editorial Advisory Board

Table of Contents

Detailed Table of Contents

consider supportive measures for firms adopting sustainability initiatives. This study provides empirical insights into the nuanced effects of triple transformation on profitability in different economic contexts.

This chapter aims to analyze the evolutionary advances in the review of the conceptual, theoretical-methodological, and empirical literature on digital economic organization from different perspectives and in the current context. The method used is meta-analytical and meta-cognitive, reflexive, and descriptive based on the review of the conceptual, theoretical-methodological, and empirical literature. It is concluded that digital economic organization is a multidimensional concept that ranges from conceptual to methodological and empirical changes.

Digital transformation is reshaping industries worldwide, and tourism is no exception. In the dynamic context of Dubai, a city recognized globally for its innovative megaprojects, integrating digital technologies into the tourism sector has transcended the status of a mere trend to become a critical element in the city's long-term strategy. This chapter examines the role of digital technologies, such as big data, artificial intelligence, and the internet of things, in promoting sustainable tourism practices. Through case studies of major megaprojects, it highlights how digital transformation initiatives have improved operational efficiency, visitor experiences, and sustainability. The chapter also discusses collaborative efforts among stakeholders and the challenges faced in implementing digital strategies. Finally, it provides insights into the future of smart tourism in Dubai, highlighting the ongoing adaptation to global demands and sustainability standards.

The concept of phygital refers to the integration of physical and digital media in our current digital era. This approach is relevant across various sectors, including marketing, education, communication, and banking. It involves delivering various services and products to consumers through both physical channels and digital technologies. Phygital applications enable firms to stand out in value delivery through multi-channel structures in an increasingly digital world. Today's banking is shifting from a model characterized by numerous branches to one where the number of branches is reduced, and the use of digital channels is emphasized. Innovations such as digital payment solutions and electronic money applications from technology companies are fundamentally changing the digitalization process within the banking sector. The journey that began with internet banking in Türkiye 30 years ago has now deepened through new areas such as the metaverse and artificial intelligence. With the amendments made to Turkish Banking Legislation in 2021, the requirement for wet signatures in individual customer transactions was eliminated, allowing customer acquisition through digital security processes. Additionally, regulations introduced in 2022 paved the way for the establishment of fully digital banks. However, existing regulations still require digital banks to maintain physical offices, indicating that in an environment where digitalization in banking is rapidly advancing, the complete abandonment of physical channels does not seem realistic. In light of this context, this study aims to develop the concept of "Phygital Banking" for the Turkish Banking sector. As the rules of the competition are being redefined, with intellectual assets and intellectual capital taking precedence over physical ones, this research examines the opportunities presented by phygital applications in the Turkish Banking industry. The study aims to analyze existing phygital tools and provide recommendations for new application areas.

The present study aims to clarify and explore the needs regarding the understanding of the essence of social entrepreneurship in Bulgaria, as well as to attempt to analyze the relationship: education, business environment, social environment. We can already define at the beginning that social entrepreneurship is an unknown area for young people, and they essentially do not put any meaning in this concept. Establishing a deficit of such knowledge in young people leads to a search for an opportunity to be familiar with social entrepreneurship. The more essential problem is their preparation for carrying out similar social activities in this direction. All this is related to the development of new models for career development and the realization of a good professional and life perspective. The problems are clear from the outset, as they relate to low awareness, educational deficits, and lack of receptivity. This further complicates the tasks and creates additional obstacles.

For the case of Slovakia in a comparative evolutionary dynamic of the Visegrad Four countries in the period 2007-2021. The results of such DDM-analysis were further used as a reasoned justification for the need of ESG transformation in the context of globalization G3.0 and G4.0 within the framework of the TT model. At the same time, these results demonstrated the extremely complicated nature of a local or regional object as a complex adaptive system (CAS) subject to such ESG transformation. And in any case, such TT in the case of live CAS is similar to the external symptoms of the body, which are the result of deeper processes driven by some internal innovative driver. At the heart of such an internal innovation engine, which requires fundamentally new knowledge as a fuel for its work, is the triple integration model (TIM).

A brief overview and analysis of the digital, cultural, and strategic transformation and the relationship between each transformation is made. A SWOT analysis is made indicating positive and negative sides and how the gaps should be corrected. The advantages of each transformation, the method of implementation, and the role of state regulation in implementing the transformations are examined. An algorithm for implementing each of the three transformations is indicated and how they

Preface

In the rapidly evolving business environment, the concept of achieving sustained business excellence is increasingly seen as a multifaceted and dynamic challenge. *Achieving Business Excellence Through Triple Transformation* seeks to address this challenge by offering a comprehensive framework that combines three essential dimensions of transformation—digital, cultural, and strategic—into a cohesive strategy for success. This book presents a novel approach by recognizing that these three critical aspects, while often treated in isolation, are interdependent and must be integrated for businesses to thrive in the long term. The primary aim is to provide business leaders, entrepreneurs, and scholars with a structured, actionable roadmap that helps organizations navigate the complexities of transformation.

One of the core contributions of this book is its emphasis on the intersection of digital innovation, cultural agility, and strategic foresight. These dimensions are not only crucial individually but also vital when considered together as part of a broader transformation process. In today's world, technological advancements, shifting organizational cultures, and the need for forward-thinking strategies have become pivotal factors influencing the performance and sustainability of businesses. However, many organizations struggle to reconcile these areas, often implementing digital or strategic initiatives without aligning them with cultural shifts or ensuring long-term sustainability. This book aims to bridge this gap, providing a multidimensional view of transformation that addresses all three areas simultaneously, thereby fostering a more holistic understanding of what it takes to achieve excellence in business.

The book draws on a wide range of case studies and empirical insights to illustrate how the integration of digital, cultural, and strategic transformations can be effectively implemented within different organizational settings. By offering practical applications, it moves beyond theoretical concepts and provides readers with actionable tools that can be applied within their own organizations. These tools and insights are designed to help businesses build resilience, improve agility, and enhance their competitiveness in an increasingly complex and unpredictable global marketplace.

Digital transformation has been a key area of focus for businesses in recent years. As technology continues to evolve at a rapid pace, organizations must adapt to these changes to stay relevant and competitive. However, digital innovation alone is not enough to ensure long-term success. Cultural transformation is equally important, as it fosters an environment that supports creativity, collaboration, and adaptability—qualities that are essential for leveraging digital advancements. This book explores how a shift in organizational culture can complement and accelerate digital transformation efforts, creating a sustainable foundation for business excellence.

Strategic foresight is the third critical component of this transformative framework. As businesses face constant change and uncertainty, having a clear, long-term vision is crucial. Strategic foresight enables organizations to anticipate potential disruptions, identify emerging opportunities, and position themselves effectively for the future. By combining digital innovation, cultural agility, and strategic foresight, businesses are better equipped to navigate the complexities of the modern business landscape and respond proactively to evolving challenges.

In addition to its practical implications, this book also serves as a valuable resource for further academic research. It invites scholars and practitioners to explore the synergies between these three domains of transformation and their collective impact on long-term business success. The growing body of research on organizational transformation has primarily focused on one of these domains at a time, but this book encourages a more integrated approach that recognizes the interdependencies between them. By contributing to this ongoing dialogue, the book lays the groundwork for future studies that examine the long-term effects of combining digital, cultural, and strategic changes.

Ultimately, *Achieving Business Excellence Through Triple Transformation* aims to provide a comprehensive framework for organizations looking to achieve sustained success in a rapidly changing world. By integrating digital, cultural, and strategic transformations into a cohesive and actionable plan, businesses can improve their ability to adapt, innovate, and thrive. This approach is not only relevant to large corporations but is equally applicable to small and medium-sized enterprises, as it offers a flexible and scalable model that can be tailored to the specific needs and challenges of any organization. As such, this book is an invaluable tool for anyone seeking to enhance their organization's resilience, agility, and competitiveness in an ever-evolving global market.

DESCRIPTION OF WHERE THE TOPIC FITS IN THE WORLD TODAY

In today's globalized and highly interconnected world, businesses are facing unprecedented challenges and opportunities. The landscape is characterized by rapid technological advancements, shifting cultural dynamics, and ever-changing strategic imperatives. In this context, the concept of achieving business excellence through the integration of digital, cultural, and strategic transformations is more relevant than ever. As organizations strive to maintain competitiveness and resilience, they are increasingly recognizing that success in the modern business environment requires a holistic approach that encompasses all three of these dimensions.

The rapid pace of technological change is perhaps the most obvious factor driving transformation in the business world today. Digitalization is no longer a luxury but a necessity for survival. From automation and artificial intelligence (AI) to big data and cloud computing, technology has revolutionized every aspect of business, from operations and supply chains to customer engagement and decision-making. However, while digital innovation offers substantial opportunities for efficiency and growth, it also presents significant challenges. Businesses must navigate not only the complexities of adopting new technologies but also the organizational and cultural shifts necessary to ensure these innovations are successfully integrated. This is where the concept of digital transformation fits into the broader picture. Digital transformation goes beyond the mere implementation of new tools; it requires a rethinking of business processes, culture, and strategy to fully leverage the potential of technology. This book addresses this critical need by integrating digital innovation with other key elements of business transformation, such as cultural agility and strategic foresight, to create a cohesive approach to achieving excellence.

While digitalization is at the forefront of contemporary business transformation, cultural agility has become an equally important factor for organizational success. In an increasingly diverse and globalized world, businesses are encountering new cultural challenges, both within their workforce and in their interactions with customers and partners. A company's ability to adapt to and embrace cultural differences has a direct impact on its ability to innovate, collaborate, and thrive. Cultural transformation involves fostering an environment that supports inclusivity, creativity, and adaptability. Companies that cultivate a culture of agility are better equipped to respond to the rapidly changing demands of the market, the expectations of their employees, and the shifting values of society at large. This aspect of transformation is particularly relevant in today's world, where social, political, and economic changes are reshaping business practices and consumer behaviors. The integration of cultural agility into business strategies is, therefore, essential for achieving long-term success in an environment that values diversity, flexibility, and continuous learning.

Strategic foresight, the third pillar of the transformation framework, plays a crucial role in guiding organizations through the uncertainties and complexities of the future. In an era of global disruption, businesses must anticipate emerging trends and adapt their strategies accordingly to stay ahead of the competition. Strategic foresight involves more than just long-term planning; it requires organizations to continuously scan the external environment, identify potential threats and opportunities, and adjust their approach to align with future realities. The ability to foresee and adapt to changes in the market, technology, and geopolitics is essential for navigating today's volatile business environment. Companies that fail to anticipate shifts in their industry risk being left behind, while those that embrace strategic foresight can better position themselves for success in the future.

The integration of digital, cultural, and strategic transformations is a natural response to the rapidly changing world in which businesses operate today. While each of these dimensions has been studied and implemented independently, the recognition that they must work together is a relatively recent development. This book fills a critical gap by offering a comprehensive framework that integrates these three areas, providing businesses with a more complete and adaptive approach to transformation. In the current business climate, where traditional models of success are being upended by technological advances, shifting societal values, and increasing global competition, this integrated approach is essential for organizations seeking to achieve sustainable excellence.

Moreover, the relevance of this topic extends beyond the business world to academia and policy-making. As organizations navigate the complexities of digital, cultural, and strategic transformations, scholars and researchers are increasingly focused on understanding how these changes intersect and influence long-term business outcomes. The integration of these transformative processes is not only a topic of academic inquiry but also one of great practical significance for businesses worldwide. Policymakers, too, have a role to play in shaping the future of business transformation. By fostering environments that encourage innovation, inclusivity, and adaptability, governments can help create the conditions necessary for businesses to thrive in an era of continuous change.

In conclusion, the topic of achieving business excellence through triple transformation fits squarely within the global discourse on organizational change and adaptation. As the world continues to evolve, the need for businesses to integrate digital innovation, cultural agility, and strategic foresight into a cohesive transformation strategy becomes increasingly critical. This integrated approach not only helps businesses navigate the complexities of today's business environment but also ensures their long-term success in an increasingly competitive and unpredictable world. The relevance of this topic is evident in the ongoing conversations among business leaders, scholars, and policymakers alike, as they seek to understand and implement the best practices for organizational transformation in the 21st century.

A DESCRIPTION OF THE TARGET AUDIENCE

The target audience for this book, *Achieving Business Excellence Through Triple Transformation*, is diverse, encompassing a broad range of individuals and organizations that are either involved in or interested in the ongoing processes of digital, cultural, and strategic transformations in business. This audience includes business leaders, entrepreneurs, scholars, and policymakers, each of whom will find valuable insights and actionable frameworks for enhancing organizational performance in the increasingly complex global market.

Business leaders, including CEOs, CFOs, COOs, and other executives, are a primary audience for this book. These individuals are tasked with steering organizations through the challenges of digital disruption, cultural shifts, and evolving market demands. They are responsible for driving strategic decision-making, managing organizational change, and ensuring the long-term success of their companies. For business leaders, this book offers a structured framework that integrates the critical dimensions of digital innovation, cultural agility, and strategic foresight. The practical tools, case studies, and empirical insights presented in the book will enable these leaders to implement transformational changes that foster resilience, competitiveness, and sustainability within their organizations. Moreover, the holistic approach outlined in the book provides business leaders with a comprehensive perspective on how these transformations intersect, allowing them to make informed decisions that align with both short-term goals and long-term objectives.

Entrepreneurs, particularly those leading small- and medium-sized enterprises (SMEs), represent another key segment of the target audience. Entrepreneurs often face unique challenges in adapting to new technologies, navigating cultural dynamics, and formulating strategies that position their businesses for growth. This book provides them with the tools and insights needed to successfully integrate digital, cultural, and strategic transformations in their businesses. By understanding how these domains interact and influence each other, entrepreneurs can develop adaptive business models that respond to market needs, customer preferences, and technological advancements. The actionable framework and practical applications offered in the book also help entrepreneurs identify opportunities for innovation and competitive advantage, enabling them to scale their businesses in a rapidly changing environment.

Academics and scholars in the fields of business, management, and organizational studies are also a critical part of the book's target audience. This book contributes to the growing body of research on organizational transformation by presenting a unique, multidimensional approach to understanding and implementing change. Scholars researching digital transformation, organizational culture, strategic management, and innovation will find this book to be a valuable resource, providing new perspectives and frameworks for future research. By exploring the intersection of digital, cultural, and strategic dimensions of transformation, the book opens up avenues for further academic inquiry into how these processes impact long-term business success. Additionally, the inclusion of empirical case studies and practical insights allows scholars to bridge the gap between theory and practice, offering a more comprehensive understanding of organizational transformation.

Policymakers and government officials also form an important part of the target audience. In today's global economy, governments play a crucial role in shaping the conditions under which businesses operate. By fostering environments that encourage innovation, inclusivity, and adaptability, policymakers can help businesses navigate the challenges of digital, cultural, and strategic transformations. This book serves as a resource for policymakers seeking to understand how technological advancements, cultural shifts, and strategic foresight can influence economic growth and social development. By offering insights into how businesses can leverage these transformative processes for long-term success, the book also provides policymakers with ideas for creating supportive policies that facilitate sustainable business practices and foster economic resilience.

In addition to these primary audiences, the book also appeals to organizational consultants, change management professionals, and human resource practitioners. These individuals are often tasked with guiding organizations through complex transformation processes and ensuring that changes are effectively implemented and sustained. The comprehensive framework and practical tools provided in the book will be valuable for consultants and professionals working with businesses on digital, cultural, and strategic transformations. The book offers a clear, structured approach to these transformations, enabling consultants to provide more targeted and effective advice to their clients. Furthermore, human resource professionals can benefit from the book's insights into cultural agility, as it provides valuable guidance on how to foster inclusive, adaptive work environments that support organizational change.

Finally, the book is intended for business students and emerging leaders who are interested in gaining a deeper understanding of the complex and interconnected processes of organizational transformation. As the next generation of business leaders, these individuals will be tasked with navigating the complexities of the modern business landscape, and the book offers them a solid foundation in the principles of digital, cultural, and strategic transformation. The book provides students with both theoretical insights and practical tools that will help them in their careers, whether they are entering established companies or starting their own ventures.

In summary, the target audience for *Achieving Business Excellence Through Triple Transformation* is broad and varied, encompassing business leaders, entrepreneurs, academics, policymakers, consultants, and students. This diverse group of individuals and organizations will benefit from the book's holistic approach to business transformation, which integrates digital innovation, cultural agility, and strategic foresight. By providing both theoretical insights and practical tools, the book aims to empower its audience to navigate the complexities of the modern business environment and drive sustained business excellence.

A DESCRIPTION OF THE IMPORTANCE OF EACH OF THE CHAPTERS

1) This chapter systematically summarizes the evolution of the digital strategy concept and related academic research. It uses bibliometric analysis to examine 737 studies published between 1999 and 2024, offering insights into publication trends, key contributors, research areas, and global distribution. The findings highlight the growing interest in digital strategy, particularly in 2022, with Linda Harrington as a prominent author and Management as the leading research area. The United States emerges as the leading country for digital strategy research, and English dominates the field. The study underscores the importance of recognizing key themes, such as "digital strategy," and how they shape the academic discourse on strategic management and technology.
2) In this chapter, each section contributes to understanding the nuanced effects of environmental, technological, and social transformations on business performance. The first section introduces the concept of triple transformation, providing a theoretical foundation by defining key variables such as Research and Development expenses (RND), Social Pillar Score (SPS), and Environmental Innovation Score (ENIS). It emphasizes the importance of these transformations for long-term sustainable growth and explains how they can yield different effects in various economic contexts. The second section outlines the methodology, detailing the panel data from 25 UK and 24 French firms between 2005 and 2023, and justifies the use of panel quantile regression models. It explains how these models help capture the varying impacts of the three key variables on profitability across different performance levels. The third section presents the empirical findings, showing that SPS and ENIS negatively affect profitability, particularly for more profitable firms, while RND does not have a significant impact. The section highlights the role of firm size, noting that it

positively influences profitability but diminishes among top performers. Finally, the last section discusses the policy implications of the findings, stressing the need for supportive measures for firms adopting sustainability initiatives, despite the short-term financial challenges. Together, these sections provide a comprehensive understanding of how triple transformation initiatives impact business performance and offer valuable insights for both academic researchers and policymakers in promoting sustainable growth across different economic contexts.

3) This chapter provides a comprehensive analysis of the evolutionary advancements in the review of the conceptual, theoretical-methodological, and empirical literature on digital economic organization from diverse perspectives in the current context. The first section outlines the conceptual framework, discussing the evolution of digital economic organization and its multidimensional nature. The second section examines the theoretical and methodological approaches used in studying this field, focusing on the key shifts in research methodologies and their impact on understanding digital economic organization. The third section presents the empirical findings, synthesizing results from various studies and offering insights into how these advancements have shaped practical applications in the field. The paper concludes by emphasizing that digital economic organization is a dynamic and evolving concept, encompassing significant changes in its conceptual, methodological, and empirical dimensions. It highlights the need for continuous reflection and adaptation of research approaches to fully capture the complexities of this field.
4) This chapter explores the transformative role of digital technologies, such as big data, artificial intelligence, and the Internet of Things, in reshaping the tourism sector in Dubai, a city renowned for its innovative megaprojects. The first section introduces the significance of digital transformation within the tourism industry, emphasizing its strategic importance beyond a temporary trend and positioning it as a core element of Dubai's long-term development goals. The second section presents case studies of major tourism megaprojects, showcasing how digital technologies have enhanced operational efficiency, visitor experiences, and sustainability practices. The third section delves into the collaborative efforts among various stakeholders, examining the challenges encountered in implementing digital strategies across the sector. Finally, the chapter concludes with insights on the future of smart tourism in Dubai, stressing the city's continuous adaptation to evolving global demands and sustainability standards. By presenting these perspectives, the chapter contributes to understanding the critical role of digital transformation in achieving sustainable tourism development in urban contexts.

5) This chapter explores the concept of Phygital, which refers to the integration of physical and digital media in the current digital era, with a focus on its relevance across multiple sectors, including marketing, education, communication, and banking. The first section examines how this approach blends physical channels with digital technologies to deliver services and products to consumers. The second section discusses how Phygital applications allow firms to distinguish themselves by adopting multi-channel structures that cater to an increasingly digital consumer landscape. The third section focuses on the shift in banking, which has moved from a traditional branch-heavy model to one emphasizing digital channels, including innovations like digital payment solutions and electronic money. The chapter highlights the evolution of banking in Turkey, tracing its journey from the early days of internet banking 30 years ago to the integration of emerging technologies such as the metaverse and artificial intelligence in shaping the digitalization process within the sector. This analysis provides insights into how Phygital applications are reshaping industries, particularly banking, in the context of evolving digital transformation trends.
6) This chapter investigates the understanding and perception of social entrepreneurship among young people in Bulgaria, aiming to analyze the relationship between education, the business environment, and the social environment. The study highlights that social entrepreneurship remains an unfamiliar concept for many young individuals, who fail to attribute significant meaning to it. The lack of knowledge about social entrepreneurship among youth triggers a search for opportunities to become more familiar with the concept. A key concern identified in the study is the inadequacy of preparation for engaging in social entrepreneurial activities, which affects career development and the realization of both professional and life goals. The study emphasizes the challenges posed by low awareness, educational deficits, and a lack of receptivity, which further complicate the development of social entrepreneurship initiatives and create additional barriers for young people in Bulgaria. Through this examination, the study seeks to identify new models for career development and contribute to the development of social entrepreneurship in the country.
7) This chapter examines the political and regulatory determinants, drivers, and motives of the market-based Triple Transformation (TT) of the ESG reality through Foreign Direct Investment (FDI) within the global digital space, with a focus on Slovakia. The analysis spans the period from 2007 to 2021 and compares the evolutionary dynamics of the Visegrad Four countries. The results of this Determinants-Drivers-Motives (DDM) analysis provide a well-grounded justification for the necessity of ESG transformation in the context of globalization 3.0 and 4.0, framed within the TT model. These findings also highlight the complex nature of a local or regional entity, viewed as a Complex Adaptive

System (CAS) undergoing ESG transformation. The study asserts that TT within a live CAS mirrors external symptoms of a body, which are the consequences of deeper, internal processes driven by innovative factors. At the core of this internal innovation engine, the study posits that the Triple Integration Model (TIM) serves as a critical driver, requiring fundamentally new knowledge to fuel its progress.

8) This chapter provides an overview and analysis of the interplay between digital, cultural, and strategic transformations, emphasizing the relationship between these distinct yet interconnected processes. A SWOT analysis is conducted to identify the strengths and weaknesses of each transformation, while also addressing the gaps that need to be corrected for effective implementation. The study explores the advantages of each transformation, the methods for their implementation, and the role of state regulation in facilitating these changes. An algorithm is proposed for executing each of the three transformations, highlighting how they complement each other in the process. The paper also examines the implementation of these transformations in Bulgaria and the Balkan Peninsula, offering insights into successful practices, existing challenges, and prospects for future implementation, particularly in light of the unique regional characteristics.
9) This chapter explores the emergence, development, and various key features of social entrepreneurship as a response to the growing social problems in society. The paper examines the opposing perspectives and opinions on social entrepreneurship, acknowledging the factors and understandings that lead to both positive and negative views. By analyzing the essential characteristics of social entrepreneurship, the study aims to provide a clear perspective on how involvement in social entrepreneurial initiatives can be both effective and efficient. It highlights the inevitable interweaving of economic theories in both socially entrepreneurial and traditional business initiatives, emphasizing the differences between "business entrepreneurship" and "social entrepreneurship," particularly in terms of their substantive aspects and result-oriented goals.
10) This study offers a comprehensive overview of organizational structure and its development potential within the context of a dynamic, modern society. Central to the study are the concepts of corporate culture, personal management, and motivation, which are explored in depth. The study also examines the potential for the growth of medical tourism and provides justifications for the effective functioning of organizations in this sector. In addition to theoretical models, the authors present practical opportunities for implementing their ideas, aiming to provide actionable insights for enhancing organizational performance and fostering growth in the medical tourism industry.

11) This paper examines the key dimensions of integrating environmental considerations into business strategy and culture, analyzing their effects on shifts within the economic landscape. A primary focus is on the motivational factors driving businesses to incorporate environmentalism into their transformation processes, emphasizing the various benefits of becoming a purpose-driven organization. The study highlights the development of the theoretical foundations for environmental trajectories within business transformation, providing insights into the evolving role of businesses in society. The author also explores the growing distinction between shareholders and stakeholders, and how this differentiation contributes to the transformation of companies into influential entities capable of driving large-scale change through value-driven approaches.

CONCLUSION

Achieving Business Excellence Through Triple Transformation makes a significant contribution to the field of business management and organizational studies by presenting a comprehensive, multidimensional approach to achieving sustained business excellence through the integration of three critical transformation domains: digital, cultural, and strategic. The book offers both theoretical insights and practical applications, thereby addressing the growing need for frameworks that can guide organizations through the complexities of the modern business environment. By bridging the gap between digital innovation, cultural agility, and strategic foresight, the book not only enhances existing literature but also provides a fresh perspective on how these domains intersect and influence each other in shaping long-term business success.

One of the book's most notable contributions to the field is its holistic framework, which integrates the three key transformation areas that are often treated in isolation. While existing literature tends to focus on individual aspects of business transformation—such as digitalization, strategic planning, or organizational culture—this book connects these areas into a unified model that emphasizes their interconnectedness and interdependence. This integrated approach reflects the reality of today's business landscape, where organizations must navigate a complex set of challenges and opportunities that span digital technologies, organizational culture, and strategic decision-making. By doing so, the book provides a more accurate and actionable representation of how businesses can achieve excellence in an increasingly dynamic and competitive market.

The practical implications of this book are far-reaching. Through empirical case studies and real-world examples, it provides actionable tools that business leaders, entrepreneurs, and consultants can use to implement the frameworks and strategies outlined in the book. The inclusion of practical applications ensures that the book is not only a theoretical resource but also a guide for real-world transformation. It empowers readers to take concrete steps toward improving their organizations, making them more agile, resilient, and competitive. The book's emphasis on actionable strategies helps bridge the gap between theory and practice, which is often a challenge in academic literature. By offering readers practical tools and frameworks that can be directly applied to their businesses, the book enhances the relevance and utility of academic research in the field of business transformation.

Another significant impact of the book is its ability to enrich the academic discourse on organizational transformation. By combining digital, cultural, and strategic perspectives, the book provides a nuanced understanding of how these domains interact and influence each other in the context of business success. This interdisciplinary approach opens new avenues for academic inquiry and invites further research into the intersections between these three critical areas. Scholars in business management, strategic studies, and organizational behavior will find the book to be a valuable resource for advancing research on transformation processes. The book encourages a shift in how organizational change is conceptualized and studied, moving away from siloed approaches to more integrated models that reflect the complexity of real-world business environments.

Moreover, the book serves as a vital resource for policymakers and government officials seeking to understand the broader implications of business transformation on economic growth, social development, and policy formulation. The book's insights into how businesses can leverage digital, cultural, and strategic transformations to drive innovation, competitiveness, and sustainability offer valuable lessons for policymakers tasked with fostering an environment that supports business growth. By demonstrating how organizations can adapt to and benefit from these transformations, the book provides actionable recommendations for creating policies that promote technological adoption, cultural agility, and strategic foresight. In this way, the book contributes to a broader understanding of how business transformation intersects with public policy and economic development, expanding its impact beyond the business community to include policymakers and government agencies.

The book also makes a significant contribution to the ongoing conversation about how organizations can navigate the challenges of a rapidly changing global economy. In today's world, businesses are constantly confronted with technological disruption, shifting cultural norms, and evolving market dynamics. This book addresses these challenges head-on by offering a framework that helps organizations not only survive but thrive in the face of uncertainty. By providing a structured pathway for integrating digital innovation, cultural transformation, and strategic foresight, the book helps businesses become more resilient and adaptable to the ever-changing demands of the global market. This contribution is particularly timely as organizations around the world grapple with the long-term effects of the COVID-19 pandemic, which has accelerated digital transformation and reshaped organizational priorities.

In summary, *Achieving Business Excellence Through Triple Transformation* makes a significant and lasting contribution to the field of business management by providing a holistic framework for achieving organizational excellence. By integrating digital, cultural, and strategic transformations, the book enhances the existing literature on business transformation and offers practical tools for implementation. It provides valuable insights for business leaders, entrepreneurs, scholars, and policymakers, helping them navigate the complexities of the modern business landscape and drive sustainable business success. The book's interdisciplinary approach, real-world applications, and actionable strategies ensure that it has a meaningful impact on both academic research and practical business practices, making it an invaluable resource for anyone interested in the future of business excellence.

Meltem Okur Dinçsoy
Trakya University, Turkey

Hamit Can
Trakya University, Turkey

Chapter 1
Bibliometric Analysis of Studies on the Concept of Digital Strategy With VOSviewer

Meltem Okur Dincsoy
https://orcid.org/0000-0002-6918-3234
Trakya University, Turkey

Hamit Can
https://orcid.org/0000-0002-6918-3234
Trakya University, Turkey

ABSTRACT

The aim of this study is to map the evolution of the concept of digital strategy and the studies conducted on this concept and to present a systematic summary of the literature within the scope of quantitative data. Bibliometric data belonging to different types of studies scanned in the Web of Science database and published between 1999-2024 were examined. When the distribution of 737 studies published on digital strategy according to the publication years is examined, it is seen that the most intensive one is in 2022; the name that produced the most studies is Linda Harrington; the publication type is mostly articles (517); in terms of research areas, the studies are published in the fields of management (130); when the distribution of publications by country is examined, it is seen that the leadership is in the USA (152); the studies are mostly published in English (690); the vast majority of the publications are indexed by the Emerging Sources Citation Index (ESCI) (227). Digital strategy is among the most frequently used keywords with 175 repetitions.

DOI: 10.4018/979-8-3693-9435-9.ch001

1. INTRODUCTION

Unlike systematic literature review, bibliometric analysis is an analytical method used to obtain formal and quantitative data on the current status of a field and facilitates tracking academic trends through visualization software. The ultimate goal of the bibliometric approach, which can be confused with concepts such as scientometric, webometric, cybermetric, altmetric, and infometric of the metrics era, is to obtain quantitative data and numerical measurement indicators on research performance. Interpretations to be made on these metrics must be inspired by the experiences and knowledge of researchers in the field. Through bibliometrics, quantitative findings are obtained on country, author, university and journal productivity, weak and strong research areas, literature gaps, collaboration networks, potential opportunities and widespread effects of outputs produced in a field. Despite all its limitations, bibliometrics, which can also be used as a preliminary stage of a systematic literature review, can be used as a preliminary step of any research, which we believe is among the factors that explain the widespread interest it has received today. The aim of the present study is to provide a systematic analysis of the evolution of the concept of "digital strategy" based on relevant publications. It is to develop an integrated approach to digital strategy, including general options. The study attempts to identify trends and gaps in relevant research by providing a systematic summary of the existing literature on post-truth as a key contemporary concept, facilitating the identification of some future research directions.

In order to keep up with the change that is a result of technology and time, to maintain their existence in some way or to move from their current situation to a desired situation, companies need to be able to manage this process correctly. Digital transformation, which is a strategic response of companies to the disruptive changes brought by digital technologies (Vial, 2019), leads to radical changes in the industry and changes the traditional understanding of competition (Zhang, Xu, & Ma, 2023). Digital transformation represents a structural change for companies and radically changes the way companies conduct their business (Balakrishnan and Das, 2020; Muduli and Choudhury, 2024; Singh, Sharma, and Dhir, 2021).

It is seen that a technological revolution is rapidly beginning. The technological revolution is expected to bring radical changes in many areas, from individuals' lifestyles to the way they do business and the methods of communication between people (Dinçsoy, 2023). Given the limited abilities and finite lifespan of humans, advancements in artificial intelligence inspire scientists to deepen their research in this domain(Can H. & Minkovska, D., 2020). This change represents an unprecedented change in human history in terms of its size and depth (Schwab, 2016). Speculations about how digitalization can have a transformative effect on business and the economy are increasing day by day (Paus, 2018). While discussions on how businesses respond to digital transformation continue, analyses are emerging on how the COVID-19 pandemic has accelerated this transformation (Forbes, 2020). Digitalization raises concerns about the role that robots, automation, artificial intelligence and machine learning algorithms will play in the business world and the potential for mass unemployment, poverty and social explosion (Okur Dinçsoy, 2020). Digitalization could significantly change economic structures, labor relations and work dynamics in the business world (Wisskirchen et al., 2017). Digital transformation refers to the integration of digital technologies into business processes and applications (Dias, Carvalho, & Sampaio, 2022), requires a strategic organizational change (Fernández, Gómez, Binjaku, & Meçe, 2023), and redefines organizational boundaries (Plekhanov, Franke, & Netland, 2023). Digital transformation, which consists of strategy, people, organization, ecosystem, innovation, customer, technology, and the corresponding sub-dimensions (Ivančić, Vukšić, & Spremić, 2019), includes both the adoption of digital technologies and change management (Dang-Pham, Hoang, Vo, & Kautz, 2022). Digital transformation refers to a deliberate change in organizations to use the latest technologies such as big data analytics, cloud computing, and mobile technologies to deliver products and services (Dinçsoy, 2023). The biggest factor that caused this organizational transformation process is that digital technologies seriously change existing industries and change all the rules of the game in the competitive environment (Ly, 2023).

Digital transformation refers to the integration of digital technologies into every area of the organization's business to create new ways to create value by going beyond the use of technology to redefine the organization's value proposition (Dang-Pham et al., 2022). Digital transformation, a change process in which companies use information technologies to increase their competitiveness and develop new values, includes improving customer experience, streamlining operations, and creating new business models through the use of new digital technologies to achieve significant business improvements (Tsai & Su, 2022). For digital transformation, companies need to determine which digital technologies they will use and how (Saarikko, Westergren, & Blomquist, 2020). This indicates that a digital transformation strategy is the starting point for digital transformation. A digital transformation strategy aims to foster a culture that supports digital technology, treats leaders, employees, or staff as customers, and fosters open innovation by developing a digital-based work culture (Rozak, Adhiatma, Fachrunnisa, & Rahayu, 2021). Digital transformation, which encompasses the combined effects of digital innovations and technologies and causes the emergence of new actors, structures, practices, values, and beliefs that affect existing institutional rules, reshapes business models and affects corporate culture (AlNuaimi et al., 2022).

Advances in business are closely linked with the information and communication sector developments. At the same time, related developments have been determining factors for e-business, including hardware and software tools, mobile and telecommunication technologies, and wireless transmission equipments (Okur Dincsoy, 2009). For this reason, revealing the organizational elements that enable digital transformation is critical both for the developing digital transformation literature and for companies.

Keeping up with the pace of technological revolutions and effectively adapting to digitalization is of vital importance for the business world. Within the scope of this importance, the article aims to guide businesses so that they can best evaluate the opportunities and overcome the challenges brought by digital transformation

2. LITERATURE REVIEW

Can and Terziev (2016) concluded that with the emergence of the Information Society, developments in information and communication technologies have had significant effects on national economies. He concluded that today, it is difficult to talk about the concept of development in a society without technological developments, and in this context, it is very important to examine how technological developments affect the economic dimension in particular. He also concluded that it reduces the economic impact of physical distances, the costs of accessing information, and the costs of establishing new small businesses, making businesses more efficient and competitive.

Yeow et al (2018) addressed the highly dynamic context of digital strategy. To address this gap, they analyzed the stages of a B2B company's B2C digital strategy implementation using the dynamic capabilities approach. They emphasized on iteratively restructuring organizational resources and refining the strategy to respond to both environmental changes and internal tensions.

Schallmo et al. (2019) expanded on this research by conducting 13 semi-structured interviews to obtain insights from digital strategy experts (researchers and consultants) and also analyzed 10 case studies collected using semi-structured interviews with company representatives. The study findings show that although digital strategy is still in its infancy, it is currently an important topic in many industries.

Chanias et al. (2019) used interpretive in-depth case study research to examine how a European financial services provider formulates and implements a DTS, concluding that a DTS is constantly under construction with no foreseeable end.

Horváth and Szabo (2019) investigated how top managers interpret the concept of Industry 4.0, the drivers for the introduction of new technologies, and the main barriers to Industry 4.0. The study findings predicted that management's desire to increase control and enable real-time performance measurement is a major driver behind Industry 4.0, along with production factors.

Eller et al. (2020) Based on the resource-based view, first investigated the impact of three main SME resources on digitalization: information technology, employee skills, and digital strategy. Second, evaluated the impact of digitalization on financial performance. The results of a survey of 193 SMEs show how digitalization can affect SME performance and that the three resources are positively related to digitalization.

Raj et al. (2020) examined the barriers to the implementation of Industry 4.0 technologies in the manufacturing sector in the context of both developed and developing economies. A comprehensive literature review following discussions with industry experts identified 15 barriers that were analyzed using the Grey Decision Making Experimentation and Evaluation Laboratory (DEMATEL) approach. Along with resource scarcity, the "lack of digital strategy" emerges as the most prominent obstacles in both developed and developing economies.

Dwivedi et al. (2020) provide a collective perspective on many of the key issues and fundamental complexities impacting organizations and society from an information systems and technological perspective due to COVID-19. Expert perspectives provide timely insights into various topics, identifying key issues and recommendations for theory and practice.

In the Akbiyik and Can (2023) study, it was examined which applications were implemented using information technologies in order to respond to the needs of the local people in a shorter and faster time thanks to the digital transformation applications implemented by local governments. The use of digital transformation technologies within the institution and in reinforced concrete buildings can be seen as an efficiency-enhancing factor(Can, et al., 2020).

3. METHOD

This section of the study includes the purpose of the research, the analyses and findings.

3.1. Purpose of the Research

As a result of the bibliometric analysis conducted on the concept of digital transformation as a result of quantitative data and numerical measurement indicators, aims to present the studies on the concept to the attention of researchers with a holistic perspective.

3.2. Data and Analysis

Different bibliometric analysis tools are used in the literature. In this study, the VOSviewer program was preferred due to its strong functional aspects. It is considered to be an important program that provides convenience to researchers in order to discover the evolutions, relationships and new concepts in the literature. In addition, it allows for in-depth analysis of data sets due to the visualization, mapping and multi-dimensional analysis opportunities it provides. The Web of Science database was used in the current study. The selection of the Web of Science database for various analyses including bibliometric analyses is an important factor in terms of the reliability of the research. The Web of Science database has advanced search indicators for advanced data analysis and uses various control mechanisms. It covers qualified and reliable studies in terms of publication ethics. In addition, it provides access to a comprehensive data collection from different disciplines. On 10.10.2024, 737 results were reached in the search made by selecting "all fields" in Web of Science with the keyword "digital strategy". By year, 517 articles from different disciplines, the oldest being 1999 and the newest being 2024, 159 Proceeding Papers, 37 Book Chapters, 37 Editorial Materials, 23 Early Access, 18 Review Articles, 4 Meeting Abstracts, and 3 Book Reviews were accessed. In terms of disciplines, the majority of the studies were seen in the fields of Management (130), Business (125), Computer Science Information Systems (78), Information Science Library Science (63), Computer Science Interdisciplinary Applications (44), Computer Science Theory Methods (43), Education Educational Research (40), Computer Science Artificial Inteligence (34), Engineering Electrical Electronic (32), Communication (31), and Economics (31). The accessed data was examined through author-citation-journal, country-institution and keyword analyzes. The contents indexed in Web of Science were taken as the criterion as the database.

4. FINDINGS

The findings obtained in the study are given under this heading.

4.1. Co-authorship of Authors

According to the co-authorship analysis of the authors, a network map was created by determining the criteria of at least 2 publications and at least 2 citations to identify the most connected and collaborating authors. According to the analysis made among the names with the highest links, 13 items, 2 clusters, 78 links and 144 total strength links are seen to be combined in a single cluster. Of the 21 most connected authors in the cluster, Tani Heap, Jenilyn Agapito, Neil Guppy, Uwe Matzat 27 and David Boud, Jamie Lee Burgess, Louise Lutze Mann, Patsie Polly, Mary Roth, Joanna Tai 21, the other 11 authors have a total link strength of 20. It is also seen that the most cited authors (Youngjin Yoo with 1469 citations, Chris Bullen with 224 citations, Simon Denny, Enid Dorey, Ralph Maddison, Hayden Mcrobbie, Anthony Rodgers, Robyn Whittaker) are not the most connected authors. The authors who produced the most work also do not appear to be among the most connected authors (Linda Harrington (22 documents), Christopher I. Tucci (5 documents), and Iryna Gureveych (5 documents)).

Figure 1. Co-Author Links Showing Collaboration Between Authors (Network Visulization)

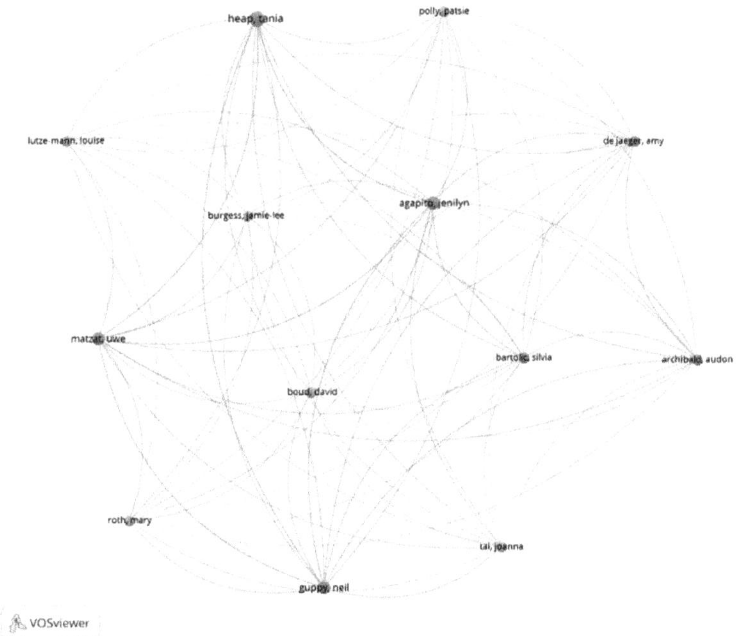

Figure 2. Co-Author Links Showing Collaboration Between Authors (Overlay Visulization)

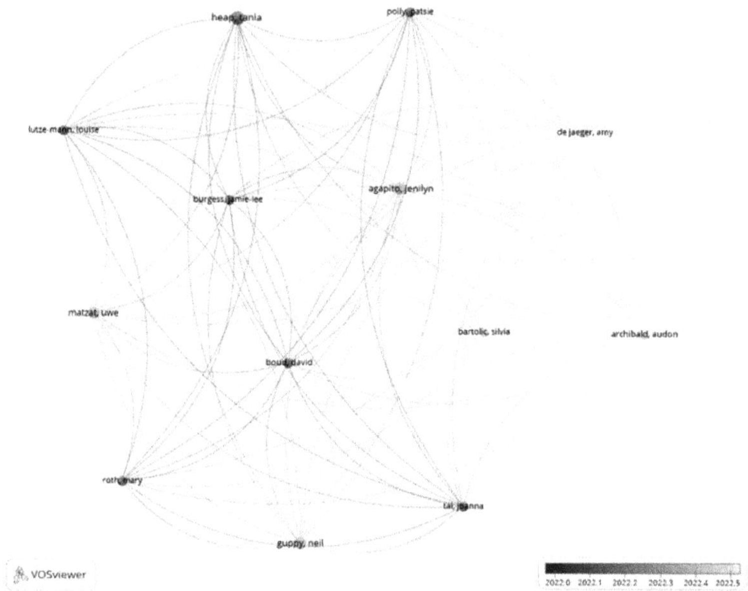

When the figure above is examined, it is seen that publications in this field are concentrated in 2022.

Figure 3. Co-Author Links Showing Collaboration Between Authors (Density Visulization)

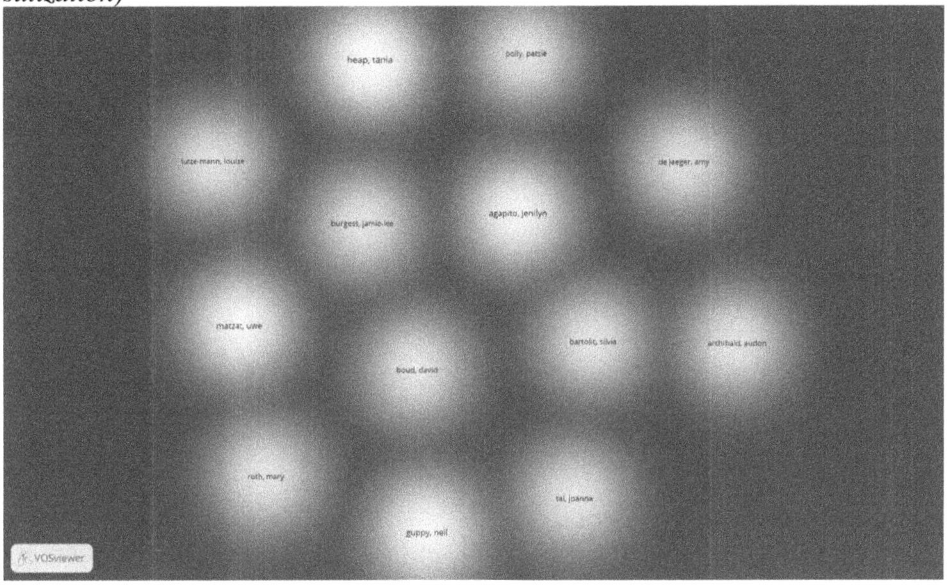

In the figure above, it is seen that the authors who have worked in this field generally concentrate on yellow tones. It would be useful to examine the works of these authors with this yellow intensity in research in these fields.

4.2. Citation of Authors

In order to determine the citation networks, a network map was created for the author citation analysis with the criteria of at least 1 publication and at least 1 citation. In the analysis conducted on 267 items that were seen to be connected to each other, a total of 16 clusters, 1485 links and a total link strength of 1504 were detected. The most cited authors were Youngjin Yoo with 1469 citations, Ola Henfridsson and Kalle Lyytinen with 1468 citations. These three authors are not in the top three in terms of total link strength (67 total link strength) Rina Hansen, Christina Soh, Adrian Yeow).

Figure 4. Authors' Citation Links

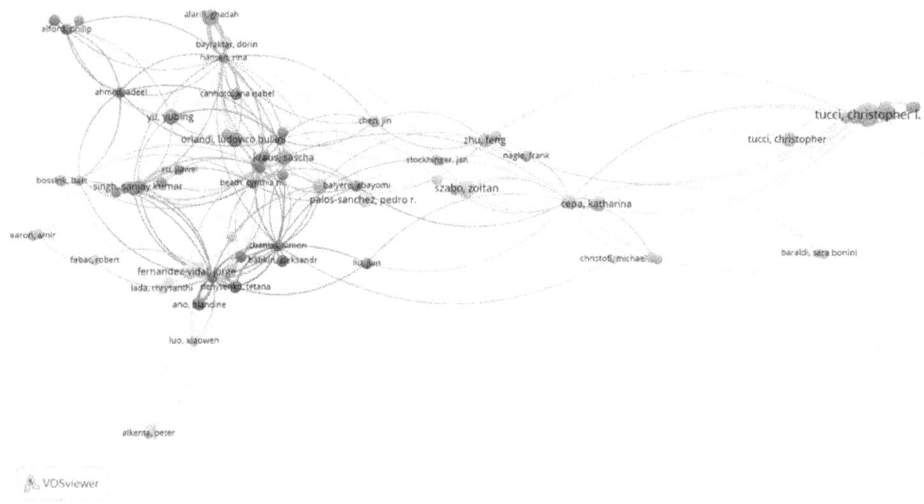

4.3. Citation of Countries

In order to create a network map regarding the citations received by the publications according to their countries of origin, an analysis was conducted on 56 items that were related to each other within the scope of the criterion that at least 1 pubication was published and a country received 1 citation. 10 clusters, 328 links and 679 total link strengths were identified. The countries with the most citations were USA (3765 citations), England (2446 citations), and Norway (1563 citations). In terms of total connection strength, England (149), USA (147), China (116) were in the top three. In terms of the number of works, the ranking was as follows: USA (151 documents), England (86 documents) and Germany (66 documents).

Figure 5. Citation Links of Countries

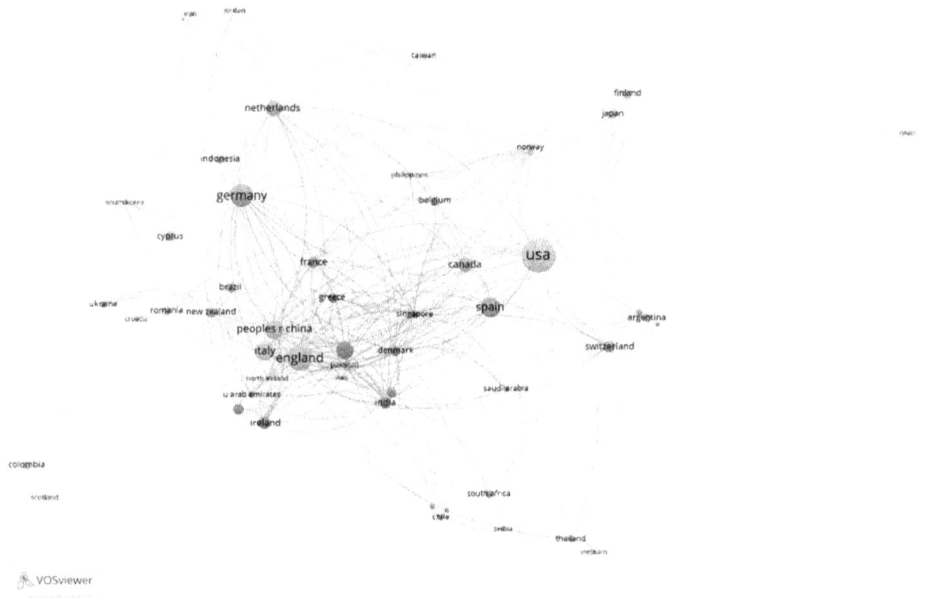

4.4. Citation of Organizations

In order to create a network map of inter-institutional citations, an analysis was conducted on 211 items that were related to each other within the scope of the criterion that an institution should publish at least 1 document and receive 1 citation. While Texas Christian University (13 documents), The Technical University of Darmstadt (12 documents), Baylor College of Medicine (10 documents) were represented by works, the address institutions of the most cited publications were University of Oslo (1475 citations), Case Western Reserve University (1472 citations) and Temple University (1468 citations). A total of 16 clusters, 1181 links and a total link strength of 1228 were identified.

Figure 6. Citation Links of Institutions

4.5. Co-Occurence of All Keywords

When looking at the most frequently used keywords in publications related to Digital Strategy, the most common ones are digital strategy with 175 repetitions, digital transformation with 112 repetitions, digitalization with 33 repetitions, social media with 23 repetitions, and digital technology with 17 repetitions. The strongest expressions in terms of total connection strength were digital strategy, digital transformation, and digitalization. As a result of the analysis conducted with 324 observation units that were seen at least twice and had a relationship between them, a total of 22 clusters, 1558 connections, and 2219 total connection strengths were determined.

Figure 7. Most Frequently Used Keyword Links (Network Visulization)

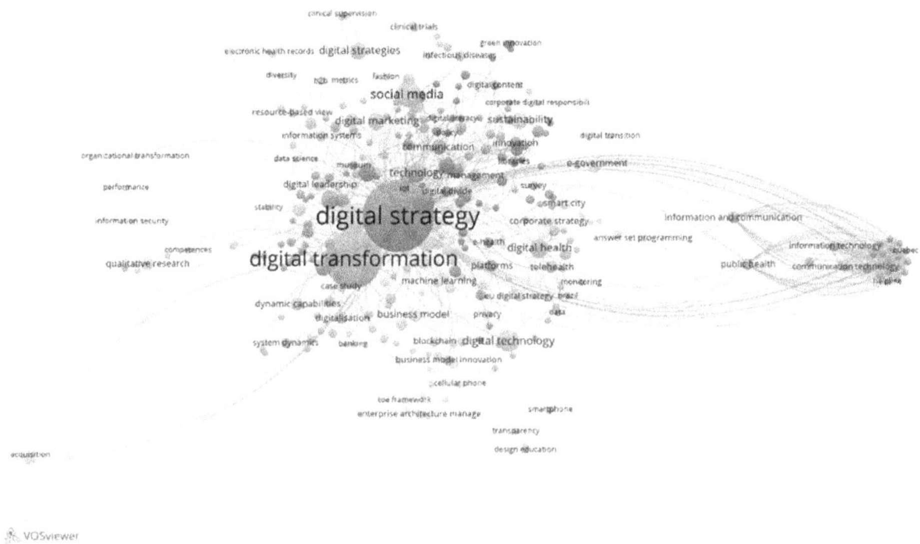

In addition, the figure shows which topics the topic of digital strategy is worked on and associated with (archives, community, COVID 19, digital behavior, digital content, digital divide, digital innovation, digital learning, digital literacy, digital video, digitization, e-health).

Figure 8. Most Frequently Used Keyword Links (Overlay Visulization)

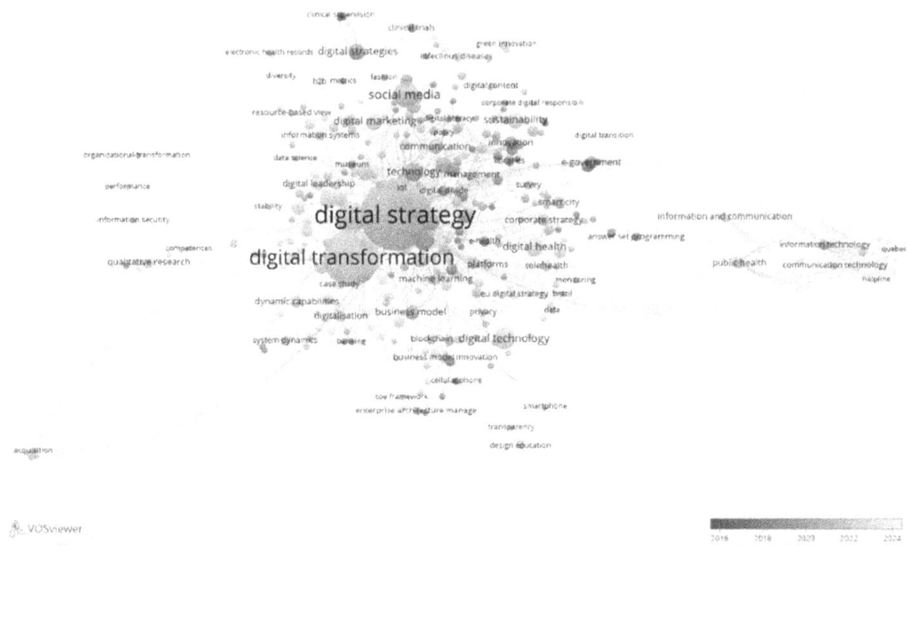

We see how the keywords are distributed. Similar ones are shown in the same color.

Figure 9. Most Frequently Used Keyword Links (Density Visulization)

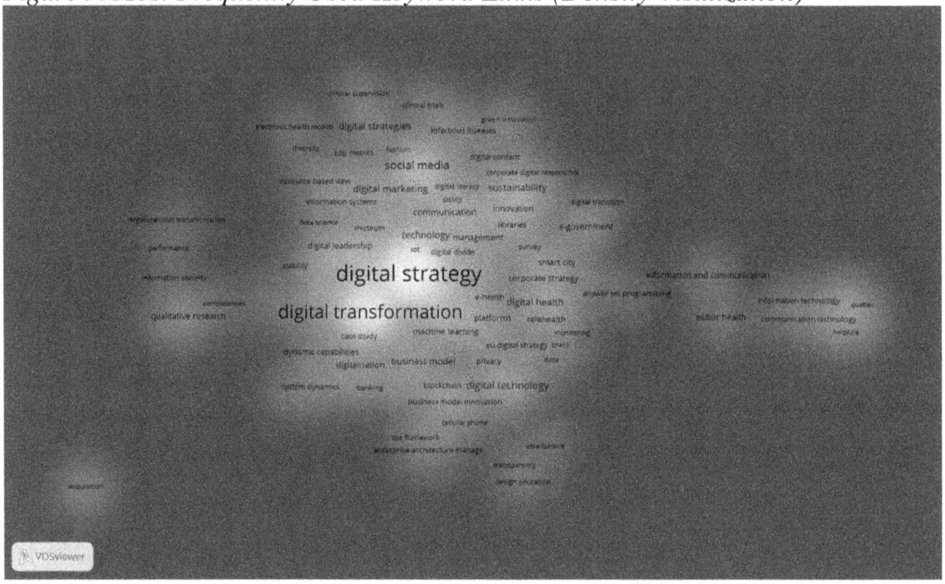

When looking at the figure above, generally digital strategy and digital transformation are the most studied topics. The concepts between yellow and blue density are transition concepts. These concepts provide information about which concepts can be used when addressing the topic you want to study.

4.6. Bibliographic Coupling of Documents

Bibliographic match refers to the situation of citing a common work cited by two independent sources. According to the analysis conducted with 351 items selected with the criterion of having at least 1 citation and having a connection between them, 16 clusters, 5748 links and 10899 total link strength were obtained. The publications with the highest bibliographic matches were Yoo (2010) with 1468 citations, Horvath (2019) with 588 citations and Raj (2020) with 481 citations. The works with the highest total link strength were Teubner (2020) with 497 total link strength, Marino - Romero (2024) with 489 total link strength and Alnoor (2023) with 372 total link strength.

Figure 10. Bibliographic Coupling Links of Documents

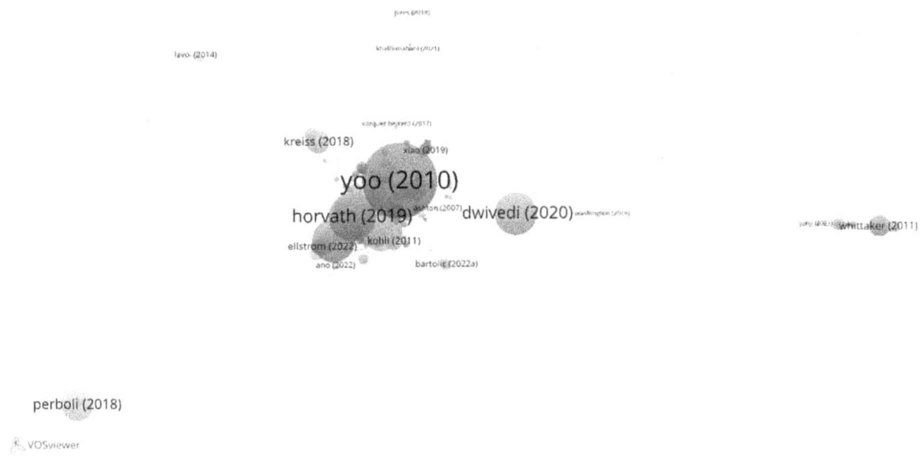

4.7. Bibliographic Coupling of Authors

According to the analysis conducted with 1147 items selected with the criteria of having at least 1 publication and 1 citation and having connections between them, 42 clusters, 59131 links and 297091 total link strength were obtained. The authors with the highest number of bibliographic matches were Youngjin Yoo with 1469 citations (729 link strength), Ola Henfridsson with 1468 citations (196 link strength) and Kalle Lyytinen with 1468 citations (196 link strength).

Figure 11. Bibliographic Coupling of Authors

4.8. Co-Citation of Co-Authors

Different sources cited in a publication are called co-citations. By selecting a minimum of 10 citations, a total of 7 clusters, 7301 links and 24615 total link strengths were identified based on the analysis conducted on 166 items. The authors with the most co-citations were identified as Dj Teece (102), European Commission (81) and A. Bharadwaj (72).

Figure 12. Co-Citation of Co-Authors

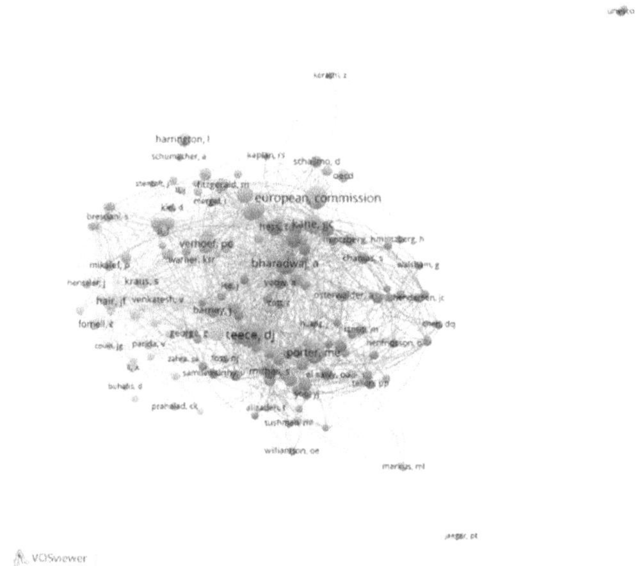

CONCLUSION

In this study, a quantitative synopsis of the studies conducted on the concept of digital strategy has been attempted. There are some results indicated by both the quantitative analysis and the theoretical review of the studies subject to the analysis. In order to understand how digital transformation can be implemented effectively, it is very important to understand the building blocks underlying the implementation of the digital transformation strategy. The concept of digital transformation draws attention as a subject that should be placed at the leading position of the individual and social agenda. Apart from the quantitative picture that a series of statistics obtained as a result of this bibliometric analysis will present to those interested in the subject, the main starting point of the study was to underline the urgency of the subject.

In the analysis covering the years 1999-2024 regarding the concept of digital strategy, it was seen that there were 517 Articles, Proceeding Paper 160, Book Chapters 37, Editorial Material 37, Early Access 23, Review Article 18, Meeting Abstract 4, Book Review 3, News Item 2, Correction 1, Letter 1 on the subject indexed in Web of Science. In addition, Linda Harrington, who has 23 studies indexed in Web of Science on this subject, is followed by Oswaldo Jose Lorenzo, Peter Kawalak, R. Collington, Leigh Wharton, Stelios Timotheuou with 6 studies, Christopher L. Tucci and Iryna Gurevych with 5 studies.

In terms of research areas; Management (130), Business (125), Computer Science Information Systems (78), Information Science Library Science (63), Computer Science Interdisciplinary Applications (44), Computer Science Theory Methods (43), Education Educational Research (40), Computer Science Artificial Inteligence (34), Engineering Electrical Electronic (32), Communication (31), Economics (31), Green Sustainable Science Technology (28),Nursing (27), Environmental Studies (24), Environmental Sciences (23), Health Care Sciences Services (20), Multidisciplinary Sciences (19), Operations Research Management Science (18), Social Sciences Interdisciplinary (18), Automation Control Systems (17), Public Administration (17), Medical Informatics (16), Regional Urban Planning (16), Political Science (15) ; when the distribution of publications by country was examined, it was determined that the leadership was with publishers from the USA (152), England (86), Germany (68), Spain (52), Italy (50), China (50), Australia (39), Netherlands (33), Canada (29), Mexico (24), Portugal (21), Ireland (19), France (18), India (18), Switzerland (18), Russia (15); the studies were mostly published in English (690), Spanish (27) and German (5); the majority of publications were scanned in the Emerging Sources Citation Index (ESCI) (227), Social Sciences Citation Index (SSCI) (205) and Science Citation Index Expanded (SCI-EXPANDED) (171) indexes. When we look at the most frequently used keywords in publications related to digital strategy, the most frequently used words are digital strategy with 175 repetitions, digital transformation with 112 repetitions, digitalization with 33 repetitions, social media with 23 repetitions and digital technology with 17 repetitions.

In an environment where artificial intelligence is on the rise and thrives on the data produced by humanity on the internet, studies on the spread of artificial intelligence and digital strategy will also be valuable. The development of digital strategies can be effective in solving current economic problems such as climate change problems (Can and Terziev, 2017), nutrition problems (Can, 2023), and energy problems (Dincsoy and Can (2023) in certain areas. The effectiveness and effects of existing social awareness strategies are among the issues that need to be examined. How strategies such as education programs, campaigns, and awareness activities for the society can be designed are potentially beneficial, especially in comparative studies that take into account differences between different cultures, demographic groups, or sectors. Of course, the study has some limitations. The most critical limitations of the study are the inclusion of studies listed in the WOS Core Collection within the scope of the analysis, the exclusion of databases such as TÜBİTAK Ulakbim and YÖK Thesis Archive in Turkey and Scopus and Pubmed in the international arena, and other sources that are not in online circulation.

REFERENCES

Akbiyik, S., & Can, H. (2023). Structural and Qualitative Defects in Adaptation to Digital Transformation in Local Governments. In Okur Dinçsoy, M., & Can, H. (Eds.), *Optimizing Energy Efficiency During a Global Energy Crisis* (pp. 327–340). IGI Global. DOI: 10.4018/979-8-3693-0400-6.ch018

AlNuaimi, B. K., Singh, S. K., Ren, S., Budhwar, P., & Vorobyev, D. (2022). Mastering Digital Transformation: The Nexus Between Leadership, Agility, and Digital Strategy. *Journal of Business Research*, 145, 636–648. DOI: 10.1016/j.jbusres.2022.03.038

Balakrishnan, R., & Das, S. (2020). How do Firms Reorganize to Implement Digital Transformation? *Strategic Change*, 29(5), 531–541. DOI: 10.1002/jsc.2362

Can, H., & Minkovska, D. (2020). Current Status and Future of Artifical Inteligence, XXIX ISTC "ADP-2020", Sozopol, Bulgaria, ISSN 2682-9584, 162-165, https://mf.tu-sofia.bg/ADP%20Magazine%20site/index.html

Can, H., Minkovska, D., & Stoyanova, L. (2020, October). Estimation of Energy Performance Classes of Concrete Structures with Artificial Intelligence Models. In *2020 III International Conference on High Technology for Sustainable Development (HiTech)* (pp. 1-3). IEEE. DOI: 10.1109/HiTech51434.2020.9364003

Can, H., & Terziev, V. (2016). The relationship economic growth and information technologies. Retrieved from *SSRN*: https://ssrn.com/abstract=3383899 or DOI: 10.2139/ssrn.3383899

Can, H., & Terziev, V. (2017, October). Climate Change Effect on Energy Production Index. In *Сборник Доклади от Научна Конференция „Актуални Проблеми на Сигурността", Електронно издание Велико Търново* (pp. 292-297). DOI: 10.2139/ssrn.3383943

Can, S. (2023). The Role of Nutrition in Social and Economic Development. In Okur Dinçsoy, M., & Can, H. (Eds.), *Optimizing Energy Efficiency During a Global Energy Crisis* (pp. 341–348). IGI Global. DOI: 10.4018/979-8-3693-0400-6.ch019

Chanias, S., Myers, M. D., & Hess, T. (2019). Digital transformation strategy making in pre-digital organizations: The case of a financial services provider. *The Journal of Strategic Information Systems*, 28(1), 17–33. DOI: 10.1016/j.jsis.2018.11.003

Dang-Pham, D., Hoang, A. P., Vo, D. T., & Kautz, K. (2022). Digital Kaizen: An Approach to Digital Transformation. *AJIS. Australasian Journal of Information Systems*, 26, 1–28. DOI: 10.3127/ajis.v26i0.3851

Dias, A. M., Carvalho, A. M., & Sampaio, P. (2022). Quality 4.0: Literature Review Analysis, Definition and Impacts of the Digital Transformation Process on Quality. *International Journal of Quality & Reliability Management*, 39(6), 1312–1335. DOI: 10.1108/IJQRM-07-2021-0247

Dinçsoy, E. E. (2023). Dijital Dünyanın Paradigmaları. In Kayapınar, Ö., & Yürük Kayapınar, P. (Eds.), *Geleceği İnşa Etmek: Metaverse ve Yapay Zeka ile İşletmelerde Dijital Dönüşüm* (pp. 1–28). Paradigma Akademi.

Dinçsoy, M. O., & Can, H. (2023). The Relationship of Renewable Energy Generation, Renewable Energy Consumption, and Economic Growth: The Case of Türkiye. In Okur Dinçsoy, M., & Can, H. (Eds.), *Optimizing Energy Efficiency During a Global Energy Crisis* (pp. 65–74). IGI Global. DOI: 10.4018/979-8-3693-0400-6.ch005

Dwivedi, Y. K., Hughes, D. L., Coombs, C., Constantiou, I., Duan, Y., Edwards, J. S., Gupta, B., Lal, B., Misra, S., Prashant, P., Raman, R., Rana, N. P., Sharma, S. K., & Upadhyay, N. (2020). Impact of COVID-19 pandemic on information management research and practice: Transforming education, work and life. *International Journal of Information Management*, 55, 102211. DOI: 10.1016/j.ijinfomgt.2020.102211

Eller, R., Alford, P., Kallmünzer, A., & Peters, M. (2020). Antecedents, consequences, and challenges of small and medium-sized enterprise digitalization. *Journal of Business Research*, 112, 119–127. DOI: 10.1016/j.jbusres.2020.03.004

Fernández, A., Gómez, B., Binjaku, K., & Meçe, E. K. (2023). Digital Transformation Initiatives in Higher Education Institutions: A Multivocal Literature Review. *Education and Information Technologies*, 28(10), 12351–12382. DOI: 10.1007/s10639-022-11544-0 PMID: 37361743

Forbes. (2020). Bernard Marr-How the covid-19 pandemic is fast-tracking digital transformation in companies. https://www.forbes.com/sites/bernardmarr/2020/03/17/how-thecovid-19-pandemic-is-fast-tracking-digital-transformation-incompanies/#449f9158a8ee/

Horváth, D., & Szabó, R. Z. (2019). Driving forces and barriers of Industry 4.0: Do multinational and small and medium-sized companies have equal opportunities? *Technological Forecasting and Social Change*, 146, 119–132. DOI: 10.1016/j.techfore.2019.05.021

Ivančić, L., Vukšić, V. B., & Spremić, M. (2019). Mastering the Digital Transformation Process: Business Practices and Lessons Learned. *Technology Innovation Management Review*, 9(2), 36–50. DOI: 10.22215/timreview/1217

Ly, B. (2023). The Interplay of Digital Transformational Leadership, Organizational Agility, and Digital Transformation. *Journal of the Knowledge Economy*. Advance online publication. DOI: 10.1007/s13132-023-01377-8

Muduli, A., & Choudhury, A. (2024). Exploring the Role of Workforce Agility on Digital Transformation: A Systematic Literature Review. *Benchmarking*. Advance online publication. DOI: 10.1108/BIJ-02-2023-0108

Okur Dincsoy, M. (2009). Can ICT Economically Catalyze a Regional GDP Per Capita Convergence? A Case Study of Major East Asian Countries. , 7(1), 45-64.

Okur Dinçsoy, M. (2020). Sustainable Development and Industry Revolutions. In New Approaches to CSR, Sustainability and Accountability, Volume I. Accounting, Finance, Sustainability, Governance & Fraud: Theory and Application (pp. 61-79). Singapore: Springer.

Paus, E. (2018). *Confronting Dystopia: The New Technological Revolution and the Future of Work*. Cornell University Press. DOI: 10.7591/9781501719868

Plekhanov, D., Franke, H., & Netland, T. H. (2023). Digital Transformation: A Review and Research Agenda. *European Management Journal*, 41(6), 821–844. DOI: 10.1016/j.emj.2022.09.007

Raj, A., Dwivedi, G., Sharma, A., de Sousa Jabbour, A. B. L., & Rajak, S. (2020). Barriers to the adoption of industry 4.0 technologies in the manufacturing sector: An inter-country comparative perspective. *International Journal of Production Economics*, 224, 107546. DOI: 10.1016/j.ijpe.2019.107546

Rozak, H. A., Adhiatma, A., Fachrunnisa, O., & Rahayu, T. (2021). Social Media Engagement, Organizational Agility and Digitalization Strategic Plan to Improve SMEs' Performance. *IEEE Transactions on Engineering Management*, 70(11), 3766–3775. DOI: 10.1109/TEM.2021.3085977

Saarikko, T., Westergren, U. H., & Blomquist, T. (2020). Digital Transformation: Five Recommendations for the Digitally Conscious Firm. *Business Horizons*, 63(6), 825–839. DOI: 10.1016/j.bushor.2020.07.005

Schallmo, D., Williams, C. A., & Lohse, J. (2019). Digital strategy—Integrated approach and generic options. *International Journal of Innovation Management*, 23(08), 1940005. DOI: 10.1142/S136391961940005X

Schwab, K. (2016). The Fourth Industrial Revolution: What It Means, How to Respond. World Economic Forum, January 16.

Singh, S., Sharma, M., & Dhir, S. (2021). Modeling the Effects of Digital Transformation in Indian Manufacturing Industry. *Technology in Society*, 67, 101763. DOI: 10.1016/j.techsoc.2021.101763

Tsai, W. Y., & Su, C. J. (2022). Digital Transformation of Business Model Innovation. *Frontiers in Psychology*, 13, 1017750. DOI: 10.3389/fpsyg.2022.1017750 PMID: 36389577

Vial, G. (2019). Understanding Digital Transformation: A Review and a Research Agenda. *The Journal of Strategic Information Systems*, 28(2), 118–144. DOI: 10.1016/j.jsis.2019.01.003

Wisskirchen, G., Biacabe, B. T., Bormann, U., Muntz, A., Niehaus, G., Soler, G. J., & von Brauchitsch, B. (2017). Artificial intelligence and robotics and their impact on the workplace. *IBA Global Employment Institute*, 11(5), 49–67.

Yeow, A., Soh, C., & Hansen, R. (2018). Aligning with new digital strategy: A dynamic capabilities approach. *The Journal of Strategic Information Systems*, 27(1), 43–58. DOI: 10.1016/j.jsis.2017.09.001

Zhang, X., Xu, Y. Y., & Ma, L. (2023b). Information Technology Investment and Digital Transformation: The Roles of Digital Transformation Strategy and Top Management. *Business Process Management Journal*, 29(2), 528–549. DOI: 10.1108/BPMJ-06-2022-0254

Chapter 2
A Tale of Two Countries:
Triple Transformation Effect on Business Performance in the United Kingdom and France

Enver Erdinç Dinçsoy
https://orcid.org/0000-0002-3927-0724
Trakya University, Turkey

Muhammet Atlas Doğan
https://orcid.org/0000-0002-4943-223X
Istanbul Technical University, Turkey

ABSTRACT

This study explores the effect of triple transformation—environmental, technological, and social initiatives—on business performance in the UK and France. The authors use panel data from 25 UK and 24 French firms (2005-2023) and employ panel quantile regression models to assess the impact of research and development expenses (RND), social pillar score (SPS), and environmental innovation score (ENIS) on return on assets (ROA). The results show SPS and ENIS negatively affect profitability, especially for more profitable firms, while RND shows no significant impact. Firm size positively influences profitability but diminishes among top performers. Triple transformation is crucial for sustainable growth, though it may pose short-term financial challenges for more profitable firms. Policymakers should consider supportive measures for firms adopting sustainability initiatives. This study provides empirical insights into the nuanced effects of triple transformation on profitability in different economic contexts.

DOI: 10.4018/979-8-3693-9435-9.ch002

1. INTRODUCTION

In the 21st century, businesses face pressures from sustainability and social expectations in addition to rapidly changing technological developments. These pressures may originate from the economic system or sectoral structure, as well as legal regulations and/or social origins. This process has evolved into a different structure with the addition of social transformation to the twin transformation, which entered the literature as the integration of digital transformation and green transformation. This concept, called triple transformation, has become a necessity for businesses not only to gain competitive advantage, but also to achieve long-term sustainable success. *Triple transformation* requires businesses to restructure their business models. In addition, businesses will provide global competitive advantage by combining innovation, environmentally friendly practices and processes that provide social benefits, and will also help them not to get stuck in tax, trade, financial, etc. prohibitive policies brought by international regulations. Consequently, triple transformation, which incorporates environmental, technological, and social changes, is progressively an essential framework for increasing business performance.

A particularly compelling framework for achieving this is the concept of triple transformation, which focuses on the integration of environmental, technological, and social transformations to drive sustainable growth and enhance overall business performance.

A range of economic, social, political, and technological changes have repercussions on businesses, leading them to change the ways they work and driving them to adopt innovative solutions. Among such changes, those linked to climate and environmental issues, referred to as the green growth or green economy, are particularly of interest. They have mainly originated from and are a part of every country's policy to fight against climate change. Innovation and the integration of new technologies are obviously considered possible ways businesses can grow and gain a competitive advantage, and the impact of environmental changes and technologies combined, known as green development innovation, has already been discussed at the theoretical and empirical level. More recently, other social trends, such as the increase in public health and quality of life expectations and the development of social media, have also emerged as a part of the new standard of society, made up of social macro trends that are a source of significant changes in economic, social, and structural infrastructures.

Environmental transformation involves integrating sustainable practices into business operations, driven by the urgent need to address climate change and ecological degradation. Companies that adopt green entrepreneurship principles not only create social and environmental value but also enhance their competitive advantage. As an illustration, businesses introducing eco-innovations are able to improve their bottom line while decreasing the level of their environmental impacts (Rabadán et al., 2019). The shift to a green economy contributes to the global sustainability agenda and enables the growing of a low-carbon economy, which is highly required for the survival of the business in the long-term (Khasanova and Saydulgerieva, 2024). Furthermore, organizations that embed environmental considerations into their corporate strategies often experience enhanced brand reputation and customer loyalty, leading to improved financial performance.

Technological transformation is characterized by the adoption of digital technologies that streamline operations, enhance productivity, and foster innovation. The digital metamorphosis of business processes cannot be regarded as only a current perspective or existing fashion but as an important part of staying afloat in the current competitive environment (Dinçsoy, 2023). With the use of such technologies, artificial intelligence, big data technologies and cloud computing, organizations can rationalize their processes and leverage on data from the analysing (Okur Dinçsoy, 2020).

The role of digital transformation in enhancing operational efficiency is evident across various sectors. Active and strategic application of the relevant digital technologies can enhance their normal operations which in turn brings positive results for business (Trollman and Colwill, 2021). For instance, the adoption of digital strategies mediated the relationship between market complexity and Small Medium Enterprise (SME) performance indicating the importance of technology meeting business needs (Prihandono et al., 2024). Additionally, firms that have implemented the digital transformation process tend to have a better ability to adapt to the changing environment or consumer needs, which gives them a good advantage over their competitors (Simbolon, 2024; Duğru, 2024).

Social transformation involves adopting more inclusive and equitable business practices that consider the needs and well-being of all stakeholders. Social entrepreneurship, which focuses on addressing social issues through innovative business models, plays a significant role in this context (Cao et al., 2023). By prioritizing social responsibility and community engagement, businesses can build stronger relationships with their stakeholders, enhance their brand reputation, and foster customer loyalty. Furthermore, integrating social considerations into business strategies can lead to improved employee satisfaction and retention, further contributing to organizational success.

The interconnectedness of these transformations creates a synergistic effect that enhances business performance. Such companies would often use digital technologies to help them monitoring the ecological reporting activities., thereby improving transparency and accountability (Burritt and Christ, 2016). Technological progress can also assist in the carrying out of social initiatives by allowing for policymakers and business decision-makers to achieve alignment between corporate digitalization and sustainability (Sang and Han, 2023).

The triple transformation is comprehensive, integrating digital, green and social transformation about the opportunities and challenges that businesses and societies have to face today. Global Powers such as the UK and France have employed different strategic paths towards adopting and actualizing triple transformation. Future transformations indeed pose similarities and distinctions which are because of the economic, political and social structures of each country. It has been suggested that companies adjusting to the requirements of eco-innovation can reduce its environmental impact and concurrently increase efficiency (Rabadán et al., 2019). The route towards sustainable economy is in line with the global sustainable development agenda and supports low carbon economic development[1] which is essential for the long term survival of enterprises (Khasanova and Saydulgerieva, 2024). Besides, firms rearranging their corporate strategies in favour of environmentally friendly policies tend to improve their brand and customer loyalty together which enhances profits.

The ongoing adjustment process is accompanied by the introduction of digital technology systems that streamline processes, increase efficiency, and enhance creative thinking. Actions and changes which modern businesses embrace willingly and actively as they understand that it is not just a fad, rather, the digital transformation of companies is essential development. With the convergence of technology such as AI, big data, and cloud computing, organizations can improve their processes and make data-based decisions. It has been observed that project-based firms with a tendency to integrate technology in their activities, perform better financially and have an improved ability to develop new products.

The role of digital transformation in improving operational efficiency is evident in most industries. Strategic activities improve sectoral efficiency which in turn leads to better overall corporate performance (Trollman and Colwill, 2021). The adoption of digital strategies mediated the relationship between market complexity and SME performance indicating the importance of technology meeting business needs.

Digital transformation allows businesses to increase efficiency by restructuring their business processes, while digital applications contribute to both improving customer experience and reducing costs (Kapoor et al., 2022; Duğru, 2023). In a period when industry 4.0 applications are widespread in many countries around the world, it is seen that digitalization efforts in France have accelerated, especially with the adoption of industry 4.0 applications (Fond-Harmant et al., 2023). Industry 4.0 applications are the main elements that increase the efficiency of production factors under limited resources in a rapidly digitalizing world. Another global trend that prevents waste of resources and increases the efficiency of production factors is the *Circular Economy*. The circular economy provides more efficient use of resources, while significantly reducing global pollution and carbon emissions (Kazaz et al.,

2023). Many telecommunications and technology companies provide transparency and accountability to companies by providing intermediary services for monitoring and reporting environmental data (Kuriyan et. al., 2011).

Companies have general and specific goals. Their general goals are similar for all countries in the world and are shaped around profit, continuity and social benefit. However, among the specific goals of companies, there are elements that support social transformation such as "protecting the health and morale of employees" and "developing good relations with neighbours and society". In this respect, social transformation is increasingly important for companies and is a qualified tool that increases social welfare. In a period when the interaction between companies' specific goals and their general goals is increasing, issues such as workforce diversity, social equality and employee satisfaction are seen to be prioritized in social transformation practices in France[2]. While state-supported initiatives encourage businesses to increase their social responsibility through educational reforms and workforce inclusiveness, social entrepreneurship also increases the brand value of companies by providing innovative solutions to social problems.

It is certain that companies that achieve the triple transformation will gain a competitive advantage. However, in order to create a broader social and environmental impact, they must increase digital technologies, environmental efficiency and social initiatives at a higher level (Han et al., 2023).

The triple transformation expresses a holistic integration and becomes a strategic necessity for companies. Companies that cannot implement this holistic integration will face significant risks such as lack of digital transformation, inefficiency, failure to meet customer expectations and failure to adapt to market conditions. Failure to properly adopt new technologies will limit companies' ability to offer innovative products and services to the market and eliminate their competitive advantage (Trollman and Colwill, 2021). In other words, companies that do not have an information and communication technology (ICT) infrastructure, especially those that do not create automation and data analytics mechanisms, will be highly likely to fall behind.

Companies that cannot achieve green transformation will have difficulty in the face of increasingly stringent environmental regulations. The most important of these challenges will be the implementation of high penalties, increased costs and negative impacts on brand value. Especially in regions such as the European Union, where regulations such as carbon footprint management and sustainability reporting are in place, it is inevitable for businesses to transition to sustainable production models (Eurostat, 2023)[3]. Therefore, companies that fail to fulfil their environmental responsibilities will not be preferred by consumers and will be replaced by more environmentally friendly alternatives (Geels, 2022).

Lack of social transformation can lead businesses to lose social trust. Companies that do not adopt values such as diversity, equality and social responsibility weaken their relationships with employees and society. Losing a social license means that a company is not accepted by local communities and loses its perception in the eyes of consumers (Cao et al., 2023). Today, consumers prefer to stay away from businesses that do not adopt business ethics practices, and this negatively affects customer loyalty (Han, 2023).

On the other hand, lack of digitalization, lack of green transformation and lack of social responsibility can reduce the interest of investors and negatively affect the financial structure of the company. For example, companies with poor ESG (Environmental, Social and Governance) performance may not receive the necessary financial support, which may increase the company's capital costs (Idris et al., 2024). Moreover, investors may give more priority to companies focused on social responsibility, which may cause the financial performance of companies that do not adapt to social transformations to decrease in the long term (Kohli and Melville, 2019).

Companies that achieve the triple transformation will be ahead in the innovation and adaptation race on a global scale. Although this situation seems to affect developed countries, this risk will also start to show its effect in the short term for rapidly developing countries. The microeconomic connections of national development plans should not be ignored, as it will be valid for developed countries that are trying to maintain their place on a global scale as well as countries with rapid development goals. In addition, companies that lose their competitive advantage due to rapidly changing market conditions will lose their talented and qualified workforce, causing the human capital quality of their countries to decrease (von Kutzschenbach, 2017) because today the young generation is more inclined to technology and prefer to work in companies with high social responsibility and environmental awareness (Greenwood et al., 2014; Gegenhuber et al., 2020).

In short, by implementing the triple transformation in a holistic way, businesses not only eliminate threats, but also have the potential to evaluate new opportunities. Therefore, triple transformation should be considered as a strategic road map for the sustainability and long-term success of businesses, and triple transformation should become a necessity rather than an option for companies.

This study seeks to extend knowledge by definitively comparing the effects of triple transformation on business in the UK and France. It aims to understand the patterns and results of management change, including digital, green, and social transformation, in two of the countries and how businesses are affected to modify their practices and what strategy is employed. The panel data encompasses such variables as Return on Asset (ROA), Research and Development Expenses to Total Revenues Ratio (RND), Social Pillar Score (SPS), Environmental Innovation Score (ENIS), and Company's Market Cap (MCAP). These indicators are very important in exploring the relationship between corporate strategies and performance measurement with a focus on digital, green and social transitions. Utilizing this extensive data set, the study hopes to establish the patterns, correlations and cause and effect which will explain how the businesses in the two countries are responding to the pressures of transformation in the three dimensions while enhancing their growth and competitiveness. For this reason, this study hopes to fill a gap in the academic literature in order to assist policymakers and businesses in formulating appropriate triple transformation strategies which will yield improved sustainable growth.

The SMEs across the European Union stress that there are great initiatives and projects that get funded for the advancement and digital transformation but there is a percentage gap on how the digitally transformed projects will be integrated to be environmentally sustainable. The success of the triple transformation can be grouped under certain headings such as strategic leadership and management, innovation and technological infrastructure strengthening, awareness of environmental and social consequences, establishing networks and partnerships, and education and talent management. However, transferring the socio-political and socio-economic order from one form to another can cause certain problems and difficulties. The resistance of people to change due to their traditions and established practices or the lack of resources or funds required to undergo a transformation, and the resistance of organizations to change are among the most difficult and problematic issues encountered during the process. In addition, legal and political obstacles can be important factors that seriously hinder/delay transformation activities.

Zero waste initiatives, renewable energy projects, and cybersecurity strategy transformations are some of the most successful and well-known examples of the triple transformation. Such projects are good examples of successful integration and use of environmental, technological, and social factors. The aim of zero waste projects and programs is to ensure more efficient use of resources and to reduce environmental impacts (Huseynov and Dinçsoy, 2023). With renewable energy programs, cleaner energy sources that will replace fossil fuels are used in production and consumption (Dinçsoy and Can, 2023). Digital transformation projects, on the other hand, increase the performance of business operations and help create a sustainable organizational structure by improving a company's technology infrastructure.

In order to successfully implement the triple transformation, organizations must increase their focus on leadership development programs, provide training aimed at encouraging innovation, and continuously improve the quality of human capital that their employees have. In addition, strategic steps such as regularly monitoring and evaluating environmental and social impacts and creating suitable environments for collaborations will support the transformation process. These measures will not only advance the competitive advantage of organizations but will also be important in terms of collaborations and sustainability issues.

2. REVIEW OF LITERATURE

The concept of triple transformation enhances the notion of twin transformation by integrating a social dimension, which emphasizes inclusivity and promotes societal welfare in conjunction with digital and ecological objectives. This more expansive framework recognizes the intricate interdependencies among economic development, technological advancement, and social equity.

He and Chen (2024) in their paper focused on the impact of digital transformation on the ESG performance of Chinese A-share listed firms from the year 2010 to 2022. The study also found out that digital transformation improved corporate ESG performance which is largely the case in private enterprises. Specifically, the key mechanisms include improvements in something like the quality of people and the skills within the organization. Environmental regulation, however, in various ways that alter the manner through which digital transformation affects labor and therefore the ESG performance of the firm, alters such outcomes. Nitlarp and Mayakul (2023) have also studied the relationship between the ESG elements and the three Business, Workforce, and Technology transformations in the energy industry and noted the importance of digital transformation in modern business as an agent of new ideas and development that is important for the improvement of competitiveness in the ever-changing environment. The research examined the relationships through which triple transformation affects ESG performance and established that the structures of relationships of causal mechanisms were such that triple transformation has a positive impact on ESG measures.

From the perspective of the Resource Based View (RBV) and Contingency Theory, Vitari and Raguseo (2020) identified links between business value derived from Big Data Analytics (BDA) and the performance of firms within their business setting. It is suggested that BDA solutions can serve as a source of competitive advantage with environmental factors playing a critical role in shaping this relationship. The findings revealed that environmental munificence positively moderates the link between BDA business value and firm performance, in contrast, environmental dynamism does not exhibit a moderating effect on the performance outcomes of BDA solutions.

The study based on the information derived from medium and large firms in France, concluded that high level adoption of BDA solutions is associated with better improved financial performance as well as greater market and customers satisfaction especially in munificent environments.

The environment external to the firm is viewed as a factor that may present opportunities, threats or resources to the firm and thus the relationship between firm's performance and the environment is salient in allowing organizations to make decisions and strategies in the face of dynamic. Institutional theory, dynamic capabilities theory and open system theory all acknowledge that amongst competing firms, those that are able to effectively tailor their operations to the gaps presented by the environment, tend to thrive over their rivals.

Das (2024) explores social and environmental practices and their implicating effects on business performance of Indian leather and chemical SMEs with a sample of 200 SMEs, a model was developed that aimed to depict how integrating collaborative operations within the industry and government policies promotes effective sustainability. The research findings therefore have been able to show that there is a connection between policies from the government and collaborative strategies implemented in organizations so that they all work towards improving sustainability and therefore organizational productivity. In addition, the size of the firm holds moderating influence over the equation of sustainability against the business performance of the firm. Achieving "triple-wins" whereby economic, social and environmental goals are integrated at the same time policy approaches in low-income countries is usually done thanks to well-designed strategies that have their roots from the top government led efforts at key points in history (Pickard and Lemma, 2023).

The frameworks of twin and triple transformation highlight the different yet complementary dimensions of the process of corporate change in the face of external imperatives. In Great Britain, the twin transformation is in line with the Net Zero Strategy and the United Kingdom's (UK) Digital Strategy, which seek to integrate technology with environmental objectives.

Such transformation is especially relevant as enterprises start recognizing the necessity of adopting sustainability in business processes. The environmental dimension of the triple transformation is mainly driven by the need for businesses to adopt sustainable practices that reduce their environmental footprint, with companies increasingly implementing green technology and sustainable resource practices to meet strict environmental legislation and the growing expectations of the green consumer (Costa et al., 2022; Kashmanian, 2022). Such policies are also aimed at achieving carbon neutrality and minimising waste generation, which makes it essential for businesses to develop and adopt more sustainable business models (Contini and Peruzzini, 2022).

On the other hand, the industrial change in UK can be characterized by the rapid integration of technologies aimed towards increasing productivity and fostering the development of new ideas and new products. The adoption of technologies such as artificial intelligence, big data or the Internet of Things (IoT) is altering the way business operations are conducted in many industries (Lei et al., 2023) enhancing supply chain management and increasing interaction with customers (Kim et al., 2024). The digital transformation not only amplifies productivity but also bolsters sustainability endeavors by facilitating improved resource management and minimizing waste generation (Costa et al., 2022). Furthermore, Industry 4.0 signifies a shift towards more organized and robotic production systems, which can lead to significant improvements in both economic and environmental performance. Businesses in France have developed innovative strategies to successfully manage this process. France has also left many European countries behind in green transformation by increasing its renewable energy investments within the framework of the European Green Deal (Fetting, 2020).

The social dimension of the triple transformation involves with practices towards greater social responsibilities. In England, there is a growing recognition of the importance of corporate social responsibility. Social issues such as inequality, employee welfare, and community engagement are increasingly expected to demonstrate their contributions to social values. Social transformation is not only about compliance but also about building trust and loyalty among stakeholders, including employees, customers, and the broader community (Arviana and Wibisono, 2023; Talattov et al., 2021). Social transformation is also supported by the UK Corporate Governance Code[4] (https://www.mccg.nl/), which encourages diversity and ethical data governance practices within organizations. Organizations are increasingly adopting the TBL5 framework to guide their strategies, ensuring that they remain competitive while contributing positively to society and the environment for navigating the complexities of modern business and achieving long-term sustainability.

In France, digital transformation studies have an important place in the strategic priorities of companies. It is revealed that French companies attach great importance to technologies such as cloud computing, AI, automation and data analytics in their digital transformation processes. Particularly, this transformation has accelerated after the COVID-19 pandemic and has become a strategy that aims to increase efficiency and innovation by going beyond customer experience.

A study conducted in France in 2023 found that IT expenditures are remarkably concentrated on investments such as cybersecurity and automation of business processes. In addition, 57% of companies reported satisfaction with digital transformation projects, which is slightly above the European average. French companies have determined reducing costs, focusing on core business functions and improving service quality as their main goals with digital transformation. Digital transformation strategies in sectors such as financial services and logistics focus on optimizing business processes and improving customer experience. These developments show that companies are increasing their R&D expenditures to increase their competitiveness with innovative technologies.

The organizational culture and innovation diffusion in technology offers strategic plans and practical recommendations to address for French SMEs, ultimately aiming to enhance operational efficiency and strengthen the national digital transformation framework (Ejjami, 2024).

In companies in France, environmental transformation is of increasing importance to achieve sustainability goals and gain competitive advantage. In this transformation process, companies are developing environmentally friendly production processes and innovation practices. Studies show that environmental innovations are closely linked to organizational changes. In particular, the implementation of environmentally sensitive innovations makes significant contributions to the training of employees, work organization and the management structure of the company. In this process, it is critical for companies to adopt environmental management systems and develop strategies to reduce their carbon footprints.

In the case of France, however, digital and environmental transformation concerns are dealt with simultaneously in the context of re-industrialization policies. In this perspective, businesses, for instance, aim to achieve the goals set out in the Paris Agreement and the Green Deal by changing their production processes and reducing carbon emissions. However, issues related to the protection of biological diversity, the management of water resources, and the design of products emerge as important factors of the transformation as well. In spite of this, environmental transformation is not seen only as a requirement for achieving sustainability, but as an area for innovation and competitiveness as well. In addition, it has been noticed that the environmental transformation policies put in place in France are coherent with the predominant industrial and environmental objectives.

In France, the focus of enterprises lies in diversity and inclusivity aspects of the efforts related to social transformation. The social transformation efforts are mainly based on the concepts of gender balance in the employment of the labour force, the employment of the migrant population, increasing bit all the economic mobility and diversity of cultures. The social transformation projects are intended to focus on gender integration within the labour forces, the incorporation of foreigners in the workforce, improving the economic status of the people, and the expansion of the cultural dimensions.

French companies that adopt socio-cultural diversity as a strategic goal implement concrete change programs at the senior management level. These programs aim not only to promote equality in the workplace but also to present a more inclusive corporate image to external stakeholders. Supporting individuals with different backgrounds, especially in terms of education levels and socio-economic mobility, can increase the contribution of employees to corporate success.

Another issue that can lead to greater changes both within the company and at the societal level is to ensure social transformation by creating more participatory governance structures in cultural and artistic life with social and solidarity economy (SSE)[6] models. In general, social transformation efforts in France prioritize approaches such as inclusive leadership, diversity programs, and participatory governance to increase the competitiveness of companies in order to contribute more to the general well-being of society.

The main reasons for choosing the UK and France for this study are both the analytical depth provided by the economic, cultural and regulatory differences of these two countries and the superiority of data access and quality. While the UK stands out with its flexible regulatory structure and its tendency towards innovative initiatives (especially after Brexit), France exhibits a more rigid regulatory and state intervention-based governance approach. These differences provide a strong basis for comparing how the triple transformation processes take shape and how businesses respond to these processes. In addition, these two countries are among the largest economies in Europe and are leaders in issues such as digitalization, environmental sustainability and social transformation. Although the UK and France adopt different strategies in these areas, both play a key role in Europe's transformation processes. The dataset used in the study provides comprehensive and reliable indicators, especially for businesses in these two countries, increasing the robustness and reliability of the analyses. Since other European countries do not offer the same level of infrastructure in terms of data quality and accessibility, the selection of the UK and France has become a scientific and rational choice in the study. In addition, the fact that these two countries have both similarities and differences in historical, political and commercial contexts creates a unique opportunity for comparative analysis. For these reasons, the selection of the UK and France as the focus of the study is not only due to a data limitation, but also due to the in-depth analysis potential they offer in analytical terms.

It should be noted that there are several reasons why the most powerful economy in Europe, Germany, was not included in the study. First, Germany's economic and institutional structure exhibits a different dynamism compared to other European countries. Germany has a strong industrial infrastructure, a highly export-oriented economy and a very strong labor market. These structural features cause digital, green and social transformation processes to take shape differently than other countries. Therefore, the inclusion of Germany was seen as a risk of reducing the depth and focus of the analyses while expanding the scope of the study. In particular, it is a fact that Germany, which operates within a much more centralized European Union policy framework, will reveal a very different transformation dynamic than the UK and France.

Secondly, Germany’s performance and strategic approaches in transformation processes have already been extensively examined by many academic studies and reports. It was thought that this situation could limit the original contribution that new research could bring.

In addition, while the dataset used in the study has a more coherent and comprehensive structure for the UK and France, similarly accessible, comparable and reliable data could not be obtained for other European countries. Since data deficiencies could affect the consistency of the analyses and the reliability of the results, it was preferred to exclude other similar countries from the analysis.

Finally, it was thought that including different countries in the study would make the comparison between countries more complex in administrative and analytical terms. Therefore, to analyse the specific transformation processes on which the study focuses in a clearer and more comparable way, the focus was on the UK and France. Considering the results obtained, it would be possible to expand the scope of the study and/or apply it to different country groups with a different model.

3. DATA AND METHODOLOGY

3.1. Discussion and Limitations

The main reasons for selecting the UK and France for the study are both the analytical depth provided by the economic, cultural and regulatory differences of these two countries and the superiority of data access and quality. While the UK stands out with its flexible regulatory structure and its tendency towards innovative initiatives (especially after Brexit), France exhibits a more rigid regulatory and state intervention-based governance approach. These differences provide a strong basis for comparing how the triple transformation processes take shape and how businesses respond to these processes. In addition, these two countries are among the largest economies in Europe and are leaders in issues such as digitalization, environmental sustainability and social transformation. Although the UK and France adopt different strategies in these areas, both play a key role in Europe's transformation processes. The dataset used in the study provides comprehensive and reliable indicators, especially for businesses in these two countries, increasing the robustness and reliability of the analyses. Since other European countries do not offer the same level of infrastructure in terms of data quality and accessibility, the selection of the UK and France has become a scientific and rational choice in the study. In addition, the fact that these two countries have both similarities and differences in historical, political and commercial contexts creates a unique opportunity for comparative analysis. For these reasons, the selection of the UK and

France as the focus of the study is not only due to a data limitation, but also due to the in-depth analysis potential they offer in analytical terms.

It should be noted that there are several reasons why the most powerful economy in Europe, Germany, was not included in the study. First, Germany's economic and institutional structure exhibits a different dynamism compared to other European countries. Germany has a strong industrial infrastructure, a highly export-oriented economy and a very strong labor market. These structural features cause digital, green and social transformation processes to take shape differently than other countries. Therefore, the inclusion of Germany was seen as a risk of reducing the depth and focus of the analyses while expanding the scope of the study. In particular, it is a fact that Germany, which operates within a much more centralized European Union policy framework, will reveal a very different transformation dynamic than the UK and France.

Secondly, Germany's performance and strategic approaches in transformation processes have already been extensively examined by many academic studies and reports. In addition, while the dataset used in the study has a more coherent and comprehensive structure for the UK and France, similarly accessible, comparable and reliable data could not be obtained for other European countries. Since data deficiencies could affect the consistency of the analyses and the reliability of the results, it was preferred to exclude other similar countries from the analysis.

Lastly, it was thought that including different countries in the study would make the comparison between countries more complex in administrative and analytical terms. Therefore, to examine the specific transformation processes on which the study focuses in a clearer and more comparable way, the focus was on the UK and France. Considering the results obtained, it would be possible to expand the scope of the study and/or apply it to different country groups with a different model.

3.2. Data and Variable Definitions

In this chapter, we present an examination of the relationship between firms' sustainability initiatives—specifically, R&D expenses, social responsibility, and environmental innovation—and their financial performance, as measured by ROA. Our analysis focuses on publicly listed firms from the UK and France, utilizing a panel quantile regression approach to capture the heterogeneous effects across different levels of firm profitability.

The dataset employed in this study comprises annual observations of publicly listed firms from the UK and France over the period from 2005 to 2023. The data were collected from the financial database Thomson Reuters Eikon, and the firm's annual reports. The initial sample included all firms listed on the main stock exchanges of the respective countries.

After applying these criteria, the final sample consists of 25 UK firms with 475 firm-year observations and 24 French firms with 456 firm-year observations.

Table 1. Variable Definitions

Indicator	Description
ROA	Return on Assets (%): Net income divided by total assets, representing firms' profitability.
RND	Research and Development Expenses to Total Revenue (%): Reflects firms' investment in innovation.
SPS	Social Pillar Score: A comprehensive measure of firms' social responsibility performance.
ENIS	Environmental Innovation Score: Assesses firms' efforts in environmental innovation and sustainability practices.
MCAP	Market Capitalization: Total market value of a firm's outstanding shares, serving as a proxy for firm size.

To provide an initial understanding of the data, we present the descriptive statistics for the key variables in Tables 2 and 3 for UK and French firms, respectively. An examination of the descriptive statistics reveals insightful differences and similarities between UK and French firms.

UK firms exhibit a higher average ROA of 9.58% compared to 4.86% for French firms, indicating that, on average, UK firms are more profitable. The standard deviation of ROA is larger for UK firms (7.69) than for French firms (4.49), suggesting greater variability in profitability among UK firms. The ROA ranges from -24.22% to 51.38% in the UK and from -19.52% to 22.60% in France, with UK firms having both lower minimums and higher maximums.

The average RND is slightly higher for French firms at 4.45% compared to 4.02% for UK firms. French firms show a wider range and higher standard deviation, with RND reaching up to 39.66%, indicating that some French firms invest substantially more in R&D.

Table 2. Descriptive Statistics for UK Firms

Variable	Obs	Mean	Std. dev.	Min	Max
ROA	475	9.58	7.69	-24.22	51.38
RND	475	4.02	6.07	0.00	25.46
SPS	475	57.69	24.83	6.45	97.30
ENIS	475	50.92	26.60	0.00	98.21
LN_MCAP	475	22.92	1.91	19.33	26.36

French firms have a higher average SPS of 68.32 compared to 57.69 for UK firms, suggesting that French firms may be more engaged in social responsibility initiatives. The standard deviations are relatively similar, indicating comparable variability in SPS across both samples.

The average ENIS is higher for French firms (55.75) than for UK firms (50.92), pointing towards a greater emphasis on environmental innovation in France. Both countries exhibit wide ranges, with maximum scores nearing 100, demonstrating that top-performing firms in both countries are highly engaged in environmental innovation.

Table 3. Descriptive Statistics for France Firms

Variable	Obs	Mean	Std. dev.	Min	Max
ROA	456	4.86	4.49	-19.52	22.60
RND	456	4.45	5.63	0.00	39.66
SPS	456	68.32	22.63	2.56	97.99
ENIS	456	55.75	26.04	6.25	99.36
MCAP_LN	456	23.18	1.45	17.64	26.31

The mean of the natural logarithm of market capitalization is slightly higher for French firms (23.18) than UK firms (22.92), indicating that the French sample includes somewhat larger firms on average. UK firms have a larger standard deviation (1.91) compared to French firms (1.45), suggesting greater diversity in firm sizes within the UK sample.

These differences may reflect varying national policies, cultural attitudes towards sustainability, and economic environments in the UK and France. The higher profitability among UK firms could reflect differences in market structures, competitive environments, or economic policies between the two countries.

The greater emphasis on social responsibility and environmental innovation among French firms may be influenced by cultural norms, stakeholder expectations, or more stringent regulatory requirements in France.

The higher RND variability and maximum values in France suggest that while the average investment in R&D is similar, certain French firms are investing significantly more in innovation, potentially seeking competitive advantages in technology-intensive industries.

The descriptive statistics provide a foundational understanding of the data and suggest that there are noteworthy differences between UK and French firms in terms of profitability, sustainability engagement, and firm size. These initial observations set the stage for a more detailed econometric analysis to uncover the underlying relationships between sustainability initiatives and financial performance across different levels of firm profitability.

3.3. Model and Estimation Technique

To examine the impact of R&D expenses, social responsibility, and environmental innovation on firm performance, we employ a panel quantile regression model. This methodology allows us to analyze how the effects of the independent variables vary across different points of the conditional distribution of the dependent variable (ROA). Unlike ordinary least squares (OLS) regression, which estimates the average effect, quantile regression provides a more comprehensive understanding of the relationships at different levels of profitability.

3.3.1. Model Specification

The panel quantile regression model is specified as follows:

$$Q\tau(ROA_{it} \mid X_{it}) = \alpha_i + \beta_{1,\tau} RND_{it} + \beta_{2,\tau} SPS_{it} + \beta_{3,\tau} ENIS_{it} + \beta_{4,\tau} ln(MCAP_{it}) + \varepsilon_{it}$$

Where, $Q\tau(ROA_{it} \mid X_{it})$ denotes the τ-th conditional quantile of ROA for firm i at time t. α_i represents unobserved firm-specific effects. $\beta_{k,\tau}$ are the quantile-specific coefficients for each explanatory variable. X_{it} is the vector of independent variables. ε_{it} is the error term.

Quantile regression, introduced by Koenker and Bassett (1978), is particularly suitable for our analysis for several reasons. It allows us to capture the differential impact of explanatory variables across the distribution of ROA, recognizing that factors influencing low-profit firms may differ from those affecting high-profit firms. Quantile regression is less sensitive to outliers and skewed distributions, which are common in financial data. Understanding the effects at different quantiles can inform targeted policy recommendations for firms at various profitability levels.

Traditional quantile regression models face challenges in panel data settings due to the incidental parameters problem when including fixed effects. To address this, we utilize the method of moments quantile regression (MM-QR) estimator developed by Machado and Santos Silva (2019). This estimator efficiently handles fixed effects in panel quantile regression models. Robust standard errors are calculated to account for potential heteroskedasticity and autocorrelation within panels.

4. RESULTS

4.1. Panel Unit Root Test Results

To ensure the reliability of our panel data analysis, it is crucial to determine whether the variables under study are stationary or contain unit roots. Non-stationary variables can lead to spurious regression results, which can mislead the interpretation of the relationships among variables. We conducted the Im–Pesaran–Shin (IPS) unit root tests for our key variables: ROA, RND, SPS, ENIS, and the natural logarithm of MCAP. The IPS test is suitable for panel data as it allows for individual unit root processes across panels (firms), testing the null hypothesis that all panels contain unit roots against the alternative that at least some panels are stationary.

Table 4. Unit root test results for France

Country	Variable	Z-t-tilde-bar
United Kingdom	ROA	-4.541***
United Kingdom	RND	-5.516***
United Kingdom	SPS	-3.846***
United Kingdom	ENIPS	-3.204***
United Kingdom	LN_MCAP	-3.447***
France	ROA	-5.768***
France	RND	-4.025***
France	SPS	-2.361***
France	ENIPS	-3.015***
France	LN_MCAP	-6.144***

Notes: p-values are indicated with stars: ***p<0.01, **p<0.05, *p<0.10.

The IPS unit root test results confirm that our key variables are stationary for at least some firms in both the UK and France. This finding supports the inclusion of these variables in our regression models without the concern of non-stationarity leading to unreliable results. The stationarity of these variables suggests that firms exhibit stability in profitability, innovation investments, social responsibility initiatives, and environmental innovation efforts over time. Consequently, any relationships identified in our analysis are more likely to reflect genuine economic phenomena rather than statistical artifacts.

By ensuring the stationarity of our variables, we strengthen the robustness of our subsequent panel data analyses, including the panel cointegration tests and quantile regression models. This foundational step enhances the credibility of our findings regarding the impact of triple transformation initiatives on business performance in the UK and France.

4.2. Panel Cointegration Test Results

To assess the long-term relationship among firm profitability (ROA), RND, SPS, ENIP, and firm size (LN_MCAP), we conducted panel cointegration tests using the methods proposed by Kao (1999), Pedroni (1999, 2004). The tests were performed both with and without demeaning to control cross-sectional dependence. The results are summarized in Table 5.

Table 5. Summary of Panel Cointegration Test Results for France

Country	Method	Test	Statistic	Statistic (Demeaned)
France	Kao Test	Modified Dickey-Fuller t	-6.41***	-6.88***
France	Kao Test	Dickey-Fuller t	-7.93***	-8.03***
France	Kao Test	Augmented Dickey-Fuller t	-4.84***	-4.56***
France	Kao Test	Unadjusted Modified DF t	-13.06***	-12.87***
France	Kao Test	Unadjusted Dickey-Fuller t	-10***	-9.81***
France	Pedroni Test	Modified Phillips-Perron t	1.46*	2.02**
France	Pedroni Test	Phillips-Perron t	-7.8***	-7.29***
France	Pedroni Test	Augmented Dickey-Fuller t	-8.18***	-7.54***
United Kingdom	Kao Test	Modified Dickey-Fuller t	-4.57***	-5.54***
United Kingdom	Kao Test	Dickey-Fuller t	-5.65***	-6.56***
United Kingdom	Kao Test	Augmented Dickey-Fuller t	-2.62***	-3.54***
United Kingdom	Kao Test	Unadjusted Modified DF t	-8.99***	-10.04***
United Kingdom	Kao Test	Unadjusted Dickey-Fuller t	-7.27***	-8.06***
United Kingdom	Pedroni Test	Modified Phillips-Perron t	3.67***	3.23***
United Kingdom	Pedroni Test	Phillips-Perron t	-2.94***	-4.05***
United Kingdom	Pedroni Test	Augmented Dickey-Fuller t	-3.1***	-3.39***

Notes: p-values are indicated with stars: ***p<0.01, **p<0.05, *p<0.10.

For both countries, the Kao test results indicate strong evidence of cointegration across all panels, with all test statistics significant at the 1% level. Similarly, the Pedroni test results support the presence of cointegration, as the majority of test statistics are significant at the 1% level.

These findings suggest that there is a stable long-term equilibrium relationship among the variables studied. The triple transformation factors, RND, ENIP, and SPS along with firm size, are interconnected with firm profitability over time. This implies that any short-term fluctuations among these variables are temporary and that they tend to move together in the long run. The results support the hypothesis that the triple transformation (digital, green, and social) is linked to business performance in both the UK and France.

This combination of stationarity and cointegration provides a solid foundation for the subsequent panel quantile regression analyses and supports the validity of the study's findings regarding the impact of the triple transformation on business performance.

4.3. Results for the Panel Quantile Regressions

The panel quantile regression results for UK firms are presented in Table 4, illustrating the effects of the independent variables—RND, SPS, ENIS, LN_MCAP on ROA across different quantiles of the profitability distribution.

4.3.1. Panel Quantile Regression Results for UK Firms

The coefficients for RND are positive at the lower quantiles (Q10 to Q50), ranging from 0.128 to 0.003, but none are statistically significant at conventional levels. At higher quantiles (Q60 to Q90), the coefficients become negative, decreasing to -0.093 at the 90th quantile, yet they remain statistically insignificant throughout. This pattern suggests that RND do not have a statistically significant impact on the profitability of UK firms across different levels of ROA within the sample period. The insignificance may be attributed to the lagged nature of returns on RND, where the benefits may materialize beyond the scope of the current analysis.

Table 6. Panel Quantile Regression Results for UK Firms

Variables	Q10	Q20	Q30	Q40	Q50	Q60	Q70	Q80	Q90
RND	0.128	0.082	0.056	0.030	0.003	-0.017	-0.037	-0.063	-0.093
	(0.218)	(0.184)	(0.165)	(0.148)	(0.133)	(0.124)	(0.118)	(0.114)	(0.116)
SPS	-0.134***	-0.124***	-0.118***	-0.113***	-0.107***	-0.103***	-0.098***	-0.093***	-0.086***
	(0.030)	(0.024)	(0.021)	(0.020)	(0.019)	(0.019)	(0.020)	(0.022)	(0.025)
ENIS	-0.018	-0.026	-0.030*	-0.035*	-0.040*	-0.043*	-0.047*	-0.052*	-0.057*
	(0.023)	(0.019)	(0.018)	(0.019)	(0.020)	(0.023)	(0.025)	(0.029)	(0.034)
LN_MCAP	5.701***	4.672***	4.074***	3.489***	2.866***	2.424***	1.971***	1.385**	0.703
	(1.236)	(0.992)	(0.875)	(0.782)	(0.690)	(0.639)	(0.610)	(0.600)	(0.609)

continued on following page

Table 6. Continued

Variables	Q10	Q20	Q30	Q40	Q50	Q60	Q70	Q80	Q90
Constant	-118.6***	-92.9***	-77.9***	-63.3***	-47.7***	-36.6***	-25.3**	-10.7	-6.3
	(27.6)	(22.1)	(19.5)	(17.5)	(15.4)	(14.2)	(13.6)	(13.4)	(13.6)

Notes: ***, **, * indicate P<0.01, P<0.05, and P<0.1 respectively. Standard errors are presented in parenthesis.

In contrast, the SPS exhibits negative and highly significant coefficients across all quantiles ($p < 0.01$). The magnitude of the coefficients slightly decreases from -0.134 at Q10 to -0.086 at Q90, indicating a persistent negative relationship between social responsibility performance and profitability. This consistent negative effect across the ROA distribution implies that higher engagement in social initiatives is associated with lower profitability for UK firms, potentially due to the costs involved in implementing such initiatives outweighing the immediate financial benefits.

The ENIS coefficients are negative and become statistically significant ($p < 0.10$) starting from the 30th quantile. The coefficients increase in magnitude from -0.030 at Q30 to -0.057 at Q90, suggesting that environmental innovation efforts have an increasingly negative impact on profitability at higher levels of ROA. This trend indicates that firms with higher profitability experience a more substantial adverse effect from environmental innovation investments, which may be due to the substantial costs associated with these initiatives not being offset by immediate returns.

The coefficients for LN_MCAP are positive and highly significant across most quantiles, with values decreasing from 5.701 at Q10 to 0.703 at Q90. The significance of LN_MCAP diminishes at the highest quantile, where it is no longer statistically significant. This diminishing effect suggests that while larger UK firms generally achieve higher profitability, the advantage conferred by firm size decreases for firms at the upper end of the profitability spectrum. The observed pattern may reflect diminishing returns to scale or that the most profitable firms rely on factors other than size, such as operational efficiency or niche market advantages.

4.3.2. Panel Quantile Regression Results for French Firms

Table 5 displays the panel quantile regression results for French firms, providing insights into how the independent variables affect profitability across different quantiles of the ROA distribution.

The RND coefficients for French firms are negative across all quantiles, ranging from -0.028 at Q10 to -0.051 at Q90, but they are not statistically significant at any level. This finding suggests that R&D expenditures do not have a significant immediate impact on the profitability of French firms within the sample period. Similar to the UK, the insignificance may be due to the time lag between R&D investments and the realization of their financial benefits.

Table 7. Panel Quantile Regression Results for France Firms

Variables	Q10	Q20	Q30	Q40	Q50	Q60	Q70	Q80	Q90
RND	-0.028	-0.033	-0.036	-0.039	-0.042	-0.044	-0.046	-0.048	-0.051
	(0.086)	(0.069)	(0.059)	(0.052)	(0.048)	(0.046)	(0.045)	(0.046)	(0.052)
SPS	-0.031*	-0.037**	-0.042***	-0.046***	-0.049***	-0.052***	-0.055***	-0.058***	-0.062***
	(0.018)	(0.0148)	(0.0129)	(0.0115)	(0.0108)	(0.0105)	(0.0106)	(0.0110)	(0.0123)
ENIS	0.009	0.002	-0.003	-0.008	-0.011*	-0.014**	-0.017**	-0.021***	-0.026***
	(0.011)	(0.0088)	(0.0076)	(0.0068)	(0.0065)	(0.0067)	(0.0070)	(0.0078)	(0.0092)
LN_MCAP	2.713***	2.615***	2.549***	2.487***	2.443***	2.397***	2.358***	2.312***	2.244***
	(0.686)	(0.563)	(0.501)	(0.460)	(0.446)	(0.446)	(0.458)	(0.484)	(0.542)
Constant	-59.9***	-55.3***	-52.2***	-49.3***	-47.2***	-45.0***	-43.2***	-41.1***	-37.9***
	(15.6)	(12.7)	(11.3)	(10.3)	(10.0)	(9.9)	(10.2)	(10.7)	(12.0)

Notes: ***, **, * indicate P<0.01, P<0.05, and P<0.1 respectively. Standard errors are presented in parenthesis.

The SPS coefficients are negative and become increasingly significant at higher quantiles. At the 10th quantile, the coefficient is -0.031 and significant at the 10% level, increasing in magnitude to -0.062 and achieving significance at the 1% level by the 90th quantile. This progression indicates that the negative impact of social responsibility performance on profitability is more pronounced for more profitable French firms. The increasing magnitude and significance at higher quantiles suggest that the costs associated with social initiatives may exert greater pressure on the profitability of firms already performing well.

The ENIS coefficients transition from positive but insignificant values at lower quantiles to negative and statistically significant coefficients starting at the median (Q50). From Q50 to Q90, the coefficients become increasingly negative and significant, with the coefficient reaching -0.026 at Q90 ($p < 0.01$). This shift implies that environmental innovation efforts begin to negatively affect profitability for firms at or above the median profitability level. The intensifying negative effect at higher quantiles suggests that the financial burden of environmental innovation is more substantial for more profitable firms in France.

The coefficients for LN_MCAP are consistently positive and highly significant across all quantiles, decreasing slightly from 2.713 at Q10 to 2.244 at Q90. This consistent positive relationship indicates that larger French firms achieve higher profitability across the ROA distribution. The slight decrease in the magnitude of the coefficients at higher quantiles suggests that while firm size remains an important determinant of profitability, its relative impact diminishes marginally for the most profitable firms.

5. FINDINGS

The quantile regression analysis reveals distinct patterns in how the independent variables affect firm profitability across different quantiles of the ROA distribution in both the UK and France. Notably, the SPS consistently exhibits a negative relationship with profitability in both countries, with the effect being statistically significant across all quantiles for UK firms and becoming increasingly significant at higher quantiles for French firms. This finding suggests that social responsibility initiatives are associated with lower profitability, and the effect is more pronounced among more profitable firms, especially in France.

The ENIS shows a negative and significant impact on profitability at higher quantiles in both countries, indicating that environmental innovation efforts may impose greater financial burdens on more profitable firms. The significance of the negative effect emerges at a lower quantile (Q30) for UK firms compared to French firms (Q50), implying that UK firms may experience the profitability impacts of environmental innovation earlier in the profitability spectrum.

RND does not display a statistically significant relationship with profitability in either country across all quantiles. This lack of significance suggests that the immediate financial benefits of R&D expenditures are not realized within the sample period, possibly due to the long-term nature of R&D investments.

Firm size, measured by LN_MCAP for UK firms and LN_MCAP for French firms, has a positive and significant effect on profitability across most quantiles. The effect diminishes at higher quantiles, particularly for UK firms where the coefficient becomes insignificant at the 90th quantile. This pattern indicates that while larger firms generally achieve higher profitability, the advantage conferred by size decreases for the most profitable firms, potentially due to diminishing returns to scale or the increasing importance of other factors such as innovation efficiency or market differentiation.

These findings highlight the heterogeneous effects of sustainability initiatives and firm characteristics on profitability across different levels of firm performance. The results underscore the importance of considering the distributional impacts when evaluating the relationship between corporate sustainability efforts and financial outcomes.

6. CONCLUSION

This study provides a comprehensive analysis of the impact of triple transformation—digital, green, and social—on business performance in the UK and France. By employing a panel quantile regression model on data from publicly listed firms between 2005 and 2023, we have uncovered insights into how sustainability initiatives and firm characteristics influence profitability across different levels of firm performance.

Our findings reveal that social responsibility initiatives, measured by SPS, consistently exhibit a negative relationship with profitability in both countries. This effect is statistically significant across all quantiles for UK firms and becomes increasingly significant at higher quantiles for French firms. The implication is that while social initiatives are essential for long-term sustainability and corporate reputation, they may impose short-term financial costs that disproportionately affect more profitable firms. This suggests that the immediate costs associated with implementing social responsibility practices may outweigh the immediate financial benefits, especially for firms operating at higher profitability levels.

Similarly, environmental innovation efforts, represented by ENIS, show a negative and significant impact on profitability at higher quantiles in both countries. The effect emerges at a lower quantile for UK firms compared to French firms, indicating that UK firms may experience the financial impacts of environmental innovation earlier in the profitability spectrum. This finding underscores the substantial investments required for environmental initiatives, which may not yield immediate financial returns, particularly for more profitable firms that might be investing more heavily in such initiatives.

RND do not display a statistically significant relationship with profitability in either country across all quantiles. This lack of significance may be attributed to the long-term nature of returns on RND, where financial benefits may materialize beyond the scope of the sample period analyzed. It suggests that firms may not experience immediate profitability gains from their RND, highlighting the need for a long-term strategic perspective when investing in innovation.

Firm size, LN_MCAP, has a positive and significant effect on profitability across most quantiles in both countries. However, the effect diminishes at higher quantiles, particularly for UK firms where the coefficient becomes insignificant at the 90th quantile. This pattern suggests that while larger firms generally achieve higher profitability, the marginal advantage conferred by size decreases for the most profitable firms. This could be due to diminishing returns to scale or the increasing importance of other factors such as operational efficiency, innovation efficiency, or market differentiation strategies in driving profitability at higher levels.

These results have important implications for both business practitioners and policymakers. For businesses, the findings highlight the need to balance sustainability initiatives with financial performance objectives. Firms, especially those with higher profitability, should carefully consider the timing and scale of their investments in social responsibility and environmental innovation to mitigate potential short-term profitability impacts. Developing strategies that integrate sustainability initiatives with core business operations may help in aligning these efforts with financial performance goals.

For policymakers, the negative association between sustainability initiatives and profitability suggests the need for supportive policies that incentivize businesses to engage in social and environmental activities without compromising their financial viability. This could include tax incentives, subsidies, or regulatory frameworks that reduce the financial burden on firms implementing sustainability initiatives, particularly for those at higher profitability levels who may be investing more heavily in these areas.

The study contributes to the existing literature by providing empirical evidence on the heterogeneous effects of triple transformation initiatives on firm profitability across different profitability levels in the UK and France. It underscores the importance of considering distributional impacts when evaluating the relationship between corporate sustainability efforts and financial outcomes.

However, the study also has limitations that offer avenues for future research. The analysis is confined to publicly listed firms, which may not capture the dynamics present in smaller or privately held companies. Additionally, the sample period may not fully capture the long-term effects of RND investments and sustainability initiatives. Future research could extend the analysis to a broader set of countries, including a longer time horizon, or examine sector-specific effects to deepen the understanding of how triple transformation influences business performance.

REFERENCES

Arviana, N., & Wibisono, M. (2023). The Effect Of Fundamental Factors On Triple Bottom Line And Firm Value. *JRAK*, 15(1), 12–18. DOI: 10.23969/jrak.v15i1.5474

Burritt, R., & Christ, K. (2016). Industry 4.0 and environmental accounting: A new revolution? *Asian Journal of Sustainability and Social Responsibility*, 1(1), 23–38. DOI: 10.1186/s41180-016-0007-y

Cao, D., Teng, X., Chen, Y., Tan, D., & Wang, G. (2023). Digital transformation strategies of project-based firms: Case study of a large-scale construction company in China. *Asia Pacific Journal of Innovation and Entrepreneurship*, 17(2), 82–98. DOI: 10.1108/APJIE-02-2023-0027

Contini, G., & Peruzzini, M. (2022). Sustainability and industry 4.0: Definition of a set of key performance indicators for manufacturing companies. *Sustainability (Basel)*, 14(17), 11004. DOI: 10.3390/su141711004

Costa, V. B. F., Capaz, R. S., Silva, P. F., Doyle, G., Aquila, G., Coelho, É. O., de Lorenci, E., Pereira, L. C., Maciel, L. B., Balestrassi, P. P., Bonatto, B. D., & da Silva, L. C. (2022). Socioeconomic and Environmental Consequences of a New Law for Regulating Distributed Generation in Brazil: A Holistic Assessment. *Energy Policy*, 169, 113176. DOI: 10.1016/j.enpol.2022.113176

Das, M. (2024). Impact of Social and Environmental Practices on SME Business Performance, *Authorea Preprints*.

Dinçsoy, E. E. (2023). Dijital Dünyanın Paradigmaları. In Kayapınar, Ö., & Yürük Kayapınar, P. (Eds.), *Geleceği İnşa Etmek: Metaverse ve Yapay Zeka ile İşletmelerde Dijital Dönüşüm* (pp. 1–28). Paradigma Akademi.

Dinçsoy, M. O., & Can, H. (2023). The relationship of renewable energy generation, renewable energy consumption, and economic growth: the case of Türkiye. In *Optimizing Energy Efficiency During a Global Energy Crisis* (pp. 65–74). IGI Global. DOI: 10.4018/979-8-3693-0400-6.ch005

Duğru, M. (2023). Bankacılık Sektöründe Dijitalleşme. In Kayapınar, Ö., & Yürük Kayapınar, P. (Eds.), *Metaverse, Yapay Zeka Ve Robotik Süreç Otomasyonlarinin Önemi* (pp. 273–297). Paradigma Academy.

Duğru, M. (2024). Innovation in the Banking World. In Abdelkader, M. S. D. (Ed.), *Social and Ethical Implications of AI in Finance for Sustainability* (pp. 228–246). IGI Global. DOI: 10.4018/979-8-3693-2881-1.ch010

Ejjami, R. (2024). The digital evolution: Strategies for overcoming cybersecurity and adoption challenges in French SMEs. International Journal For Multidisciplinary Research, 6(3).

Fetting, C. (2020). The European Green Deal. In *ESDN Report, December 2020*. ESDN Office.

Fond-Harmant, L., Philippart, A., Megherbi, S., Pereaux, P., & Gavrila-Ardelean, M. (2023). Digitalization of the European society: Challenges for social work. *Social Work Research*, 1, 141–155.

Geels, F. W. (2022). Conflicts between economic and low-carbon reorientation processes: Insights from a contextual analysis of evolving company strategies in the United Kingdom petrochemical industry (1970–2021). *Energy Research & Social Science*, 91, 102729. DOI: 10.1016/j.erss.2022.102729

Gegenhuber, T., Logue, D., Hinings, B. C., & Barrett, M. (2020). Digital transformation and institutional theorizing: Consequences, opportunities and challenges. Research in the Sociology of Organizations. Call for papers.

Greenwood, R., Hinings, C. R., & Whetten, D. (2014). Rethinking institutions and organizations. *Journal of Management Studies*, 51(7), 1206–1220. DOI: 10.1111/joms.12070

Han, Y., Li, Y., & Wang, Q. (2023). Digital finance, environmental regulation, and green development efficiency of China. *Frontiers in Environmental Science*, 11, 1131058. DOI: 10.3389/fenvs.2023.1131058

He, X., & Chen, W. (2024). Digital Transformation and Environmental, Social, and Governance Performance from a Human Capital Perspective. *Sustainability (Basel)*, 16(11), 4737. DOI: 10.3390/su16114737

Huseynov, N., & Dinçsoy, M. O. (2023). Döngüsel Ekonomi ve COVID-19 Pandemisinin Etkileri. *Balkan and Near Eastern Journal of Social Sciences*, 9(Special Issue), 262–279.

Idris, S. H., Chang, L. W., Prihandono, I., & Rasidi, S. A. (2024). Green financing and climate change: Challenges and regulatory mechanisms in Malaysia and Indonesia. *Clean Technologies and Environmental Policy*, 26(12), 1–12. DOI: 10.1007/s10098-024-02829-8

Im, K. S., Pesaran, M. H., & Shin, Y. (2003). Testing for unit roots in heterogeneous panels. *Journal of Econometrics*, 115(1), 53–74. DOI: 10.1016/S0304-4076(03)00092-7

Kao, C. (1999). Spurious regression and residual-based tests for cointegration in panel data. *Journal of Econometrics*, 90(1), 1–44. DOI: 10.1016/S0304-4076(98)00023-2

Kapoor, K., Bigdeli, A. Z., Schroeder, A., & Baines, T. (2022). A platform ecosystem view of servitization in manufacturing. *Technovation*, 118(102248), 1–12. DOI: 10.1016/j.technovation.2021.102248

Kashmanian, R. M. (2022). Scaling Up Transformational Change: Facing Up to Global Megatrends and Their Environmental Impacts. *Environmental Management and Sustainable Development*, 11(3), 13–60. DOI: 10.5296/emsd.v11i3.19875

Kazaz, D., Okur Dinçsoy, M., & Şenalp, U. E. (2023). Doğrudan Yabanci Yatirim, Ekonomik Büyüme Ve Karbon Emisyonu İlişkisinin Yeşil ve Kahverengi Alan Yatirimlari Açisindan Analizi. Trakya Üniversitesi Sosyal Bilimler Dergisi, 25(Özel Sayı), 429-446.

Khasanova, S. S., & Saydulgerieva, M. A. (2024). Green economy as a tool for sustainable development and a factor contributing to the formation of a low-carbon economy. In BIO Web of Conferences, 82(04003), 1-8. DOI: 10.1051/bioconf/20248204003

Kim, J. W., Rhee, J. H., & Park, C. H. (2024). How Does Digital Transformation Improve Supply Chain Performance: A Manufacturer's Perspective. *Sustainability (Basel)*, 16(7), 3046. DOI: 10.3390/su16073046

Koenker, R. (2004). Quantile Regression for Longitudinal Data. *Journal of Multivariate Analysis*, 91(1), 74–89. DOI: 10.1016/j.jmva.2004.05.006

Kohli, R., & Melville, N. P. (2019). Digital innovation: A review and synthesis. *Information Systems Journal*, 29(1), 200–223. DOI: 10.1111/isj.12193

Kuriyan, R., Bailur, S., Gigler, S., & Park, K. R. (2011). *Technologies for Transparency and Accountability: Implications for ICT policy and Implementation. Open Development Technology Alliance*. World Bank.

Lei, Y., Liang, Z., & Ruan, P. (2023). Evaluation on the impact of digital transformation on the economic resilience of the energy industry in the context of artificial intelligence. *Energy Reports*, 9, 785–792. DOI: 10.1016/j.egyr.2022.12.019

Machado, J. A. F., & Santos Silva, J. M. C. (2019). Quantiles via Moments. *Journal of Econometrics*, 213(1), 145–173. DOI: 10.1016/j.jeconom.2019.04.009

Nitlarp, T., & Mayakul, T. (2023). The Implications of Triple Transformation on ESG in the Energy Sector: Fuzzy-Set Qualitative Comparative Analysis (fsQCA) and Structural Equation Modeling (SEM) Findings. *Energies*, 16(5), 1–26. DOI: 10.3390/en16052090

Okur Dinçsoy, M. (2020). Sustainable Development and Industry Revolutions. In New Approaches to CSR, Sustainability and Accountability, Volume I. Accounting, Finance, Sustainability, Governance & Fraud: Theory and Application (pp. 61-79). Singapore: Springer.

Pedroni, P. (1999). Critical values for cointegration tests in heterogeneous panels with multiple regressors. *Oxford Bulletin of Economics and Statistics*, 61(s1, S1), 653–670. DOI: 10.1111/1468-0084.61.s1.14

Pedroni, P. (2004). Panel cointegration: Asymptotic and finite sample properties of pooled time series tests with an application to the PPP hypothesis. *Econometric Theory*, 20(3), 597–625. DOI: 10.1017/S0266466604203073

Pickard, S., & Lemma, A. (2023). In search of nexus triple wins: Planning for and evidence of economic transformation, social inclusion and ecological sustainability in Sri Lanka, Thailand and the Dominican Republic. *The Journal of Poverty and Social Justice : Research, Policy, Practice*, 31(3), 351–371. DOI: 10.1332/175982721X16916833771132

Prihandono, D., Wijaya, A. P., Wiratama, B., Prananta, W., & Widia, S. (2024). Digital transformation to enhance Indonesian SME performance: Exploring the impact of market competition and digital strategy. *Problems and Perspectives in Management*, 22(2), 103–113. DOI: 10.21511/ppm.22(2).2024.09

Rabadán, A., González-Moreno, Á., & Sáez-Martínez, F. J. (2019). Improving Firms' Performance and Sustainability: The Case of Eco-Innovation in the Agri-Food Industry. Sustainability, 11(20), 5590, 1-13

Sang, Y., & Han, E. (2023). A win-win way for corporate and stakeholders to achieve sustainable development: Corporate social responsibility value co-creation scale development and validation. *Corporate Social Responsibility and Environmental Management*, 30(3), 1177–1190. DOI: 10.1002/csr.2412

Simbolon, A. N. (2024). Innovative Trends in Economic Development: Towards a New Era of Creativity and Productivity. *Innovative Economics Journal*, 1(1), 16–24.

Talattov, A. P., Wibowo, M. R., & Kallman, M. (2021). Corporate Transformation Towards Sustainability: The case of the Indonesian pulp and papers industry. *Sustainability Science and Resources*, 1(1), 107–134. DOI: 10.55168/ssr2809-6029.2021.1005

Trollman, H., & Colwill, J. (2021). The imperative of embedding sustainability in business: A model for transformational sustainable development. *Sustainable Development (Bradford)*, 29(5), 974–986. DOI: 10.1002/sd.2188

Vitari, C., & Raguseo, E. (2019). Big data analytics business value and firm performance: Linking with environmental context. *International Journal of Production Research*, 58(18), 5456–5476. DOI: 10.1080/00207543.2019.1660822

Von Kutzschenbach, M. (2017). "And then a miracle occurs ..." - Engaging the challenge of operationalizing theories of success in digital transformation. Systemics. *Cybernetics and Informatics*, 15(6), 101–105.

ENDNOTES

1 European Union sets the goal of maximizing the reduction of carbon emissions by 2050

2 https://economy-finance.ec.europa.eu/system/files/2023-06/ip234_en.pdf

3 https://ec.europa.eu/eurostat/documents/276524/16747589/EU-SDG-indicators-2023-final.pdf/0d79cdec-5813-16d6-4161-e21d19cae2d2?t=1683812427141

4 A corporate governance code is a guide for board members and directors, setting out how they should approach governance in their organisation. Corporate governance codes are relatively recent in modern business.

5 The triple bottom line (TBL) maintains that companies should commit to focusing as much on social and environmental concerns as they do on profits.

6 The Social and Solidarity Economy (SSE) encompasses economic activities and relationships that emphasize social and frequently environmental goals over the pursuit of profit. It also involves collective action by citizens working in solidarity to democratize both economic structures and societal systems, including the participation of producers, workers, and consumers in fostering more inclusive and equitable approaches to economic and social development.

Chapter 3
Conceptual, Theoretical–Methodological, and Empirical Analysis of Digital Economic oOganization

José G. Vargas-Hernandez
https://orcid.org/0000-0003-0938-4197
Tecnológico Nacional de México, ITS Fresnillo, Mexico

Francisco J. Gonzàlez-Àvila
Tecnològico Nacional de Mèxico, ITS Fresnillo, Mexico

Omar C. Vargas-Gonzàlez
https://orcid.org/0000-0002-6089-956X
Tecnològico Nacional de Mèxico, Ciudad Guzmàn, Mexico

Carlos Rodriguez-Maillard
https://orcid.org/0000-0003-2406-196X
Universidad Cristóbal Colón, Mexico

ABSTRACT

This chapter aims to analyze the evolutionary advances in the review of the conceptual, theoretical-methodological, and empirical literature on digital economic organization from different perspectives and in the current context. The method used is meta-analytical and meta-cognitive, reflexive, and descriptive based on the review of the conceptual, theoretical-methodological, and empirical literature. It

DOI: 10.4018/979-8-3693-9435-9.ch003

is concluded that digital economic organization is a multidimensional concept that ranges from conceptual to methodological and empirical changes.

INTRODUCTION

Over the years, organizations have been the subject of multiple studies to understand how they are structured and function in digital environments, especially in response to the growing digital transformation and the digital economy has gained the attention of researchers, consultants, journalists, policymakers, and business managers as an area of high potential (Li et al., 2020).

Digital organization refers to the integration of digital technologies into organizational structures and processes, transforming the way companies operate and relate to their customers. From various perspectives, the conceptualization of the digital organization can be addressed through definitions and approaches that highlight its importance in the current context.

From a technological perspective, a digital organization is characterized by the intensive use of digital technologies, such as artificial intelligence, big data, and the Internet of Things (IoT). These technologies are essential for automating processes, improving efficiency, and creating new forms of interaction and communication within the organization. The digital economy is seen as an essential force to drive structural changes and transformations in economies, especially in Latin American contexts.

Digital economic organizations tend to have more agile and less hierarchical structures, allowing them to quickly adapt to new opportunities and challenges. This translates into a greater capacity to form interdependent teams that collaborate on specific projects. It is considered a catalyst for reducing inequality and strengthening processes of social inclusion (ECLAC, 2013). This approach emphasizes the transformative role of the digital economy in social and economic development. From this perspective, digital transformation is not just a matter of technological adoption but of a fundamental change in organizational culture and the way of doing business (Bharadwaj et al., 2013).

Digital transformation, on the other hand, involves the integration of digital technologies into all areas of an organization, which fundamentally changes how it operates and delivers value to customers. This process not only involves adopting new technologies, but also a profound cultural and organizational change.

The digital economy enables disintermediation in trade, removing barriers between producers and consumers. This means that companies can interact directly with their customers through digital platforms, improving communication and reducing costs. The digital economy disrupts traditional business models by enabling the creation of new digital markets that operate with digital products and services (Tapscott, 1996). This change implies a continuous review of business strategies to remain competitive in a dynamic environment.

Organizational theory offers you various definitions and conceptualizations of "digital organization" from different perspectives. Below are various definitions and conceptualizations from different perspectives. These definitions and conceptualizations highlight how digital organization not only involves technology but also profound changes in organizational culture, structure, and processes to adapt to an increasingly digitalized environment. According to sociotechnical theory, the digital organization is the result of the interaction between technical systems (technological infrastructure) and social systems (people, practices, and culture). This approach emphasizes how workers and digital technologies coexist and co-evolve to achieve a balance that maximizes both technical efficiency and social satisfaction at work (Mumford, 2006).

From the perspective of organizational transformation, the digital organization is the result of a profound organizational transformation, where organizational processes, structures and cultures are redesigned to adapt to the digital environment. This approach considers the digital organization as a dynamic entity where traditional boundaries disappear and interconnected value networks are established through the use of digital technologies (Hess et al. 2016).

From the perspective of digitalization and digital transformation, digitalization involves the conversion of analog information into digital formats. In contrast, digital transformation goes further, integrating digital technologies into all aspects of an organization to optimize processes and improve the customer experience. Digitalization refers to the conversion of analog information into digital formats, such as transforming paper documents into PDF files. This process allows electronic access and management of information. Digitalization presents both challenges and opportunities for organizations. ILO/Cinterfor (2020) mentions that increasing access to digital technologies requires companies to adapt to a new, customer-centric environment, which implies a significant organizational transformation.

From a structuralist perspective, a digital organization is defined as an entity whose design and structure are based on advanced technological platforms, allowing for process automation, greater flexibility and organizational agility. This type of organization is capable of integrating multiple digital channels, enabling decentralized and real-time decision-making (Zammuto et al., 2007).

The digital economy is described as an ecosystem where technological infrastructure, processing services, and end users converge. The digital economy is defined as "the part of economic output derived solely or primarily from digital technologies with a business model based on digital goods or services" (Bukht & Heeks, 2017). This approach highlights how digital technologies have become the core of contemporary economic activities. This approach highlights how organizations must adapt to an interconnected environment in order to thrive (Mesenbourg, 2001).

The digital economy includes fundamental components such as the ICT industry, e-commerce between companies, and the digital distribution of goods and services. This definition highlights the interconnection between technology and economic infrastructure in the digital context (Margherio, 1998).

From an organizational perspective, digitalization is seen as a process that improves operational efficiency and enables greater agility in responding to market demands. Digital transformation is seen as a cultural shift that affects how employees interact and how decisions are made (HubSpot, 2023). From this organizational perspective, digital transformation is seen as a process that redefines business models and improves operational efficiency. This includes the adoption of tools such as artificial intelligence, data analytics, and automation to optimize processes and improve customer experience.

Digital organization seeks to have an impact on improving the customer experience by using technologies such as artificial intelligence and data analytics. This allows companies to personalize their services and respond quickly to consumer needs (SAP, 2023). Digital organizations are designed to be agile and adaptive, allowing for a rapid response to market demands and changing consumer expectations.

From an innovation perspective, digital organizations are seen as those that take a proactive approach to technological change and constant innovation. These organizations not only react to the digital environment but anticipate and take advantage of it to create new business opportunities and operating models. The ability to adapt quickly to emerging digital trends is crucial to their survival and success (Yoo et al., 2012). The digital organization fosters an environment of continuous innovation, where companies must be willing to experiment and adapt to new technologies to remain competitive.

This implies a constant commitment to learning and improvement (AWS, 2023). Continuous innovation is a key component in the digital economy. Organizations must commit to the constant renewal of products, processes, and business models to remain competitive in a changing environment.

In the context of the digital economy, a relationship of cooperation and interdependence between actors in academia, business, and government is recognized to foster the development of digital organizations. This approach suggests that success in digitalization requires a joint effort (UASB, 2020).

Digital organizations often have distinctive characteristics, such as leveraging the intensive use of information and communication technologies to optimize their operations through continuous innovation, adapting quickly to changes in the environment, offering new services and constantly improving their processes. They promote fluid communication in agile structures between departments and allow for faster decision-making.

From a strategic perspective, the digital organization seeks not only to survive in an increasingly digitalized environment but also to thrive by creating sustainable competitive advantages through the effective use of data and technology. The digital economy not only transforms the business environment but also has a significant impact on social and political organization, promoting structural changes in how goods and services are produced and consumed.

These definitions and conceptualizations highlight how digital economic organization involves not only technology but also profound changes in organizational culture, structure, and processes to adapt to an increasingly digitalized environment. The digital economic organization represents a radical change in how companies operate, interact with consumers, and adapt to an increasingly digitalized environment. This phenomenon not only redefines business models but also has profound implications for the global social and economic structure.

This study contributes to clarifying the existing literature on the subject and leaving measures that can improve the performance of digital economies and is organized as follows: First, it examines the concepts and definitions of the digital economic organization, leading to the analysis of theories and empirical literature review. The study presents two tables aiming to synthesize the findings. A section on discussion examines some of the implications, developments and advances in the conceptual, theoretical and empirical issues related to digital economic organization. Finally, some concluding remarks are offered.

BACKGROUND

Digital Economic Organization

"Digital economic organization" is a complex concept that has been addressed from various perspectives in the academic literature. Digital economic organization refers to the integration of digital technologies into economic and business processes, transforming the way companies operate and relate to their customers. This type of organization refers to the set of activities, institutions, and economic actors that use digital technologies to create, distribute, and consume goods and services. Below are several definitions and conceptualizations of digital economic organization from different perspectives.

A digital economic organization is one that has adopted an intensive focus on the use of digital technologies to optimize its operations. This includes the implementation of technological solutions that allow for greater efficiency, innovation and adaptation to market changes. It is defined as a branch of the economy that combines the benefits of the Internet with the marketing and manufacturing of products and services. This implies that commercial transactions are carried out mainly on digital platforms, which transforms traditional market dynamics.

From a collaborative economy perspective, digital economic organization is understood as a system in which digital platforms connect users to shared resources, allowing the exchange of goods and services without the need for traditional intermediaries. This organization leverages digital technology to create new business models that decentralize control and ownership of resources, as in the cases of Airbnb or Uber (Sundararajan, 2016).

Digital economic organization, from the perspective of the platform economy, refers to the emerging economic structure where digital platforms act as intermediaries that coordinate interactions between users, producers and consumers. These platforms (such as Amazon, Google, or Facebook) create value by facilitating transactions (Kenney & Zysman, 2016).

From a critical perspective of digital capitalism, digital economic organization is defined as an extension of capitalism, where capital is accumulated mainly through the control of data and information. The digital economy is also characterized by the interaction between information and economic activity, where "the asset on which transactions are made is information" (Orkestra Deusto, 2017). This aspect underlines how information has become a key resource for generating economic value. Dominant digital firms extract value by collecting, analyzing, and trading personal data, giving rise to new forms of economic power and digital monopolization (Srnicek, 2017).

The digital economic organization can also be conceptualized as an economic system based on technological innovation. In this context, digital technologies (such as artificial intelligence, blockchain, and big data) enable greater efficiency in markets, facilitate the creation of new forms of value, and enable the emergence of entirely new industries. Digital firms are seen as organizations that thrive through continuous innovation and rapid adoption of new technologies (Brynjolfsson & McAfee, 2014).

Digital economic organization, from the perspective of globalization, refers to a system in which geographic and political barriers are less relevant to economic exchange. Digital companies can operate and scale their businesses globally more quickly and efficiently, using digital technologies to optimize logistics, communication, and the sale of products and services across borders (Baldwin, 2016).

In the conceptualization of the attention economy, digital economic organization focuses on how digital platforms and companies capitalize on users' attention as a fundamental economic resource. Companies operating in this economy design products and services (such as social media, mobile apps, or online content) to capture and monetize consumers' time and attention (Wu, 2017).

Digital economic organization is a multifaceted phenomenon that can be understood from several perspectives, whether as part of a new platform-based exchange model, a driver of technological innovation or as a central component of data-driven capitalism. This economic model facilitates access to global connectivity for products and services, allowing small businesses to reach international markets without the need for a physical presence. Constant connectivity between businesses and consumers improves brand loyalty and enables a faster response to market needs.

The digital organizational economy is an ecosystem that combines telecommunications infrastructure, information and communication technology (ICT) industries, and economic activities facilitated by the Internet. This ecosystem allows individuals and organizations to interact, collaborate, and create value through digital platforms. As an important driving force and new kinetic energy, digital economy is promoting the development of economy in the direction of high quality, and brings new opportunities and challenges to the development of real economy and the upgrading and optimization of industrial structure (Zhang, 2024).

Digital economic organization has been studied from various theoretical and methodological perspectives. Different conceptualizations allow us to understand how digital technology redefines economic relations, business models and value creation in the global economy. Below, several theories are presented that address this phenomenon, highlighting their characteristics and approaches. These new digital technologies are prompted by big data analytics, artificial intelligence (AI), platform economy, digital trade, fintech innovation, and societal and economic sustainability. (Li et al, 2020)

Theories on Digital Economic

The digitization of the economy has been on the rise in recent years and continues to evolve. The latest wave of the IT revolution is based on radical mobility, with an emphasis on intangible capital, big data management, and machine learning-based digital platforms that help businesses as well as individuals (Byrne, 2022). Using digital technology and developing a digital mindset, companies can make big changes to existing business models and management methods and give them the power of data, thus making the digital economic organization more competitive (Wang & Qi, 2024). The successful operation of the digital economy relies on the close collaboration of numerous core elements. Urgently, a unified theoretical framework is needed to thoroughly explore and analyze the foundational aspects of the digital economy (Xie et al., 2023)

Organization Theories on digital economic organization address the fundamental changes that digital technologies have introduced in economic structures and dynamics. There are various theories that address digital economic organization from different conceptual and theoretical-methodological perspectives. Below, several relevant theories are presented from different conceptual and theoretical-methodological approaches; all focused on analyzing how digitalization is transforming the nature of economic organizations.

Complex systems theory is applied to understanding how different actors interact in a digital ecosystem. This approach views digital economic organizations as operating within an interconnected system where changes in one component can affect others, requiring adaptability (Holland, 1995).

New economics theory, popularized by Don Tapscott and others, argues that the digital economy represents a fundamental shift in how goods and services are created and distributed. This theory emphasizes the role of the Internet as a facilitator of disintermediation and reintermediation, allowing firms to interact directly with consumers, reducing costs and improving efficiency (Tapscott, 1996).

Theories on digital economic organization highlight how digital technologies have transformed not only the structure and functioning of firms but also markets and the economy as a whole. These theoretical perspectives provide tools to analyze the new dynamics of power, innovation, and value that are emerging in the digital economy.

Platform economics theory focuses on how digital platforms mediate economic interactions between multiple groups (users, producers, consumers). Platforms, such as Amazon, Uber, or Airbnb, not only facilitate transactions but also create value networks through network effects. The success of these organizations lies in their ability to reduce transaction costs, increase scale, and generate network value, where the value of the platform grows as more users adopt it (Parker et al., 2016).

Information Theory focuses on how digitalization transforms the flow of information within organizations. This theory suggests that effective management of large volumes of data is crucial for decision-making and market adaptation (Cohen et al., 2000). According to this perspective, the ability to manage large volumes of data through digital technologies is crucial for economic development. Companies that manage to optimize the use of information can make more informed decisions and adapt quickly to market conditions.

The theory of surveillance capitalism is proposed by Shoshana Zuboff, this theory analyzes how digital economic organizations use personal data to obtain economic benefits. Instead of creating value solely through products or services, digital companies, especially large technology platforms, extract data from their users, process it, and commercialize it, which Zuboff (2019) calls “surveillance capitalism.” This theory questions the ethical and social impact of mass data collection and how it affects the privacy and autonomy of individuals.

The theory of organizational change focuses on how companies must transform internally to adapt to the digital economy. This theory addresses aspects such as organizational culture, the development of digital skills in employees, and the implementation of new technologies as critical factors for success in a digitalized environment (Kotter, 1996).

Clayton Christensen proposes the theory of disruptive innovation; this theory describes how digital technologies are transforming traditional markets by introducing innovations that displace established companies. In the context of digital economic organization, disruptive technology startups offer more accessible or affordable products or services through digital platforms, which changes the rules of the game in industries such as transportation, hospitality, or retail (Christensen, 1997). Innovation is more critical than ever in the digital economy era. Innovation should concern not just technology but organizations, management methods, and business models as well (Li et al., 200).

Research on digital business models focuses on how firms can create value in a digital environment. This includes studies on digital platforms, e-commerce, and their implications for business competitiveness. Different models ranging from traditional e-commerce to collaborative platforms that enable new forms of business interaction are explored, analyzing their implications for business competitiveness (Chesbrough, 2007).

Digital innovation ecosystem theory suggests that digital economic organizations function as part of complex innovation ecosystems where multiple actors (technology companies, startups, governments, universities) interact and co-create value. Collaboration between these actors is crucial for the development of emerging technologies such as artificial intelligence, blockchain, and the Internet of Things (IoT), which enable new forms of economic organization and value creation (Jacobides, et al. 2018).

Product life cycle theory is adapted to the digital economy by considering how digital technologies affect each stage of the product cycle. This theory allows us to understand how digital innovations alter traditional cycles and facilitate rapid adaptation to market demands (Kotler, 1997). In this context, it analyses how digital technologies enable innovations in the development, marketing and distribution of products, altering traditional cycles and allowing rapid adaptation to market demands.

Actor-Network Theory (ANT) is proposed by Bruno Latour and Michel Callon to analyze how digital economic organizations are complex networks of human and non-human actors (such as algorithms, technologies, and data). ANT argues that digital firms should be viewed not only as economic entities, but as sociotechnical networks that include technologies as key actors in the organization and distribution of resources and power in the digital economy (Latour, 2005).

The institutional approach examines how normative and regulatory structures affect the development of digital economic organizations. This theory suggests that public policies and institutions play a crucial role in facilitating or restricting the growth of the digital economy, affecting aspects such as innovation, investment, and access to technologies (North, 1990).

From the theory of social capital, it is argued that digital networks facilitate new forms of collaboration and exchange between individuals and organizations. This perspective emphasizes how digital platforms can build meaningful relationships that generate economic value (Putnam, 2000). This theory highlights how digital platforms enable meaningful relationships to be built that can be leveraged to generate economic value, especially in environments where trust and collaboration are critical.

Transaction cost theory in the digital economy based on Oliver Williamson's transaction cost theory is applied to digital economic organization to explain how digital technologies significantly reduce the costs associated with economic transactions (such as information search, negotiation, and monitoring). Digital platforms allow transactions to be carried out more efficiently and at lower cost, transforming the structure of markets and facilitating the creation of global digital markets (Williamson, 1981).

The attention economy theory argues that in the digital economy, users' attention has become a crucial economic resource. Digital organizations compete to capture and retain consumers' attention, using personalized algorithms, engaging content, and advertising-based business models. The attention economy highlights how technology companies monetize users' time and focus across various platforms (Davenport & Beck, 2001).

In summary, these theories provide a diverse conceptual framework for understanding the dynamics that shape digital economic organization, addressing technical, social, and institutional aspects and their implications for business development in an increasingly digitalized environment. Each approach offers a unique perspective on how companies can navigate this new economic landscape driven by digital technology.

Empirical Research on Digital Organizational Economics

Even though there are few literatures based on theoretical models and empirical analysis to study the impact of digital economy development (Zhang, 2024), the available empirical research on organizational economics in the digital context has produced significant findings in key areas such as organizational efficiency, the impact of digital platforms, value creation, and innovation. From the perspective of organizational economics, several empirical investigations have been carried out that address digital economic organization. Below are some relevant findings, results, and conclusions from these investigations.

In a study by Armijos-Orellana et al. (2023) on digital economy and value creation, it was investigated how the digital economy can be a driver of growth in Latin America. The findings indicate that the adoption of digital platforms and the use of data are fundamental for the creation and capture of economic value. The research concludes that digital transformation is crucial to improve productivity and foster innovation in interdependent productive sectors.

Another empirical research on the Attention Economy and Monetization in Digital Platforms, carried out by Wu (2017) explored the "attention economy" and how digital organizations, such as social networks and media outlets, monetize users' attention. Through an empirical analysis of how technology companies use strategies to capture and retain users' attention, Wu found that these organizations earn most of their revenue through targeted advertising. Platforms optimize content design to maximize the time users spend on the platform, creating new forms of attention-based value.

Previous research found that digital organizations monetize users' attention through targeted advertising models. Furthermore, the attention economy may be unsustainable in the long term due to market saturation and user burnout. The research concludes that digital platforms have created a business model based on capturing attention, which poses ethical and sustainability challenges as consumers become saturated with content.

An empirical research by Sundararajan (2016) explored the impact of platforms on labor markets and how sharing economy platforms, such as Uber and Airbnb, are transforming labor markets. Through a series of case studies and data analysis of platforms, it was found that these digital organizations are challenging traditional employment structures by offering flexibility and reducing intermediation. However, the research also highlighted the increasing prevarication of employment and the lack of social benefits in platform-based jobs.

The main findings of this research show an increase in labor flexibility, but with lower guarantees of job security, as well as digital platforms facilitating entry into the labor market but creating unstable working conditions. Among the conclusions, it highlights that digital platforms represent a significant transformation in the way work is organized, with benefits for some workers in terms of flexibility but with risks in the quality of employment.

A study on digital business models suggests that organizations must adapt their strategies to make the most of the opportunities offered by digitalization. According to Pérez and Guzmán (2015), companies that implement effective digital models achieve greater operational efficiency and a better relationship with their customers, which is essential for their long-term sustainability.

Research conducted by Sieglin (2014) on organizational conditions in Mexican public universities and their challenges in implementing digital technologies reveals that there are significant limitations in infrastructure and human resources that affect scientific development. The results indicate that these limitations hinder the effective adoption of digital technologies, which in turn negatively impacts the innovative capacity of these institutions.

Empirical research on open innovation and co-creation in digital ecosystems is empirical research conducted by Chesbrough (2006), who studied how digital organizations take advantage of open innovation and innovation ecosystems to generate value. Through case studies of technology companies such as IBM and Google, it was found that organizations that allowed open collaboration with external actors (users, competitors and startups) managed to accelerate innovation and reduce R&D costs.

Among the findings found in this research, it is found that open innovation allows digital organizations to reduce costs and accelerate the development of new products. In addition, organizations that are part of open digital ecosystems tend to be more competitive and resilient. The research concludes that organizations that encourage open innovation and collaboration with external actors are better positioned in the digital economic environment, generating value more efficiently and sustainably.

Empirical research on platform economics and network effects in value creation, conducted by Rochet and Tirole (2003) conducted empirical research on the behavior of two-sided platforms, such as credit cards and online platforms, analyzing how network effects influenced value creation. By collecting data on different platforms, they found that digital organizations create value when they manage to attract users on both sides of the platform, generating positive network effects. The larger the user base, the greater the value perceived by new users.

The findings of this research revolve around network effects that are essential for the success of platforms, which manage to balance the participation of the two sides (consumers and suppliers) and generate a positive feedback loop in value creation. The research concludes that the theory of two-sided platforms is crucial to understand how digital organizations can maximize value by creating dynamic markets in which users attract each other.

An analysis of the impact of the role of information and knowledge in the digital economy highlights that these elements are considered strategic resources in organizations. According to Blanco et al. (2001), knowledge becomes a key factor for competitiveness, as it allows companies to quickly adapt to changes in the environment and improve their capacity for innovation.

Brynjolfsson and Hitt (2000) conducted empirical research to measure the impact of information technology (IT) on company productivity in the transformation of productivity and efficiency in digital organizations. Analyzing data from American companies, they discovered that organizations that invested in IT showed a significant increase in productivity. However, the benefits materialized only when these investments were accompanied by organizational changes, such as restructuring processes and the adoption of more agile organizational models.

In the findings, researchers found that IT boosts productivity, but only when aligned with changes in organizational structure and that IT implementation without organizational transformation can lead to stagnant productivity. The research concludes that the adoption of digital technologies is critical to improving organizational efficiency, but must be accompanied by structural redesign and innovation processes in organizations.

Research on the knowledge economy highlights how this paradigm has transformed organizational dynamics. According to Kogut and Zander (1992), organizations that foster continuous learning and the development of innovative capabilities are more likely to succeed in a digitalized economic environment. The findings from the general digital economic theory reveal that in a socially optimal equilibrium, consumers should share their data with firms until the marginal benefits equal the marginal costs (Xi et al., 2023).

Empirical research in digital organizational economics highlights the transformative impact of digital technologies in areas such as productivity, labor markets, value creation, and innovation models. This research reflects how digital economic organizations face challenges and opportunities in an environment increasingly influenced by digital technologies and knowledge as a key resource for their strategic success.

This research provides evidence on how organizations must adapt to the digital environment to maximize their benefits, but also highlights the challenges related to job insecurity, the sustainability of the care model, and competition in platform markets.

Table 1 below summarizes the definitions and concepts, theories, and empirical research related to digital economic organization from the perspective of organizational economics sciences.

Table 1.

Categories	Content
Definitions and Concepts	**1. Digital Economy:** "The part of economic production derived solely or mainly from digital technologies" (Bukht & Heeks, 2017). **2. Components of the Digital Economy:** Includes the ICT industry and e-commerce (Margherio, 1998). **3. Structural Transformation:** The digital economy acts as a catalyst to reduce inequality and strengthen social inclusion (ECLAC, 2013). **4. Interaction between Information and Economy:** Information becomes a key resource to generate economic value (Orkestra Deusto, 2017). **5. Challenges and Opportunities:** Digitalization requires significant adaptations in companies (ILO/Cinterfor, n.d.). **6. Impact on Business Models:** Digitalization alters traditional business models (Tapscott, 1996).
Theories	1. **New Economy Theory**: Highlights the role of the Internet in disintermediation and reintermediation (Tapscott, 1996). 2. **Information Theory**: Emphasizes effective data management as a key to competitiveness (Cohen et al., 2000). 3. **Social Capital Theory**: Digital networks facilitate new forms of collaboration (Putnam, 2000). 4. **Complex Systems Theory**: Analyzes interactions in a digital ecosystem (Holland, 1995). 5. **Institutional Approach**: Examines how regulatory structures affect digital development (North, 1990).
Empirical Research	1. **Digital Economy and Value Creation**: Armijos-Orellana et al. (2023) conclude that digital transformation improves productivity and innovation in Latin America. 2. **Impact of Information and Knowledge**: Blanco et al. (2001) indicate that knowledge is key to organizational competitiveness. 3. **Challenges in Technological Implementation**: Sieglin (2014) reveals limitations in infrastructure that affect the innovative capacity in Mexican public universities. 4. **Digital Business Models**: Pérez and Guzmán (2015) highlight that effective digital models improve operational efficiency and customer relations. 5. **Knowledge Economy**: Kogut and Zander (1992) suggest that continuous learning is essential for success in a digitalized environment.

The table above provides a structured overview of the key definitions and concepts related to digital economic organization, as well as the relevant theories and significant empirical findings in this field of study.

Table 2 is presented below, which organizes the information previously provided into three categories: Definitions and Conceptualizations, Theories on Digital Economic Organization, and Empirical Research with Findings, Results, and Conclusions.

Table 2.

Category	Description	References
Definitions and conceptualizations		
Collaborative Economy	The digital economic organization focuses on platforms that facilitate collaboration and the exchange of goods and services between peers without intermediaries.	Sundararajan (2016).
Platform Economy	Digital platforms such as Amazon and Uber act as intermediaries, connecting consumers and producers, and creating value through network effects.	Kenney & Zysman (2016). Parker et al (2016).
Digital Capitalism	Digital companies generate capital by controlling data and extracting value by commercializing users' personal information.	Srnicek (2017).
Technological Innovation	The digital economic organization is characterized by a rapid adoption of new technologies such as AI, blockchain, and big data to improve efficiency and create value.	Brynjolfsson & McAfee (2014).
Globalized Digital Economy	Digital companies operate globally, minimizing geographic barriers and optimizing logistics and distribution through technological platforms.	Baldwin (2016).
Attention Economy Digital	organizations capitalize on users' attention, designing platforms to maximize the time consumers spend on them	Wu (2017).
Theories on Digital Economic Organization		
Platform Economy	Two-sided platforms mediate transactions between multiple actors (consumers and suppliers), maximizing value through network effects.	Parker et al (2016); Rochet & Tirole (2003)
Surveillance Capitalism	Digital firms extract value by surveillance and commercialization of personal data.	Zuboff (2019).
Disruptive Innovation	Disruptive organizations challenge established firms by using digital technologies that offer more accessible products or services	Christensen (1997).
Digital Innovation Ecosystem	Digital organizations co-create value as part of innovation ecosystems that include diverse actors, from startups to universities	Jacobides et al (2018).
Actor Network Theory	Digital organizations are socio-technical networks, where both humans and technologies play a role in creating and distributing value	Latour (2005).
Transaction Cost Theory	Digital platforms reduce transaction costs by facilitating information search and coordination among market actors	Williamson (1981).
Attention Economy	In the digital environment, attention is a key economic resource; technology companies compete to capture and retain users' attention.	Davenport & Beck (2001); Wu (2017).

This table and the references provide a structured summary that facilitates the understanding of the different definitions, theories and empirical research on digital economic organization. Digital economic organization is a topic of growing relevance today, given the impact that digitalization has had on all economic sectors.

This analysis focuses on the conceptual, theoretical-methodological, and empirical advances in research on this phenomenon.

Discussion on Digital Economic Organization: Conceptual, Theoretical, and Methodological Advances

Digital economic organization is a concept that has gained increasing relevance in recent years due to the transformative impact of technology on economic models, organizational structures, and market dynamics.

This phenomenon has been the subject of research from different conceptual, theoretical and methodological approaches, with the aim of understanding the economic, social and political implications of digitalization. The main advances in the matter are discussed below.

Conceptual Advances

The digital economy refers to the integration of information and communication technologies (ICT) into economic activities, modifying the patterns of production, distribution and consumption of goods and services. For authors such as Manuel Castells (1996), the digital economy is a manifestation of the network society, where digital networks transform economic relations by facilitating global connectivity and the interdependence of actors.

Digital economic organization refers to the way in which digital technologies transform the structure and functioning of organizations. According to authors such as Castells (2000), the digital economy is characterized by interconnection and globalization, which allows companies to operate in a more dynamic and competitive environment. This concept has evolved to include not only electronic commerce but also the use of digital platforms, big data, and artificial intelligence.

Another important conceptual advance is the focus on the collaborative economy, where platforms such as Uber and Airbnb have redefined the concept of ownership and consumption. Botsman and Rogers (2010) highlight how these platforms facilitate the exchange of goods and services between individuals, leading to a reconfiguration of traditional economic relations.

From a conceptual approach, digitalization has been understood as a process of dematerialization, where goods and services move from the physical to the digital world. This includes the emergence of digital platforms, the monetization of data and the creation of new online markets (Evans & Schmalensee, 2016). Platforms such as Amazon, Google and Facebook have become new intermediaries, which has transformed power structures in the global economy (Srnicek, 2016).

In terms of organization, Brynjolfsson and McAfee (2014) argue that digitalization has given rise to a new form of business organization based on platforms and networks, in which the traditional hierarchical structure has been replaced by horizontal interactions and labor flexibility.

Theoretical-Methodological Advances

From a theoretical-methodological point of view, various approaches have been developed to study digital economic organization. Social network theory, for example, has been used to understand how digital interactions affect organizational dynamics. Authors such as Granovetter (1973) have been fundamental in this field, analyzing how relationships between actors influence access to resources and information. In addition, the systemic approach has gained relevance by considering organizations as part of a broader system that includes consumers, suppliers, and competitors.

This approach allows for a better understanding of interdependencies and information flows in a digital environment.

The theoretical analysis of digital economic organization has been based on various approaches. From the firm's theory, authors such as Coase (1937) suggest that new technologies reduce transaction costs, allowing companies to outsource activities that were previously carried out internally. Digitalization has intensified this process, facilitating the coordination of activities through smart contracts and platforms that connect suppliers and consumers globally (Tapscott, 2016).

Another important approach comes from network theory, which argues that the digital economy is organized around nodes and information flows rather than traditional hierarchies (Castells, 1996). Digital networks allow for decentralized coordination and control, which translates into new forms of corporate governance, where digital platforms have a dominant role.

On the other hand, from the perspective of human capital, Acemoglu and Restrepo (2020) propose that digitalization needs to automate certain tasks, which increases productivity but also displaces employment. However, digital organizations depend not only on technology but also on the adaptation of workers' capabilities and skills to the digital environment.

The study of digital economic organization requires the adoption of new methodological tools that capture the emerging dynamics of digital economies. One of the most significant advances in this field is the use of big data and network analysis to map and understand economic interactions on digital platforms. This approach has allowed researchers to quantify the magnitude of digital transactions, study user behavior patterns, and measure the economic impact of digitalization in real time (Einav & Levin, 2014).

Machine learning and big data processing techniques are also being used to model complex economic phenomena, such as consumer behavior in digital environments, predicting market trends, and identifying competitive dynamics in platform markets (Athey, 2017). Furthermore, the study of the digital economy has involved increasing interdisciplinarity, incorporating knowledge from economics, computer science, sociology, and data science. This convergence has allowed for the development of more comprehensive theoretical frameworks and the application of quantitative and qualitative models to explore the impact of technology on economic organization.

Empirical Developments

Empirically, numerous studies have addressed how organizations are implementing digital technologies. A study by Brynjolfsson and McAfee (2014) shows that companies that adopt digital technologies tend to be more innovative and efficient. Likewise, research on the impact of teleworking during the COVID-19 pandemic has revealed significant changes in employee productivity and well-being (Kässi & Lehdonvirta, 2020).

On the other hand, it has been documented how small and medium-sized enterprises (SMEs) face specific challenges when adopting digital technologies. According to a study by the European Commission (2020), many SMEs lack the necessary resources to implement effective digital strategies.

From an empirical point of view, research on the digital economy has provided evidence that digital platforms are transforming traditional sectors such as retail, financial services and transportation (Cohen & Sundararajan, 2015). For example, the rise of e-commerce has disrupted traditional supply chains, reducing entry costs for small sellers and facilitating access to global markets.

A notable empirical example is the analysis of the digital labor market, where studies have shown that the platform economy is generating new forms of work (Uber, Deliveroo, etc.), but also poses challenges in terms of labor protection, social security and workers' rights (De Stefano, 2016). The impact of digitalization on labor inequalities has also been the subject of study, with some researchers suggesting that automation tends to polarize the labor market, favoring highly skilled workers while displacing less skilled workers (Goos, Manning and Salomons, 2014).

On the other hand, research on the impact of the digital economy on competition has revealed that, although digital platforms tend to increase efficiency and reduce costs, they can also lead to the concentration of market power in a few technology companies (Autor, Dorn, Katz, Patterson, & Van Reenen, 2020). These companies, referred to as "superstars," have accumulated a significant amount of economic power, leading to concerns about monopolies and anticompetitive practices.

METHODOLOGY

The metacognitive and reflective analysis presented in this paper through the investigation of theories and concepts leads us to reflect on the thought processes that have led us to understand that the digital economic organization is multidimensional. A bibliometric review was used, through which a quantitative analysis of publications related to digital economic organizations, theories, and empirical research on digital economics. The bibliometric indicators taken as inclusion factors were the quality of the publications where the research is presented, the context covered by the publication, and the relevance of the topic in the research.

This bibliometric review was conducted in two stages. In the first stage, the search criteria used in the different databases were defined, including temporality, date of consultation, type of document and journal, topic and keywords. The second stage consisted of classifying and analyzing the papers based on the identification criteria; these were grouped to identify the connections between the papers, selecting the most relevant ones in order to prepare the discission presented.

RESULTS AND DISCUSSION

Nowadays, the realization of the digital economy is occurring all around the globe, in Asian nations due to the need to revamp traditional business processes, extensive technology innovation, supportive government policies for economic growth, and the high capacity for digital entrepreneurship (Li et al., 2020), in the other hand, European countries have been changing their policies over the past three decades to improve their innovative performance (Gomes et al., 2022).

According to ILO/Cinterfor (2020), digital transformation redefines work processes, profoundly challenging organizational culture. Digital transformation not only affects technological processes but also transforms organizational culture. It implies a change in the mindset of employees and how they interact with each other and with customers. This cultural change is crucial to the success of any digital initiative. Digital transformation involves not only technological changes but also cultural changes within organizations. This includes the need to develop digital skills in employees and foster an open mindset to change (PowerData, 2023). The digital economy can indeed improve the level of upgrading and optimization of industrial structures (Zhang, 2024).

The digital economy is a challenge that countries have been working on to develop and accelerate the digital single market (Szeles & Simionescu, 2020). To accelerate the development of the digital economy, the different regional actors (government, academia, and companies) must work to increase the levels of qualification in the higher education of the population, the development of R&D partnerships, and incentives (Gomes et al., 2022). It is necessary to promote the healthy development of the platform economy and sharing economy, digital industrialization and industrial digitization, and deep integration of the digital economy and real economy (Zhang, 2024).

Digitalization presents both challenges and opportunities. Organizations must face the challenge of implementing new technologies while managing the cultural change necessary for their effective adoption. However, those who manage to do so can benefit significantly by improving their competitiveness. In short, digital organization is a multifaceted concept that ranges from simple process digitization to a profound transformation that redefines how organizations operate as a whole.

CONCLUSION

The digital economic organization represents a multidimensional field ranging from conceptual to methodological and empirical changes. As we move towards an increasingly digitalized future, it is crucial to continue researching how these transformations affect both organizations and the economy at large. This analysis provides a comprehensive view on the developments in digital economic organization and its impact on the contemporary business environment.

It is essential for companies seeking to adapt to a world where technology plays a central role in all business interactions. Digital organizations can be understood from various perspectives, all of which highlight the importance of digital technologies not only as operational tools but also as drivers of organizational transformation. From structure and processes to culture and innovation, the digital environment redefines how organizations interact with their internal and external environments.

The study of digital economic organization has advanced significantly in recent decades, providing new conceptual, theoretical and methodological approaches that allow us to better understand the changing nature of economic activities in the digital age. However, despite progress, this field continues to evolve and raise new questions, especially regarding the impact of digitalization on employment, inequality and economic competition.

REFERENCES

Acemoglu, D., & Restrepo, P. (2020). The Race Between Man and Machine: Implications of Technology for Growth, Factor Shares, and Employment. *The American Economic Review*, 108(6), 1488–1542. DOI: 10.1257/aer.20160696

Armijos-Orellana, A., González, M., Maldonado-Matute, J., & Guerrero, P. (2023). Un acercamiento teórico a la economía digital. *Estudios de la Gestión*, 14, 78-90. https://revistas.uasb.edu.ec/index.php/eg/article/download/4116/3999/16300

Athey, S. (2017). Beyond prediction: Using big data for policy problems. *Science*, 355(6324), 483–485. DOI: 10.1126/science.aal4321 PMID: 28154050

Autor, D., Dorn, D., Katz, L., Patterson, C., & Van Reenen, J. (2020). The Fall of the Labor Share and the Rise of Superstar Firms. *The Quarterly Journal of Economics*, 135(2), 645–709. DOI: 10.1093/qje/qjaa004

AWS. (2023). *¿Qué es la transformación digital?* Recuperado de https://aws.amazon.com/es/what-is/digital-transformation/

Baldwin, R. (2016). *The great convergence: Information technology and the new globalization*. Harvard University Press. DOI: 10.2307/j.ctv24w655w

Bharadwaj, A., El Sawy, O. A., Pavlou, P. A., & Venkatraman, N. (2013). Digital business strategy: Toward a next generation of insights. *Management Information Systems Quarterly*, 37(2), 471–482. DOI: 10.25300/MISQ/2013/37:2.3

Blanco, F., Eaton, B., & Bawden, D. (2001). La información y el conocimiento: factores de producción en la actividad económica. *Revista Base*, 2(1), 186-200. https://www.redalyc.org/pdf/3372/337228632009.pdf

Botsman, R., & Rogers, R. (2010). *What's Mine Is Yours: The Rise of Collaborative Consumption*. HarperBusiness.

Brynjolfsson, E., & Hitt, L. M. (2000). Beyond computation: Information technology, organizational transformation, and business performance. *The Journal of Economic Perspectives*, 14(4), 23–48. DOI: 10.1257/jep.14.4.23

Brynjolfsson, E., & McAfee, A. (2014). *The second machine age: Work, progress, and prosperity in a time of brilliant technologies*. W.W. Norton & Company.

Bukht, R., & Heeks, R. (2017). Defining, Conceptualising and Measuring the Digital Economy (2017). *Development Informatics Working Paper no. 68*. DOI: 10.2139/ssrn.3431732

Byrne, D. (2022). The Digital Economy and Productivity. *Finance and Economics Discussion Series (FEDS)* DOI: 10.17016/feds.2022.038

Castells, M. (1996). *The Rise of the Network Society*. Blackwell.

CEPAL. (2013). *La economía digital: Un motor para el desarrollo sostenible*. Retrieved from https://www.cepal.org/es/publicaciones/25756-economia-digital-motor-desarrollo-sostenible

Chesbrough, H. (2006) *Open Innovation: A New Paradigm for Understanding Industrial Innovation. 10th Anniversary Summer Conference on Dynamics of Industry and Innovation: Organizations, Networks and Systems*, 1-12. DOI: 10.1093/oso/9780199290727.003.0001

Chesbrough, H. W. (2007). Business Model Innovation: It's Not Just About Technology Anymore. *Strategy and Leadership*, 35(6), 12–17. DOI: 10.1108/10878570710833714

Christensen, C. M. (1997). *The innovator's dilemma: When new technologies cause great firms to fail*. Harvard Business Review Press.

Coase, R. H. (1937). The nature of the firm. *Economica*, 4(16), 386–405. DOI: 10.1111/j.1468-0335.1937.tb00002.x

Cohen, M., & Sundararajan, A. (2015). Self-regulation and innovation in the peer-to-peer sharing economy. *University of Chicago Law Review Online*, 82.

Cohen, S., de Long, D., & Zysman, J. (2000). *The New Economy: A New Perspective on the Economic Landscape*.

Davenport, T. H., & Beck, J. C. (2001). *The attention economy: Understanding the new currency of business*. Harvard Business Review Press.

De Stefano, V. (2016). The rise of the "just-in-time workforce": On-demand work, crowdwork, and labor protection in the gig-economy. *Comparative Labor Law & Policy Journal*, 37, 471–504.

Deusto, O. (2017). *Por qué la Economía Digital*. Retrieved from https://www.orkestra.deusto.es/euskadi-economia-digital/2017/por-que-economia-digital.phtml

Einav, L., & Levin, J. (2014). Economics in the age of big data. *Science*, 346(6210), 1243089. DOI: 10.1126/science.1243089 PMID: 25378629

European Commission. (2020). *Digital Economy and Society Index 2020*.

Evans, D., & Schmalensee, R. (2016). *Matchmakers: The New Economics of Multisided Platforms*. Harvard Business Review Press.

Gomes, S., Lopes, J., & Ferreira, L. The impact of the digital economy on economic growth: The case of OECD countries. *RAM Revista de Administração Mackenzie* https://doi.org/DOI: 10.1590/1678-6971/eRAMD220029.en

Goos, M., Manning, A., & Salomons, A. (2014). Explaining job polarization: Routine-biased technological change and offshoring. *The American Economic Review*, 104(8), 2509–2526. DOI: 10.1257/aer.104.8.2509

Granovetter, M. (1973). The Strength of Weak Ties. *American Journal of Sociology*, 78(6), 1360–1380. DOI: 10.1086/225469

Hess, T., Matt, C., Benlian, A., & Wiesböck, F. (2016). Options for formulating a digital transformation strategy. *MIS Quarterly Executive*, 15(2), 123–139.

Holland, J. H. (1995). *Hidden Order: How Adaptation Builds Complexity*. Addison-Wesley.

HubSpot. (2023). *Qué es la transformación digital: características, proceso y ejemplos*. Recuperado de https://blog.hubspot.es/sales/transformacion-digital

Jacobides, M. G., Cennamo, C., & Gawer, A. (2018). Towards a theory of ecosystems. *Strategic Management Journal*, 39(8), 2255–2276. DOI: 10.1002/smj.2904

Kässi, O., & Lehdonvirta, V. (2020). Digital labor and the pandemic: The case of platform work. *Socio-economic Review*, 18(4), 1001–1025.

Kenney, M., & Zysman, J. (2016). The rise of the platform economy. *Issues in Science and Technology*, 32(3), 61–69.

Kogut, B., & Zander, U. (1992). Knowledge of the firm, combinative capabilities, and the replication of technology. *Organization Science*, 3(3), 383–397. DOI: 10.1287/orsc.3.3.383

Kotler, P. (1997). *Marketing Management*. Prentice Hall.

Kotter, J. P. (1996). *Leading Change*. Harvard Business Review Press.

Latour, B. (2005). *Reassembling the social: An introduction to actor-network-theory*. Oxford University Press. DOI: 10.1093/oso/9780199256044.001.0001

Li, K., Kim, D. J., Lang, K. R., Kauffman, R. J., & Naldi, M. (2020). How should we understand the digital economy in Asia? Critical assessment and research agenda. *Electronic Commerce Research and Applications*, 44, 101004. DOI: 10.1016/j.elerap.2020.101004 PMID: 32922241

Margherio, C. (1998). *The Emerging Digital Economy*. U.S. Department of Commerce.

Mesenbourg, T. L. (2001). *Measuring the Digital Economy*. U.S. Bureau of the Census.

Mumford, E. (2006). The story of sociotechnical design: Reflections on its successes, failures and potential. *Information Systems Journal*, 16(4), 317–342. DOI: 10.1111/j.1365-2575.2006.00221.x

North, D. C. (1990). *Institutions, Institutional Change and Economic Performance*. Cambridge University Press. DOI: 10.1017/CBO9780511808678

OIT/Cinterfor. (2020). *Digitalización en las organizaciones*. Recuperado de https://www.oitcinterfor.org/digitalizacion/digitalizacion-organizaciones

Parker, G. G., Van Alstyne, M. W., & Choudary, S. P. (2016). *Platform revolution: How networked markets are transforming the economy and how to make them work for you*. W.W. Norton & Company.

Pérez, A., & Guzmán, M. (2015). Los estudios organizacionales como programa de investigación. *Revista Latinoamericana de Estudios Organizacionales*, 2(1), 1-20. https://www.scielo.cl/scielo.php?pid=S0717-554X2015000200001&script=sci_arttext

PowerData. (2023). *Transformación digital: Qué es y su importancia*. Recuperado de https://www.powerdata.es/transformacion-digital

Putnam, R. D. (2000). *Bowling Alone: The Collapse and Revival of American Community*. Simon & Schuster.

Rochet, J. C., & Tirole, J. (2003). Platform competition in two-sided markets. *Journal of the European Economic Association*, 1(4), 990–1029. DOI: 10.1162/154247603322493212

SAP. (2023). *¿Qué es la Transformación Digital? | Importancia y Beneficios*. Recuperado de https://www.sap.com/latinamerica/insights/what-is-digital-transformation.html

Sieglin, V. (2014). Economía de conocimiento y culturas organizacionales en la academia. *Ciencia UANL*, 17(69), 45-60. https://cienciauanl.uanl.mx/?p=2590

Srnicek, N. (2016). *Platform Capitalism*. Polity Press.

Srnicek, N. (2017). *Platform capitalism*. Polity Press.

Sundararajan, A. (2016). *The sharing economy: The end of employment and the rise of crowd-based capitalism*. MIT Press., DOI: 10.7551/mitpress/10425.001.0001

Tapscott, D. (1996). *The Digital Economy: Promise and Peril in the Age of Networked Intelligence*. McGraw-Hill.

Tapscott, D. (2016). *Blockchain Revolution: How the Technology Behind Bitcoin is Changing Money, Business, and the World*. Penguin.

UASB. (2020). *Un acercamiento teórico a la economía digital*. Recuperado de https://revistas.uasb.edu.ec/index.php/eg/article/download/4116/3999/16300

Wang, X., & Qi, M. (2024). A Study of the Impact of Digital Transformation on the Risk Level of Commercial Banks. Proceedings of the 2024 3rd International Conference on Artificial Intelligence, Internet and Digital Economy (ICAID 2024). DOI: 10.2991/978-94-6463-490-7_29

Williamson, O. E. (1981). The economics of organization: The transaction cost approach. *American Journal of Sociology*, 87(3), 548–577. DOI: 10.1086/227496

Wu, T. (2017). *The attention merchants: The epic scramble to get inside our heads*. Vintage.

Xie, D., Wei, W., & Li, Y. (2023). A General Theory of Digital Economy: The World after Turing. DOI: 10.2139/ssrn.4531884

Yoo, Y., Boland, R. J.Jr, Lyytinen, K., & Majchrzak, A. (2012). Organizing for innovation in the digitized world. *Organization Science*, 23(5), 1398–1408. DOI: 10.1287/orsc.1120.0771

Zammuto, R. F., Griffith, T. L., Majchrzak, A., Dougherty, D. J., & Faraj, S. (2007). Information technology and the changing fabric of organization. *Organization Science*, 18(5), 749–762. DOI: 10.1287/orsc.1070.0307

Zhang, C. (2021). An empirical study on the impact of digital economy development on the upgrading and optimization of industrial structure. *E3S Web of Conferences*, 275, 01046. DOI: 10.1051/e3sconf/202127501046

Zuboff, S. (2019). *The age of surveillance capitalism: The fight for a human future at the new frontier of power*. PublicAffairs.

Chapter 4
From Vision to Reality:
Digital Transformation for Sustainable Tourism in Dubai's Megaprojects

Seda Karagoz Zeren
https://orcid.org/0000-0003-3466-0421
University of Massachusetts, Amherst, USA

ABSTRACT

Digital transformation is reshaping industries worldwide, and tourism is no exception. In the dynamic context of Dubai, a city recognized globally for its innovative megaprojects, integrating digital technologies into the tourism sector has transcended the status of a mere trend to become a critical element in the city's long-term strategy. This chapter examines the role of digital technologies, such as big data, artificial intelligence, and the internet of things, in promoting sustainable tourism practices. Through case studies of major megaprojects, it highlights how digital transformation initiatives have improved operational efficiency, visitor experiences, and sustainability. The chapter also discusses collaborative efforts among stakeholders and the challenges faced in implementing digital strategies. Finally, it provides insights into the future of smart tourism in Dubai, highlighting the ongoing adaptation to global demands and sustainability standards.

INTRODUCTION

Digital transformation is reshaping industries worldwide, and tourism is no exception. In the dynamic context of Dubai—a city globally recognized for its innovative megaprojects—integrating digital technologies into the tourism sector

DOI: 10.4018/979-8-3693-9435-9.ch004

has transcended the status of a mere trend, becoming a critical element in the city's long-term strategy. Dubai's unique landscape of rapid technological advancements combined with a significant tourism-driven economy necessitates a comprehensive approach to digital transformation that not only enhances the tourist experience but also aligns with broader sustainability objectives. The emergence of digital platforms, big data, artificial intelligence (AI), and Internet of Things (IoT) technology has redefined how tourism services are delivered, consumed, and managed. This transition from vision to reality is increasingly placing a focus on sustainable tourism practices, aligning both economic growth and environmental stewardship within Dubai's megaproject framework.

Dubai's tourism industry stands at the intersection of rising visitor demand and expanding technological capabilities. As consumer preferences shift towards more personalized and eco-conscious travel experiences, digital tools enable businesses to adapt effectively to these evolving demands. According to research by Li et al. (2022), effective use of big data in the tourism sector is instrumental for businesses aiming to provide tailored services and improved customer experiences. Real-time data analysis allows for swift adjustments to service offerings, thereby optimizing operational efficiency and fostering personalized tourist experiences. In a competitive landscape like Dubai's, personalization is critical, and digital transformation provides the mechanisms to achieve it. This approach aligns with the global trend of responsible tourism, which places sustainability at the core of its business models, fostering both environmental protection and economic growth. Furthermore, the adoption of AI plays a pivotal role in enhancing these personalized experiences and driving green innovation within the sector. As highlighted by Le & Nguien (2024), AI's impact on green innovation and the performance of new ventures underscores its importance in achieving sustainability goals in tourism.

Building on the benefits of personalization and data-driven insights, digital transformation in Dubai's tourism sector is not limited to individual businesses but extends across large-scale, government-backed megaprojects. As these projects aim to serve millions of visitors, they rely on advanced digital frameworks that enable seamless, sustainable experiences on a vast scale. This broader application of technology, from real-time data analytics to AI and IoT integration, allows Dubai to not only meet diverse visitor preferences but also to enhance resource efficiency across high-traffic sites. These interconnected digital systems, powered by big data, provide the foundation for implementing large, complex projects that prioritize both sustainability and visitor satisfaction, marking a significant evolution in Dubai's tourism strategy.

A core aspect of Dubai's digital transformation strategy is its implementation across megaprojects such as Dubai Expo 2020 (EXPO 2020 Dubai UAE, 26.10.2024), Dubai Creek Harbour (Dubai Creek Harbour, 26.10.2024), and the Museum of the

Future (Museum Of The Future, 26.10.2024). These projects serve as more than tourist attractions; they act as case studies in integrating digital strategies for sustainable development. For instance, the Dubai Expo 2020 showcased innovative applications of AI and IoT, which managed everything from resource allocation to crowd control, enhancing visitor experiences while minimizing environmental impact. Such projects illustrate how digital transformation can be harnessed to meet sustainability goals by reducing waste and optimizing resource consumption, setting a benchmark for future tourism-oriented infrastructure in Dubai and beyond.

The success of Dubai's megaprojects in embedding digital solutions for sustainable operations is not only a showcase of technological prowess but also a driver for a data-centric approach that supports long-term environmental goals. The integration of AI and IoT in these projects demonstrates how digital infrastructure can handle the complexities of tourism on a massive scale, collecting and transmitting data that aids in fine-tuning services and managing resources efficiently. This data-driven approach extends into broader applications across the tourism sector, where big data analytics provide stakeholders with real-time insights into visitor behaviors. Such insights enable proactive decision-making and sustainable resource allocation, laying the groundwork for continuous innovation and operational sustainability in Dubai's tourism ecosystem. This holistic use of digital transformation in both large projects and daily operations underlines Dubai's commitment to advancing tourism sustainably while adapting to evolving visitor preferences. Moreover, Dubai's strategy also aligns with findings from Mohsin et al. (2024), who emphasize the role of digitalization and public-private partnerships in fostering sustainable economic development in Asian economies. This comparison underscores the broader applicability of Dubai's digital transformation initiatives within the context of sustainable development.

Big data analytics enables deeper insights into consumer behaviors, helping stakeholders in Dubai's tourism sector make informed decisions that support sustainability. The capacity to analyze massive datasets in real time allows tourism operators to identify and respond to patterns, thereby reducing operational inefficiencies. This has a direct impact on sustainability, as resources are allocated more effectively, energy consumption is minimized, and the environmental footprint is reduced.

Beyond efficiency, big data also enables better planning for sustainable tourism. For example, understanding tourist foot traffic can help optimize visitor flow, reducing crowding and wear on natural and built environments. This kind of application is particularly pertinent in Dubai, where the concentration of tourist activity is high due to the city's landmark attractions. With predictive analytics, tourism managers can forecast peak periods, adjust resources, and deploy green practices such as energy-efficient transport, thereby reducing the ecological impact of tourism while enhancing the visitor experience. The evolving trends in using digitalization for sustainable development, as reviewed by Pan et al. (2024), further support the integration of such practices in Dubai's tourism, offering a pathway to align with global sustainability standards.

Dubai's tourism transformation also aims to enrich visitor experiences through technologies like augmented reality (AR) and virtual reality (VR), providing immersive interactions with the city's culture and heritage. According to Han et al. (2019), AR and VR can offer tourists unique ways to experience Dubai's historical and cultural sites, allowing them to connect more deeply with the local culture while minimizing the need for physical modifications to heritage sites. This technological application aligns with sustainable tourism goals by balancing preservation with experiential engagement, ensuring that tourists can appreciate the city's legacy without impacting its structural integrity.

For example, visitors to the Museum of the Future can explore interactive exhibits that integrate AR and VR to present Dubai's history and its vision for the future (Museum Of The Future, 26.10.2024). Such technology not only captures visitors' attention but also fosters a deeper understanding of Dubai's cultural narrative and environmental goals. This approach allows for cultural preservation while promoting a sustainable, low-impact tourism experience, aligning with broader global trends toward responsible and culturally enriching travel.

The success of Dubai's digital transformation in tourism relies heavily on collaboration among key stakeholders, including government entities, private businesses, and local communities. Majeed et al. (2020) emphasize the importance of coordination among stakeholders to achieve seamless and sustainable service delivery. Digital platforms that facilitate communication among these diverse parties allow for a more cohesive approach to tourism management. For example, platforms that link government regulatory bodies, tourism operators, and community representatives create a shared space for resource allocation and environmental accountability, fostering a unified and sustainable tourism ecosystem.

Digital platforms are also crucial for engaging communities in Dubai's tourism strategy, ensuring that locals have a voice in tourism development and feel the benefits of increased visitor activity. In this way, technology serves as a bridge between tourism growth and community well-being, promoting social sustainability alongside economic and environmental goals.

Implementing digital transformation strategies within Dubai's tourism sector is not without its challenges. Issues such as data privacy, technological disparities among stakeholders, and the need for a skilled workforce capable of managing complex digital systems pose significant hurdles. As more data is collected from tourists, the question of privacy becomes paramount, necessitating robust data governance and regulatory oversight (Ioannou, Tussyadiah, & Miller, 2021). Technological disparities among stakeholders also present a challenge, as smaller enterprises may struggle to keep up with the digital capabilities of larger organizations, potentially widening the gap in sustainable practices.

On the flip side, these challenges present opportunities for growth and innovation. Developing a skilled workforce trained in the latest digital tools will not only benefit the tourism sector but also create job opportunities and support the broader economy. Addressing data privacy concerns and fostering transparent practices will build trust with tourists, making Dubai a model of responsible and secure tourism in the digital age.

As Dubai looks to the future, its commitment to digital transformation for sustainable tourism continues to evolve. Emerging technologies like blockchain, augmented reality, and AI-enhanced data analysis are expected to play a significant role in Dubai's tourism landscape. Blockchain, for instance, could be used to ensure transparency in sustainable practices, giving tourists insight into the environmental impact of their activities and promoting informed decision-making (Rani, Sharma, & Gupta, 2024). Moreover, as visitor expectations shift towards more eco-friendly travel options, AI-powered insights can help tourism operators in Dubai anticipate and adapt to these trends, maintaining Dubai's status as a world leader in sustainable tourism (Generis Global, 27.10.2024).

In conclusion, Dubai's journey from vision to reality in the realm of digital transformation for sustainable tourism in megaprojects reflects a sophisticated approach that balances economic growth with environmental responsibility. The convergence of technology, stakeholder collaboration, and sustainability principles positions Dubai to redefine the future of tourism in a digital era. As Dubai's tourism sector continues to evolve, digital transformation will play an instrumental role in fostering sustainable practices, enhancing visitor experiences, and ensuring long-term viability. This strategic integration of technology, culture, and sustainability provides a roadmap for other cities seeking to harmonize tourism with the demands of a modern, environmentally conscious world.

In the book chapter, this chapter that follows will explore the transformative impact of digital technologies on sustainable tourism, using Dubai as a prime example. Beginning with an analysis of digital tools' role in promoting environmentally responsible tourism, it will delve into case studies of Dubai's megaprojects, such as Expo 2020, the Museum of the Future, and Dubai Creek Harbour. These projects showcase the city's efforts to embed sustainability into tourism through innovative technologies. The book chapter will also examine the collaborative ecosystem emerging in Dubai's tourism industry, emphasizing the roles of stakeholders and the digital synergies they create. Additionally, it will discuss the challenges and opportunities that Dubai faces in navigating its digital transformation for tourism, highlighting both obstacles and areas for growth. Finally, the book chapter will highlight its insight into future trends in digital sustainability and Dubai's vision to become a leader in tourism excellence. Each chapter builds on these interconnected themes, offering a comprehensive view of how digital transformation shapes sustainable tourism in Dubai.

1. THE ROLE OF DIGITAL TECHNOLOGIES IN SHAPING SUSTAINABLE TOURISM

This section will explore the various digital technologies that are being integrated into Dubai's tourism sector, including big data analytics, AI, and IoT. It will discuss how these technologies contribute to sustainable practices by enhancing operational efficiency, reducing waste, and improving visitor experiences.

In the contemporary landscape of tourism, digital technologies have emerged as transformative forces that not only enhance operational efficiency but also promote sustainable practices. This is particularly evident in Dubai, a city known for its megaprojects and commitment to innovation. The integration of technologies such as big data analytics, AI, and IoT is reshaping the tourism sector, allowing for a more sustainable approach to managing resources and improving visitor experiences. The application of IoT for creating smart environments, as discussed by Ghazal et al. (2024) in the context of smart healthcare, offers valuable insights into how similar strategies can be adopted in smart tourism to enhance sustainability and operational efficiency.

Big data analytics plays a crucial role in the tourism industry by enabling stakeholders to make informed decisions based on real-time data (Yallop & Seraphin, 2020). According to Archi et al., the ability to analyze vast amounts of data allows for a deeper understanding of tourist behavior, preferences, and trends, which can lead to more tailored services and experiences (Archi, et al., 2023). This data-driven approach not only enhances operational efficiency but also minimizes waste by optimizing resource allocation. For instance, hotels and attractions can use predictive analytics to manage staffing levels and inventory more effectively, thereby reducing unnecessary costs and environmental impact.

Moreover, the insights gained from big data analytics can facilitate the development of targeted marketing strategies that resonate with environmentally conscious travelers. By understanding the demographics and preferences of visitors, tourism operators in Dubai can promote sustainable practices that align with the values of their target audience. This alignment is essential in fostering a culture of sustainability within the tourism sector, as highlighted by Eichelberger et al. (2023), who emphasize the importance of organizational learning in adapting to changing consumer expectations. The role of corporate social responsibility (CSR) and social media in enhancing this alignment is further underscored by Abbas et al. (2024), suggesting that digital platforms are crucial for promoting sustainable practices among businesses.

Al is another pivotal technology that is reshaping the tourism landscape in Dubai. AI applications, such as chatbots and virtual assistants, are increasingly being utilized to enhance customer service and engagement. These tools can provide instant responses to inquiries, assist in booking processes, and offer personalized recommendations based on individual preferences. As noted by Buhalis, technology innovations empower travelers to co-create value throughout their journey, enhancing their overall experience (Buhalis, 2019).

Furthermore, AI can analyze visitor data to identify patterns and preferences, allowing tourism operators to tailor their offerings accordingly. This personalization not only improves visitor satisfaction but also encourages repeat visits, contributing to the long-term sustainability of the tourism sector. The integration of AI in tourism also extends to operational processes, where machine learning algorithms can optimize pricing strategies and inventory management, further enhancing efficiency and reducing waste.

The IoT is revolutionizing the way tourism services are delivered and experienced. By connecting various devices and systems, IoT enables seamless communication between tourists and service providers. For instance, smart sensors can monitor visitor flows in real time, allowing attractions to manage crowd levels effectively and enhance the visitor experience. As highlighted by Morais et al., the IoT facilitates advanced analytics that can improve tourism management and development (Morais, Cunha, & Mendonça, 2022, September).

Integrating AI and the IoT creates a powerful synergy that can transform the tourism sector by enhancing both personalization and operational efficiency. While AI tailors experience based on visitor data, IoT connects devices and systems, enabling real-time data collection and interaction between tourists and service providers. This interconnected approach allows tourism operators to dynamically respond to visitor needs, manage crowd flows, and optimize resource allocation. Together, AI and IoT provide actionable insights, enabling smarter decision-making and a more responsive, satisfying experience for tourists, thereby fostering long-term sector growth and sustainability.

In Dubai, IoT technologies are implemented in various megaprojects, where smart infrastructure is designed to enhance sustainability (Sheikh Mohammed bin Rashid Al Maktoum, 28.10.2024). For example, smart waste management systems can optimize collection routes based on real-time data, reducing carbon emissions associated with waste transport. Additionally, IoT-enabled applications can provide tourists with real-time information about local attractions, transportation options, and environmental conditions, empowering them to make informed decisions during their visit.

The convergence of big data analytics, AI, and IoT creates a robust framework for promoting sustainable tourism practices in Dubai. By leveraging these technologies, tourism stakeholders can enhance operational efficiency, reduce environmental impact, and improve visitor experiences. As noted by Mehraliyev et al., the integration of smart technologies in tourism is essential for creating sustainable value propositions that resonate with modern travelers (Mehraliyev, Choi, & Köseoğlu, 2019).

Moreover, the collaborative nature of these technologies fosters a more integrated approach to tourism management. Stakeholders can share data and insights, enabling a coordinated response to challenges such as overcrowding and resource depletion. This collaborative effort is crucial in ensuring that the growth of the tourism sector aligns with sustainability goals, as emphasized by Baggio et al., who highlight the importance of smart tourism development in achieving better outcomes (Baggio, Micera, & Chiappa, 2020).

In conclusion, the role of digital technologies in shaping sustainable tourism in Dubai is multifaceted and transformative. The integration of big data analytics, AI, and IoT not only enhances operational efficiency but also promotes sustainable practices that benefit both visitors and the environment. As Dubai continues to position itself as a leading global tourism destination, the ongoing adoption of these technologies will be essential in ensuring that the sector remains resilient, sustainable, and responsive to the evolving needs of travelers

2. CASE STUDIES OF DUBAI'S MEGAPROJECTS: A DIGITAL TRANSFORMATION PERSPECTIVE

This chapter will present specific examples of megaprojects in Dubai, such as the Dubai Expo 2020, Dubai Creek Harbour, and the Museum of the Future. Each case study will analyze how digital transformation initiatives have been implemented in these projects to promote sustainability and enhance the overall tourist experience.

Dubai has emerged as a global city characterized by its ambitious megaprojects that have redefined urban landscapes and economic paradigms. The rapid urbanization and development in Dubai have been driven by a combination of factors, including substantial oil revenues and a strategic pivot towards diversification and innovation in various sectors, particularly in technology and infrastructure. This chapter explores the critical success factors (CSFs) that underpin the successful execution of megaprojects in Dubai, the implications of digital transformation on urban planning, and the socio-economic impacts of these developments.

Due in large part to Expo 2020 plans and other urban developments that aim to improve social responsibility and environmental sustainability, Dubai has become a global pioneer in sustainable megaprojects. The planning and execution of these projects reflect a strategic approach to integrating sustainability into urban development, which is essential for addressing the challenges posed by rapid urbanization and climate change.

One of the most significant examples of Dubai's commitment to sustainability is Expo 2020, which was designed not only as a major international event but also as a catalyst for long-term sustainable development. Taha and Allan emphasize that the planning for Expo 2020 included a comprehensive framework aimed at maximizing cost-effectiveness while ensuring a lasting legacy of sustainability (Taha & Allan, 2022). This event showcased various mega projects that were developed with sustainability principles at their core, including energy-efficient buildings and sustainable transport systems. The legacy of Expo 2020 is expected to influence future urban planning and development in Dubai, setting a benchmark for sustainable practices in mega events globally.

In addition to Expo 2020, Dubai has implemented the Green Building Regulations, which align with international efficiency standards while being tailored to the specific needs of the region. Athapaththu and Karunasena highlight that these regulations drive contractors towards adopting sustainable construction practices, which is crucial for reducing the environmental impact of new developments (Athapaththu & Karunasena, 2018). The integration of sustainability into the construction sector is not merely a regulatory requirement but a fundamental aspect of Dubai's broader strategy to position itself as a leader in sustainable urban development.

The phenomenon of megaprojects in Dubai can be traced back to the late 20th century, where the city began to establish itself as a hub for tourism, trade, and finance. The critical success factors for these projects are multifaceted, encompassing economic, social, and environmental dimensions. Abdalla et al. (2023) highlight the importance of multiple-criteria decision analysis in identifying CSFs that are specific to the unique context of Dubai's development boom, emphasizing the need for a tailored approach to project management in the region. The authors argue that while CSFs have been extensively studied in construction and urban projects globally, there remains a significant gap in the literature concerning the Middle East, particularly Dubai. This gap is starting to be addressed with studies like that by Mohammad and Rahmat (2024), which explores the application of AI in enhancing the tourism and hospitality industry in the UAE, providing specific examples relevant to Dubai's context.

As Dubai's megaprojects evolved to address complex challenges in economic, social, and environmental dimensions, a shift toward digital transformation became increasingly evident. While early projects focused primarily on establishing Dubai as a global hub, recent initiatives recognize the potential of advanced technologies to enhance project management and sustainability. By incorporating digital tools and data-driven decision-making, Dubai is not only refining its approach to managing critical success factors but is also paving the way for smart, sustainable urban environments. This integration of technology has become essential, as seen in projects like Internet City, which underscore Dubai's commitment to leveraging digital infrastructure for growth and innovation (Rethinking The Future, 28.10.2024).

Digital transformation plays a pivotal role in Dubai's urban megaprojects, integrating advanced technologies such as IoT, AI, and big data to enhance efficiency and sustainability. Projects like Dubai Internet City and the Dubai Smart City initiative showcase how digital infrastructure fosters economic growth while addressing resource optimization and environmental challenges. These efforts align with global trends emphasizing innovation-driven urban design and sustainability, including the use of technologies like blockchain to improve transparency and scalability (Zaidan & Abulibdeh, Master planning and the evolving urban model in the gulf cities: principles, policies, and practices for the transition to sustainable urbanism, 2020). The potential for energy efficiency improvements in the region, as explored by Alarefi et al. (2024), further supports the integration of these digital technologies, suggesting substantial benefits for sustainability in Dubai's megaprojects.

However, challenges persist, including disparities in technology adoption among stakeholders and concerns over data privacy and governance. Addressing these issues and expanding the application of emerging technologies can enhance inclusivity and sustainability. Dubai's digital transformation journey offers valuable insights into balancing technological advancement with environmental and social responsibility, serving as a model for urban development worldwide (Abdelfattah, Bazzoni, & Choubassi, 2021).

2.1 Fostering Sustainable Urbanism: The Social Impact of Sustainable Development in Dubai's Evolving Urban Landscape

The concept of sustainable neighborhoods has also gained traction in Dubai, with projects like the Sustainable City serving as a model for future developments. El-Khateeb discusses how this project incorporates various sustainability principles, such as energy efficiency, water conservation, and community engagement, to create a livable and environmentally responsible urban space (El-khateeb, 2019). This aligns with the United Nations' Sustainable Development Goal 11: Sustainable cities and comunities, which aims to make cities inclusive, safe, resilient, and sustainable (UN Enviromental Programme, 28.10.2024). The Sustainable City exemplifies how urban design can promote sustainability while enhancing the quality of life for residents.

Dubai's urban landscape is undergoing a profound transformation characterized by megaprojects that aim to foster sustainable urbanism. Notably, the Dubai Expo 2020, Dubai Creek Harbour, and the Museum of the Future exemplify this shift towards sustainability, integrating social, economic, and environmental dimensions. Expo 2020, with its theme of "Connecting Minds, Creating the Future," aimed to foster a collaborative environment that encourages innovation and sustainability (Nadkarni, Conclusions: Expo 2020 and its impact on Dubai, 2019). This event not only showcased cutting-edge technologies but also emphasized the importance of social equity and community engagement, thereby enhancing the vibrancy of Dubai's diverse socio-economic landscape (Nadkarni, The pre- and post-event planning roadmap for expo 2020: dubai's coming-out-party, 2019). This initiative has not only attracted global attention but has also fostered a sense of belonging among local residents, thereby enhancing social cohesion and community identity (Aguerrebere, 2023: Hallaq, Ninov, & Dutt, 2020: Nadkarni, The pre- and post-event planning roadmap for expo 2020: dubai's coming-out-party, 2019). The digital transformation associated with these projects has further amplified their social impact by facilitating real-time communication and engagement among stakeholders, thus promoting a sense of community ownership and participation (Noori, Hoppe, & Jong, 2020).

The Dubai Creek Harbour project further exemplifies the integration of sustainable practices within urban planning. By prioritizing green spaces, pedestrian-friendly environments, and mixed-use developments, it aims to create a vibrant community that balances urban density with livability. The emphasis on high-density neighborhoods, despite cultural resistance, is crucial for achieving urban sustainability goals (Alawadi & Benkraouda, The debate over neighborhood density in dubai: between theory and practicality, 2017). This resistance often stems from a preference for low-density living, which poses challenges to planners seeking to implement sustainable urban policies. However, the potential benefits of high-density living, such as reduced carbon footprints and enhanced public transport accessibility, are significant (Alawadi & Benkraouda, 2017; Alawadi, 2016).

Digital transformation plays a critical role in fostering sustainable urbanism in Dubai. The integration of smart technologies in urban planning and management enhances the efficiency of resource use and improves the quality of life for residents. For instance, the Museum of the Future incorporates cutting-edge technologies to create interactive experiences that educate visitors about sustainability and innovation (Zaidan & Abulibdeh, 2020; Taha & Allan, 2022). This digital approach not only supports the city's sustainability goals but also aligns with the broader vision of establishing Dubai as a global hub for innovation and technology.

Moreover, the Museum of the Future serves as a beacon of innovation, focusing on sustainable practices and digital technologies to create immersive experiences that educate visitors about future challenges and solutions (Al-Shihabi, 2023). This aligns with the broader goals of sustainable urbanism, where public spaces are designed to foster social interactions and community well-being. The integration of smart technologies in urban planning, as seen in Dubai Creek Harbour, enhances the livability of urban environments by improving accessibility and reducing environmental footprints (Noori, Hoppe, & Jong, 2020). Thus, the social impact of these megaprojects is profound, as they not only contribute to the urban landscape but also promote a culture of sustainability and community engagement.

Additionally, the social impact of these megaprojects extends beyond immediate community benefits. They serve as platforms for cultural exchange and knowledge sharing, which are essential for fostering a diverse and inclusive urban environment. The Expo 2020, for example, has positioned Dubai as a melting pot of cultures, showcasing innovations from around the world while promoting local heritage and values (Aguerrebere, 2023: Sharma, Stranjančević, & Kleber, 2019). This cultural dimension is vital for social sustainability, as it encourages mutual respect and understanding among diverse populations.

Furthermore, the societal awareness of sustainability in Dubai has been shown to influence business practices significantly. Eltoum et al. found a direct correlation between the public's understanding of sustainability and the adoption of responsible business practices within the local business sector (Eltoum, Yatiban, Omar, & Islam, 2022). This awareness is crucial as it drives consumer demand for sustainable products and services, thereby encouraging businesses to adopt more sustainable practices. The interplay between societal awareness and corporate responsibility is vital for fostering a culture of sustainability in Dubai.

The media's role in shaping public perception of sustainability initiatives is also noteworthy. Ayoub's analysis reveals that media coverage often reflects government narratives on sustainability, which can sometimes lead to a lack of critical discourse on the effectiveness of these initiatives (Ayoub & Freeman, 2023). This highlights the importance of fostering a more diverse media landscape that can provide a balanced view of sustainability efforts in Dubai, ensuring that all voices are heard in the conversation about sustainable development.

In terms of urban planning, Zaidan and Abulibdeh (2020) argue that there is a need for policies that are sensitive to the local socio-cultural context while promoting sustainable urbanism (Zaidan & Abulibdeh, Master planning and the evolving urban model in the gulf cities: principles, policies, and practices for the transition to sustainable urbanism, 2020). The authors emphasize that the current planning practices often overlook the unique dynamics of the Gulf region, which can lead to inconsistencies in the implementation of sustainable practices. By developing policies that are more attuned to local conditions, Dubai can enhance its sustainability efforts and ensure that they are effective and inclusive.

The impact of mega-projects on sustainability is further explored by Wu et al., who discuss the critical importance of delivering these projects in a sustainable manner (Wu, Chong, Wang, & Li, 2018). The authors argue that the construction industry must prioritize environmental protection and social equity to ensure that mega projects contribute positively to the urban landscape. This perspective is essential as Dubai continues to expand its infrastructure to accommodate its growing population and economic ambitions.

The challenges associated with sustainable neighborhood development are also significant. Dessouky et al. identify various controversies surrounding market-driven sustainable neighborhoods, emphasizing the need for a more holistic approach to post-occupancy evaluation (Dessouky, Wheeler, & Salama, 2023). By understanding the complexities of these developments, stakeholders can better address the challenges and enhance the sustainability of urban environments in Dubai.

In conclusion, Dubai's approach to sustainable mega projects is multifaceted, involving regulatory frameworks, societal engagement, media representation, and urban planning strategies. The city's commitment to sustainability is evident in initiatives like Expo 2020 and the Sustainable City, which serve as benchmarks for future developments. As Dubai continues to navigate the complexities of urbanization and sustainability, it must remain vigilant in addressing the challenges and opportunities that arise, ensuring that its growth is both environmentally responsible and socially equitable.

The interplay between sustainable development and digital transformation in Dubai's megaprojects significantly influences the social fabric of the city. By prioritizing community engagement, promoting high-density living, and leveraging digital technologies, Dubai is not only reshaping its urban landscape but also fostering a more sustainable and inclusive society. The successful integration of these elements will be crucial for the long-term viability of Dubai as a leading global city.

2.2 Balancing Growth and Ecology: The Environmental Impact of Sustainable Development in Dubai's Megaprojects

The concept of ecological modernization has gained traction in the Gulf Cooperation Council (GCC) region, with a growing emphasis on renewable energy and sustainable practices in urban development (Al-Saidi, Zaidan, & Hammad, 2019). Al-Saidi and Elagib discuss how the GCC countries, including Dubai, are increasingly adopting renewable energy projects as part of their diversification strategies (Al-Saidi & Elagib, 2018). These initiatives not only address environmental concerns but also enhance the region's geopolitical standing in the global energy landscape.

The environmental impact of Dubai's megaprojects, particularly the Dubai Expo 2020, Dubai Creek Harbour, and the Museum of the Future, reflects a growing commitment to sustainable development. These projects are designed not only to stimulate economic growth but also to address ecological concerns by integrating sustainable practices into their planning and execution. The Dubai Expo 2020, for instance, has been recognized for its emphasis on sustainability, with a significant portion of its infrastructure designed to minimize environmental footprints through energy-efficient technologies and sustainable materials (Zaidan & Abulibdeh, 2020; Manikas, Sundarakani, Madmoune, & Alvares, 2022; Giardina, 2019).

Dubai Creek Harbour is another prime example of balancing growth with ecological considerations. The project aims to create a sustainable urban environment by incorporating green spaces, water conservation measures, and biodiversity enhancement strategies. The development includes extensive waterfront areas that promote ecological resilience while providing recreational spaces for residents and visitors (Amrousi, Elhakeem, Paleologos, & Misuri, 2019; Jung, Awad, & Al Qassimi, 2021). Such initiatives are essential for mitigating the environmental impacts of rapid urbanization, which has historically posed challenges to ecological integrity in the region.

While Dubai's megaprojects have contributed significantly to its economic growth, they have also raised concerns regarding environmental sustainability. Binshakir points out that the construction boom has resulted in a substantial environmental footprint, with construction waste accounting for nearly 70% of the total solid waste generated in the UAE (Binshakir, 2023). This situation necessitates a critical examination of the sustainability practices employed in megaprojects and the implementation of strategies to mitigate their environmental impact.

The environmental implications of Dubai's megaprojects are significant, particularly in the context of sustainable development. Expo 2020 has been recognized for its commitment to sustainability, utilizing innovative technologies to minimize environmental impacts and promote ecological awareness among visitors (Manikas, Sundarakani, Madmoune, & Alvares, 2022). The event's infrastructure was designed with sustainability at its core, incorporating renewable energy sources and sustainable materials, which set a precedent for future developments in the region (Al-Shihabi, 2023). This approach not only mitigates the ecological footprint of such large-scale projects but also serves as a model for integrating sustainability into urban planning.

Dubai Creek Harbour, another pivotal project, emphasizes the balance between urban growth and ecological preservation. The development incorporates green spaces and water management systems that enhance biodiversity while providing recreational areas for residents (Noori, Hoppe, & Jong, 2020). The use of digital technologies in these projects facilitates better environmental monitoring and management, allowing for real-time data collection and analysis that informs sustainable practices (Jung, 2023). This integration of technology not only aids in reducing resource consumption but also enhances the resilience of urban ecosystems against climate change impacts.

Digital transformation is pivotal in enhancing the environmental sustainability of these megaprojects. Smart technologies facilitate efficient resource management, enabling real-time monitoring of energy consumption, waste management, and water usage. For example, the Museum of the Future employs advanced building management systems that optimize energy use and reduce greenhouse gas emissions (Zaidan & Abulibdeh, 2020; Noori, Hoppe, & Jong, 2020). This integration of technology not only supports environmental sustainability but also positions Dubai as a leader in smart urban development.

Furthermore, the environmental impact of these projects extends to their legacy. The planning for Expo 2020 has included considerations for long-term sustainability, ensuring that the infrastructure developed will continue to benefit the environment and the community long after the event concludes (Zaidan & Abulibdeh, 2020; Manikas, Sundarakani, Madmoune, & Alvares, 2022). This foresight is critical in addressing the challenges posed by climate change and urban sprawl, as it promotes a model of development that prioritizes ecological health alongside economic growth.

In summary, the environmental impact of Dubai's megaprojects is characterized by a commitment to sustainable development that balances growth with ecological integrity. Through the integration of smart technologies and sustainable practices, these projects not only address immediate environmental concerns but also lay the groundwork for a more sustainable urban future. The ongoing challenge will be to maintain this balance as Dubai continues to evolve and expand.

2.3 Economic Growth and Social Equity: The Economic Impact of Sustainable Megaprojects in Dubai's Urban Development

The socio-economic implications of Dubai's megaprojects are profound, influencing various aspects of urban life. Buckley and Hanieh argue that the nexus between urbanization and financial markets has reshaped the economic landscape of Dubai, with real estate megaprojects catalyzing financial re-engineering (Buckley & Hanieh, 2013). The authors highlight how these developments have led to the emergence of new capital groups that are intricately linked to both the real estate and financial sectors, thereby driving economic diversification.

However, the rapid pace of development has also resulted in social inequalities, particularly concerning the treatment of migrant workers involved in construction projects. Buckley critiques the socio-economic divide that characterizes Dubai's urban landscape, where the affluent consumer class coexists with a marginalized workforce (Buckley, 2012). This dichotomy raises important questions about the inclusivity of urban development and the need for policies that address social disparities.

The economic impact of Dubai's megaprojects is multifaceted, contributing to both growth and social equity. Expo 2020 is projected to significantly boost the local economy by attracting millions of visitors and creating thousands of jobs, thereby enhancing the economic landscape of Dubai (Nadkarni, 2019). The event has catalyzed investments in infrastructure and services, which are essential for sustaining long-term economic growth. Furthermore, the emphasis on sustainability within these projects ensures that economic benefits are distributed equitably among diverse communities, promoting social inclusion (Manikas, Sundarakani, Madmoune, & Alvares, 2022).

The economic impact of sustainable megaprojects in Dubai, particularly the Dubai Expo 2020, Dubai Creek Harbour, and the Museum of the Future, is profound and multifaceted. These projects are designed to stimulate economic growth while promoting social equity, thereby addressing the needs of diverse communities within the city. The Expo 2020 is expected to generate significant economic benefits, including job creation, increased tourism, and enhanced global visibility for Dubai as a leading destination for business and innovation (Aguerrebere, 2023; Nadkarni, 2019; Sharma, Stranjančević, & Kleber, 2019).

Moreover, the economic strategies employed in these megaprojects emphasize inclusivity and accessibility. For instance, the Dubai Creek Harbour project aims to create a mixed-use community that caters to various income levels, ensuring that the benefits of economic growth are equitably distributed (Amrousi, Elhakeem, Paleologos, & Misuri, 2019; Qatawneh, Adnan, AlZoughool, & AlQudah, 2020). This approach is essential for fostering social equity, as it mitigates the risks of gentrification and displacement that often accompany large-scale urban developments.

Digital transformation plays a crucial role in enhancing the economic impact of these projects. The integration of smart technologies not only improves operational efficiencies but also creates new business opportunities in sectors such as technology, tourism, and hospitality. The Museum of the Future, for example, serves as a hub for innovation and entrepreneurship, attracting startups and established companies alike to collaborate on sustainable solutions (Zaidan & Abulibdeh, 2020; Noori, Hoppe, & Jong, 2020). This focus on innovation is vital for maintaining Dubai's competitive edge in the global economy.

By leveraging data analytics and smart technologies, Dubai can optimize resource allocation and improve service delivery, which enhances the overall efficiency of urban operations (Noori, Hoppe, & Jong, 2020). This not only supports economic growth but also fosters an environment where social equity can thrive, as marginalized communities gain access to improved services and opportunities (Nadkarni, 2019). The Museum of the Future, for instance, not only serves as a cultural landmark but also as a hub for innovation and entrepreneurship, further driving economic diversification and resilience in Dubai's economy (Al-Shihabi, 2023).

Furthermore, the economic impact of these megaprojects extends beyond immediate financial gains. They contribute to the long-term sustainability of Dubai's economy by diversifying its economic base and reducing reliance on oil revenues. The emphasis on sustainable tourism and green technologies aligns with global trends towards sustainability, positioning Dubai as a forward-thinking city that is responsive to changing market demands (Anthonisz & Mason, 2019; Jong, Hoppe, & Alawadi, 2019).

In conclusion, the economic impact of sustainable megaprojects in Dubai is characterized by a commitment to growth that is inclusive and equitable. By leveraging digital transformation and prioritizing social equity, these projects not only stimulate economic development but also contribute to the overall well-being of the community. As Dubai continues to evolve, the challenge will be to sustain this momentum while ensuring that the benefits of growth are shared by all residents.

3. BUILDING A COLLABORATIVE TOURISM ECOSYSTEM: STAKEHOLDER ROLES AND DIGITAL SYNERGIES IN DUBAI

The tourism sector is increasingly recognized as a pivotal contributor to economic development and cultural exchange. However, the sustainability of tourism practices has become a pressing concern, particularly in rapidly growing destinations like Dubai. This chapter explores the collaborative efforts among various stakeholders-government entities, private organizations, and local communities-that are essential for fostering sustainable tourism in Dubai. It further examines how digital platforms enhance stakeholder communication, enabling coordinated planning, resource sharing, and accountability towards environmental goals. This integrated approach is crucial for creating a resilient tourism ecosystem in the digital era.

Sustainable tourism necessitates the active participation of multiple stakeholders, including government agencies, private sector entities, and local communities. Each stakeholder plays a unique role that contributes to the overarching goal of sustainability. Government entities are responsible for establishing regulatory frameworks that promote sustainable practices while also providing financial support and infrastructure development (Saarinen, 2020). Private organizations, including hotels and tour operators, are increasingly adopting sustainable practices in response to consumer demand for responsible tourism options (Mondal & Samaddar, 2020). Local communities, on the other hand, are vital for preserving cultural heritage and natural resources, which are essential for attracting tourists (McNaughton, Rao, & Verma, 2020). In the digital age, the perspectives of these stakeholders are evolving rapidly. Tourists, for instance, are increasingly tech-savvy, expecting seamless digital experiences throughout their travel journey, from online booking to mobile apps providing real-time information. Policymakers, particularly in Dubai, have been proactive in promoting digital innovation and sustainable development. They play a crucial role in shaping the digital landscape through investments in infrastructure, smart city initiatives, and regulatory frameworks that address data privacy and security. They are also focused on fostering digital literacy, supporting local businesses, and aligning digital transformation with sustainability goals. The role of government policies and regulations is vital in creating an enabling environment for digital innovation while ensuring equitable benefits for all stakeholders (Dąbrowska, Al-Mawali, Wilson, & Gore, 2024).

The collaboration among these stakeholders is facilitated by digital platforms that enhance communication and coordination. For instance, social media platforms allow stakeholders to share information, best practices, and success stories, thereby fostering a culture of collaboration (Sultan, Sharmin, Bădulescu, Ştiubea, & Xue, 2020). Moreover, digital tools enable real-time data sharing, which is critical for effective decision-making and resource allocation (Abdelrady, 2023). The integration of these digital solutions into the tourism ecosystem not only enhances stakeholder engagement but also promotes transparency and accountability in sustainability efforts (Samuel, Lucivero, & Croxatto, 2022). This is particularly important given the diverse perspectives and needs of stakeholders in the digital age, as discussed above. For example, digital platforms can be used to address tourists' concerns about data privacy by providing transparent information about data collection and usage practices. They can also support local businesses in their digital transformation by providing access to training resources and facilitating knowledge sharing.

Digital platforms have revolutionized the way stakeholders in the tourism sector communicate and collaborate. These platforms serve as a nexus for information exchange, enabling stakeholders to coordinate their efforts towards common sustainability goals. For example, the use of big data analytics allows stakeholders to understand visitor behavior and preferences, which can inform the development of sustainable tourism strategies (Li, Liu, & Zhang, 2022). Additionally, digital marketing tools enable stakeholders to reach a wider audience, promoting sustainable tourism initiatives effectively (Aman, & Papp-Váry, 2022).

The emergence of user-generated content on social media has also transformed stakeholder interactions. Travelers increasingly rely on reviews and recommendations from fellow tourists, which can significantly influence their travel choices (Sultan, Sharmin, Bădulescu, Ştiubea, & Xue, 2020). This shift in consumer behavior underscores the importance of engaging with digital platforms to promote sustainable practices and enhance the overall visitor experience. By leveraging these platforms, stakeholders can foster a sense of community among tourists and locals, encouraging responsible tourism behaviors (Firdausi, 2023).

Effective planning and resource sharing are critical components of a sustainable tourism ecosystem. Digital platforms facilitate these processes by providing stakeholders with access to valuable data and insights. For instance, collaborative platforms can enable stakeholders to share resources such as transportation, accommodation, and tour services, thereby reducing operational costs and environmental impacts (Yuniarta, Purnamawati, & Suwena, 2023). This sharing economy model not only enhances efficiency but also promotes a more sustainable approach to tourism development (Mondal & Samaddar, 2020).

Moreover, coordinated planning efforts can lead to the development of integrated tourism strategies that align with local sustainability goals. For example, stakeholders can collaborate on initiatives that promote eco-friendly practices, such as waste reduction and energy conservation (Eichelberger, Eller, Kallmuenzer, & Peters, 2023). By working together, stakeholders can create a unified vision for sustainable tourism that benefits both the local community and the environment. This collaborative approach is essential for addressing the complex challenges and opportunities of digital transformation, taking into account the evolving perspectives of tourists, local businesses, and policymakers.

Accountability is a crucial aspect of sustainable tourism, as it ensures that stakeholders are held responsible for their actions and commitments. Digital platforms can enhance accountability by providing transparent metrics and reporting mechanisms that track progress towards sustainability goals (Samuel, Lucivero, & Croxatto, 2022). For instance, stakeholders can utilize digital dashboards to monitor key performance indicators related to environmental impacts, such as carbon emissions and resource consumption (Archi, et al., 2023).

Furthermore, the integration of digital technologies can facilitate stakeholder engagement in sustainability initiatives. For example, mobile applications can empower tourists to make informed choices about their travel behaviors, such as opting for eco-friendly transportation options or supporting local businesses (Chen, Jiang, Pu, Li, & Hong-mei, 2022). By fostering a culture of accountability, stakeholders can collectively work towards achieving their sustainability objectives and enhancing the overall resilience of the tourism ecosystem. Digital tools can also help bridge the digital divide among local businesses by providing access to information, training, and support for technology adoption. This is crucial for ensuring that all businesses, regardless of their size or resources, can participate in and benefit from the digital transformation of the tourism sector.

While the potential of digital platforms to enhance stakeholder collaboration in sustainable tourism is significant, several challenges must be addressed. One major challenge is the digital divide, which can hinder the participation of smaller businesses and local communities in the digital tourism landscape (Alford & Jones, 2020). To overcome this barrier, it is essential to provide training and resources that enable all stakeholders to effectively utilize digital tools (Adekuajo, 2023).

Additionally, there is a need for regulatory frameworks that govern the use of digital technologies in tourism. As digital platforms continue to evolve, stakeholders must navigate complex issues related to data privacy, security, and ethical considerations (Marino & Pariso, 2021). By establishing clear guidelines and best practices, stakeholders can ensure that digital transformation contributes positively to sustainable tourism development.

Despite these challenges, the opportunities presented by digital transformation are vast. The ability to harness big data and analytics can lead to more informed decision-making and improved visitor experiences (Li, Liu, & Zhang, 2022). Furthermore, the rise of immersive technologies, such as VR and augmented reality, can enhance the way tourists engage with destinations, promoting a deeper understanding of local cultures and environmental issues (Nazare, Moldoveanu, & Moldoveanu, 2023). These technologies can also contribute to a more inclusive tourism ecosystem by providing accessible and engaging experiences for a wider range of tourists, including those with disabilities or limited mobility.

Building a collaborative tourism ecosystem in Dubai requires the active participation of various stakeholders, supported by digital platforms that facilitate communication, coordinated planning, and accountability. By leveraging these digital tools, stakeholders can work together to promote sustainable tourism practices that benefit both the local community and the environment. While challenges remain, the potential for digital transformation to enhance stakeholder collaboration and drive sustainable tourism development is significant. As the tourism sector continues to evolve, embracing these digital synergies will be essential for creating a resilient and sustainable tourism ecosystem in the digital era.

4. CHALLENGES AND OPPORTUNITIES IN DUBAI'S DIGITAL TRANSFORMATION FOR TOURISM

Dubai's tourism sector has emerged as a significant contributor to its economy, attracting millions of visitors annually. However, the rapid advancement of digital technologies presents both challenges and opportunities for this sector. As Dubai seeks to position itself as a leading global tourism destination, understanding the implications of digital transformation is crucial. This subject explores the challenges faced by Dubai's tourism sector in implementing digital transformation strategies, including data privacy concerns, technological disparities, and the need for a skilled workforce. Additionally, it discusses the opportunities that arise from overcoming these challenges, ultimately contributing to a more resilient and innovative tourism ecosystem.

One of the most pressing challenges in the digital transformation of Dubai's tourism sector is the issue of data privacy. As businesses increasingly rely on digital platforms to collect and analyze customer data, concerns about the security and ethical use of this information have intensified. The General Data Protection Regulation (GDPR) and similar frameworks highlight the importance of protecting personal data, yet many tourism businesses may lack the necessary infrastructure to comply with these regulations (Cheng, Xue, Yang, & Ma, 2023). The potential for data breaches not only jeopardizes customer trust but also poses significant legal and financial risks for organizations (Alrawadieh, Alrawadıeh, & Çetin, 2020). Furthermore, the ethical use of big data and AI in managing supply chains, as reviewed by Kamble et al. (2024), raises similar concerns about data privacy and algorithmic bias that are pertinent to the tourism industry.

Moreover, the diverse demographic of tourists visiting Dubai complicates data privacy issues. Different cultures have varying expectations regarding privacy, which can lead to misunderstandings and potential conflicts (Kumar, Kumar, Bhatt, Kumar, & Attri, 2023). For instance, tourists from regions with stringent data protection laws may be more sensitive to how their information is handled compared to those from areas with less stringent regulations. This disparity necessitates a nuanced approach to data management that respects the privacy concerns of all stakeholders involved. As highlighted earlier, tourists are increasingly aware of data privacy issues, and their willingness to share data may depend on the perceived trustworthiness of the businesses and organizations collecting and using their information.

To address these challenges, Dubai's tourism sector must invest in robust cybersecurity measures and establish transparent data management practices. This includes educating both employees and customers about data privacy rights and responsibilities (Kallou & Kikilia, 2021). By fostering a culture of transparency and accountability, the tourism sector can enhance customer trust and loyalty, ultimately benefiting from the digital transformation process.

Another significant challenge in Dubai's digital transformation journey is the technological disparity among various stakeholders in the tourism sector. While large hotel chains and established travel agencies often have the resources to invest in advanced digital technologies, smaller businesses and local operators may struggle to keep pace (Muñiz, Vila, & Brea, 2021). This disparity can lead to an uneven playing field, where larger entities dominate the market, potentially stifling innovation and competition from smaller players. This is particularly relevant to local businesses in Dubai's tourism sector, many of which are small to medium-sized enterprises (SMEs) striving to adapt to the digital age. As discussed earlier, these businesses often face challenges related to digital literacy, technology adoption costs, and the need for training and support.

The COVID-19 pandemic has further exacerbated these disparities, as SMEs faced financial hardships that hindered their ability to invest in digital tools (Eichelberger, Eller, Kallmuenzer, & Peters, 2023). Without access to essential technologies, these businesses may find it challenging to adapt to changing consumer preferences and market demands, ultimately risking their survival in an increasingly competitive landscape.

To mitigate these disparities, it is crucial for Dubai's tourism sector to foster an inclusive digital ecosystem that supports the growth of all stakeholders. This can be achieved through public-private partnerships that provide training, resources, and funding for SMEs to adopt digital technologies (Li, Liu, & Zhang, 2022). Additionally, initiatives aimed at enhancing digital literacy among local operators can empower them to leverage technology effectively, ensuring that they remain competitive in the evolving tourism landscape. Policymakers play a critical role in fostering such an inclusive ecosystem. Their efforts in promoting digital literacy, supporting local businesses, and establishing regulatory frameworks are essential for bridging the digital divide and ensuring that the benefits of digital transformation are shared equitably.

The successful implementation of digital transformation strategies in Dubai's tourism sector hinges on the availability of a skilled workforce. As businesses adopt new technologies, the demand for employees with digital skills is rapidly increasing (Shehade & Stylianou-Lambert, 2020). However, there is often a gap between the skills possessed by the current workforce and those required to navigate the complexities of digital transformation.

Many educational institutions in Dubai are beginning to recognize the importance of equipping students with the necessary digital competencies to thrive in the tourism industry. However, there remains a need for more comprehensive training programs that focus on practical applications of digital technologies in tourism (Lei, Indiran, & Kohar, 2023). This includes not only technical skills but also soft skills such as adaptability, problem-solving, and customer service, which are essential in a digital-first environment.

To address the skills gap, collaboration between educational institutions, industry stakeholders, and government entities is vital. By developing targeted training programs and internships that expose students to real-world digital challenges in tourism, Dubai can cultivate a workforce that is well-prepared to meet the demands of a rapidly evolving industry (Chiang, 2020). Furthermore, ongoing professional development opportunities for existing employees can ensure that the workforce remains agile and capable of adapting to new technologies as they emerge.

Despite the challenges associated with digital transformation, there are numerous opportunities for innovation and growth within Dubai's tourism sector. The integration of advanced technologies such as AI, big data analytics, and the IoT can enhance operational efficiency and improve the overall visitor experience (Zerrer & Sept, 2020). For instance, AI-powered chatbots can provide personalized customer service, while data analytics can help businesses better understand consumer preferences and tailor their offerings accordingly.

Moreover, the rise of digital platforms has facilitated the emergence of new business models, such as the sharing economy, which allows individuals to monetize their assets and provide unique experiences for tourists (Nur, Niswaty, Mustafa, & Guntur, 2021, September). This shift not only diversifies the tourism offerings in Dubai but also fosters a sense of community and local engagement, enhancing the overall visitor experience.

Additionally, the COVID-19 pandemic has accelerated the adoption of digital technologies in tourism, prompting businesses to rethink their operations and embrace innovative solutions (Saleh, Bassil, & Safari, 2021). For example, contactless payment systems and virtual tours have become increasingly popular, allowing businesses to adapt to changing consumer preferences while ensuring safety and convenience (Zhang, 2023). By leveraging these opportunities, Dubai's tourism sector can position itself as a leader in digital innovation, attracting a new generation of tech-savvy travelers.

In conclusion, the digital transformation of Dubai's tourism sector presents both challenges and opportunities. Addressing data privacy concerns, technological disparities, and the need for a skilled workforce is essential for ensuring a successful transition to a digital-first environment. However, by embracing innovation and leveraging advanced technologies, Dubai can enhance its tourism offerings and create a more resilient and competitive sector. As the tourism landscape continues to evolve, the ability to adapt and thrive in the digital era will be crucial for the long-term sustainability and growth of Dubai's tourism industry.

5. FUTURE TRENDS IN DIGITAL SUSTAINABILITY: DUBAI'S VISION FOR TOURISM EXCELLENCE

As Dubai positions itself as a global leader in tourism, the integration of digital sustainability into the tourism framework is becoming increasingly critical. This topic explores emerging trends in digital transformation, focusing on technologies such as blockchain, AR, and AI. These innovations not only enhance customer experiences, but also align Dubai with its sustainable tourism goals. Furthermore, this topic on the future of smart tourism in Dubai highlights the ongoing adaptation to global tourism demands and sustainability standards. Additionally, this section will examine the future of mega projects in Dubai and highlight the role of digital transformation and sustainability initiatives in shaping urban development.

Blockchain technology has emerged as a transformative force across various sectors, including tourism (Demirel, Karagöz Zeren, & Hakan, 2022). Its decentralized nature enhances transparency and security, which are essential for building trust among consumers and service providers (Saarinen, 2020). In the context of tourism, blockchain can facilitate secure transactions, streamline supply chains, and improve service traceability, thereby enhancing customer confidence. For instance, blockchain can be utilized to verify the authenticity of travel packages, ensuring that consumers receive what they pay for, thus aligning with Dubai's commitment to sustainable tourism practices. The convergence of blockchain with IoT and AI, as highlighted by Prakash et al. (2024), further suggests that these technologies can collectively enhance the efficiency and sustainability of tourism operations.

Moreover, blockchain can support eco-friendly initiatives by enabling the tracking of carbon footprints associated with travel activities. This capability allows stakeholders to implement more sustainable practices and promote responsible tourism. As Dubai seeks to position itself as a leader in sustainable urban development, the adoption of blockchain technology will be crucial in mitigating the environmental impacts of tourism.

AR is another technology that holds significant potential for enhancing the tourism experience in Dubai. AR can provide immersive experiences that enrich visitors' understanding of cultural and historical sites. For example, AR applications can overlay digital information onto physical landmarks, offering tourists interactive and educational content that enhances their visit. This aligns with Dubai's goal of promoting cultural heritage while providing innovative experiences that attract tech-savvy travelers (Paramita, 2023).

Furthermore, AR can facilitate personalized experiences by allowing tourists to customize their itineraries based on their interests. This level of personalization not only enhances visitor satisfaction but also encourages longer stays and increased spending, contributing to the overall economic growth of the tourism sector. As Dubai continues to innovate in its tourism offerings, AR will play a pivotal role in creating engaging and memorable experiences for visitors (Nadkarni & Morris, 2019).

Al is revolutionizing the tourism industry by providing insights that enhance customer experiences and operational efficiency. AI-driven analytics can help businesses understand consumer preferences, enabling them to tailor services and marketing strategies accordingly. For instance, AI can analyze data from social media and online reviews to gauge customer sentiment, allowing tourism operators to make informed decisions that improve service quality (Alexis-Thomas, 2020). This transformative power of AI on service delivery and value co-creation, as discussed by Okumus et al. (2024), highlights the ongoing impact of technological advancements on the tourism and hospitality sectors, further emphasizing the importance of integrating AI into Dubai's tourism strategy.

Moreover, AI-powered chatbots and virtual assistants can enhance customer service by providing instant responses to inquiries, thereby improving the overall visitor experience. This technology not only streamlines operations but also allows human staff to focus on more complex tasks, ultimately leading to higher levels of customer satisfaction.

As Dubai embraces AI, it must also address the challenges associated with its implementation, such as workforce displacement and the need for reskilling. By investing in training programs that enhance AI literacy among employees, Dubai can ensure that its workforce is equipped to thrive in an increasingly automated environment (Zaidan, 2015).

The integration of blockchain, AR, and AI into Dubai's tourism sector aligns seamlessly with its sustainable tourism goals. These technologies facilitate transparency, enhance visitor experiences, and promote responsible practices, all of which are essential for sustainable development. For instance, by leveraging blockchain for carbon tracking, Dubai can provide tourists with information on the environmental impact of their travel choices, encouraging more sustainable behaviors (Saarinen, 2020).

Additionally, the use of AR can promote cultural awareness and appreciation, fostering a deeper connection between tourists and the local community. This connection is vital for ensuring that tourism benefits both visitors and residents, contributing to the long-term sustainability of the sector (Paramita, 2023).

Looking ahead, the future of smart tourism in Dubai will be characterized by continuous adaptation to global tourism demands and sustainability standards. As consumer preferences evolve, Dubai must remain agile in its approach to tourism development. This includes embracing new technologies and innovative practices that enhance the visitor experience while minimizing environmental impacts. The exploration of the metaverse and its potential impact on tourism, as analyzed by Nawaz et al. (2024), indicates that virtual and augmented reality technologies will play a significant role in shaping future tourist experiences in Dubai.

The ongoing digital transformation will enable Dubai to position itself as a leader in smart tourism, attracting a diverse range of travelers seeking unique and sustainable experiences. By leveraging emerging technologies, Dubai can create a more resilient tourism ecosystem that responds effectively to changing market dynamics.

The future of megaprojects in Dubai will be significantly influenced by the integration of smart technologies and sustainability initiatives. As urban planning continues to evolve, the incorporation of digital solutions will enhance the efficiency of urban services and infrastructure development (Shevchenko & Petrushenko, 2021). For instance, smart city technologies can optimize resource management, reduce energy consumption, and improve transportation systems, contributing to a more sustainable urban environment.

Moreover, the collaborative approach advocated by Denicol et al. emphasizes the need for stakeholder engagement in the planning and execution of megaprojects. By involving government entities, private enterprises, and civil society, Dubai can ensure that the benefits of megaprojects are equitably distributed, fostering inclusive growth and community development (Denicol, Davies, & Pryke, 2021).

As Dubai seeks to position itself as a global leader in sustainable urban development, the adoption of eco-friendly practices will be paramount in mitigating the environmental impacts of construction. This includes utilizing sustainable materials, implementing energy-efficient designs, and incorporating green spaces into urban planning. The integration of these practices not only enhances the environmental performance of megaprojects but also contributes to the overall quality of life for residents and visitors alike (Khitskov, et al., 2017).

Furthermore, the evolving urban model in Gulf cities suggests a shift towards more sustainable and inclusive urban practices. This transition will require a collaborative approach that involves stakeholders from various sectors, ensuring that the benefits of megaprojects are equitably distributed (Haneef, Ansari, & Bhavani, 2019).

In conclusion, the future of digital sustainability in Dubai's tourism sector is promising, driven by emerging technologies such as blockchain, augmented reality, and Al. These innovations align with Dubai's sustainable tourism goals and will play a crucial role in shaping the future of smart tourism. As the city continues to evolve, the integration of sustainable practices and smart technologies will be essential in creating a resilient urban future. The lessons learned from Dubai's experience can serve as valuable insights for other cities embarking on similar journeys toward sustainable tourism excellence.

CONCLUSION

Dubai's journey towards digital transformation in the tourism sector is a multifaceted endeavor that intertwines technological innovation with sustainable practices. As the city continues to evolve, the integration of digital technologies such as big data analytics, AI, and IoT is reshaping the tourism landscape, enhancing operational efficiency, and promoting sustainable practices. This transformation is not merely a response to global trends but a proactive strategy aimed at positioning Dubai as a leader in sustainable tourism.

The case studies of prominent megaprojects, such as the Dubai Expo 2020 and the Museum of the Future, exemplify how digital transformation initiatives can be effectively implemented to foster sustainability and enhance visitor experiences. These projects illustrate the potential of digital technologies to create smart urban environments that prioritize ecological balance and social equity. The Sustainable City project, for instance, serves as a model for integrating sustainability principles into urban design, demonstrating that economic growth can coexist with environmental stewardship.

Moreover, the collaborative efforts among stakeholders—government entities, private organizations, and local communities—are crucial for building a resilient tourism ecosystem. Digital platforms facilitate communication and resource sharing, enabling coordinated planning and accountability towards environmental goals. However, challenges such as data privacy concerns, technological disparities, and the need for a skilled workforce must be addressed to fully realize the potential of digital transformation in tourism.

Looking ahead, the future of megaprojects in Dubai will be significantly influenced by ongoing digital transformation and sustainability initiatives. The integration of smart technologies into urban planning will redefine the megaproject landscape, fostering innovation and enhancing the efficiency of urban services. As Dubai seeks to position itself as a global leader in sustainable urban development, the adoption of eco-friendly practices will be paramount in mitigating the environmental impacts of construction.

In conclusion, Dubai's vision for tourism excellence is intricately linked to its commitment to digital sustainability. The lessons learned from Dubai's experience can serve as valuable insights for other cities embarking on similar journeys towards sustainable tourism. By embracing digital transformation and prioritizing sustainability, Dubai is not only enhancing its tourism sector but also setting a benchmark for global best practices in the industry.

Future Research Directions

As digital transformation continues to reshape the tourism sector in Dubai, particularly within its ambitious megaprojects, there is a growing need for research that addresses the evolving challenges and opportunities associated with sustainable tourism. This section outlines several promising directions for future research, each aimed at deepening our understanding of how digital tools can be leveraged to create a sustainable, resilient, and inclusive tourism ecosystem in Dubai and similar global cities.

1. Evaluating the Long-Term Environmental Impact of Digital Transformation in Tourism

While current research highlights the potential of digital tools for enhancing operational efficiency and sustainability, there remains a gap in understanding the long-term environmental impacts of these technologies. Future studies should examine the actual carbon footprint reductions achieved through digital innovations in tourism, assessing whether energy-efficient practices implemented in megaprojects like Dubai Expo 2020 and Dubai Creek Harbour have tangible, measurable effects.

Comparative studies with other urban regions could also reveal broader implications and best practices for sustainable urban tourism development globally.

2. Digital Transformation and Social Equity in Tourism

Digital transformation in tourism has the potential to foster inclusivity by making resources and services more accessible. However, disparities in access to technology among different segments of society, such as low-income groups and smaller tourism operators, can reinforce social inequalities. Future research could investigate how digital transformation can bridge these gaps by promoting equitable access to resources and opportunities within the tourism sector. Case studies might focus on digital literacy initiatives and affordable tech solutions that empower underserved communities and SMEs in Dubai's tourism ecosystem.

3. Impact of Artificial Intelligence (Al) and Big Data on Visitor Experiences and Personalization

AI and big data analytics are instrumental in shaping personalized visitor experiences. While personalization can significantly enhance satisfaction, more research is needed to explore the optimal balance between personalization, privacy, and data security in tourism. Specifically, studies could examine tourists' preferences and privacy concerns, as well as the effectiveness of AI-driven personalization in improving visitor satisfaction. Investigating how different demographic groups respond to these tailored experiences could provide valuable insights for designing inclusive and culturally sensitive tourism strategies.

4. Collaborative Stakeholder Ecosystems and Digital Platforms

The role of digital platforms in fostering collaboration among stakeholders—government, private entities, and local communities—is crucial to sustainable tourism. However, limited empirical research has analyzed the dynamics and efficacy of these collaborative systems. Future research could focus on evaluating specific digital platforms used in Dubai's tourism sector, analyzing their impact on coordinated planning, resource sharing, and stakeholder accountability. Additionally, studies could examine the potential of blockchain technology to improve transparency and trust in multi-stakeholder collaborations, particularly in complex megaprojects with varied interests.

5. Technological Resilience and Cybersecurity in Smart Tourism Infrastructure

As digital transformation advances, so does the risk of cybersecurity threats, especially in sectors involving high volumes of sensitive data, such as tourism. Research is needed to explore how Dubai's tourism sector can enhance cybersecurity measures to protect data and ensure operational continuity. Studies could focus on developing and assessing cybersecurity frameworks tailored to tourism, examining best practices for data protection and privacy regulations. Additionally, exploring resilience strategies for technology-based tourism systems, including contingency planning and disaster recovery, could provide insights for securing the longevity of smart tourism infrastructures.

6. Role of Emerging Technologies in Enhancing Environmental Sustainability

Emerging technologies, such as blockchain, AR, and VR, have the potential to support sustainable tourism by offering immersive, low-impact alternatives to physical tourism and facilitating eco-friendly transactions. Future research could evaluate the environmental benefits of these technologies within Dubai's tourism sector, examining how AR and VR experiences can reduce the environmental footprint of tourism activities. Moreover, studies could investigate the application of blockchain for sustainable resource management, analyzing its potential to streamline supply chains, reduce waste, and foster transparent, eco-friendly tourism practices.

7. Adoption and Adaptation of Digital Sustainability Standards

As global sustainability standards evolve, understanding how Dubai's tourism sector can adopt and adapt them within its unique socio-economic and environmental context is essential. Research could focus on identifying gaps between international sustainability frameworks and Dubai's current practices, assessing the adaptability of standards like the UN Sustainable Development Goals (SDGs) to Dubai's megaprojects. Additionally, studies could explore the development of context-specific sustainability metrics that account for the technological advancements and urbanization patterns unique to Dubai, providing a model for similar rapidly growing cities.

8. Quantifying the Economic Impact of Digital Transformation on Tourism

While digital transformation is often associated with improved efficiency and visitor experiences, its broader economic impacts within Dubai's tourism sector are not fully understood. Future research could quantify the financial benefits of digital initiatives in tourism, examining metrics such as cost savings, revenue growth, and job creation. Comparative studies between digitally transformed and non-transformed tourism entities could shed light on the return on investment in digital technologies, providing insights for policymakers and investors. Additionally, research could analyze the economic impact of digital tourism on local communities, assessing whether technology-driven growth translates into local economic resilience and benefits.

The digital transformation of Dubai's tourism sector presents numerous opportunities to create a more sustainable, resilient, and inclusive ecosystem. However, realizing this vision requires further investigation into key areas, including long-term environmental impacts, social equity, data privacy, collaborative platforms, cybersecurity, emerging technologies, sustainability standards, and economic metrics. By addressing these future research directions, scholars and practitioners can contribute to a comprehensive framework for sustainable digital tourism in Dubai, offering valuable insights not only for Dubai but also for other cities undergoing similar transformations.

REFERENCES

Abbas, J., Mahmood, S., Ali, H., Ali, R., Aman, J., Bano, S., & Nurunnabi, M. (2024). The effects of corporate social responsibility practices and environmental factors through a moderating role of social media marketing on sustainable performance of business firms. *Sustainability*, 13(18), 10463. DOI: 10.3390/su131810463

Abdalla, S., Mushtaha, E., Rashid, M., Opoku, A., Hamad, R., Dweiri, F., & El-mualim, A. (2023). Pre-design CSFs (critical success factors) of building projects for Dubai's development boom. *Built Environment Project and Asset Management*, 13(3), 359–374. DOI: 10.1108/BEPAM-09-2022-0144

Abdelfattah, L., Bazzoni, F., & Choubassi, R. (2021). The redemptive potential of the street. a multi-angular analysis of dubai's pedestrian infrastructure. *The Journal of Public Space*, 6(1), 67–94. DOI: 10.32891/jps.v6i1.1326

Abdelrady, H. (2023). Exploring the effectiveness of using digital tourism platforms in egyptian tourist destination. *Journal of Association of Arab Universities for Tourism and Hospitality*, 24(1), 389–405. DOI: 10.21608/jaauth.2023.235547.1499

Adekuajo, I. (2023). The digital evolution in hospitality: A global review and its potential transformative impact on u.s. tourism. *International Journal of Applied Research in Social Sciences*, 5(10), 440–462. DOI: 10.51594/ijarss.v5i10.633

Aguerrebere, P. (2023). Dubai expo 2020's impact on the united arab emirates brand: A quantitative analysis of american and european media companies. *Journal of Advanced Research in Social Sciences*, 6(4), 16–29. DOI: 10.33422/jarss.v6i4.1122

Al-Saidi, M., & Elagib, N. (2018). Ecological modernization and responses for a low-carbon future in the Gulf Cooperation Council countries. *Wiley Interdisciplinary Reviews: Climate Change*, 9(4), e528. DOI: 10.1002/wcc.528

Al-Saidi, M., Zaidan, E., & Hammad, S. (2019). Participation modes and diplomacy of Gulf Cooperation Council (GCC) countries towards the global sustainability agenda. *Development in Practice*, 29(5), 545–558. DOI: 10.1080/09614524.2019.1597017

Al-Shihabi, S., Aydin, R., Hadj-Alouane, A., & Alshanasi, A. (2023). Sustainable technologies, mega-events, and environmental awareness—Lessons from expo 2020 dubai. *Frontiers in Sustainable Cities*, 5, 1192295. Advance online publication. DOI: 10.3389/frsc.2023.1192295

Alarefi, A. H., Ameerbakhsh, O., Ab Ghani, M. K., & Zidan, Y. A. (2024). Energy efficiency in the GCC region: Prospects, challenges and opportunities. *International Journal of Thermofluids*, 21, 1000511. DOI: 10.1016/j.ijft.2023.100511

Alawadi, K. (2016). Place attachment as a motivation for community preservation: The demise of an old, bustling, dubai community. *Urban Studies (Edinburgh, Scotland)*, 54(13), 2973–2997. DOI: 10.1177/0042098016664690

Alawadi, K., & Benkraouda, O. (2017). The debate over neighborhood density in dubai: Between theory and practicality. *Journal of Planning Education and Research*, 39(1), 18–34. DOI: 10.1177/0739456X17720490

Alexis-Thomas, C. (2020). An examination of issues related to tourism and health and well-being as a sustainable development goal by tourism providers in tobago. *Worldwide Hospitality and Tourism Themes*, 12(3), 293–303. DOI: 10.1108/WHATT-02-2020-0006

Alford, P., & Jones, R. (2020). The lone digital tourism entrepreneur: Knowledge acquisition and collaborative transfer. *Tourism Management*, 81, 104–139. DOI: 10.1016/j.tourman.2020.104139

Alrawadieh, Z., Alrawadıeh, Z., & Çetin, G. (2020). Digital transformation and revenue management: Evidence from the hotel industry. *Tourism Economics*, 27(2), 328–345. DOI: 10.1177/1354816620901928

Aman, E., & Papp-Váry, A. (2022). Digital marketing as a driver for sustainable tourism development. *Multidiszciplináris Kihívások Sokszínű Válaszok*, 2(2), 3–33. DOI: 10.33565/MKSV.2022.02.01

Amrousi, M., Elhakeem, M., Paleologos, E., & Misuri, M. (2019). Engineered landscapes: The new dubai canal and emerging public spaces. *International Review for Spatial Planning and Sustainable Development*, 7(3), 33–34. DOI: 10.14246/irspsd.7.3_33

Anthonisz, A., & Mason, G. (2019). Reinventing tourism: The dubai phenomenon. *Worldwide Hospitality and Tourism Themes*, 11(3), 279–286. DOI: 10.1108/WHATT-01-2019-0004

Archi, Y., Benbba, B., Zhu, K., Andaloussi, Z., Pataki, L., & David, L. (2023). Mapping the nexus between sustainability and digitalization in tourist destinations: A bibliometric analysis. *Sustainability (Basel)*, 15(12), 9717. DOI: 10.3390/su15129717

Athapaththu, K., & Karunasena, G. (2018). Framework for sustainable construction practices in sri lanka. *Built Environment Project and Asset Management*, 8(1), 51–63. DOI: 10.1108/BEPAM-11-2016-0060

Ayoub, E., & Freeman, B. (2023). People, Planet, and Profits: Comparing Media Treatment of Dubai Sustainable City. *SAGE Open*, 13(3). DOI: 10.1177/21582440231190299

Baggio, R., Micera, R., & Chiappa, G. (2020). Smart tourism destinations: A critical reflection. *Journal of Hospitality and Tourism Technology*, 11(3), 407–423. DOI: 10.1108/JHTT-01-2019-0011

Binshakir, O., AlGhanim, L., Fathaq, A., AlHarith, A. M., Ahmed, S., & El-Sayegh, S. (2023). Factors affecting the bidding decision in sustainable construction. *Sustainability (Basel)*, 15(19), 14225. DOI: 10.3390/su151914225

Buckley, M., & Hanieh, A. (2013). Diversification by urbanization: Tracing the property-finance nexus in dubai and the gulf. *International Journal of Urban and Regional Research*, 38(1), 155–175. DOI: 10.1111/1468-2427.12084

Buhalis, D. (2019). Technology in tourism-from information communication technologies to etourism and smart tourism towards ambient intelligence tourism: A perspective article. *Tourism Review*, 75(1), 267–272. DOI: 10.1108/TR-06-2019-0258

Chen, L., Jiang, S., Pu, R., Li, L., & Hong-mei, Y. (2022). Knowledge map of digital tourism: A bibliometric approach using citespace. *Problems and Perspectives in Management*, 20(4), 573–587. DOI: 10.21511/ppm.20(4).2022.43

Cheng, X., Xue, T., Yang, B., & Ma, B. (2023). A digital transformation approach in hospitality and tourism research. *International Journal of Contemporary Hospitality Management*, 35(8), 2944–2967. DOI: 10.1108/IJCHM-06-2022-0679

Chiang, C. (2020). Developing an emarketing model for tourism and hospitality: A keyword analysis. *International Journal of Contemporary Hospitality Management*, 32(10), 3091–3114. DOI: 10.1108/IJCHM-03-2020-0230

Dąbrowska, J., Al-Mawali, H., Wilson, R., & Gore, T. (2024). The role of digital social identity in the stakeholder engagement process. *Journal of Business Research*, 172, 114442. DOI: 10.1016/j.jbusres.2023.114442

Demirel, E., Karagöz Zeren, S., & Hakan, K. (2022). Smart contracts in tourism industry: A model with blockchain integration for post pandemic economy. *Current Issues in Tourism*, 25(12), 1895–1909. DOI: 10.1080/13683500.2021.1960280

Denicol, J., Davies, A., & Pryke, S. (2021). The organisational architecture of megaprojects. *International Journal of Project Management*, 39(4), 339–350. DOI: 10.1016/j.ijproman.2021.02.002

Dessouky, N., Wheeler, S., & Salama, A. (2023). The five controversies of market-driven sustainable neighborhoods: An alternative approach to post-occupancy evaluation. *Social Sciences (Basel, Switzerland)*, 12(7), 367. DOI: 10.3390/socsci12070367

Dubai Creek Harbour. (2024). Retrieved from https://properties.emaar.com/en/our-communities/dubai-creek-harbour/

Eichelberger, S., Eller, R., Kallmuenzer, A., & Peters, M. (2023). Organisational learning and sustainable tourism: The enabling role of digital transformation. *Journal of Knowledge Management*, 27(11), 82–100. DOI: 10.1108/JKM-06-2022-0434

El-khateeb, S. (2019). Sustainable neighborhoods in arab world; a path towards sustainability. *The Academic Research Community Publication*, 3(1), 153–166. DOI: 10.21625/archive.v3i1.437

Eltoum, A., Yatiban, A., Omar, R., & Islam, M. (2022). Sustainability awareness in society and its impact on the level of responsible business adoption in the business sector of dubai. *Problems and Perspectives in Management*, 20(3), 540–551. DOI: 10.21511/ppm.20(3).2022.43

EXPO 2020 Dubai UAE. (26.10.2024). Retrieved from https://www.expo2020dubai.com/

EXPO 2020 Dubai UAE. (2024). Retrieved from Our commitment to sustainability: https://www.expo2020dubai.com/en/understanding-expo/expo-initiatives/sustainability-at-expo

Firdausi, F. (2023). Digital activism for sustainable tourism: management of social media instagram @travelxism through voluntrip activities. *Symposium of Literature Culture and Communication (Sylection) 2022, 3*(1), 106.

Generis Global. (2024). Retrieved 05.08.2023, from The Growing Role of AI in Dubai's Tourism Sector: https://generisonline.com/the-growing-role-of-ai-in-dubais-tourism-sector/

Ghazal, T. M., Hasan, M. K., Alshurideh, M. T., Alzoubi, H. M., Ahmad, M., Akbar, S. S., Al Kurdi, B., & Akour, I. A. (2024). IoT for smart cities: Machine learning approaches in smart healthcare—A review. *Future Internet*, 13(8), 218. DOI: 10.3390/fi13080218

Giardina, G. (2019). Expo 2020 and sustainability: Luxury hotel properties challenges and future outlook. *Worldwide Hospitality and Tourism Themes*, 11(3), 314–326. DOI: 10.1108/WHATT-01-2019-0005

Hallaq, A., Ninov, I., & Dutt, C. (2020). The perceptions of host-city residents of the impact of mega-events and their support: The expo 2020 in dubai. *Journal of Policy Research in Tourism, Leisure & Events*, 13(3), 374–396. DOI: 10.1080/19407963.2020.1839088

Han, D., Weber, J., Bastiaansen, M., Mitas, O., & Lub, X. (2019). Virtual and augmented reality technologies to enhance the visitor experience in cultural tourism. *Augmented reality and virtual reality: The power of AR and VR for business*, 113-128.

Haneef, S., Ansari, Z., & Bhavani, G. (2019). Attractions of dubai and expo 2020: An exploratory study. *Worldwide Hospitality and Tourism Themes*, 11(3), 266–278. DOI: 10.1108/WHATT-01-2019-0007

Ioannou, A., Tussyadiah, I., & Miller, G. (2021). That's private! Understanding travelers' privacy concerns and online data disclosure. *Journal of Travel Research*, 60(7), 1510–1526. DOI: 10.1177/0047287520951642

Jong, M., Hoppe, T., & Alawadi, N. (2019). City branding, sustainable urban development and the rentier state. how do qatar, abu dhabi and dubai present themselves in the age of post oil and global warming? *Energies*, 12(9), 1657. DOI: 10.3390/en12091657

Jung, C., Abdelaziz Mahmoud, N. S., & Alqassimi, N. (2023). Enhancing indoor air quality and sustainable living in newly constructed apartments: Insights from dubai. *Frontiers in Built Environment*, 9, 1292531. Advance online publication. DOI: 10.3389/fbuil.2023.1292531

Jung, C., Awad, J., & Al Qassimi, N. (2021). Analyzing the users' satisfaction levels and perceptions of the dubai water canal for future waterfront development in uae. *Future Cities and Environment, 7*(1).

Kallou, S., & Kikilia, A. (2021). A transformative educational framework in tourism higher education through digital technologies during the covid-19 pandemic. *Advances in Mobile Learning Educational Research*, 1(2), 37–47. DOI: 10.25082/AMLER.2021.01.005

Kamble, S., Kaushik, D., Bhat, I. A., & Alfalou, A. (2024). The role of big data analytics and artificial intelligence in sustainable supply chain management: A survey. *Global Transitions*, 6, 100151. DOI: 10.1016/j.glt

Khitskov, E., Veretekhina, S., Medvedeva, A., Mnatsakanyan, O., Shmakova, E., & Koteney, A. (2017). Digital transformation of society: Problems entering in the digital economy. *Eurasian Journal of Analytical Chemistry*, 12(5b, 5B), 855–873. DOI: 10.12973/ejac.2017.00216a

Kumar, S., Kumar, V., Bhatt, I., Kumar, S., & Attri, K. (2023). Digital transformation in tourism sector: Trends and future perspectives from a bibliometric-content analysis. *Journal of Hospitality and Tourism Insights*, 7(3), 1553–1576. DOI: 10.1108/JHTI-10-2022-0472

Le, D. N., & Nguien, S. H. (2024). Unveiling the impact of artificial intelligence adoption intention on green innovation and new venture performance: The mediating effect of green dynamic capability. *Journal of Innovation & Knowledge*, 100504. Advance online publication. DOI: 10.1016/j.jik.2024.100504

Lei, J., Indiran, L., & Kohar, U. (2023). Barriers to digital transformation among msme in tourism industry: Cases studies from bali. *International Journal of Academic Research in Business & Social Sciences*, 13(3), 844–858. DOI: 10.6007/IJARBSS/v13-i3/16575

Li, N., Liu, Z., & Zhang, X. (2022). A study on the impact of dynamic visitor demand on the digital transformation of enterprises—Considerations based on the regional innovation environment and the level of big data. *Sustainability (Basel)*, 15(1), 261. DOI: 10.3390/su15010261

Majeed, S., Zhou, Z., Lu, C., & Ramkissoon, H. (2020). Online tourism information and tourist behavior: A structural equation modeling analysis based on a self-administered survey. *Frontiers in Psychology*, 599, 11. DOI: 10.3389/fpsyg.2020.00599 PMID: 32373008

Manikas, I., Sundarakani, B., Madmoune, A., & Alvares, R. (2022). Integrated supply chain sustainability for mega-events: An empirical study of dubai expo 2020. *Event Management*, 26(6), 1409–1432. DOI: 10.3727/152599522X16419948391032

Marino, A., & Pariso, P. (2021). Digital government platforms: Issues and actions in europe during pandemic time. *Journal of Entrepreneurship and Sustainability Issues*, 9(1), 462–485. DOI: 10.9770/jesi.2021.9.1(29)

McNaughton, M., Rao, L., & Verma, S. (2020). Building smart communities for sustainable development. *Worldwide Hospitality and Tourism Themes*, 12(3), 337–352. DOI: 10.1108/WHATT-02-2020-0008

Mehraliyev, F., Choi, Y., & Köseoğlu, M. (2019). Progress on smart tourism research. *Journal of Hospitality and Tourism Technology*, 10(4), 522–538. DOI: 10.1108/JHTT-08-2018-0076

Mohammad, N., & Rahmat, M. K. (2024). Exploring the potential of artificial intelligence in augmenting tourism and hospitality industry in United Arab Emirates (UAE). *SHS Web of Conferences. 189*, p. 03007. EDP Sciences.

Mohsin, M., Taghizadeh-Hesary, F., Iqbal, N., & Saydaliev, H. (2024). The role of digitalization and public-private partnerships in sustainable economic development: Evidence from selected Asian economies. *Journal of Risk and Financial Management*, 16(9), 397. DOI: 10.3390/jrfm16090397

Mondal, S., & Samaddar, K. (2020). Issues and challenges in implementing sharing economy in tourism: A triangulation study. *Management of Environmental Quality*, 32(1), 64–81. DOI: 10.1108/MEQ-03-2020-0054

Morais, E., Cunha, C., & Mendonça, V. (2022, September). Tourism and Internet of Things: A bibliometric analysis of scientific production from the Scopus database. In *International Conference on Advanced Research in Technologies, Information, Innovation and Sustainability* (pp. 244-255). Cham: Springer Nature Switzerland. DOI: 10.1007/978-3-031-20316-9_19

Muñiz, D., Vila, N., & Brea, J. (2021). Changes in consumption patterns and tourist promotion after the covid-19 pandemic. *Journal of Theoretical and Applied Electronic Commerce Research*, 16(5), 1332–1352. DOI: 10.3390/jtaer16050075

Museum Of The Future. (2024). Retrieved from https://museumofthefuture.ae/en)

Museum Of The Future. (2024). Retrieved from Inhabit The Skies: https://museumofthefuture.ae/en/experience

Nadkarni, S. (2019). Conclusions: Expo 2020 and its impact on Dubai. *Worldwide Hospitality and Tourism Themes*, 11(3), 341–345. DOI: 10.1108/WHATT-02-2019-0011

Nadkarni, S. (2019). The pre- and post-event planning roadmap for expo 2020: Dubai's coming-out-party. *Worldwide Hospitality and Tourism Themes*, 11(3), 259–265. DOI: 10.1108/WHATT-02-2019-0009

Nadkarni, S., & Morris, S. (2019). Innovation-centric courses in hospitality management education in dubai. *Worldwide Hospitality and Tourism Themes*, 2(2), 166–172. DOI: 10.1108/WHATT-12-2018-0084

Nawaz, M., Dinc, M. S., Qureshi, M. B., & Magda, R. (2024). Metaverse and tourism in the digital age: A bibliometric analysis. *Technological Forecasting and Social Change*, 202, 123298. DOI: 10.1016/j.techfore.2024.123298

Nazare, A., Moldoveanu, A., & Moldoveanu, F. (2023). Virtual Journeys, Real Engagement: Analyzing User Experience in a Virtual Traveling Social Platform. *Information 2024, 15*, 396.

Noori, N., Hoppe, T., & Jong, M. (2020). Classifying pathways for smart city development: Comparing design, governance and implementation in amsterdam, barcelona, dubai, and abu dhabi. *Sustainability (Basel)*, 12(10), 4030. DOI: 10.3390/su12104030

Nur, A., Niswaty, R., Mustafa, D., & Guntur, M. (2021, September). The role of technology in development policy in the era of globalization in south sulawesi indonesia. *3rd Annual International Conference on Public and Business Administration (AICoBPA 2020)* (pp. 126-132). Atlantis Press. Retrieved from DOI: 10.2991/aebmr.k.210928.026

Okumus, F., Buhalis, D., & Taheri, B. (2024). The transformative power of technological advancements on service delivery, experiences and value co-creation in tourism, hospitality, leisure, and events. *Journal of Service Management*. Advance online publication. DOI: 10.1108/JOSM-11-2023-0496

Pan, S., Yang, M., Li, Y., & Gao, M. (2024). Digitalization for sustainable development: A systematic literature review of evolving trends and practices. *Heliyon*, 24974. Advance online publication. DOI: 10.1016/j.heliyon.2024.e24974

Paramita, A., Winarso, H., Hudalah, D., & Syabri, I. (2023). Path dependency and development impacts of megaproject: A case study of north jakarta bay reclamation. *International Journal of Sustainable Development and Planning*, 18(11), 3477–3490. DOI: 10.18280/ijsdp.181113

Prakash, O., Solanki, P., Shekhawat, R. S., & Dhiman, G. (2024). Revolutionizing Industries With Blockchain-Based Internet of Things and Artificial Intelligence Based Applications. *Computers & Electrical Engineering*, 115, 109287.

Qatawneh, D., Adnan, A., AlZoughool, S., & AlQudah, T. (2020). A study of the leading factors that induced confidence in the foreign investors for investing in real estate business for the period 1970- 2019. *Scholars Journal of Economics Business and Management*, 07(01), 39–43. DOI: 10.36347/sjebm.2020.v07i01.007

Rani, P., Sharma, P., & Gupta, I. (2024). Toward a greener future: A survey on sustainable blockchain applications and impact. *Journal of Environmental Management*, 120273, 354. DOI: 10.1016/j.jenvman.2024.120273 PMID: 38350276

Rethinking The Future. (2024). Retrieved from Smart Cities: Exploring how technology is being integrated into urban infrastructure and services: https://www.re-thinkingthefuture.com/architectural-community/a10783-smart-cities-exploring-how-technology-is-being-integrated-into-urban-infrastructure-and-services/

Saarinen, J. (2020). Tourism and sustainable development goals: Research on sustainable tourism geographies. In *Tourism and Sustainable Development Goals* (pp. 1–10). Routledge. DOI: 10.1201/9780429324253-1

Saleh, A., Bassil, C., & Safari, A. (2021). Tourism research for the gcc region: Current status and future research directions. *Tourism Economics*, 28(6), 1626–1646. DOI: 10.1177/1354816621999968

Samuel, G., Lucivero, F., & Croxatto, L. (2022). The environmental sustainability of digital technologies: Stakeholder practices and perspectives. *Sustainability (Basel)*, 14(7), 3791. DOI: 10.3390/su14073791

Sharma, S., Stranjančević, A., & Kleber, D. (2019). The effects of hosting events on destination branding: Dubai expo 2020. *Kinerja*, 23(2), 91–102. DOI: 10.24002/kinerja.v23i2.2390

Shehade, M., & Stylianou-Lambert, T. (2020). Revisiting authenticity in the age of the digital transformation of cultural tourism. *Cultural and tourism innovation in the digital era: Sixth international IACuDiT conference* (pp. 3-16). Springer International Publishing.

Sheikh Mohammed bin Rashid Al Maktoum. (2024). Retrieved from Mohammed bin Rashid Launches Digital Wealth Initiative and Dubai IoT Strategy: https://sheikhmohammed.ae/en-us/news/details?nid=25236&cid=

Shevchenko, H., & Petrushenko, M. (2021). Rural tourism within the sustainable development goals: the case of ukraine. *SHS Web of Conferences, 95*. DOI: 10.1051/shsconf/20219501004

Sultan, M., Sharmin, F., Bădulescu, A., Ştiubea, E., & Xue, K. (2020). Travelers' responsible environmental behavior towards sustainable coastal tourism: An empirical investigation on social media user-generated content. *Sustainability (Basel)*, 13(1), 56. DOI: 10.3390/su13010056

Taha, B., & Allan, A. (2022). Planning for Legacy–A Cost Effective and Sustainable Approach. Case Study: Dubai Expo 2020. *ISPRS Annals of the Photogrammetry, Remote Sensing and Spatial Information Sciences*, 10, 237–244. DOI: 10.5194/isprs-annals-X-4-W3-2022-237-2022

UN Enviromental Programme. (2024). Retrieved from GOAL 11: Sustainable cities and communities: https://www.unep.org/topics/sustainable-development-goals/why-do-sustainable-development-goals-matter/goal-11

Wu, X., Chong, H., Wang, G., & Li, S. (2018). The influence of social capitalism on construction safety behaviors: An exploratory megaproject case study. *Sustainability (Basel)*, 10(9), 3098. DOI: 10.3390/su10093098

Yallop, A., & Seraphin, H. (2020). Big data and analytics in tourism and hospitality: Opportunities and risks. *Journal of Tourism Futures*, 6(3), 257–262. DOI: 10.1108/JTF-10-2019-0108

Yuniarta, G., Purnamawati, I., & Suwena, K. (2023). The effect of using digital marketing platforms, optimizing potential assets on the inclusive and sustainable economy improvement. *International Journal of Organizational Behavior and Policy*, 2(1), 35–44. DOI: 10.9744/ijobp.2.1.35-44

Zaidan, E. (2015). Tourism shopping and new urban entertainment. *Journal of Vacation Marketing*, 22(1), 29–41. DOI: 10.1177/1356766715589426

Zaidan, E., & Abulibdeh, A. (2020). Master planning and the evolving urban model in the gulf cities: Principles, policies, and practices for the transition to sustainable urbanism. *Planning Practice and Research*, 36(2), 193–215. DOI: 10.1080/02697459.2020.1829278

Zerrer, N., & Sept, A. (2020). Smart villagers as actors of digital social innovation in rural areas. *Urban Planning*, 5(4), 78–88. DOI: 10.17645/up.v5i4.3183

Zhang, Z. (2023). Digital operational strategies in the post-pandemic era for travel companies: A case study of ctrip. *Highlights in Business Economics and Management*, 23, 521–525. DOI: 10.54097/h0w3ar97

ADDITIONAL READING

Al-Saidi, M., & Elagib, N. A. (2018). Ecological modernization and water resource management in the Gulf Cooperation Council (GCC) countries: Identifying challenges and opportunities. *Environmental Science & Policy*, 80, 107–115.

Alegre, J., & Sard, M. (2019). Tourism innovation and smart destinations: Insights from the tourism industry in Dubai. *Journal of Destination Marketing & Management*, 14, 100374.

Buhalis, D., & Amaranggana, A. (2015). Smart tourism destinations enhancing tourism experience through personalisation of services. *Information and Communication Technologies in Tourism*, 2015, 377–389. DOI: 10.1007/978-3-319-14343-9_28

Chong, A. Y. L., & Chan, F. T. S. (2018). Structural equation modeling for multi-stage analysis on big data analytics adoption in the tourism and hospitality industry. *Tourism Management*, 68, 27–39.

Choudhury, A., & Tavares, N. (2019). Digital platforms and megaproject collaboration: Creating synergy in cross-sector partnerships. *Journal of Urban Technology*, 26(2), 43–64.

Dubai Electricity and Water Authority. (2024). *DEWA's contribution to Dubai's smart tourism vision.* DEWA. Retrieved from https://www.dewa.gov.ae/

El-Khateeb, S. (2019). Sustainable urbanism and tourism megaprojects in Dubai: The role of digital transformation in sustainable urban neighborhoods. *Urban Studies Journal*, 56(14), 2784–2801.

Sigala, M. (2020). Tourism and COVID-19: Impacts and implications for advancing and resetting industry and research. *Journal of Business Research*, 117, 312–321. DOI: 10.1016/j.jbusres.2020.06.015 PMID: 32546875

World Tourism Organization (UNWTO). (2023). The role of digital transformation in Dubai's sustainable tourism development. UNWTO Journal. Retrieved from https://www.unwto.org/

Yigitcanlar, T., Kamruzzaman, M., Foth, M., Sabatini-Marques, J., da Costa, E. M., & Ioppolo, G. (2018). Can cities become smart without being sustainable? A systematic review of the literature. *Sustainable Cities and Society*, 45, 348–365. DOI: 10.1016/j.scs.2018.11.033

Chapter 5
A New Client Experience Area in Banking Evolving From Physical to Digital: Phygital Banking Applications in Türkiye

Yunus Bölükbaşı
Trakya University, Turkey

ABSTRACT

The concept of phygital refers to the integration of physical and digital media in our current digital era. This approach is relevant across various sectors, including marketing, education, communication, and banking. It involves delivering various services and products to consumers through both physical channels and digital technologies. Phygital applications enable firms to stand out in value delivery through multi-channel structures in an increasingly digital world. Today's banking is shifting from a model characterized by numerous branches to one where the number of branches is reduced, and the use of digital channels is emphasized. Innovations such as digital payment solutions and electronic money applications from technology companies are fundamentally changing the digitalization process within the banking sector. The journey that began with internet banking in Türkiye 30 years ago has now deepened through new areas such as the metaverse and artificial intelligence. With the amendments made to Turkish Banking Legislation in 2021, the requirement for wet signatures in individual customer transactions was eliminated, allowing customer acquisition through digital security processes. Additionally, regulations introduced in 2022 paved the way for the establishment of fully digital banks. However, existing regulations still require digital banks to maintain physical offices, indicating that in an environment where digitalization in banking is rapidly

DOI: 10.4018/979-8-3693-9435-9.ch005

advancing, the complete abandonment of physical channels does not seem realistic. In light of this context, this study aims to develop the concept of "Phygital Banking" for the Turkish Banking sector. As the rules of the competition are being redefined, with intellectual assets and intellectual capital taking precedence over physical ones, this research examines the opportunities presented by phygital applications in the Turkish Banking industry. The study aims to analyze existing phygital tools and provide recommendations for new application areas.

1. INTRODUCTION

The concept of "phygital" emerges in this era where every stage of life rapidly becomes digital, integrating both physical and digital channels. Derived from combining the words "physical" and "digital," phygital refers to the simultaneous use of these two channels to create a unique added value (Çelik, 2021; Sloviov&Danilov, 2020; Aydın & Öztürk, 2022; Averbek & Türkyılmaz, 2021; Johnson & Barlow, 2021).

Phygital, which has entered our lives through the science of marketing, is a conceptual combination that can be explored across various dimensions such as education, communication, and banking. Through this integration, consumers receive services and products from companies via physical channels, while also accessing similar or distinct offerings through digital technologies. Thus, phygital applications enable firms to stand out in the value proposition they offer to their customers with multi-channel structures in a completely digital world.

Rapid advancements in smart technologies, along with innovations such as Industry 5.0 and Society 5.0, are driving large-scale transformations and facilitating the integration of digitization as a significant phenomenon in contemporary society (Dinçsoy, 2023). In this context, digital technologies continue to exert a growing influence across various facets of modern life, and the prevalence of phygital examples is also expected to increase. This study seeks to investigate this emerging domain by analyzing current digital innovations and phygital examples, with a particular emphasis on the banking sector. The banking industry, as a key representative of digital transformation, plays a crucial role in the broader trend towards digitization. Given the limited academic research available on this topic and the pressing need to establish a new conceptual framework, this study also aims to address this gap. So, the goal of this research is to enrich the conceptual literature with practical examples, while also providing a methodological foundation for qualitative research. Hence this study also aims to serve as a basis for further research in this rapidly evolving domain.

The banking and finance world is constantly evolving with new technology and consumer demand. Banks fully leverage technological advancements in their marketing activities to reach customers (Duğru & Dinçsoy, 2014). These technological advancements facilitate the development of new channels for customers to interact with financial services, while also contributing to the reduction of financial risks. In this regard, rapidly developing new technologies always provide new phygital channels.

Phygital banking concepts and practices can be examined theoretically within the framework of the Technology Acceptance Model (TAM) (Davis, 1989) and Disruptive Innovation Theory (Bower & Christensen, 1995; Christensen, 2006). The Technology Acceptance Model suggests that customers accept new banking technologies based on ease of use and benefits. Also, the Disruptive Innovation Theory explains how new technologies can challenge established practices with technological innovations by meeting consumer demands in innovative ways. Together, these two theories theoretically reveal how phygital banking meets existing customer needs and how it transforms the sector by forcing traditional banks to innovate, thus putting them at risk of extinction.

Garg and Kumar (2024), in their bibliometric analysis conducted within the context of banking, digital technologies, and sustainability, highlight the research gap between these three areas. They point out that the evolution of banking, starting from the Internet and mobile applications and advancing with a wide range of digital technologies, has facilitated operations, reduced errors, expanded services, and contributed to regulating illegal activities through digital records. Additionally, they argue that digital technologies pave the way for permanent financial stability and contribute to social sustainability by reducing income inequality. In the relevant research context, it is emphasized that digital advancements in banking will create social benefits in terms of sustainability, supporting the research focus of this paper.

Based on the relevant literature research, the main question of the research is to examine the new phygital medium created in the post-digital era in terms of banking and what phygital services are offered to clients. In this context, it is also aimed to introduce the concept of phygital banking to the literature as a new research area and to try to create a curiosity that will lead to further research. In addition, it is aimed to show how the technological transformation in the triple transformation is undertaken by banking and the social benefit and sustainability dimension created by the phygital applications that emerged in this way.

With all these purposes, this paper is organised into several distinct sections, each addressing key components of the research. The introduction, summarises the literature and research background, highlighting its scope, significance and the identified research gap. In subsequent sections, the concepts of phygital, digital banking and phygital banking are defined respectively. Following this, the conceptual research model is presented, supported by relevant theories from the literature. The research section includes examples of phygital banking applications in Türkiye. Finally, the 'conclusion and recommendations' section provides theoretical and practical explanations, along with suggestions for further research.

2. DEFINING PHYGITAL

This new concept, which expresses the integration of physical and digital environments, was first articulated as "phygital" by Chris Weil, CEO of Momentum, at the American Advertising Agencies Association in 2007, and it was explained as the inseparability of the two worlds (www.aaaa.org). With the blurring of sharp lines between the physical and digital realms, a completely new space and experience area called the "Phygital World" is emerging (Çakın & Yaman, 2020; Çelik, 2021; Lehy, 2017 as cited in Köse & Yengin, 2018).

Through phygitalization, a bridge is being established between the physical and digital worlds, allowing online and offline environments to coexist with economic activity (Soloviov & Danilov, 2020). Phygital tools effectively bridge the gap between the digital and physical environments, thereby offering consumers new and different experiences. Technologies such as virtual reality (VR), augmented reality, QR codes, contactless payment methods, near field communication (NFC), radio frequency identification (RFID), interactive touch screens, the Internet of Things, beacon devices, facial and voice recognition systems, virtual dressing rooms in retail, location-based services (LBS), artificial intelligence and machine learning are making significant contributions to enhancing the customer experience (Gedik, 2021; Johnson & Barlow, 2021; Klaus, 2021; Moravcikova & Kliestikova, 2017).

3. DIGITAL BANKING

The concept of electronic banking services encompasses all electronic distribution channels through which customers can perform transactions remotely or provide transaction instructions. The digital process begins with Internet banking services and includes mobile banking, telephone banking, open banking services, banking transactions conducted at ATMs, and kiosk devices (tbb.org.tr). In 1997, İşbank became the first bank in Türkiye to offer Internet banking services, after which other banks also began to provide various services through their websites (isbank.com.tr).

With the entry of smartphones and tablets into our lives, specialized Internet banking distribution channels that enable customers to perform banking transactions through banks' dedicated mobile applications on these devices are referred to as mobile banking (The Banks Association of Türkiye, 2024a). Due to the development of mobile banking applications facilitated by the rapid advancement of technology, the digitalisation process in banking continues unabated. A considerable proportion of banking transactions are now conducted by customers through digital banking applications. In Türkiye, the number of digital banking customers who have logged in at least once within the past year exceeds 136 million[1]. Furthermore, in the last three months, the number of active digital banking customers who have conducted at least one transaction has exceeded 114 million (The Banks Association of Türkiye, 2024b).

In addition to digital banking activities, a new generation of banks that operate exclusively through digital channels has begun to emerge worldwide. These new generation banks, known as neobanks, can be defined as institutions that operate with their banking licenses, differentiating themselves from fintechs, but without any physical branches (Balkan & Aydın, 2021). As in other parts of the world, regulations have been developed in our country for the establishment of fully digital banks. In this regard, the "Regulation on the Operating Principles of Digital Banks and Banking As a Service Model" came into effect in 2022. According to this regulation, a digital bank is defined as "*a credit institution that provides banking services through electronic banking service distribution channels instead of physical branches*" (Bddk.gov.tr, 2022)[2].

After the implementation of regulations enabling banking operations without the necessity of a physical branch, the Turkish banking sector has experienced the introduction of new digital banks starting in 2022. The common characteristics of these banks are that they have been established according to the new digital banking regulations and, unlike traditional banks, do not have branch structures. The banks that are established and operating completely digitally include Hayat Finans Participation Bank and T.O.M. Participation Bank. Furthermore, the digital banks that have received establishment authorization from the Banking Regulation and Supervision Agency but have yet to commence operations include FUPS Bank, Ziraat Dinamik Bank, Colendi Bank and Adil Participation Bank (Bddk.gov.tr, 2024)[3].

In addition to permitting banking operations without any physical branches, digital banking regulations impose a requirement for physical infrastructure. According to the relevant digital banking regulations, while digital banks are prohibited from establishing physical branches, they are mandated to set up a physical office to address customer complaints. Consequently, even for next-generation digital banks that are designed to operate entirely in a digital format, having physical touchpoints to resolve customer issues is regarded as a necessity.

In this era of rapid technological advancements, it is evident that digital developments are influencing every aspect of life. However, the process of digitalization does not imply a complete abandonment of the physical realm. On the contrary, the convergence of digital and physical elements is generating new experiences and competitive landscapes. This new era has been articulated as "phygital" in the preceding discussion. The concept of "Phygital Banking," as it relates to this new phase in the banking sector, is proposed in this academic study and will be examined in the subsequent section.

4. PHYGITAL BANKING

It has been conceptually established in previous sections that the phygital represents a convergence point of the physical and digital worlds. This section proposes a new concept called "Phygital Banking," which differs from traditional digital banking. Additionally, examples of applications and tools relevant to this new era are presented.

Traditional banks' digital banking services provide practical solutions for various aspects of daily life. Factors such as a youthful population, technological adeptness, and unforeseen circumstances particularly the global pandemic, have positively influenced the increasing adoption of digital channels for financial transactions. While the digitalization process is progressing rapidly, as previously discussed, a complete transition away from physical channels is neither feasible in the context of everyday life nor compliant with regulatory requirements, which necessitate the maintenance of physical contact points.

Phygital approaches not only offer unique experiences but also enhance customer loyalty and trust in banking institutions (Ergen et al., 2024). Therefore, this study aims to elucidate the significance of the "Phygital Banking" era, which can be considered a new phase in the field of banking.

According to Rasheed K. (2023), phygital banking approaches combine the strongest features of physical and digital processes to create a new communication channel in service delivery. In this way, the conveniences offered to customers who cannot physically go to a branch, who need assistance due to security reasons in digital transactions, or who cannot access the necessary services in their environment due to infrastructural deficiencies contribute significantly to the creation of social benefits. Additionally, the widespread adoption of innovative phygital applications in regions with low financial literacy will also provide benefits in terms of financial sustainability.

According to Chaudhary and Nalwaya (2021), banking is in a disruptive technological development process. A new hybrid banking system is emerging with the combination of physical and digital banking services. As a result of this new combination, there will be a positive increase in customer experience in the banking sector. In addition, banks that use disruptive technologies better will be able to offer more qualified solutions to their customers in the evaluation of investment risks and opportunities. Furthermore, these banks will be better equipped to proactively address issues such as fraud. In this world where the physical and digital merge, an increase in customers' financial well-being will be observed.

4.1. Conceptual Model of the Research

Developing technologies are increasingly bridging the gap between the physical and the digital day by day. While both areas are getting closer to each other, they are also creating a new common area where they are connected. This new intersection, as defined in the above sections, is referred to as phygital. This study proposes the combination of traditional physical banking and digital banking fields as a new concept for the banking field in the form of phygital banking and presents it in the following model. There are many studies in the literature emphasizing the importance of digital banking (Nnaomah et al., 2024; Starnawska, 2021), and attention is also drawn to the research gap in the field of digital technologies and banking (Garg and Kumar (2024). In this regard, the research model is considered important and supported in the literature.

Figure 1. Conceptual Model

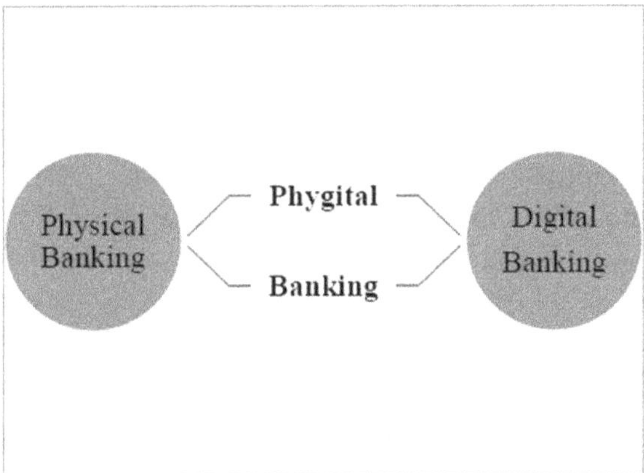

4.2. Evaluation From a Theoretical Perspective

The integration of phygital banking practices can be examined through the lenses of the Technology Acceptance Model (Davis, 1989) and Disruptive Innovation Theory (Bower & Christensen, 1995; Christensen, 2006). The Technology Acceptance Model posits that perceived ease of use and perceived usefulness significantly influence users' acceptance of new technologies. In the context of phygital banking, customers' willingness to adopt hybrid banking solutions, such as QR code transactions and queue management applications, relies heavily on their perceptions of how these services enhance their banking experience compared to traditional methods. Additionally, Disruptive Innovation Theory, emphasizes how innovations can initially serve a niche market but eventually displace established market leaders. As phygital banking evolves, traditional banks may find themselves challenged by new entrants that leverage technology to meet consumer demands in novel ways. Integrating the Technology Acceptance Model and Disruptive Innovation Theory provides a nuanced understanding of how the adoption of phygital banking solutions addresses immediate consumer demands while simultaneously transforming the competitive dynamics within the banking sector. This interplay compels established financial institutions to engage in continuous innovation to meet evolving consumer expectations, thereby mitigating the risk of becoming obsolete in a rapidly changing marketplace. Viewed through this perspective, we can recognize that phygital banking not only addresses contemporary consumer demands but also serves as a driving force for strategic transformation within traditional banks, compelling them to evolve or confront the possibility of decline.

5. PHYGITAL BANKING APPLICATIONS

This section will present examples of phygital banking applications. While some of these applications remain actively operational and accessible to customers, others are no longer maintained or updated. As a result, some applications have evolved in response to industry advancements, while others have gradually become obsolete.

5.1. QR Code-Based Financial Transactions at ATMs

Phygital Banking is partially integrated into the solutions currently implemented by traditional banks (Santosh, 2019). For instance, the process of withdrawing cash from ATMs using QR codes is not merely a digital or physical solution; rather, it exemplifies an application where the physical and digital realms converge, serving as an illustration of phygital banking. Although the transaction may be initiated via mobile banking, the subsequent integration with a physical touchpoint, such as an ATM, underscores that this transaction represents a phygital banking solution. To provide concrete examples, Figure 2 presents a screenshot of the QR code and ATM interface from Garanti BBVA, while Figure 3 displays the corresponding interface from Yapı Kredi Bank.

Figure 2. Garanti BBVA QR Code Cash Withdrawal from ATM

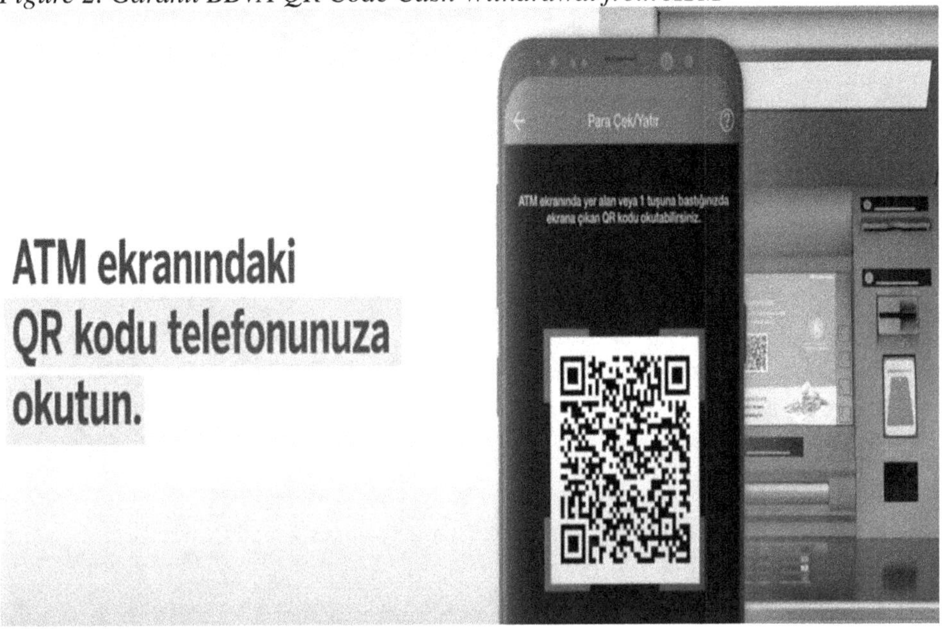

Source: www.garantibbva.com.tr

Figure 3. Yapı Kredi Bank QR Code Cash Withdrawal from ATM

Source: www.yapikredi.com.tr

5.2. Transformation of Physical Money Box into Phygital Banking Solutions

Initially introduced by Türkiye İşbank in 1929, the physical money box played a significant role in fostering savings habits among children until the 2000s (isbank.com.tr). With the increasing prevalence of computers in daily life during the 2000s, Ersin Özince, who was the General Manager of Türkiye İşbank at the time, stated the necessity for the money box to transition to an electronic format (hurriyet.com).

In 2017, Türkiye İşbank developed the Digital Money Box to enhance savings awareness among "Digital Natives"[4]. The traditional physical money box was redesigned to incorporate digital displays. Consequently, while the money transferred through digital banking accumulates in the money box account, the total savings amount is simultaneously displayed on the digital screen of the money box. This application can be regarded as a contemporary example of Phygital Banking, where digital and physical banking practices are seamlessly integrated. Figure 4 depicts the digital money box developed by Türkiye İşbank.

Figure 4. Türkiye İşbank Digital Money Box Phygital Banking Application

Source: www.isbank.com.tr

5.3. Fuel Purchase Without Exiting the Vehicle: Phygital Payment Solutions

Another example of Phygital Banking is Garanti Bank's in-car payment transactions at gas stations. This process offers a phygital solution that enables users to make payments while refuelling their vehicles without exiting the vehicle. At participating gas stations, customers can enter the station and pump information via a mobile application. The BonusFlaş application installed on users' phones detects their location and the gas station at which they are located. In the first step, users log into the application and select the in-car payment option. In the second step, they enter the station number and gas pump number. Finally, in the third step, payment is processed from the card without requiring the user to exit the vehicle. Figure 5 illustrates the steps of the application process.

Figure 5. Garanti BBVA BP In-Car Payment Application

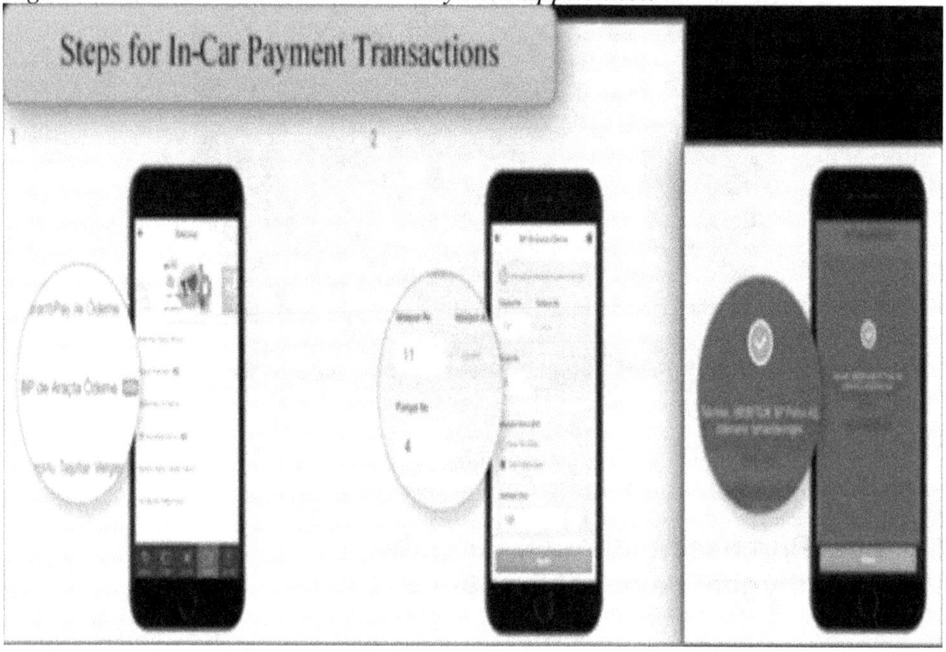

Source: www.bp.com.tr

5.4. Queue Management Without Visiting the Branch: Arrival Confirmation

The process implemented by Deniz Bank, which allows customers to obtain a queue number for their desired branch without physically visiting, is another example of the integration of physical and digital banking. In this process, customers who download Deniz Bank's queue management application on their smartphones can view the waiting times at their chosen branches and obtain a queue number for their desired branch directly from their mobile devices. Figure 6 presents a visual representation of the application.

Figure 6. Deniz Bank Mobile Queue Management Application (Queumatic)

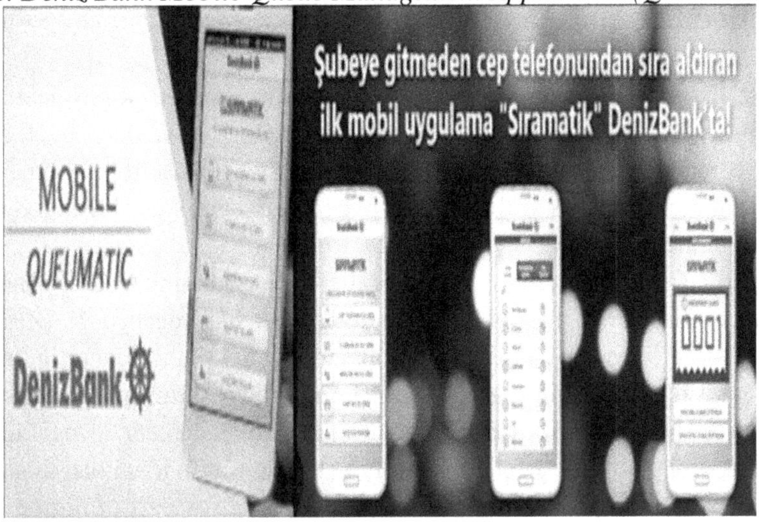

Source: https://www.denizbank.com/dijital-bankacilik/siramatik

Additionally, through a collaboration with Blesh[5], Deniz Bank has implemented beacon devices installed in its branches. These devices enable communication with customers who have the Deniz Bank Fastpay application installed on their smart devices, provided that prior permissions have been obtained. As a result, queue numbers are directly transmitted to their mobile phones. This process is illustrated in Figure 7.

Figure 7. Integration Process of Deniz Bank Fastpay App and Queue Management System

Source: Deniz Bank Internet of Things Promotional Video[6]

5.5. Phygital Branches in Conjunction With Video Banking Centers

One of the most significant examples of the convergence of physical and digital realms is the "Video Banking Centers" technology developed by T.C. Ziraat Bank. This technology enables customers to conduct transactions by engaging in audio-visual consultations with banking experts at centers established outside of traditional branches.

In 2009, T.C. Ziraat Bankası launched the Video Banking Centers, the first of their kind in the world, and by 2011, their number had reached 78 (Ziraatbank.com.tr, 2024). However, it appears that this application is no longer in use today. The project was not sustained due to insufficient interest during the period when these centers, which constituted a revolutionary advancement in banking, were established, along with cost-related factors. Although individual banking services are now offered through video calls on mobile phones as part of digital banking applications, during the days when branches are closed, these centers can effectively meet significant needs in secure environments such as shopping malls where people gather. Furthermore, they can provide important accessibility for small and medium-sized enterprises (SMEs) seeking to connect with banking experts. Additionally, this solution offers considerable convenience for customer segments that may be technologically averse or prefer not to use digital banking and video conferencing options due to security concerns or other constraints. Figure 8 illustrates an example of a Video Banking Center.

Figure 8. T.C. Ziraat Bank Video Banking Center Technology

*Source: Ziraatbank Sustainability Report 2013[7] and Tumsaş**

6. CONCLUSION AND RECOMMENDATIONS

In this section, distinct conclusions are drawn from both theoretical and practical viewpoints. This approach not only supports the advancement of the theoretical framework of digital banking but also seeks to offer useful recommendations that enhance customers' daily lives.

The evolution of phygital banking signifies a pivotal transformation in the financial sector, reflecting a broader trend towards the integration of physical and digital experiences. Through the lens of the Technology Acceptance Model and Disruptive Innovation Theory, it becomes clear that the successful adoption of phygital solutions relies not only on their perceived ease of use and usefulness but also on their capacity to challenge and redefine existing market paradigms. As customers increasingly seek seamless and enhanced banking experiences, traditional financial institutions must adapt by leveraging technology to meet evolving consumer expectations. This ongoing transformation presents both opportunities and challenges: while disruptive entrants may threaten established banks, they also compel these institutions to innovate and refine their service offerings frequently. Ultimately, the phygital banking landscape serves as a critical case study of how technological advancements can reshape industries, urging stakeholders to reconsider their strategies in a rapidly changing environment. Embracing this unique hybrid approach is not merely an option but a necessity for future competitiveness in the banking sector.

In a period where technological developments have been rapidly experienced in recent years, phygital channels, which are the combination of physical and digital, should definitely be taken into consideration for the future of Turkish Banking. Banks should develop financial technologies for phygital touchpoints or establish the necessary collaborations with fintech companies (Omarini, 2018). In this context, this study has proposed the concept of phygital banking to the finance and banking literature.

It is recommended that the applications mentioned in previous sections be further developed and promoted for broader usage in phygital banking. This approach will enable digitally native consumers to become more loyal customers of your bank. Additionally, the developed phygital applications will facilitate a smoother transition for your customers, who are accustomed to traditional banking services and may identify as digital immigrants, allowing them to adapt to digital environments more quickly.

When developing phygital banking applications, particular attention should be given to gamification strategies aimed at new-generation consumer groups. By leveraging NFC technology and beacon devices, initiatives such as point-collection activities and store collaborations can be implemented in shopping mall campaigns, coffee chains frequented by younger demographics, and university campuses. Furthermore, similar to GoTyme Bank's operations in the Philippines, placing kiosks in strategic locations can facilitate customer acquisition through phygital channels (Asian Development Bank, 2024). GoTyme Bank successfully reached two million customers within just fourteen months through its strategically placed 462 kiosks (GoTyme Bank, 2024)[8].

Further research can significantly advance the literature by emphasizing conceptual development. Quantitative studies may further enrich the existing body of knowledge, providing empirical insights. Collaborative research with financial technology firms can yield additional examples of the phygital area and its applications. As observed in various disciplines, the emerging field of phygital banking, building after the digital phase, will evolve by fostering a desire and motivation for phygital experiences that exceed traditional digital interactions. The convenience afforded by this new paradigm is likely to drive increased demand as consumers become more aware of their evolving needs. As a result, banks will have the opportunity to create distinctive and engaging value propositions for a new generation in a competitive landscape. In addition, banks participating in the triple transformation will create new phygital channels as a result of their digitalized processes, facilitating access to the financial system, and thus creating added value to social benefits and sustainability processes.

REFERENCES

aaaa.com. (2024, Apr 10). American Association of Advertising Agencies: https://www.aaaa.org/050608_momentum/

Asian Development Bank. (2024, Jul 15). *Leveraging Fintech for Women Entrepreneurs in Indonesia, the Philippines, and Viet Nam*.https://www.adb.org/publications/leveraging-fintech-women-entrepreneurs

Aydın, Ö., & Öztürk, A. (2022). Pazarlamada Yeni Trend Fijital Pazarlama. M. Kısa (Dü.) içinde, *Sosyal. Beşeri ve İdari Birimler Alanında Uluslararası Araştırmalar.*, 4, 155–168.

Balkan, H., & Aydın, M. (2021). Neobank: Kavram, Gelişim ve İş Modelleri. *Bankacılar Dergisi*, (116), 104–126.

Bddk.gov.tr. (2022, Jun 01). Regulation on the Operating Principles of Digital Banks and Banking As a Service Model: https://www.bddk.org.tr/Mevzuat/DokumanGetir/1128

Bddk.gov.tr. (2024, Sept 15). Digital Banks Establishment and Operation Permits: https://www.bddk.org.tr/Mevzuat/Liste/55

Bower, J. L., & Christensen, C. M. (1995). Disruptive Technologies: Catching the Wave. *Harvard Business Review*.

Çakın, Ö., & Yaman, D. (2020). Fijital (Phygital) Pazarlama Uygulamaları Üzerine Bir İnceleme: Amazon Go Örneği. *Middle Black Sea Journal of Communication Studies*, 5(1), 1–10.

Çelik, Z. (2021). *Fijital (Phygital) Pazarlama. Dijitalleşen Dünyada Pazarlama*. Nobel Yayınevi.

Chaudhary, R., & Nalwaya, N. (2021). Hybrid Banking: The Convergence of Physical with Digital Banking - An Evolving Transformation. *International Journal of Scientific Research*, 10(6), 101–105.

Christensen, C. M. (2006). The Ongoing Process of Building a Theory of Disruption. *Journal of Product Innovation Management*, 23(1), 39–55. DOI: 10.1111/j.1540-5885.2005.00180.x

Davis, F. D. (1989). Perceived Usefulness, Perceived Ease of Use, and User Acceptance of Information Technology. *Management Information Systems Quarterly*, 13(3), 319–340. DOI: 10.2307/249008

Dinçsoy, E. E. (2023). *Dijital Dünyanın Paradigmaları. Geleceği İnşa Etmek: Metaverse ve Yapay Zeka ile İşletmelerde Dijital Dönüşüm*. Paradigma Akademi.

Duğru, M., & Dinçsoy, E. E. (2014). Bankacılık Hizmetlerinin Pazarlanmasında Bölgesel Müşteri Profilinin Önemi Üzerine Bir Alan Çalışması. *Trakya Üniversitesi İktisadi ve İdari Bilimler Fakültesi E-Dergi*, 3(2), 46–72.

Ergen, A., Girginkaya Akdağ, S., & Ekin, G. (2024). Rethinking The Servicescapes of New Generation Banks: Evidence From Türkiye. *New Design Ideas*, 8(1), 97–115. DOI: 10.62476/ndi.8197

Garg, M., & Kumar, P. (2024). Harnessing Digital Technologies for Triple Bottom Line Sustainability in the Banking Industry: A Bibliometric Review. *Future Business Journal*, 10(62), 1–23. DOI: 10.1186/s43093-024-00336-2

Gedik, Y. (2021). Pazarlamada Yeni Bir Dönem: Fijital Pazarlama. *Hacettepe University Journal of Social Sciences*, 3(2), 99–131.

GoTyme Bank. (2024, Jul 0). https://www.gotyme.com.ph/media/news/gotyme-bank-2-million/

Hürriyet Gazetesi. (2024, Apr 4). www.hurriyet.com.tr: https://www.hurriyet.com.tr/ekonomi/turk-sanayiini-kumbaralar-kurdu-39100486

Johnson, M., & Barlow, R. (2021). Defining the Phygital Marketing Advantage. *Journal of Theoretical and Applied Electronic Commerce Research*, 16(6), 2365–2385. DOI: 10.3390/jtaer16060130

Klaus, P. (2021). Viewpoint: Phygital – The Emperor's new clothes? *Journal of Strategic Marketing*, (September), 1–8.

Köse, N., & Yengin, D. (2018). Dijital Pazarlamadan Fijital Pazarlamaya Geçişe Örnek Olarak Artırılmış Gerçeklik ve Sanal Gerçeklik Uygulamalarının Pazarlama Üzerindeki Katkılarının İncelenmesi. *İstanbul Aydın Üniversitesi Dergisi, 10*(1), 77-111.

Moravcikova, D., & Kliestikova, J. (2017). Brand Building with Using Phygital Marketing Communication. *Journal of Economics, Business and Management, 5*(3).

Nnaomah, U. I., Aderemi, S., Olutimehin, D. O., Orieno, O. H., & Ogundipe, D. O. (2024). Digital Banking and Financial Inclusion: A Review of Practices In The Usa And Nigeria. *Finance & Accounting Research Journal*, 3(6), 463–490. DOI: 10.51594/farj.v6i3.971

Omarini, A. E. (2018). Banks and Fintechs: How to Develop a Digital Open Banking Approach for the Bank's Future. *International Business Research*, 11(9), 23–36. DOI: 10.5539/ibr.v11n9p23

Participation Banks Association of Türkiye. (2024, Apr 10). Digital Banking Statistics: https://veripetegi.tkbb.org.tr/

Prensky, M. (2001). Digital Natives, Digital Immigrants Part 1. *On the Horizon*, 9(5), 1–6. DOI: 10.1108/10748120110424816

Rasheed, K. A. (2023). Enabling Financial Inclusion in Rural India Through a Phygital Model. 06 10, 2024 tarihinde iimk.ac.in/uploads/publications/IIMKWPS569FIN202303.pdf

Santosh, K. (2019). Phygital Banking – A Game Changer In Indian Banking Sector. *International Journal of Innovative Technology and Exploring Engineering*, 8(9), 289–292. DOI: 10.35940/ijitee.H7283.078919

Soloviov, E., & Danilov, A. (2020). The beginning of phygital world. *South Asian Journal of Engineering and Technology*, 10(2), 1–4. DOI: 10.26524/sajet.2020.2.7

Starnawska, S. E. (2021). *Sustainability in the Banking Industry Through Technological Transformation. The Palgrave Handbook of Corporate Sustainability in the Digital Era*. Palgrave Macmillan.

Sula Averbek, G., & Aysuna Türkyılmaz, C. (2021). *Sanal evrende markaların geleceği: yeni internet dünyası metaverse ve marka uygulamaları. Sosyal Bilimlerde Multi Disipliner Çalışmalar: Teori, Uygulama ve Analizler*. İstanbul Efe Akademi.

The Banks Association of Türkiye. (2024a, Apr 14). Electronic Banking Terms: https://www.tbb.org.tr/terimler.asp

The Banks Association of Türkiye. (2024b, Apr 10). Digital Banking Statistics: https://www.tbb.org.tr/Content/Upload/istatistikiraporlar/ekler/4437/Dijital-Internet-Mobil_Bankacilik_Istatistikleri-Haziran_2024.pdf

Tümsaş. (2024, Jan 5). https://tumsas.com.tr/en/about-us/index.htm

Türkiye Cumhuriyeti Ziraat Bankası. (2024, May 10). Ziraat Bank 2013 Sustainability Report: https://www.ziraatbank.com.tr/tr/Bankamiz-ZB/surdurulebilirlik/Documents/SurdurulebilirlikRaporu2013.pdf

Türkiye İşbank. (2024, Mar 5). www.isbank.com.tr

ENDNOTES

1 *The data from the Banks Association of Türkiye and the Participation Banks Association of Türkiye for June 2024 have been considered together. According to the Banks Association of Türkiye data, deposit banks and development and investment banks are included. The customer numbers reported do not account for duplicates among banks. The digital banking customer counts include those who use only internet banking, only mobile banking, and customers who use both channels.

* https://www.tbb.org.tr/tr/bankacilik/banka-ve-sektor-bilgileri/istatistiki-raporlar/59 (Digital banking statistic June 2024)

* https://veripetegi.tkbb.org.tr/

2 https://www.bddk.org.tr/Mevzuat/DokumanGetir/1128 Regulation on the Operating Principles of Digital Banks and Banking As a Service Model.

3 https://www.bddk.org.tr/Mevzuat/Liste/55 Digital Banks Establishment and Operation Permits

4 *Digital Natives:* This term refers to the new generation born into the rapidly evolving technological era, who have grown up with innovations such as smart-phones, the internet, and video games, and thus know digital technology as their native language. Those who encounter and attempt to adapt to all these innovations later are referred to as *digital immigrants* (Prensky, 2001, pp. 1-2).

5 Bluetooth Low Energy Smart Hub: The initiative abbreviated as Blesh creates a variety of communication channels through beacon devices, developing significant solutions in the field of the Internet of Things (IoT). Beacon devices utilize low-energy Bluetooth signals to connect with smart devices, providing location-based information.

6 https://www.youtube.com/watch?v=NZBUXj2wDkc 01:46. minutes.

7 https://www.ziraatbank.com.tr/en/OurBankZB/Sustainability/Documents/SustainabilityReport2013.pdf *https://tumsas.com.tr/en/about-us/index.htm Tümsaş is a solution partner company of Ziraat Bank in Video Banking Center (Video Teller Machine) technology.

8 https://www.gotyme.com.ph/media/news/gotyme-bank-2-million/

Chapter 6
Social Enterprise Is Often a Part of the Strategic Development of a Country

Venelin Terziev
https://orcid.org/0000-0003-1115-8877
Black Sea Institute, Bourgas, Bulgaria

Marusya Lyubcheva
Black Sea Institute, Bourgas, Bulgaria

Olga Valentinovna Andreeva
Rostov State University of Economics, Rostov-on-Don, Russia

Marin Georgiev
https://orcid.org/0000-0002-4530-6471
Black Sea Institute, Bourgas, Bulgaria

Simeon Simeonov
https://orcid.org/0009-0007-1433-0931
University Hospital Kaneff, Rousse, Bulgaria

Milen Dimitrov
https://orcid.org/0009-0003-6499-3742
Black Sea Institute, Bourgas, Bulgaria

ABSTRACT

The present study aims to clarify and explore the needs regarding the understanding of the essence of social entrepreneurship in Bulgaria, as well as to attempt to analyze the relationship: education, business environment, social environment. We can already define at the beginning that social entrepreneurship is an unknown area for young people, and they essentially do not put any meaning in this concept. Establishing a deficit of such knowledge in young people leads to a search for an opportunity to be familiar with social entrepreneurship. The more essential problem is their preparation for carrying out similar social activities in this direction. All this is related to the development of new models for career development and

DOI: 10.4018/979-8-3693-9435-9.ch006

the realization of a good professional and life perspective. The problems are clear from the outset, as they relate to low awareness, educational deficits, and lack of receptivity. This further complicates the tasks and creates additional obstacles.

1. INTRODUCTION

The main elements of the present study are related to establishing the attitudes and awareness of young people, what young people need and what the opposite view is, the subjective view of young people - reflection on the personal, how they relate to public opinion, how they understand public attitudes, ready are they to reflect the attitude towards social entrepreneurship in their personal development and others.

The main objectives of the study are the following: The attitude of young people towards social entrepreneurship; Young people's assessment of the social significance of social entrepreneurship; What needs to be done to make social entrepreneurship appealing to young people? What will the research help for?

The respondents are aged between 30-60 years. Male and female persons who declared that they live in the capital and in a large city were included. Graduates and workers in the capital and in the big cities. The marital status of the study participants was wide-ranging. There are both married (married) and single (not married). All people, without exception, are employed.

This research will not answer all the problematic questions, nor does it have a prior expectation to attract all young people to the cause of social entrepreneurship, but rather to get true and reliable information about - what young people think about social entrepreneurship and what are their interests in ongoing social processes. The opinions of those already involved in this process are also interesting - what are their attitudes and whether society needs it.

2. STRATEGIC FRAMEWORK FOR THE DEVELOPMENT OF SOCIAL ENTREPRENEURSHIP IN BULGARIA

The social economy and social entrepreneurship have been the subject of special attention by the European Commission (EC), especially in recent years. This is due to their potential to find solutions to society's problems related to the creation of sustainable jobs, the facilitation of social and labor integration, the provision of social services, and the improvement of the quality of life, including the fight against poverty and social isolation.

Social enterprises and social entrepreneurship occupy a central place in the EC's agenda and in particular in its Europe 2030 Strategy for "smart, sustainable and inclusive growth". They are also a key element of the European social model and contribute to the implementation of the socially significant goals of the strategy. Their growing importance - especially in the context of the economic and financial crisis - is primarily the result of Europeans' need for a more ethical and social dimension to their work, consumption, savings, and investments. In recent years, the EC started the creation of a political framework in support of the social economy and social entrepreneurship, which found expression in many political documents outlining the boundaries and opportunities for their development.

Among the specific goals that Europe sets for itself are ensuring employment for 20-60-year-olds, reducing school dropouts, and ensuring at least fewer people are at risk of poverty or social exclusion. Social entrepreneurship is recognized as a measure of achieving the stated goals and as a "tool for achieving sustainable development". The analysis of social policies shows that when direct support decreases, the effectiveness decreases accordingly, and the sustainability of "successful" models remains reciprocal to the invested resource. This trend can only be stopped by promoting innovative social models that overcome unemployment, poverty, and social exclusion permanently. Social payments and services, promotion of education, qualification, and skills in various fields, and improvement of access to public services as impact measures should be complemented by targeted efforts and resources to maintain forms that for socially vulnerable groups would serve as a bridge to the primary labor market. It is precisely as a successful solution for achieving effective long-term results that the role of social entrepreneurship is recognized.

Support and promotion of social enterprises can contribute to the maximum use of their growth potential and capacity to create social added value, expressed through job creation, creative approaches to small business, new opportunities for social inclusion, and income for the development of the activity of civil organizations. The social economy already plays an important role in the European Union, and its contribution can be illustrated as follows:

– Over 2 million active social enterprises in the member states of the European Union;
– Employer of 11 million people or nearly 6% of all employed persons;
– Accelerated growth of new social enterprise creation – 1 out of every 4 new companies are social enterprises.

Based on the above, the following wording is required: Social enterprises cover a wide range of enterprises with different legal forms that provide social services or goods to vulnerable or marginalized persons. These services include access to housing, health care, assistance for the elderly or disabled, childcare, access to employment and training, and addiction management. Social enterprises also include enterprises that use a method of producing goods or services with a social purpose, but whose activity may be outside the scope of providing social goods or services. This activity includes social and professional integration through means of access to employment for disadvantaged people, in particular, due to insufficient qualifications or social or professional problems leading to exclusion and marginalization.

The strategic objectives to support the Commission's response to unemployment and low labor market participation rates in the EU with cutting-edge and innovative policy ideas are:

– giving a "new impetus to the mix of flexibility and security" by engaging all stakeholders in strengthening the elements of this mix and by strengthening the control mechanisms of national agreements in the area of the mix of flexibility and security;
– self-employment.

Despite the rapid development of the social economy sector in the European Union and the growing role of social enterprises in combating poverty and social exclusion, social entrepreneurship remains almost invisible in Bulgaria. Although still modest in scale, social enterprises in Bulgaria carry the charge of changing attitudes towards the so-called "welfare state" and provide opportunities for mobilizing additional resources in the social sphere through the development of entrepreneurial potential and innovation.

Each member state of the European Union has adopted its strategy for reforms, which identifies key national goals and actions for their achievement within the framework of common European ones. According to the National Reform Program of Bulgaria, some of the main areas of structural reforms concern the modernization of services for access to the labor market, social support, health care, and education. The introduction of active employment measures, including for persons from vulnerable groups, through mechanisms to ensure sustainable employment, incentives for employers to open new jobs, programs for qualification, retraining and acquisition of key skills, etc. is foreseen.

Four priority areas are identified:

– better infrastructure;

– competitive youth (decreasing the share of early school leavers, increasing the number of young people who have completed higher education, stimulating young scientists, realization of young people in Bulgaria);
– better business environment (higher employment, more investments, including R&D innovations);
– greater trust in state institutions (protection of the interests of citizens and businesses, social justice, and security).

In 2011, the Bulgarian government adopted a political document – "The National Concept for Social Economy", which presents the vision and priorities for the promotion and development of the social economy in the country. This concept is an expression of the social commitment of the state to create and strengthen a favorable environment for the implementation and development of models and practices in the field of social economy in Bulgaria. The social economy is perceived both as a part of the real economy and of civil society, in which natural and/or legal persons, associations of volunteers, or other organized entities carry out economic activity for the public benefit and reinvest profits to achieve social goals.

The national concept of social economy is an expression of the social commitment of the state to create and strengthen a favorable environment for the implementation and development of models and practices in the field of social economy in the Republic of Bulgaria. It is an expression of the intention and determination to affirm awareness, culture, and values related to enterprises and organizations in the social economy sphere. The national concept is a document that presents a vision and priority goals for promoting the development of the social economy in the country. In this way, the active position of the state, formed as a result of the joint efforts of a wide range of interested parties, is presented. As a result of the activity of forming a national position on social economy issues through the National Concept, it is expected that policies will be developed that will improve the quality of life and well-being of vulnerable groups of citizens in society. It is expected that a sustainable sector will be formed, which will help to overcome the social exclusion of disadvantaged groups of people. Expectations are also for changes in the model of social inclusion of a wide range of citizens in society who have fallen into a difficult situation in terms of access to work, services, and resources.

The national concept refers to the understanding of the social economy reflected in European Union documents and other international documents. It is also in line with national strategic documents, which are directly or indirectly related to the tasks resulting from the objectives defined in the concept.

This document is a contribution to achieving the goals of the strategy for smart, sustainable, and inclusive growth, which offers a vision for a social market economy of Europe for the 21st century. In the context of what is indicated in the strategy, economic realities develop faster than political ones. The concept concretizes mature processes from the real economy, which should be separated into an independent sector of development in order to become visible both to the government in the context of the policy to increase the life level of the people, as well as for the general public, which sympathizes with the social situation of marginalized groups from the labor market.

The national concept provides an anticipatory vision regarding future changes in the regulatory framework and practice of state bodies, as well as a vision for the integration of sectoral policies. It is a document for the development of which an approach based on good national and international practices in this field was applied, systematized, and analyzed within the framework of an interdepartmental expert working group and with the broad participation of representatives of state and international institutions, organizations of social partners, non-governmental organizations.

The state strives to create a harmonious society by promoting the development of the social economy in the country to achieve sustainability, economic growth and increase the quality of life of people and especially disadvantaged groups. The establishment of a favorable environment for the development of the social economy sector is achieved through adequate policies and partnerships at international, national, regional, and local levels. All stakeholders are actively involved in this process.

In the process of establishing a social economy model in the country, the state plays an active role in popularizing, promoting, and supporting the introduction of successful practices of social enterprises, including those based on voluntary activities developed within civil society. For the realization of these commitments, the state creates an appropriate legal and institutional environment and coordinated sectoral policies for accelerated implementation of successful models of social enterprises. In fulfillment of this, the state will implement measures to increase the productivity and competitiveness of these enterprises, as well as monitor the correct acquisition and observance of the "Product of a social enterprise" mark.

A prerequisite for the development of the Concept is the achievement of a general agreement within a wide range of interested parties on key issues related to the nature, scope, limits, and possibilities of the social economy in the country to achieve better chances for the social inclusion of disadvantaged groups; pooling resources to increase the employment of groups of society with limited access to services and resources or outside the labor market; development of territorial and local cohesion.

The concept has the following specific objectives:

– To serve as a starting point when introducing criteria for the identification of enterprises and organizations from the social economy;

- To serve as an ongoing "standard" helping to support the development of the social economy and to stimulate implementers and supporters to apply and spread the spirit of social solidarity;
- To serve as a basis for the creation of a favorable administrative and legal environment for the development of social economy enterprises (access to financing, social clauses in public procurement, tax benefits, etc.).

The development and establishment of a sustainable social economy sector in the country will be achieved by applying the leading principles of good governance and the specific principles related to the implementation of good practices and models of social enterprises.

The specific principles on which the good practices and models of social economy enterprises are based are related to ensuring unity between economic efficiency and specific social goals, developing activity in conditions of public transparency, and applying solidary principles of internal management and decision-making.

The state introduces the brand "Product of a social enterprise" with an appropriate logo and procedure for awarding business entities whose activity results correspond to the indicators introduced with this Concept. The brand is used by the awarded enterprise to designate goods from its product specification, production sales areas and sites, documents, advertisements, production clothing, etc.

The purpose of trademark appropriation and its application is to draw public attention to the cause for which such enterprises work in order to attract the sympathy of the mass customers of consumer goods and services in the form of preferred purchases from preferred outlets.

Social economy enterprises with an assigned brand are considered users of a public resource and should provide statistical information upon request.

Within the framework of the National Concept, the social enterprise is defined as the basic economic unit of the social economy, which stands between the private and public sectors. Activities carried out by social enterprises include:

- Promotion of employment opportunities and career development of unemployed people, persons with disabilities, and other vulnerable persons, as well as assistance in finding or returning to work;
- Encouraging opportunities for self-employment, entrepreneurship, and starting an independent business.

The objectives of the Concept are to introduce criteria for the identification of enterprises and organizations from the social economy and to serve as a basis for the creation of a favorable (administrative and legal) environment for the development of social enterprises (access to financing; social clauses in public procurement; tax reliefs, etc.).

Although the Bulgarian legislation lacks a definition of a social enterprise, as well as norms governing the status, form, and activity of social enterprises, in real life and practice there are many examples of functioning social enterprises that, on the one hand, pursue social goals, and on the other another - apply economic mechanisms and market principles in their activities. The dynamic processes of social and economic development in recent years have clearly shown the following trends, which strengthen the role and importance of the social economy in Bulgaria:

– First of all, the inability of the state to cope with the growing social needs of the population, as well as the ever-increasing number of the population that need support;
– The debunked myth about the ability of the market economy to solve all the problems of society through the application of market principles;
– Strengthening the role of local communities and civil organizations in the development process and provision of innovative social services to support the most vulnerable part of the population.

Reforms and the implementation of innovative measures are needed to develop new approaches and models to tackle poverty and social exclusion. Social economy and entrepreneurship are the key tools to supplement the currently implemented state policy for social support and smart and sustainable growth.

There is a lack of a comprehensive and systematic policy for the promotion of the social economy, including a legal framework and financing, as well as concrete sustainable measures for starting and supporting social enterprises and creating an environment conducive to the development of the social economy.

The monitoring of the available practices from recent years in Bulgaria gives reason to conclude that the structures operating in the social economy sector receive an incentive for development when there is a targeted program for their support, financing, and development at the national level. There is still a lack of recognition of social enterprises as an innovative model for creating employment for disadvantaged groups in the labor market, as well as a new form of active social inclusion. It is important to define the areas and policies where the potential of social enterprises is still highly underestimated and untapped:

According to the National Strategy for Combating Poverty and Social Exclusion 2020, lack of employment is one of the main causes of poverty and social exclusion. That is why the main priority is the promotion of the active inclusion of persons remote from the labor market - economically inactive, young people, long-term unemployed, persons on social assistance, with primary or lower education and without professional qualification or lack of key competencies, people with permanent disabilities, elderly workers and others. Through the development of viable social enterprises, access to employment can be facilitated and support for the social inclusion of vulnerable groups can be provided by creating appropriate conditions for their professional integration in the sphere of the social economy.

In addition, social enterprises can be a key tool for the implementation of the European Employment Strategy, as they combine measures to increase suitability, access to the labor market, support social services and the provision of adequate incomes and thus contribute to the prevention of the transmission of poverty between generations. While it is important to provide services to help people "enter" the labor market, it is equally important to integrate people with complex needs into society, even if it is difficult to offer them employment opportunities. Despite their potential to reduce poverty and include the chronically unemployed and inactive in the labor market, social enterprises are hardly recognized at the policy and program level and thus remain undervalued and underutilized. There is a huge deficit in this area of organizations that can provide integrated services necessary for the social inclusion of groups furthest from the labor market with an emphasis on social skills and improving individual social work with these individuals (Andreeva et al., 2023; Vovchenko et al., 2023a; Muratova et al., 2023b; Ivanova et al., 2023c; Vovchenko et al., 2023d; Vovchenko et al., 2022).

3. WHAT DO SOCIAL ENTREPRENEURS WHO HAVE ALREADY STARTED WITH SUCH A BUSINESS THINK?

According to the respondents, the reasons for starting a social entrepreneurship are mainly personal interest and, to a high degree, the interest aroused by friends. The respondents are categorical that the provocation is not a factor to be interested in the topic of social entrepreneurship. They also do not believe in the power of family tradition.

Regarding the facilities that are in favor of starting a social entrepreneurial initiative, the respondents ranked the presence of the following factors as priorities: the appropriate economic environment; a higher degree of confidence; support from the family. However, they do not exclude start-up capital and the necessary knowledge and skills as important factors for motivation towards social entrepreneurship.

There are no definite answers to the question related to obtaining basic information about social entrepreneurship. The respondents consider it of great importance to provide initial knowledge on the subject at the university, on social networks, on specialized sites, or at narrowly profiled events. The possibilities of the non-governmental sector and print media follow the logic of the respondents in order of importance. The institution: The school is at the bottom of the respondents' preferences.

The reluctance to start a social entrepreneurship initiative, according to the respondents, is due to the low level of awareness of the essence of social entrepreneurship and insufficient knowledge and skills. The next place is the deficit of the subject in the curricula, the fear of the new, and the lack of interest that would bring a certain kind of benefit.

Regarding the profit from starting a social entrepreneurial initiative, the respondents are hesitant. Although they prioritize the opportunity for creating and personal development, they put the opportunity for profit and a great career in the background. The prestigious position is not only at the bottom of the ranking of preferences, but it is marked as part of the negative aspect by the respondents.

One important issue related to skills, respondents ranked as follows. According to them, the most important skill is teamwork, followed by initiative and communication. One unnecessary element for them is critical thinking, followed by empathy and creativity.

The opinion of the respondents about the attitude towards social entrepreneurship is primarily related to the different types of thinking towards social problems and processes; the support of the local community in the effort for this individual challenge that can develop within the framework of big business. The respondents manage to distinguish social entrepreneurship from other entrepreneurial initiatives and equally believe that as much as this type of initiative is accepted, it is not accepted by the community and/or by the closest circle.

The respondents see the directions for developing social entrepreneurial initiatives mostly in solving the problems of the local community and the problems of people with limited opportunities. Next, they pointed out the environmental problems and the problems of people from vulnerable groups.

The prerequisites for the development of this type of initiative are contained, according to the respondents, in financial incentives combined with education and training and understanding of the issue. They put legislative issues, people's motivation, and the development of the IT structure in a lower position.

The respondents see institutional support for social entrepreneurship only at the European level, where there is also good regulation, according to them. The disagreement is that there is good support and regulation at the national and local levels.

The figure of the social entrepreneur in the perceptions of the respondents is that of a "profit maker". However, in subsequent positions, they note that the social entrepreneur is a developer of new ideas, and only then that he is an innovator with a high culture and sensitivity to social problems and processes.

The social entrepreneur's capability capacity, according to the respondents, includes the necessary professional qualification, the habit of learning continuously with a built-in model for maintaining competencies, and the habit of learning continuously. Next comes the knowledge in his professional field and the hard skills required. In the last place, the respondents put the amount of necessary soft skills.

4. THE BUSINESS OF SOCIAL ENTREPRENEURSHIP

The surveyed social entrepreneurs categorically state that they engage in social entrepreneurship because they were provoked. To a very low degree, personal interest had an influence, and family tradition and being intrigued by friends fell as a negative choice in the eyes of the respondents.

Acting social entrepreneurs determine that the important factors that would facilitate their initiative are: the economic environment; the starting capital; confidence and the required knowledge and skills. For them, support from the family does not appear as a significant factor, while a personal problem to solve is a negative aspect for the respondents - it is not decisive.

The location of obtaining basic information on social entrepreneurship for respondents is evenly distributed as follows; school; university; Published editions; Internet; social media; and specialized events related to entrepreneurship. According to the surveyed social entrepreneurs, the role of the non-governmental sector is too small.

The reasons that determine the low level of desire to start social entrepreneurship, according to the respondents, are due to the following factors: low level of awareness of the essence of social entrepreneurship; absence of social entrepreneurship in curricula and programs; insufficient knowledge about social entrepreneurship; fear of the new and unpreparedness to deal with difficulties; insufficient skills; education (secondary or higher education) does not offer the necessary knowledge and skills to start social entrepreneurship. Lack of interest (benefit) does not take place among the main reasons.

The profit for social entrepreneurs implementing social entrepreneurial initiatives is contained equally in the possibility of a good career; personal development; the opportunity to create and participate in the transformation of the economy. Next is the prestigious position and the profitability does not participate in the effectiveness of an activity of this type.

The most important skills that the surveyed social entrepreneurs believe they possess are more evenly distributed in terms of importance as follows: initiative; communicativeness; quick decision-making; teamwork and empathy. Not so important to them are skills such as flexibility, critical thinking, and creativity.

According to the respondents, their attitude towards social entrepreneurship varies in their assessments from extremely positive to extremely negative. They believe that social entrepreneurship needs the support of the local community, adopted by the close social circle, and can develop within the framework of big business. At the other pole is the disagreement that social entrepreneurship is an individual challenge and is associated with a different type of thinking about societal problems.

The respondents' opinion is unanimous about the direction of social entrepreneurship development. They noted all the proposed options as current and priority-risk groups of people; people with disabilities; environmental issues; pressing problems of the local community.

Social entrepreneurs see that the development of successful initiatives is dependent on the development of the IT infrastructure; financial mechanisms; motivation of people; social receptivity, and education and training. Legislative changes are important but not a priority, according to their answers.

Based on the opinion of the respondents about the institutional attitude, there is regulation and support at the European level. On the contrary, at the national and local level, it is neither well regulated nor does it exist as a support for social entrepreneurship.

The figure of the social entrepreneur, according to the respondents, is anything but a "profit maker" or a person with additional income. On the other hand, they define themselves as highly cultured innovators who are sensitive to social issues and develop new ideas.

According to the respondents, they absolutely possess all the listed skills - sufficient knowledge in their professional field; qualification; availability of the necessary hard and soft skills; habits of continuous learning; availability of competence in several areas; own model for maintaining competencies.

The research was conducted using the interview method in an informal setting with a separate focus group. The group is composed of individuals engaged in various business initiatives with more than 10 years of experience in this direction. The participants in the focus group are aged 40-50 years, one person is female, and the others are male. The spheres of employment are of a different nature. During the talk, no discrimination was allowed, and the persons were informed about the purpose, subject, and tasks of the talk. In the course of the communication, interesting perspectives emerged, some of which are typical of the Bulgarian reality, and others outlined unforeseen directions for entrepreneurship.

In an overall aspect, there is unanimity regarding the motive for starting one's own initiative in Bulgaria. Entrepreneurs start an initiative because it's a "mostly - no one tells me what to do" way. It can be assumed that self-interest from the point of view of occupying a kind of leadership position in life is a guiding principle. Another analysis is the ability of a person to have independence and to be able to act alone (in the sense of being one's own boss). Obviously, the action is important, for something to happen, but for this action to be "in the field of control" of the person. Another element stated by the group that is highly motivating is the hobby. This can serve as the start of an initiative.

An important factor that is also key when starting initiatives is the environment. However, the majority of participants in the focus group determined that support from other people (social environment) rather than family is decisive for starting initiatives. It is particularly successful when it is implemented in informal ways and is composed of people who have a certain experience. This important trait that "a person needs to help and be in a group" allows Kropotkin's ideas to be used to some extent. Support from the environment turns out to be in a better position than the availability of start-up capital. This is natural because, in recent times, financing has not had such a great value from the point of view of "there are already ways to and of financing". The support of the close environment, combined with intensive and trusting communication in it, can result in an idea for starting a business initiative. Information, a kind of start for a business idea, is obtained in an informal setting, which leads to the conclusion of a kind of requirement for an informal source of information. However, regardless of when, where, and how the business idea will arise and how it will be launched, the group is unanimous that it is important to "know how to do the math".

Regarding knowledge and skills, it is clear (to the participants) that they are acquired and, in this sense, do not matter so much to them. However, it is important for them to have a certain confidence, to have an idea and know-how. This fact may be due to the age characteristics of the focus group. Bearing in mind that it is organized by middle-aged people with a certain life experience, it can be assumed that for them, knowledge and skills are not of primary importance. However, this should be considered as an exception and considered only as a characteristic of the studied group. In addition to the problem that "literate people are out", there is also the opinion that there is an urgent need for retraining, especially in the present time, which in turn is directly related to lifelong learning.

At the same time, a very important skill is important for starting a business - discipline, as far as it can be considered as a skill. In the Bulgarian context, the skill "flexibility" is also a priority to possess. Overall, the requirements for qualities to possess are discipline, initiative, creativity, and persistence. An entrepreneur, in order to achieve its goals, needs enthusiasm. And the evolution is based on the experience gained during the small steps taken. One opinion makes an impression, and it largely describes the characteristics of an entrepreneur, as well as the (Bulgarian) environment in which he is - "you must be ready to tremble - that is being an entrepreneur".

Gender does not have a significant impact on starting a business initiative, but it is important to have mathematical skills (in the sense of being able to do the math). However, one specific feature is noticeable in females - they have a clear idea and vision of the goal. That is, they need clarity about the pursued goals and desires in order to launch an initiative. Those of the female gender think that how we look from the side is defining (a kind of competition). Because "success is measured by the opinions of others." Also, for the female gender, success matters, and it ranks among the leading motivating factors. They pursue it intuitively, combined with self-interest. However, what is important for both sexes is the opinion that "having a business so as not to work is harmful".

The main profit for a person engaged in business is the time he earns and the hobby he realizes. But this is related to the basic presence of priority, a good social environment (friends), and having many conversations in an informal setting and of an informal nature. A new factor emerges when it comes to the success of an initiative. This is the pedantry combined with trust between the partners with whom one works and interacts and the presence of partners in general to support the achievement of the goals. This condition is valid for a group with similar characteristics, such as the focus group participants.

The participants also state something very important. It is tied to the opinion that entrepreneurship is associated with speculation. This opinion deserves attention, and the participants for this definition reason that it is fast-acting in the field of entrepreneurship and is likened to commerce. An important conclusion that arises from the last finding is that social entrepreneurship needs a clear and precise definition that is consistent with the linguistic and essential characteristics of the population. Social entrepreneurship itself is more about helping a group and/or groups of people than it is about a cause.

The group emphasizes that in Bulgarian conditions the state is unnecessarily burdensome. Moreover, extreme opinions such as "the state is better off not helping" are expressed. Although there is unanimity regarding the need for adequate legislation. The obstacle to the initiative is bureaucracy and the aspect of conservative bureaucracy. What the state can and should provide is the infrastructure to have a suitable business environment according to the participants. Of course, there must be competition. It is appropriate to implement the so-called good practices in business. For example: "mentorship", implies the presence of a person to help you in the process of starting an initiative. This initiative is not new and some European countries have some experience in this direction. This and other practices, however, need to be tested for Bulgarian conditions and then implemented in the business environment. Last but not least, the need for political will to provide certainty for the future of each initiative is categorical. The lack of a suitable environment for business allows the power (central or local government) to fail.

The opinion about the topic of folk psychology is unanimous. It is believed that there is more and more differentiation at the regional level (areas on a national scale). According to the participants, "Bulgaria is already parceled out into clear and bright zones". This identification can serve in the definition of mechanisms to involve the local community in the implementation of a certain idea. In Bulgaria, the creation and maintenance of traditions was the duty of the state. The power of the local community was isolated (removed). One solution option is to reverse this process with appropriate mechanisms. As a resource for increasing initiative, the power of propaganda and/or the so-called informational radiation can be used. Last but not least, it is good to research the interests of the local community. It turns out that the informal approach to presenting information is more effective, according to the participants. In this way, trust, and hence the tendency to listen, grows. Social entrepreneurship affects and differentiates as well as determines the relationship between the environment and the group with defined problems. The problem to be solved needs to clearly give the link between the one helping to solve problems and its benefit.

A good mechanism for growth when starting an initiative is to have a competitive environment. In addition, the availability of sufficient information turns out to be important. Social entrepreneurship must be realized in relation to the social conditions in the current environment, taking into account all the available factors of the environment.

The findings of the results are intriguing and can serve as a basis for the different directions towards the different groups that will and/or are engaged in social entrepreneurial initiatives.

Obviously, provocation is the real mechanism by which the impetus for initiative is given. This motivating mechanism intuitively leads to a form of independence regarding the life and professional path of a given individual. This statement is reinforced by the result, which demonstrates that the family as an institution has no influence on the initiative decision expressed in the answers of all the studied groups. The opposite is the opinion that the main motivating factor is personal interest. It can be perceived as a boundary line between business and social entrepreneurial initiatives. When an initiative is to a greater extent under the influence of self-interest, then it is business in its essence. In cases where the initiative has a purpose other than personal interest, it is socially entrepreneurial in nature.

A key element that is important not only for social entrepreneurial initiatives is the right environment. This includes many factors, for example, fair competition, friendly support, trust in partners, etc. Of course, the description of the majority of factors that relate to a suitable environment for starting a social entrepreneurial initiative is subject to another in-depth analysis.

It is the categorical opinion of all participants in the studies that schools, universities, and specially created thematic events are the main information carriers of knowledge on the subject. This position determines the importance of these institutions and obliges us to take immediate measures in this direction. Experience-enforced programs such as those at Stanford and Cambridge universities can be used as relevant examples. An important circumstance that needs to be taken into account is the factor of informality in obtaining knowledge. This topic implies a serious academic discussion about the organization of a curriculum, as well as a deepening of the interrelationships and interactions between the acquisition of knowledge and its practical transformation. The last finding is confirmed by the unanimous answers of the respondents that the reason for the low desire to start initiatives of a social entrepreneurial nature is due to both a low level of awareness about the essence of social entrepreneurship and insufficient knowledge about social entrepreneurship. This issue can be solved with the introduction of specialized programs that offer information about this kind of initiative in an appropriate way. And at the same time, to give an idea of the possibilities provided by the future university programs.

The prospects for profit from starting a social entrepreneurial initiative are clearly outlined. They are mainly expressed as an opportunity for personal growth, which inevitably leads to a good career. All this is combined with the ability to create a good end product or offer a good service.

The need for a set of certain skills to engage in social entrepreneurship is unquestionable. Although there are differences in the ranking of respondents' answers, they are negligibly small. In addition, other skills appear on the horizon that need to be properly offered for a future social entrepreneur, such as initiative, decision-making, teamwork, and communication. These are the skills that the surveyed groups consider important. Such skills as flexibility, critical thinking, and creative approach are not in the field of view of the respondents. However, discipline, persistence, enthusiasm, and creativity emerge. The development of precisely these skills has been underestimated until now. Until now, they have been acquired on the basis of life and professional experience.

There are fluctuations in the answers of the respondents, which refer to the attitude towards social entrepreneurship. Despite everything, they are united around the opinion that social entrepreneurship is perceived by the close circle and the family and local community, and it is possible to develop social entrepreneurship within the framework of big business. The difference is that those who do not engage in social entrepreneurship believe that social entrepreneurship is an individual challenge, while those engaged in this kind of initiative strongly disagree. A diametrical opposite is also observed in the relationship that emerges that social entrepreneurship is associated with a different type of thinking about societal problems and processes. While the current social entrepreneurs do not agree with this, the other group of respondents absolutely agree with this opinion. However, there is unanimity among both groups - they distinguish social entrepreneurship from other types of entrepreneurial initiatives.

The emphasis on the direction of development of social entrepreneurship is an important nuance in the study. From the answers, the perspective is outlined, and a future framework is created for the transfer of necessary knowledge. Observing unanimity in the responses of all respondents rather gives a higher level of complexity to the task for the required knowledge framework. Let's note that, unanimously, as a priority for the direction of development of social entrepreneurship, risk groups, people with disabilities, environmental problems, and urgent problems of the local community are noted.

The contrast in the answers regarding what is most necessary for the successful development of social entrepreneurship among the respondents is understandable. The point of view of non-entrepreneurial respondents is that there is a need for financial instruments, education, and training. For those who deal with entrepreneurial initiatives, the most important thing is to provide a good environment, know-how, and an idea with which to start. All are unanimous in the low degree of influence of the legislation. This opinion is reinforced and emphasized in the answers to the next question, which refers to the attitude of institutions towards social entrepreneurship. There are even statements like “It's best if the state doesn't help”. This sentiment is supported by the responses to the survey, which noted the huge weaknesses in the legislation, both nationally and insufficient support at the local level. These weaknesses require urgent and competent intervention because they are a significant obstacle to the development of social entrepreneurial initiatives.

Regarding the figure of the social entrepreneur, there are extreme assessments. Those who have not implemented social entrepreneurship, associate this activity and the operator with profit-making. However, true social entrepreneurs are of the opinion that they are innovative, highly cultured, and sensitive to societal issues. These differences imply not so much an intensive information campaign to reduce social distance, but an information campaign to spread the understanding of the essence of social entrepreneurship, its specific characteristics, and differences from other types of entrepreneurship. Understandably, those who are social entrepreneurs noted that they have all the listed skills. However, this needs to be specified and introduced into the framework that, for example, Radulov proposes. According to V. Radulov, it is particularly important for adolescents and young people to acquire special professional skills that are required for initial entry into the working society. The person, according to him, must master three groups of skills: general work skills; adaptive skills, and productive skills.

Another researcher provides a detailed reading of the skills situation. According to K. Hoyt, everyone must reach several types of skills:

– Basic academic skills related to oral or written communication and mathematics;
– Productive work habits, including coming to work on time; doing things the best way possible, and following directions given by management;
– A sincere desire to work, which is due to the acquisition of personal significance of the imposed work values as part of the general system of personal values of the person;
– Basic understanding and appreciation of the system in the given country by private enterprises;
– Skills related to job search and finding;
– Skills for productive use of free time;
– Skills for humanizing the workplace for yourself.

The survey results point to the need for career development specialists to supervise and support the skills-building process. Their mission will be to favor the choice and practice of a profession. These specialists need to know well the needs and specifics of each person participating in the program. Also, in terms of skills that need to be mastered for successful implementation are most often teamwork skills and communication skills. These findings lead to an indisputable conclusion of universality in the necessary skills for professional realization. The deficit of the so-called "flexible skills" is the same for everyone and needs to be filled with appropriate forms. With this feature, the delivery of the learning material to different individuals has features dictated by different levels of knowledge, skills, gender, religion, or disability.

Expectations for a different attitude of young people towards social entrepreneurship have their reasons. But above all, they shape and give meaning to the understanding of the environment and direction for development. Surprisingly, young people are not guided by recommendations, opinions of society, other people's evaluations, and recommendations to like or not social entrepreneurship. Not even as a phenomenon but as a real economic process. Young people ask questions but do not find answers to all of them. They would engage in social entrepreneurship for personal success because it will bring them successful personal development. Approximately 52.00% are ready to do so under certain conditions (Diagram 1).

Figure 1. I do social entrepreneurship because

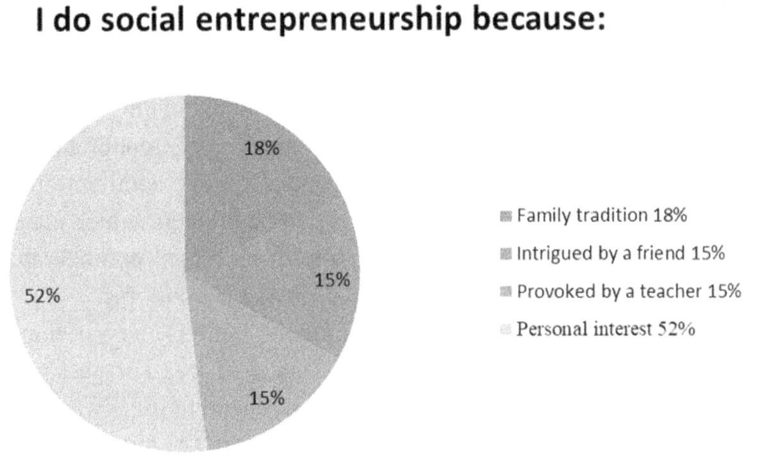

Source: authors

They engage or would engage in social predominance out of personal interest, 15.00% would follow a family tradition, and another 15.00% provoked by someone. Even in the unknown social entrepreneurship, neither the school nor the university gave them enough information. They look for this information, and above all from universities, but they also rely heavily on social networks, various Internet platforms, and others. Generation Z has its idiosyncrasies, perhaps quirks, but with a trusting attitude towards digital tools. The question here is whether there are these digital possibilities to a sufficient extent. To obtain sufficient information assessing the school's deficits in terms of awareness, they treat non-governmental organizations with higher trust, which is indicative of the relationship of young people with society.

Young people hide that their lack of awareness hinders them in the "social entrepreneurship" endeavor, but they are frank enough to admit the deficits in their knowledge and skills. They unequivocally talk about fear of the unknown, about fears that they will not cope, they emphasize that they are not prepared for this undertaking. It is obvious that if the school and the university lend a hand to the idea of entrepreneurship, including social entrepreneurship, the picture is likely to be quite different. "The absence of curricula and the fact that education does not offer enough knowledge and skills to start social entrepreneurship" makes a serious assessment of existing deficits in our education system. To what extent it meets public needs, certain priorities and strategies and market interests is another question.

Young people have their own opinions built into the way they observe social processes and the immediate environment, but they are also willing to share them to seek a solution. They already know that social entrepreneurship is not ordinary entrepreneurship it involves a different type of thinking, and it has a cause and its mission. They still do not dare to engage because they consider that it does not have sufficient support, and the external environment is not yet so favorable for this undertaking. There is an expectation of development, perspective, and even optimism, which is evident from the responses received from the respondents. Most of the respondents have the understanding that social entrepreneurship is different from the ordinary one and that it has a clear social need. Social entrepreneurship is a tool through which such business models can be created, which are according to new and different standards. By participating in social entrepreneurship, young people become participants in the transformation of the economy.

Undoubtedly, even with a favorable environment, there is fear – of the unknown, of the new, fear of themselves, whether they will succeed or fail in these new circumstances. The most frequently missed questions are related to this - what will happen to the dream career? Support is sought - in the answer to the question "Does social entrepreneurship need support" the need for personal support for young people to start this new venture is apparent. Support is needed for your different thinking and understanding of societal issues (Diagram 2).

Figure 2. In which direction is it most acceptable to develop social entrepreneurship

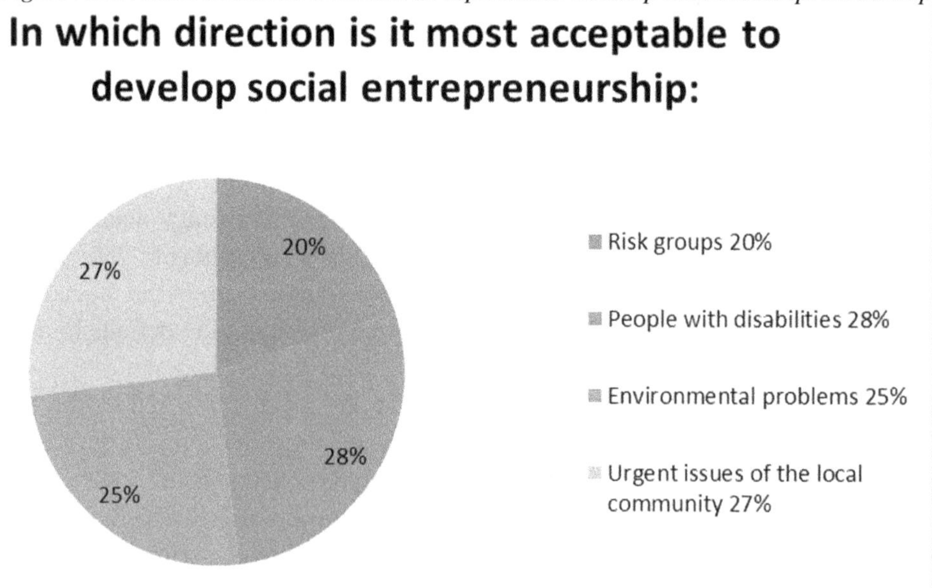

Source: authors

However, insufficient awareness does not prevent young people from considering that social entrepreneurship is not intended only for risk groups and people with disabilities, as is the understanding in society. They, by their logic, link social entrepreneurship with environmental issues, which may seem strange at first glance. Environmental protection is an issue that has an extremely social presence in people's lives, reaching security and safety, and they have realized this. It is a matter of future development that this idea of theirs finds development. Even more so, it refers to "pressing issues of the local community" - this is of high social importance, and young people appreciate this (Diagram 3).

Figure 3. What is needed for the successful development of social entrepreneurship

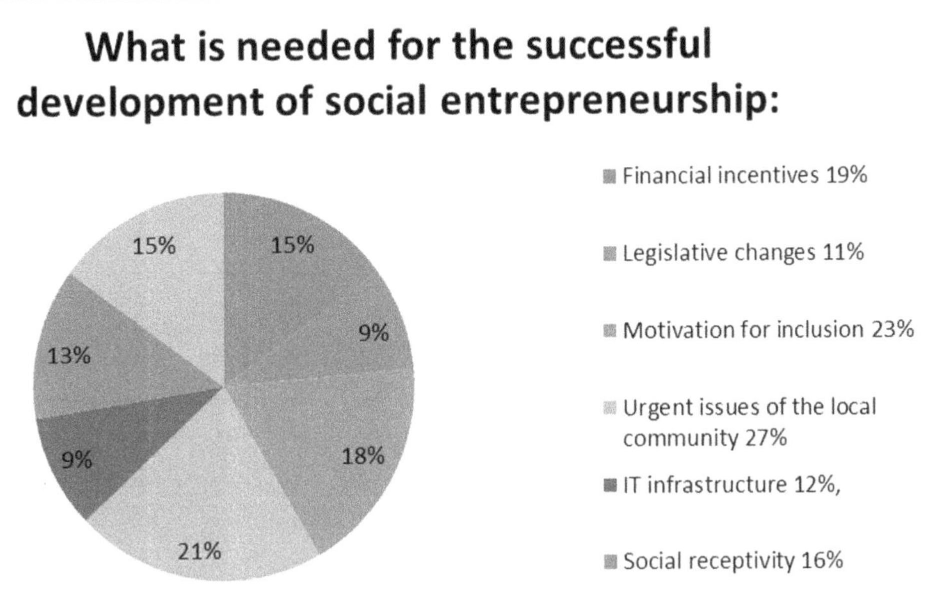

Source: authors

The environment for the development of youth social entrepreneurship includes many problems, and their solution can also change the understanding of social economy. Each zone needs to be "liberated" to a level of familiarity and opportunities for inclusion. The environment for the development of social entrepreneurship includes several factors and resources that young people value as important to support social entrepreneurs in their work and efforts to solve social problems. The provision of educational programs, courses, and training in social entrepreneurship would play an important role in the preparation of future social entrepreneurs. Bearing in mind the deficits assessed by young people in the previous elements of the survey, it is more than clear that non-formal education and training should be relied upon. Here, the resourcefulness of non-formal education will connect with the non-governmental sector and the opportunities it creates. This can include formal education at universities and informal training and workshops. Financial incentives are associated with various financial resources and investments designed specifically for social entrepreneurs, which is essentially a financial investment for the future. This area, apart from being a social investment received from foundations, grants, and other sources, can also be connected to personal development and investment in one's career. Two of the areas - "information resources" and "legislative changes" are an important part of the national support that young people "dream about". Without them, social entrepreneurship will move at a very slow pace and develop with difficulty. Young people see the role of the state as particularly important - in support and in the regulations that are created. Even though only 10% of the respondents answered the question "attitude of the state towards social entrepreneurship", the reference point is there - the national level is best known, the local level is in second place and the European Union is in third place. This is probably related to the lack of sufficient information or young people's understanding that social entrepreneurship is an issue that also has a national and local understanding and receptivity.

Figure 4. The social entrepreneur is..

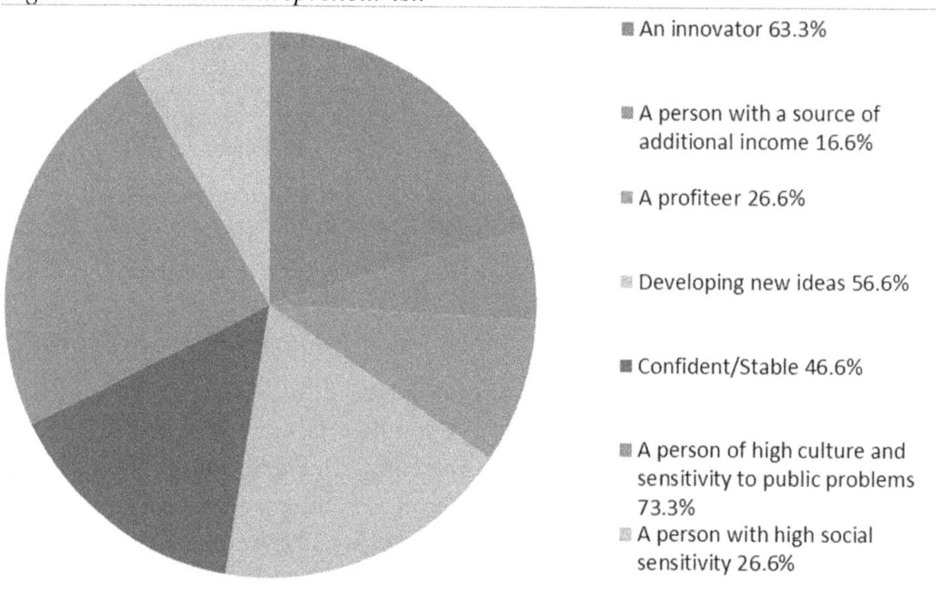

Source: authors

The power of social entrepreneurship lies in the power of personal cause, empathy, and personal social sensitivity. Sometimes to the point of giving up any financial result, but with a definition that satisfies the idea or cause with which it is developed. And often, ignoring the negative energy that some social entrepreneur definitions carry, such as "profit maker". The imperative positivism towards the adoption of social entrepreneurship can concentrate much of this energy in the direction of creating new business models subject to high culture and social sensitivity (Diagram 4).

5. CONCLUSION

All this can also be understood as a synergy between pure social entrepreneurship helping certain groups in society with big business generating social sensitivity. Therefore, many skills are needed that young people recognize, understand, and try to generate. It is no coincidence that when answering the question "The social entrepreneur has the following skills", more than 50% of the respondents put all the mentioned skills in the first position, i.e. necessary and most important.

A final emphasis in the survey, which was also answered by very few respondents, "I would easily become an entrepreneur if I had..." gives precedence to the right economic environment and personal confidence, followed by family support, the availability of start-up capital, as well as the availability of knowledge and skills.

Many opportunities for the young generation require rethinking choices and starting a career path that corresponds to intrinsic motivation based on sufficient awareness that is guided by knowledge and skills (Terziev et al., 2020a; Terziev et al., 2020b; Terziev et al., 2021a; Terziev et al., 2021b; Terziev et al., 2021c; Terziev and Lyubcheva, 2022a; Terziev et al., 2024).

The present study was developed under project: 2021-2-BG01-KA210-YOU-000049806 Laboratory for Youth Social Entrepreneurship "Hot Zone", implemented under the EU programme for education, training, youth and sport "Erasmus+".

REFERENCES

Andreeva, O. V., Vovchenko, N. G., Galazova, S. S., Sukhoveeva, A. A., & Kravchenko, E. V. (2023). Benefits and Risks of Digitalization of Providing Social Services by the State. In Popkova, E. G., & Sergi, B. S. (Eds.), *Anti-Crisis Approach to the Provision of the Environmental Sustainability of Economy. Approaches to Global Sustainability, Markets, and Governance*. Springer. DOI: 10.1007/978-981-99-2198-0_14

Ivanova, O. B., Vovchenko, N. G., Andreeva, O. V., Chernobay, O. S., & Kostoglodova, E. D. (2023c). Innovative Green Finance Tools. In Popkova, E. G. (Ed.), *Smart Green Innovations in Industry 4.0 for Climate Change Risk Management. Environmental Footprints and Eco-design of Products and Processes*. Springer. DOI: 10.1007/978-3-031-28457-1_52

Muratova, E., Muratov, D., Kravchenko, E., Sukhoveeva, A., & Andreeva, O. (2023b). Forecasting the Technical and Economic Parameters of the Combine Harvester Operation Using Pneumatic and Inertia Separator. In *XV International Scientific Conference "INTERAGROMASH 2022". INTERAGROMASH 2022. Lecture Notes in Networks and Systems, vol 575*. Springer, Cham. DOI: 10.1007/978-3-031-21219-2_154

Terziev, V., & Lyubcheva, M. (2022a). Shared knowledge and changes in the higher education system in Bulgaria. *79th International Scientific Conference on Economic and Social Development – Rabat, 25-26 March, 2022, Economic and Social Development (Book of Proceedings)*, 228-237.

Terziev, V., Lyubcheva, M., Andreeva, O., & Georgiev, M. (2020b). Revolution in industry and evolution in education or development of intelligence. *63rd International Scientific Conference on Economic and Social Development – "Building Resilient Society" - Zagreb, 11-12 December, 2020, Economic and Social Development (Book of Proceedings)*, 133-142.

Terziev, V., Lyubcheva, M., & Georgiev, M. (2021b). Domestic and international challenges in higher education. *7 th ITEM Conference – "Innovation, Technology, Education and Management" and 67th International Scientific Conference on Economic and Social Development – Sveti Martin na Muri, 29-30 April, 2021, Economic and Social Development (Book of Proceedings)*, 88-97

Terziev, V., Lyubcheva, M., & Georgiev, M. (2021c). The contemporary strategic challenges facing higher education. *Proceedings of SOCIOINT 2021 8th International Conference on Education and Education of Social Sciences 14-15 June, 2021*, 134-141.

Terziev, V., Lyubcheva, M., & Mihailova, M. (2021a). The necessity of changes in the higher education in Bulgaria. *Proceedings of INTCESS 2021 8th International Conference on Education and Education of Social Sciences 18-19 January, 2021*, 646-657. DOI: 10.51508/intcess.202104

Terziev, V., Lyubcheva, M., & Solovev, D. (2020a). The interaction: business-education- investment for development. *Proceedings of INTCESS 2020- 7th International Conference on Education and Social Sciences 20-22 January, 2020 - DUBAI (UAE)*, 865-869.

Terziev, V. K., Lyubcheva, M. I., Andreeva, O. V., & Simeonov, S. V. (2024). Creating an analytical model for the study of social entrepreneurship. *Economics & Society: Contemporary Models of Development*, 14(2), 91–112. DOI: 10.18334/ecsoc.14.2.121514

Vovchenko, N. G., Andreeva, O. V., Dmitrieva, V. D., Galazova, S. S., & Terziev, V. K. (2022). Modelling of Economic Clusters in the Russian Regions in the Context of Formation of the Industry 4.0. In Trifonov, P. V., & Charaeva, M. V. (Eds.), *Strategies and Trends in Organizational and Project Management. DITEM 2021. Lecture Notes in Networks and Systems* (Vol. 380). Springer. DOI: 10.1007/978-3-030-94245-8_91

Vovchenko, N. G., Andreeva, O. V., Dmitrieva, V. D., Kaptsova, V. S., & Terziev, V. K. (2023d). Technological, Economic, and Social Changes: The Role of End-to-End Technologies. In Makarenko, E. N., Vovchenko, N. G., & Tishchenko, E. N. (Eds.), *Technological Trends in the AI Economy. Smart Innovation, Systems and Technologies* (Vol. 625). Springer. DOI: 10.1007/978-981-19-7411-3_2

Vovchenko, N. G., Andreeva, O. V., Dmitrieva, V. D., Zaruk, N. F., & Sulzhenko, S. A. (2023a). Financial Aspects of Decarbonization of the Russian and Central Asian Economies in the Context of Climate Change: Comparative Analysis. In Popkova, E. G. (Ed.), *Smart Green Innovations in Industry 4.0 for Climate Change Risk Management. Environmental Footprints and Eco-design of Products and Processes*. Springer. DOI: 10.1007/978-3-031-28457-1_51

Chapter 7
From Triple Integration to Triple Transformation Through FDI:
The Case of Slovakia

Ninel Seniuk
https://orcid.org/0000-0002-7425-9029
Bratislava University of Economic and Management, Slovakia

Michal Fabus
https://orcid.org/0000-0002-3792-179X
Bratislava University of Economics and Management, Slovakia

ABSTRACT

For the case of Slovakia in a comparative evolutionary dynamic of the Visegrad Four countries in the period 2007-2021. The results of such DDM-analysis were further used as a reasoned justification for the need of ESG transformation in the context of globalization G3.0 and G4.0 within the framework of the TT model. At the same time, these results demonstrated the extremely complicated nature of a local or regional object as a complex adaptive system (CAS) subject to such ESG transformation. And in any case, such TT in the case of live CAS is similar to the external symptoms of the body, which are the result of deeper processes driven by some internal innovative driver. At the heart of such an internal innovation engine, which requires fundamentally new knowledge as a fuel for its work, is the triple integration model (TIM).

DOI: 10.4018/979-8-3693-9435-9.ch007

INTRODUCTION

The problem of Triple Transformation (TT), minimizing cross-sectoral barriers between the Economic, Social, and Governmental (ESG) spheres in the interests of creating a single space for stimulating positive global evolutionary dynamics, has become especially acute in connection with the adoption of the 17 Sustainable Development Goals (SDG) by U.N. in 2015. The first SDG is overcoming poverty alleviation, essentially the flip side of wealth polarization. Poverty due to lack of resources leads to social exclusion of more and more people from development processes, exacerbating the problem of polarization, both economic and social. Meanwhile, the solution to this problem does not come down to a simple redistribution of resources from rich to poor, because poverty is not cured by money, but by changing the way of life and management. Undoubtedly, the focus of such a way of life should be human health and the corresponding ecosystem with an adequate role of public administration, declaring human life and health as the main values, the protection of which should be the main concern of the state. Therefore, it is no coincidence that at the centre of the 17 SDGs is Goal 3 (Good health and well-being), the achievement of which precisely requires the integration of the synchronized capabilities of all these 17 components of inclusive human-centric sustainable development. This happens because, by the WHO definition, health is understood not as the absence of diseases threatened by doctors, but as a state of complete physical, mental, and social well-being, the achievement of which goes beyond the scope of the specific capabilities of medicine, but requires, at a minimum, comprehensive, and ideally, a holistic intersectoral approach. And since our knowledge is substantively differentiated, and public governance in industrial society has a sectoral division, then from the point of view of creating external conditions for human-centric ESG well-being, TT is needed. However, human health is not reduced only to external well-being. It is an internal state, predetermining by deep internal, including energy-informational and spiritual potential. This means that within the framework of a human-centric approach to sustainable inclusive development on a post-industrial base, a holistic vision will be required.

At the same time, such development is always a living holistic self-development in co-development with a partner/s. Within the framework of the previously introduced definitions, such co-development presupposes the presence of spiritual and creative frictions aimed at mutual improvement of each other's well-being according to subjectively assessed criteria. In the process of such frictional interaction, aimed at improving the well-being of everyone through the generation of joint interdependent well-being, based on such a partnership, a new subjectivity is created. This creation in the life of a new partner subjectivity against the backdrop of an existing individual one, in the economy corresponds to trade and investment interaction, including with the participation of Foreign Direct Investment (FDI). However, the goals pursued by Multinational Enterprises (MNEs) are primarily economic in nature, focused on maximizing profits and/or increasing their fixed capital. Meanwhile development, especially inclusive, presupposes a holistic and subject-oriented character. It is precisely this integrity that is only capable of giving the above-mentioned SDGs that existential value, the achievement of which requires ESG-driven TT, and most importantly, the creation of a new holistic subject based on intersectoral Public Private Partnership (PPP). Such a PPP-based entity can initially increase the jointly created added value by minimizing intersectoral barriers, but then improving its well-being is achieved by going beyond both geographic/administrative and state borders throughout FDI frictional interaction. In turn, when implementing this type of corporate "Go Global" strategy and for the further transition from Economic Growth (EG) to Economic Development (ED), its own multi-level vertical, horizontal, and cross-sectoral Integration will be required, carried out within the framework of the so-called Triple Integration Model (TIM) (Seniuk, 2017). The further transition to subject-oriented inclusive development makes it possible to form, in the process of interactive iterations, a request for parameters and institutional architecture of the ESG-driven Triple Transformation, indicating a strategic course in the direction from TIM to TT.

Modern Globalization, which began after WWII and has consistently enriched its evolutionary forms during this time, from post-war Globalization 2.0 (G1.0 - rule-based "Trade without borders") to G2.0 ("Production without borders") of the 1970s-80s and G3.0 ("Service without borders") of the 90s, coupled with the rapid development of digitalization and the emergence of Digital Economy (DE) since the beginning of the 21st century, dramatically expanded both the capabilities of TIM and the request and requirements for TT. As a consequence, this led to the overpriced growth of international trade, which lasted until 2012 for more than 60 years (Degain et al., 2017) and turned it into the leading engine of accelerated domestic EG, a clear example of which was China. In principle, the same kind of effect, but on a smaller scale, was characteristic of the "Visegrád Four" (V4) countries, which consisted of the Czech Republic, Hungary, Poland, and Slovakia, especially in the first decade after they accede to EU membership. Along with this, with the formation and growth of G3.0 at the end of the last century and the intensive expansion of G4.0 at the beginning of the 21st century, the structure of trade changed towards an increase in the share of manufactured intermediate goods and services, which to 2016-2017 reached 2/3 total turnover (Ahmad and Primi, 2017). At the same time, significant changes are taking place in the structure of added value created in the country and exported outside its borders, primarily due to the rapid growth of the share of services, especially within the framework of G4.0. So, in particular if in 1980 the ratio between the share of goods and services in the total volume of International Trade was 80% versus 20%, although in terms of the added value it was 70%/30%, then by 2009 this ratio became 60%/40%, developed economies demonstrated service dominance in its exports in terms of added value (Dollar and Thornton 2017, p.11). All this taken together meant that, along with the evolution of Globalization and its transition to innovation-driven forms G3.0 and G4.0, the national economies of the most developed countries were transitioning to post-industrial stages of their further progress, radically different like the added value distribution between participants in technological chains of international production and service cooperation, usually known in IB theory as Global Value Chains (GVCs). Moreover, it was said that in the framework of the industrial type of economy, the main beneficiary of the added value distribution, described by the so-called "frown curve" is the producer of goods, while at the post-industrial stage, the nature of this distribution is already described by the so-called "smile curve" and now the producer finds themself in the least advantageous position (Ahmad and Primi 2017, p.70).

It seems, as our further analysis will show, that the last case is precisely the most typical of the situation in which the Slovak economy currently finds itself. As official statistics shows (SYSR2024, tables 3-17, 3-18), in terms of GDP growth rates, the Slovak economy in the post-pandemic period demonstrates a downward trend, significantly lower than the rather high level of 2020 (4.8%). In terms of per capita indicators in purchasing power parity (PPP) base, at the end of 2023 it managed to reach the 2021 figure (73% from the EU-27 average), but not reaching the level of 2020 (74%). It was also not possible to increase the Industrial index production, which in 2023 amounted to 96.9% of the 2021 level, although labor productivity increased to 79.5% of the European average level compared to 73.5% in 2019 (Ibid, tables 31-19; 31-26). Coupled with the far-from-rosy economic prospects for the EU made by the IMF, when it is expected that by 2025 the economy of emerging and developing European countries will decline (to 2.3%) and only by 2029 should slowly rise to 2.5% against the backdrop of lower dynamics of the most developed economies (IMF2024, pp.67, 113), this gives rise to a serious request for more diversified strategies for further development (see, for example, the Yearbooks of Slovak Foreign Policy (SFP) published by the SFP Association over the past years). In particular, the Yearbook 2021 draws attention to the fact that in the context of an epochal post-pandemic shift in the centers of economic activity from the North Atlantic area to the Indo-Pacific region, special attention should be paid to Eastern Europe and Eastern Asia cooperation (Korcok, 2022, p.8). In this sense, given into account the low level of institutional development of the V4 countries and the noticeable differences in the political priorities of its member states, it is proposed to strengthen the pragmatic focus of cooperation using, among other things, its new formats. As such, in particular, it is proposed to more actively use the S3 (Austria,

Czechia, and Slovakia), 3SI (Three Seas Initiative), and V4+EaP (Eastern Partnership) formats with the participation of EU candidate countries (Strafzahlungen 2022, p.121). In any case, the practical promotion of cooperation formats of this kind, in turn will to one degree or another require multilateral TT development and synchronization.

The events associated with the Russia and Ukraine in February 2022 and which extremely aggravated the VUCA (Volatility, Uncertainty, Complexity, and Ambiguity) characteristics of the modern world, hit Europe especially hard, primarily in the field of energy security and its price consequences, which undermine the competitiveness and economic dynamics of the EU. Added to this is the difficult demographic situation in Europe and in developed countries in general, and even in China in 2021 zero population growth was observed for the first time. All this means that the European economy can hardly count on the macro influx of cheap labor as a long-term factor of EG, but mainly only on the influx of capital and talents. However, Europe also has problems with this, especially noticeable at the level of CEE and V4. There was a consequence of the fact that gas prices in Europe are 3 times higher than in the US, EG rates are noticeably lower. As a result, only 11 European MNEs were on the list of the global TOP100 in 2023, and among the TOP10 in 2024 were 6 American, 3 Chinese, and one from Saudi Arabia (Aramco), and not a single from the EU (GFM 2024). All these circumstances indicate that "economic relations in the world will change ... [and] countries that do not have sufficient supplies of capital will not be able to rely on economic models based on the extensive use of cheap labor, whether in industry (China) or services (India). There will be sectoral shift, with health, wellness and social services accounting for much larger share of GDP than they do today" (Vlachynsky 2024, p.66).

Thus, the focus of practical resolution of SDG-oriented problems is attracting FDI flows, and most importantly, the presence of innovative economic models and talents that are adequate to the global challenges of the time, capable of developing and implementing them in conditions of the modern digitalization and VUCA world. This problem, as we show further, is especially acute in Slovakia. It is in this spirit of searching for practical solutions that one should consider the visit of a representative government delegation to China led by Prime Minister of Slovakia Robert Fico from October 31 to November 5, 2024. Its main result, reflected in the joint statement on the establishment of strategic partnership relations between both countries, based on "principles of mutual respect, equality, mutual benefit, and win-win cooperation" (Joint Statement 2024). According to clause 2.4 of this Statement, it is intended to "strengthen cooperation on green development in such fields as new materials, new infrastructure, clean energy and sustainable development... in green technology, recycling, waste treatment and other such fields .... on CO2 emission reduction technologies ... and ... on the diversification of energy resource supply, thereby enhancing energy security and promoting transition to sustainable low-carbon energy sources such as solar, vehicles, geothermal and wind power" (Ibid). Undoubtedly, this kind of innovation-oriented cooperation opens up enormous opportunities for the Slovak economy, but at the same time carries with the Great risk. And this risk is associated, first of all, with the objective consequences of the distribution of the results of such cooperation, which by so-called Gravity Model (GM) (Isard 1956; Tienbergen 1962), used to describe the processes of both trade (see, for example, Badarinza et al., 2022) and investment interaction (Zwickels and Beugelsdijk 2010; Korsita et al., 2023). A win-win result, strictly speaking, is achieved in the case of equal-sized interacting partners. In the case of the Chinese-Slovak strategic partnership, we are dealing with participants of extremely different sizes, which casts doubt on the very theoretical possibility of achieving a win-win effect, unless it is necessary to create a special subject-oriented redistribution or balancing institutional mechanism. Moreover, when it comes to partner interaction in fundamentally different, heterogeneous ESG environments (see, for example, Baier and Standart, 2024). In this case, it is hardly possible to do without the appropriate institutional suitable TIM within the framework of the firm-centric holistic AI-based approach, using the Slovak economy as a conceptual heterogeneous case study.

The conceptual justification of the need and feasibility of such a transition from TIM to TT as a single living ecosystem capable of multi-level inclusive sustainable development in co-development with in general different-sized partners in heterogeneous environments in a globally integrated approach is the main goal of this research. Due to the innovative nature of this kind of problem statement, it is hardly possible to apply a traditional approach using proven theoretical models and critical analysis of more or less extensive literature, aimed at obtaining either theoretical results for improvement of the original model or at upgrading the methodology for its application to an empirical data. Therefore, in this case for better perception and understanding of the part of IB practice, we took a reverse approach, starting with an analysis of the developmental problems and needs for restructuring of the Slovak economy, focusing on the very traditional problem of goal-oriented attraction of FDI, however about the Digital Economy (DE) and in terms that are fundamentally amendable to algorithmization and use of Artificial Intelligence (AI).

1. FDI AS THE MEANS AND CRITERIA FOR THE SUCCESS OF TRIPLE TRANSFORMATION AND TRIPLE INTEGRATION. STATEMENT OF THE PROBLEM

Foreign Direct Investment (FDI) represents a very effective means of transforming the fixed capital of the host party at the micro level of the firm, and their generalized flows carry restructuring opportunities for the quantitative and qualitative transformation of the country's national wealth at the macro level. In this sense, Outward Foreign Direct Investment (OFDI) is also the main instrument of Economic Globalization and an essence of soft power, transforming the economic and social landscape of the region or country. Due to this role and the complex nature of their internal and external influences, OFDI is the focus of attention of various scientific disciplines and above all International Business (IB), which considers the investment behavior of MNEs in the global political and economic space. And since the main function of science is to reveal general patterns and specific features of the phenomenon under study, then within the IB framework the problem of analyzing OFDI in the simplest (dyadic) case comes down to describing processes and results of investment interactions between two firms from different countries: the parent MNE as an investor from the home country and the recipient company from the host economy. Ultimately, the conceptual framework of such global dyadic interaction forms the basis of the Theory of the Firm, whose investment behavior in the Global Political Economy (GPE) space is determined by the imposition of a complex set of objective (primarily macroeconomic) and subjective (institutional and political and regulatory) factors, as well as internal corporate preferences and socio-psychological motives, which in IB are called as determinants, drivers and motives (DDM) respectively (UNCTAD1998). Since it was not possible to construct a mathematically rigorous theory of such a Firm within the framework of classical scientific rationality (Seniuk et al, 2023), and simplified theoretical models of MNEs and their OFDI do not cover the entire set of typical cases of investment interaction in heterogeneous environments (Seniuk, 2012 (PhD dissertation thesis)), in practice it is necessary to use empirical approaches with using the UNCTAD modified determinants, drivers and motives (DDM) methodology (UNCTAD 2006).

At the same time, despite the lack of a mathematically rigorous theory of the firm (TF), during the formation of IB, starting from the 1960s-70s of the last century, a whole family of simplified, mainly neoclassical FDI models was created. They also primarily based their consideration on the classic case of dyadic investment interaction between a home and host firm as a FDI recipient. However, the rapid development of ICT and the emergence of the Digital Economy (DE) had a serious transformation impact on the World Economy, even giving rise to new types of Globalization in the form of G3.0 and G4.0. Undoubtedly, such profound transformations are not limited only to the economic field, but also carry with them significant socio-cultural consequences, starting with the incorporation of new knowledge (K) and skills (S), and ending with institutional innovations both at the micro level of the firms, and the macro level of sectors and countries. And of course, FDI became the main means of these transformations and their social and cultural impact. As a result, the very forms of business interaction were enriched when, in addition to the traditional classical local dyadic interaction in the global competitive space, non-classical cluster spatially distributed forms of cooperative interaction and even post-non-classical forms of Global Production Networks (GPN) and Global Innovation Network (GIN) began to grow at an accelerated pace. In turn, such a transformation of the economic landscape led to a corresponding growth of urban agglomerations as centers of business internationalization and support for Global Value Chains (GVC), as well as to the formation of Global Cities and Global Regions as new Digital Innovation Hubs (DIH). Consequently, all this created a demand for a corresponding transformation of the strategies of these new subjects of the IB in the spirit of a win-win approach.

Thus, we are talking about the external form of the Triple Transformation (TT) associated with the digitalization of the economy, institutional innovative transformation of the socio-cultural sphere, and strategically oriented Globalization of the activities of all old and new players in the modern interdependent world. However, these external TT symptoms must contain their deep mechanism, the focus of which must be a form and its corresponding internal transformation, which requires, in addition to attracting the necessary financial and technological funds, also new own and/or foreign knowledge, competencies, and skills. Moreover, we are talking about such knowledge, competencies, and skills that allow us to create and capture a significantly higher quantity and quality of added value through PPP-based intersectoral partnerships of businesses, Non-Government Organizations, and Governments. Although this kind of approach is key to achieving the 17 SDGs, it is still a reliable internal mechanism of such partnership and integration, despite its apparent simplicity from the macro level view, which represents a very serious problem at the micro level. Solving this problem requires identifying and bringing together the necessary data regarding DDM, taking into account the whole variety of new institutional and digital forms of globally integrated ESG activity in the context of digitalization. We are talking about creating an "innovative knowledge-based engine" to solve the problem at the local/regional level.

As a conceptual basis for such an engine, the Triple Integration Model (TIM) can be considered (Seniuk, 2017). It is especially promising to use such a model for the analysis of transformational trends at the border of heterogeneous environments, for example the former post-socialist EU transborder countries. For these reasons, we choose Slovakia as the object of study in the context of comparative economic and investment dynamics of the V4 Group. Such analysis, in the modern VUCA conditions, seems to be a very non-trivial task. From such a point of view, solving this task requires a unique diagnosis of the objective state and investment needs of the Slovak economy against FDI for the economic and institutional transformation in the context of the V4 group macroeconomic dynamics.

2. SLOVAK ECONOMY AND ITS INVESTMENT TRENDS IN THE CONTEXT OF THE EVOLUTIONARY DYNAMICS OF THE VISEGRAD FOUR (V4) GROUP (2007-2021)

The current state of the Slovak economy and the results of a comparative analysis of its structural transformation against the backdrop of similar dynamics of the other V4 members in the global context, relative to the middle of the last decade (2015) are presented in Table 1.

Table 1. Comparative analysis of the V4 economies in the global context: 2022 versus 2015

Country, Region	Agriculture, %		Industry, %		Manufacturing, %		Service, %	
	2015	2022	2015	2022	2015	2022	2015	2022
Czechia	2,2	2,1	33,8	30,7	23,9	21,2	54,1	57,9
Hungary	3,8	2,7	26,4	25,8	20,2	17,2	54,1	56,4
Poland	2,5	2,1	31,1	29,8	17,9	17,7	55,1	56,8
Slovakia	2,2	2,2	30,6	28,6	19,6	20,3	57,3	58,3
World	4,2	4,3	26,8	28,0	16,4	16,2	64,3	63,9
High-income countries	1,3	1,3	22,8	22,4	13,9	13,2	69,9	70,0
Upper-middle income countries	7,2	6,9	35,2	36,6	22,4	22,8	53,4	53,0

Source: World Bank

From the data presented in Table 1, a generally positive structural transformation is visible, more or less inherent in all economies from the V4 group, occupying an intermediate position between high-income countries, demonstrating a steady trend towards a decrease in the share of agriculture and industry in their economies and accordingly increasing the share of service sectors, gradually moving closer to the level of high developed countries. At the same time, against the backdrop of a consistent decline in the share of manufacturing in the structure of the economies of 3 out of 4 members of the V4 group, it is Slovakia demonstrates the opposite trend, increasing this ratio, albeit slightly from 19.6% to 20.3%, which brings it closer to the middle-income countries with increased such share from 22.4% to 22.8%, respectively. A more in-depth understanding of the current place and role of Slovakia in international flows of goods and capital in a group and global comparative approach can be obtained from the analysis of the data presented in Table 2.

Table 2. Current place and weight of the V4 countries in the Intra-regional and International Trade and Capital movement and their top partner economies

Country	Flows	Trade		Capital		TOP partners
		Rank	Level	Rank	Level	Countries
Czechia	Intra*	18	83%	11	79%	1.Germany- 73% 2.Poland- 7% 3.Slovakia- 7% 4.USA- 5% 5.China -5%
	USA**	11	82%	27	86%	
	China***	141	9%	161	1%	
Hungary	Intra	38	84%	17	77%	1.Germany – 7% 2.USA- 6% 3.Austria -6% 4.Poland- 4% 5.Romania- 4%
	USA	12	82%	11	89%	
	China	139	9%	135	2%	
Poland	Intra	21	81%	16	77%	1.USA- 20% 2.China-10% 3.Japan-8% 4.Singapore -5% 5.Rep.of Korea -4%
	USA	18	80%	31	85%	
	China	131	10%	158	1%	
Slovakia	Intra	9	87%	2	87%	1.Czechia- 15% 2.Germany -14% 3.Austria -8% 4.Hungary- 7% 5.Poland -6% 6.China-3%
	USA	20	79%	8	90%	
	China	154	7%	164	1%	

Source: DHL Global Connectedness Report 2024, pp.151,180, 239,253
*Intra -Intra-regional flows
**USA-flows with USA and its close allies
***China—flows with China and its close allies

The data presented here shows that Slovakia leads in terms of participation in Intra-regional trade with a share of 87% in total turnover and ranks 9th in the region, ahead of the Czech Republic, Hungary, and Poland. However, in terms of trade with the United States and its closest allies, Slovakia shepherds the rear, taking 20th place in Europe, albeit with a high relative ratio (79%) in trade flows, and last 154th in the world, in trade with China with a share of 7% compared with 9% for Hungary and Czechia each and 10% for Poland.

Meanwhile, Slovakia is an almost absolute leader (2nd place in the world) with 8th global place in investment interaction with the United States. At the same time, Slovakia is in the last place in the group (164 places in the world with a share of

1%) in capital exchange with China against the backdrop of a noticeable more active role of Hungary (135th place with a share of 2%). Interestingly, China is included in the list of top 5 trade and investment partners only with Poland (2nd place with a share of 10%) and the Czech Republic (5th place and 5% ratio), whereas in the case of Slovakia it found itself only in the 10th place, whereas Germany is in the top 2, most significantly represented as the leader in trade and investment flows in case of Czechia (73%) and Hungary (7%), while firmly occupying 2nd place, but with shares of 14% went to Slovakia. It is curious that in the case of a well-diversified partner structure of Poland, the leading place with a share of 20% is occupied by the United States, Germany does not even make it into top 5, and only Slovakia was the Czech Republic in the first place with a share of 15%, somewhat displacing Germany. All this indicates the differences in the dominant preferences of the V4 countries when 3 out of 4 countries are guided by leading centers of generation, configuration, and coordination of GVCs. Among them the Czech Republic has a strongly pronounced dominant role of Germany, similar to Hungary, although an order of magnitude weaker, Poland has an undoubted priority in the United States, and only in the case of Slovakia the leadership position is occupied by the former "big sister" within the framework of the previously existing Czechoslovakia. This means that Slovakia is also focused on the German center of GVC generation, but indirectly through the Czechia and with a smaller share of added value accruing when it is distributed within joint value chains.

Since we are primarily focusing on the analysis of investment trends and their impact on the economic dynamics of Slovakia, a more detailed analysis can be done using the data shown in Table 3.

Table 3. Current place of the V4 countries in International Capital Flows

Country	FDI	Structure of FDI flows				Distribution of FDI flows			
		Rank		Level		Rank		Level	
		Outward	Inward	Outward	Inward	Outward	Inward	Outward	Inward
Czechia	GF*	12	101	4,1%	0,75%	38	35	41%	63%
	M&A**	27	36	0,5%	0,38%	42	45	34%	47%
	Stock***	49	50	19%	70%	77	60	18%	36%
	Flows****	51	78	3,2%	13%				
Hungary	GF	73	13	0,24%	7%	43	47	38%	57%
	M&A	158	170	-0,23%	-0,21%	34	49	39%	45%
	Stock	44	67	24%	59%	18	47	43%	38%
	Flows	26	56	8,5%	17%				

continued on following page

Table 3. Continued

Country	FDI	Structure of FDI flows				Distribution of FDI flows			
		Rank		Level		Rank		Level	
		Outward	Inward	Outward	Inward	Outward	Inward	Outward	Inward
Poland	GF	65	42	0,34%	2,6%	31	8	47%	77%
	M&A	156	69	-0,18%	0,027%	44	28	33%	59%
	Stock	99	102	4,4%	39%	30	39	35%	41%
	Flows	71	40	1,9%	25%				
Slovakia	GF	58	34	0,45%	3,1%	52	59	33%	51%
	M&A	67	64	0	0,052%	83	50	13%	44%
	Stock	97	81	4,7%	50%	68	73	20%	32%
	Flows	72	80	1,9%	13%				

Source: DHL Global Connectedness Report 2024, pp.151,180, 239,253
*GF- Announced Greenfield FDI (% of GDP)
**M&A – transactions (% of GDP)
***Stock – FDI stock (% of GDP)
****Flows-FDI flows (% of GFCF- Gross Fixed Capital Formation)

Data from Table 3 are very eloquent and indicate that Slovakia is in the last place in group V4 in terms of participation of inward FDI flows (80s rank in the world with a 13 percent share in gross fixed capital formation) and outward ones (72nd place and 1.9%, respectively), as well as penultimate (97th rank with a share of 4.7% in GDP) in OFDI stock and in terms of accumulated FDI (81st rank, although with a significant 50 percent share in GDP). It is characterized that the leader in the group in terms of current investment of its capital abroad, with a significant gap from the rest is Hungary (26th place in the world with a share of 85% in gross fixed capital formation), as well as in terms of their OFDI (44th global rank with 24% ration in GDP), while Poland took the leading position in receiving current FDI flows (with 40th place and 25 percent share in gross fixed capital formation), and the Czech Republic is leading in accumulation foreign investment (50th rank with a record 70% share compared to GDP). From the point of view of the structure of current FDI flows, with a significant gap from the rest both in greenfield investment abroad (12th place in the world with a level of 4.1% of GDP) and in mergers and acquisitions (M&A) of foreign assets, the leader is Czech Republic, and behind it what is interesting is Slovakia (ranked 58th and 67th, respectively), with Hungary coming as last (with 73rd and 158th global rank, respectively). At the same time, in terms of FDI distribution, the leading role in greenfield both external and internal flows belong to Poland, and it is also the leader in selling its own M&A to foreigners, losing the leadership in brownfield overseas investment to Hungary.

This whole picture requires a more thorough analysis of historical dynamics, the results of which are presented in Table 4.

Table 4(a). Comparative analysis of the dynamics of GDP, wealth, and the efficiency of its use by V4 countries in the global context (2007-2021)

Country	Thousands, USD	2007	2008	2009	2010	2011	2012
Czechia	GDP, p/a	22,2	28,4	24,7	24,7	27,0	24,5
	wealth, p/a	33,7	42,2	38,6	43,6	48,6	45,1
	ROW*,%	65,9	67,3	64,0	56,6	55,6	54,3
Hungary	GDP, p/a	17,8	20,2	16,7	16,9	18,1	16,4
	wealth, p/a	32,9	35,7	32,4	32,5	35,0	33,1
	ROW, %	54,1	56,6	51,5	52,0	51,7	49,5
Poland	GDP, p/a	14,5	17,9	14,7	15,8	17,4	16,4
	wealth, p/a	33,0	30,04	28,4	31,2	29,9	32,9
	ROW, %	43,9	58,9	51,8	50,6	58,2	49,8
Slovakia	GDP, p/a	20,9	24,2	21,3	21,6	23,5	22,2
	wealth, p/a	44,6	45,5	45,3	42,8	42,7	44,9
	ROW, %	46,9	53,2	47,0	50,5	55,0	49,4
World	GDP, p/a	13,7	14,7	13,7	14,8	16,1	16,2
	wealth, p/a	54,6	49,7	52,5	55,8	56,9	59,3
	ROW, %	25,1	29,6	26,1	26,5	28,3	27,3

Source: author's, based on World Bank data and Global Wealth Databook 2022
*ROW-Return on Wealth, p/a- per adult

Table 4(b). Comparative analysis of the dynamics of GDP, wealth, and the efficiency of its use by V4 countries in the global context (2007-2021)

2013	2014	2015	2016	2017	2018	2019	2020	2021
24,8	24,5	22,0	22,9	25,6	29,1	29,6	28,4	33,2
48,0	52,3	47,2	52,1	56,9	64,9	67,1	73,7	82,2
51,7	46,8	46,6	44,0	45,0	44,8	44,1	38,5	40,4
17,3	18,0	15,9	16,4	18,3	20,6	21,0	19,6	23,8
34,3	35,6	33,6	37,3	42,8	50,4	56,1	58,0	70,7
50,4	50,6	47,3	44,0	42,8	40,9	37,4	33,8	33,7
17,0	17,7	15,7	15,4	17,2	19,4	19,6	19,3	21,2

continued on following page

Table 4(b). Continued

2013	2014	2015	2016	2017	2018	2019	2020	2021
36,6	**36,1**	**32,6**	**33,3**	**42,4**	**41,2**	**44,0**	**48,3**	**50,4**
46,4	**49,0**	**48,2**	**46,2**	**40,6**	**47,1**	**44,5**	**40,0**	**42,1**
23,0	**23,5**	**20,6**	**20,7**	**22,0**	**24,4**	**24,3**	**23,4**	**25,3**
47,6	**44,9**	**41,1**	**42,8**	**51,1**	**50,4**	**54,4**	**64,7**	**63,5**
48,3	**52,3**	**50,1**	**48,4**	**43,0**	**48,4**	**44,7**	**36,2**	**39,8**
16,4	**16,6**	**15,4**	**15,4**	**16,2**	**17,2**	**17,0**	**16,3**	**17,9**
62,3	**61,9**	**61,0**	**63,0**	**70,5**	**70,5**	**75,3**	**80,7**	**87,5**
26,3	**26,8**	**25,2**	**24,4**	**23,0**	**24,4**	**22,6**	**20,2**	**20,4**

Source: author's, based on World Bank data and Global Wealth Databook 2022
*ROW-Return on Wealth, p/a- per adult

As can be seen from the data in Table 4, in 2007 in terms of wealth per adult, the most relatively rich was Slovakia ($54.6 thousand), while the lowest level ($32.9 thousand) was demonstrated by Hungary. At the same time, the Czech Republic used its existing assets most productively (65.9% against 54.1% for Hungary, 46,9% for Slovakia, and 43.9% for Poland compared to 25.1% of the world average), due to which it was the leader in terms of GDP per adult ($22.2 thousand). However, by 2021 the picture has become significantly different. Czechia became the relatively richest during this time, having increased its assets per adult to the level of $82.2 thousand, followed by Hungary ($70.7 thousand) and Slovakia, which increased this figure by only 1.43 times ($63.5 thousand), while Poland had the worst indicator ($50.4 thousand). Together with the data from Table 3, this indicates a serious need for FDI, both in Poland, which has the lowest level in the V4 group in their stock (39% in GDP), and Slovakia (50%) against 70% for Czech Republic and 59% for Hungary, 50% for Slovakia and 39% for Poland. At the same time, Poland has recently been leading in the current attraction of investment inflows (25% of GDP), followed by Hungary (17%), and least of all with an equal share in Czechia and Slovakia (13% in GDP each). It is not surprising that in the last two years, Poland has become the leader in the group of asset productivity (42.1%), ahead of the Czech Republic (40,4%), Slovakia (39,8%), and Hungary (33.7%) against the background of the world average of 20,4%. At the same time, it is characteristic that in the area of OFDI, both in terms of their stock (24% in GDP) and current outflows (8.5% in GDP), Hungary is in the lead, followed by the Czechia (19% and 3.2%, respectively), and then with a significant gap come Slovakia (4.7/1.9%) and Poland (4.4%/1.9%).

It should be noted that both in terms of participation in the international movement of goods and capital (see Table 2), V4 countries occupy a fairly high position. First of all Slovakia, which ranks second globally in terms of the share of intraregional FDI flows (87%) in their total inflow, with a strong dominance (90%) of American capital among its external import against the backdrop of the last in the group 164th place in the world in attracting Chinese OFDI. Slovakia also leads the group in a fairly high position (9th in the world)) in participation in intraregional foreign trade, although last in trade with the United States (20th globally) and China (154th). The country also leads in the share of Foreign Trade in GDP (180-200% in 2019-2023) against the background of 160-180% for Hungary, 140-150% for Czechia, and 100-120% for Poland (Macrotrends 2024). Such a high ratio of International Trade in the Slovak GDP combined with a low position in terms of own OFDI stock, suggests that the lion's share of added value exported from the country is of a transit nature. Of course, this situation requires more in-depth studies of the structure of both Foreign Trade and Investment. However, within the framework of the Industrial Development Path model (IDP) (Narula and Dunning 2010; Sawitri Ana Brennan 2023), qualitatively we can safely say that the country's economy is in a phase of regionalization with an emphasis on maximum exploration of existing assets, rather than creating new ones. Moreover, taking into account the fact that Slovakia was the only one in the V4 group during the period of membership in the EU, the restructuring shift, as already shown in Table 1, occurred towards strengthening the industrializing role of manufacturing, this indicates the need to make post-industrial development a higher priority due to DE, as shown schematically in Fig. 1

Figure 1. Digital Economy Schematic

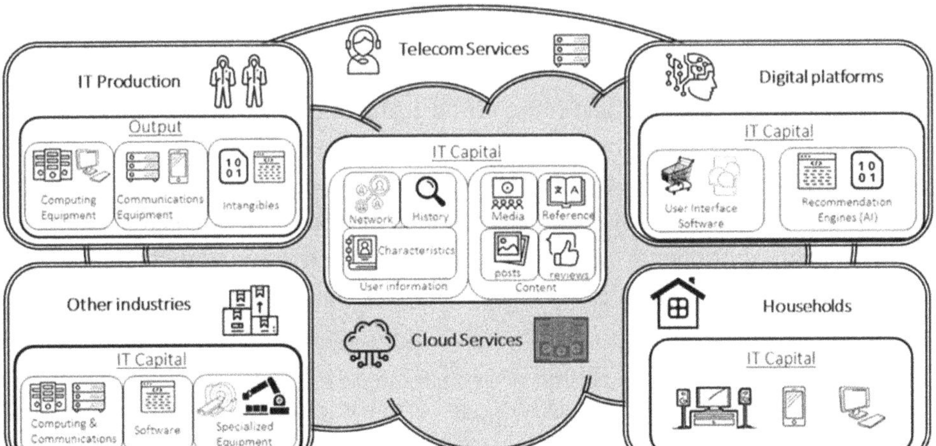

Source: Byrne 2022

As follows from Figure 1, the creation of new digital assets, primarily due to their intangible component, could open up the prospect of leveling out the current situation, which as it was shown in Table 4, in terms of the wealth per adult, the Slovak economy demonstrates a relative sliding, having moved during the period of membership in the European Union from a leading position in group V4 in penultimate third place. Meanwhile, digitalization itself relatively weakens the role of traditional industrial OLI components of the global competitiveness of the country's economy (in terms of the eclectic FDI model), which until now has served as a serious motive for attracting Foreign Investment. This means, that to achieve a win-win effect within the framework of international investment cooperation, it is necessary to find a very non-trivial theoretical and methodological solution to this problem. In addition, taking into account the practical absence of Slovak's world-class MNEs, it is necessary to create new PPP-based global players, for which TIM and the corresponding TT will be required.

3. THEORETICAL AND METHODOLOGICAL INSTRUMENTS FOR THE TT AND TIM WITHIN THE FRAMEWORK OF THE "FIRM-CENTRIC" APPROACH: CRITICAL ANALYSIS

3.1. General Context

The analysis of empirical macroeconomic trends carried out in the previous section and their results made it possible to understand the Slovak economy within the framework of a comparative approach with the V4 countries in the context of its objective needs for FDI, including OFDI from China. However, since the real driver of any market economy is the firm, a critical analysis of the theoretical and methodological micro-level tools at IB's disposal is accordingly required. At the same time, the neoclassical approach dominant in the theory and statistical modeling forms the limiting frames at various higher meso-, macro-, and global mega-levels, set by the characteristic neoclassical ideas about the stationary economic system for each of these levels, subject to the requirement of a general balance. Using the so-called Computable General Equilibrium (GCE) models, we obtain a corresponding multi-level set of such balances, leaving up for the emergent EG only those possibilities that are allowed by the elasticity of the productive factors used in the GDP modeling (see, for example, Johansen 1974; Burfisher 2021). This kind of balanced approach is a "zero-sum game", which means that one's gain automatically entails the other's loss. Therefore, there is simply no room for a win-win result.

Meanwhile, the intensive development of G3.0 and G4.0 processes with the increasingly deeper investment of developing economies, primarily from Asia, including South and Southeast Asia, clearly indicated the emergence of new innovative and creative effects that do not fit into the neoclassical picture of a closed and balanced global economy of the late 20th and early 21st centuries. First of all, the emergence of the phenomenon of "East Asian Tigers" and their involvement in GVCs led to the emergence of a new economic and investment reality that does not fit, as in the case of South Korea (Fu, 2017), into this old picture. At the same time, special attention is focused on the real limits of this elasticity within the framework of global market equilibrium, which can explain both the phenomenon of "Emerging economies that violate these boundaries, and the emergence of a new global and also rapidly growing direction of international capital movement from the South to the South and to the North, instead of the usual North-North and North-South direction" (Cai et al. 2022). This familiar and widely used neoclassical methodology for economic forecasting has been further confused by modern post-non-classical networking forms of GPN and GIN. This means that to study the theoretical possibilities for the formation of scientific and methodological foundations for the modeling of win-win strategies, a critical analysis of existing theories and models will be required as a necessary condition.

3.2. Theories and Models of the Firm and Its Investment Behavior in the Context of Analysis of the State and Needs of the Slovak Economy in FDI

The firm, as a corporate system of managed transformational activity using production facilities and natural resources, was generated by the era of industrialization and the development of Foreign Trade. From the position of general theory, the firm is usually considered in one of three aspects: Ontological, Teleological, and Epistemological (OTE) (Suszynski, 2013, p.30). Although the construction of a fundamentally complete picture, it is necessary to consider it in the OTE-unity of all three components. Meanwhile, due to their constant complication occurring under the influence of evolution, if it is possible to do this, then only at the level of general philosophical reasoning. Therefore, a unified universal theory of the firm, even within the narrower framework of ontological approaches, limited to consideration of its nature, structure, and components, has not yet been created [ibid, 43]. It is even more difficult, within the framework of classical scientific rationality, to do this in a teleological approach, the focus of which is on the goals of the firm and the objectives of its activity, not to mention the epistemological consideration, focused on the subjective nature of the firm, its content, and methods of extracting and concentration of tacit knowledge as a source of radical innovation (Suszynski, 2013, p.30). Under these circumstances, it is necessary to use differentiated within the framework of the subject specialization of the multifaced packages of the firm, primarily economic, financial, organizational, and sociological, as well as technological, legal, etc. (ibid, pp.32-36).

Naturally, in the course of evolution, such models became correspondingly more complicated and transformed. Originating at the dawn of industrialization, first in the form of small, mostly family-owned, trading companies, and then trading and manufacturing firms, by the end of the 19th and beginning of the 20th century, they acquired a more recognizable form of a manufacturing enterprise, including one that went abroad in form of MNC within the framework of Globalization 1.0 (G1.0 - Free trade). As a consequence, the first pre-war half of the 20th century produced a package of three basic and economic theories of the firm. Among them, the fundamental role belongs to the neoclassical approach of A. Marshall (Marshall, 1920). In which the company is considered as a black box, that has an individualized set of factors of production (labor and capital), capable of providing a stationary reproduction process, characterized by a constant flow input in the beginning and outputs at the end. The means of production determine the capital value of the firm, while the output determines its gross income, and with it minus costs, the firm's profit. At the same time, the main goal of the activity of such a company, within the framework of the trading logic, becomes profit maximization while minimizing costs, which is achieved by observing the equilibrium principle. In which the company provides a stationary output at stable prices when marginal cost is equal to marginal revenue. Thus, in the neoclassical approach, the attention of the company's management is focused on obtaining maximum profit through the price mechanism of balancing the volume of production (supply) according to market demand, as the basis of microeconomic equilibrium. From a methodological point of view, this neoclassical approach is based on 4 key principles: individualism, rationality, local equilibrium, and price mechanism (Walker, 2019).

Against the background of this rather static version, the more dynamic innovative approach was developed by J. Schumpeter in its English version for the first time and published in 1934 (Schumpeter,1934, (2008)). Within the framework of his approach the company, in its desire to maximize profits, is forced to organize and timely change its original system of innovation-oriented cyclic reproduction activities accordingly. Its factor base, in addition to the traditional external (exogenous), including natural resources, labor, and technology as the basis of productive capital, also includes an internal, endogenous development factor, the source of which is innovative entrepreneurial ability. Thanks to this factor, the firm acquires the ability to respond to the imperfection of the market equilibrium through both intra-firm transformation and making appropriate changes to the environment (Schumpeter, 1939), which today we would call the business ecosystem, and the changes themselves - institutional innovations. Thanks to such institutional innovations, it is possible to build horizontally integrated cluster technological chains that can quickly implement technological innovations in a cooperative approach, and at the same time reach new, higher levels of local equilibrium. At the same time, going beyond the initiating firm in this way, the implementation cycle of such technological and institutional innovations has a devastating effect on the existing production structure and institutional architecture of the business ecosystem, simultaneously generating innovation waves and encouraging others to innovate development.

A more accounting-oriented approach to the theory of the firm is the basis for Transaction Cost Theory (Coase, 1937). Within this framework, R. Coase highlights the distinction in understanding the term "firm" from an ideal economic perspective, particularly in terms of transaction costs and the time required for activities such as research, negotiation, enforcement, and coordination of contract preparations. This contrasts with the typical representation of real production processes. The theory posits that, through effective internal organization and strategic utilization of external transactions, a firm can produce goods at a lower cost than what the market offers. Additionally, it addresses the critical question of whether it is more advantageous to create a company or to purchase necessary goods from the market (the "Make or Buy" decision). Furthermore, it explores the limits of a company's growth, specifically when the total costs of external transactions and internal transactions equal the market price.

This triad of theories has indeed laid a predominantly neoclassical basis for ideas about a firm, where in the simplest case its owner is at the same time a rationally acting entrepreneur in the interests of maximizing profits, who has fairly complete information both about the production, technological and organizational and economic capabilities of his own company, and about needs, requirements, and conjuncture of the external market. From a theoretical point of view, we are talking about an idealistic picture of a firm seeking to find a local economic equilibrium in the external field of influence of market forces and price impulses, aimed at extracting maximum profit through the implementation of the marginalist principle. Within the framework of such a rather static picture and the simplest company, whose structure in the first approximation is considered as a black box, mainly exogenous factors are taken into account. While endogenous ones, related to the internal structure of the company, are only indicated in Schumpeter's innovative approach. It is clear that in reality the picture differs and often quite significantly, from the idealistic one. And the demand for accounting for such a reality began to grow rapidly in the post-war period of the formation of G2.0.

The global consequences of WWII and the needs of post-war reconstruction required the ordering of the international movement of goods and capital, which in turn led to both the complication of the very structure of the firms participating in such movement, and the need to adapt them to the requirements of the rules of the game in G2.0 conditions. The complication of the internal organization of the post-war firm required a distinction between its structure and the interest of various groups and motivations not only of owners but also of managers and other staff. Undoubtedly, all this was reflected in the market behavior of the firm, seeking to balance such interests and optimize this behavior. Therefore, the first works of this second wave, starting with the pioneering work of H. Simon (1947), and further work began as early as 1952 by Carnegie Mellon University (March 1958; Cayert and March 1963), formed the basis of the Behavioral theories of the firm. Within its framework, the firm ceases to be a black box, but is a system of a complex interaction between groups with different interests and motives, and the management of the firm is reduced not only and not so much to maximizing profits received on the foreign market, as ensuring a balance of interests and maintaining the internal unity of the company, as a result of which the problem of profit maximization is rather replaced by the problem of optimizing the main economic parameters of the company (profits, costs, and other people indicators) in conditions of information incompleteness.

The seminal paper of E. Penrose (1958) had a significant impact on the further evolution of scientific research in this area. Despite its descriptive nature, this approach goes beyond the behavioral one and proceeds from the activity structure of the firm, where its management acts as the main driving force and is quite creative at that. Moreover, the possibility of economic growth of the company is already laid here. Of course, thanks to investments in the expansion of its business activities. In this case, which is fundamentally important, it is necessary to consider already non-equilibrium processes.

The main building blocks of such a company capable of self-organized growth, in a slightly modified by the author form, are presented in Table 5.

Table 5. Explanation of the Edith Penrose's "The Theory of the Growth of the Firm"

The Concept of Firm and Its Purpose
1) Firms are institutions that are created by people to serve the purpose of people
2) Firms operate in a disequilibrium model of firm growth, and seek to maintain administrative coordination within a multistakeholder environment
The Firm as a Bundle of Resources and the Central Role of Managers

continued on following page

Table 5. Continued

The Concept of Firm and Its Purpose
3) The firm is a collection of productive resources and the services made available from these resources are the drivers of a firm's uniqueness
4) Managers play the central role—a catalyst role—in the resource-service conversion process
5) A firm's managers provide both entrepreneurial and managerial services. Versatility of managers' entrepreneurial services matters as they shape their creative imagination and vision for the firm
6) Managers with firm-specific experience are vital in identifying the subjective growth opportunity and executinggrowth projects for the firm
7) Managers' experiential knowledge of the firm's resources and their entrepreneurial imagination jointly shape how the firm "sees" the demand and which opportunities it will pursue
Unused/Underutilized Resources as Drivers of Growth, Diversification, and Innovation
8) Unused and underutilized productive services of resources are a key source of firm expansion, learning, innovation, and profitable growth
9) The specialized resources and the specialize use of resources lead to a firm's
diversification of products and services, which provide a basis for firms to achieve long-run survival and profitability
growth in a changing and competitive environment
Managerial Experience as a Key Bottleneck for the Rate of Firm Growth
10) Penrose dares to be different. By going beyond the economic research literature on firm growth, she asks a new research question. Instead of the conventional question: "What is the optimal size of
the firm?" She asks: What is the optimal growth rate of the firm? (1959, p. 2).
11) Managerial capability is the binding constraint that limits the growth of the firm – the so-called Penrose effect orPenrose theorem.
12) If a firm deliberately or inadvertently grows faster than the rate at which
managers and employees in the expanding organization can obtain the experience with each other and with the firm
that is necessary for the effective operation of the group, the efficiency of the firm will suffer.
Penrose Effect on Acquisitions and International Expansion as the Mechanisms for Firm Growth
13) There is a limit to the rate of firm growth via the expansion mode of acquisitions.
14) Availability of management capability also serves as a bottleneck for the rate of international growth. However, insome cases, acquisitions of subsidiaries in foreign countries can help to reduce the need for direct administrative co-ordination, and thus, the firm can grow at a higher rate than what is possible through organic international growth (greenfield entry form).

Source: authors modifications based on Yasemin Y.Kor, Joseph T. Mahoney, Enno Siemsen, Danchi Tan " Penrose's The Theory of the Growth of the Firm: An Exemplar of Engaged Scholarship" https://www.researchgate.net/publication/301774842_Penrose's_The_Theory_of_the_Growth_of_the_Firm_An_Exemplar_of_Engaged_Scholarship

Within the framework of this table, we will pay special attention to some important construction blocks of Edith Penrose's firm growth theory. First of all, this would seem to be an obvious statement that a company is built from people and for people (Item 1), which indirectly indicates that the potential of those who build a company and manage it should be explicitly taken into account because it is the underused part, as well as the unused part of the company's resources and production capacities, are the source of its further growth and expansion (Item 8). However, it is especially important to note the difference presented in (Item 5) between managerial and entrepreneurial functions, the main advantage of which is the ability to see, and therefore form the metaphysical foundations for making innovative decisions. From this part, it follows that managers are responsible for the stable market functioning of the firm, while the entrepreneurial component is responsible for innovations and their implementation in the interests of sustainable growth on an innovative basis.

Therefore, it is not surprising that the idea of E. Penrose of the key role of managers reflected in the Managerial Theories of the Firm. First of all, we are describing the work of W. Baumol (1959), who was the first to introduce the model of a structured firm to the world, where in the general case, the interests of managers and owners of the company do not coincide, since if the owners are interested in maximizing profits. Managers are in the stability of their position, maintaining current profitability and maximizing self-utility function. Of course, this has to be considered in the company's economic growth strategy and the choice of management tactics. Further development of this approach was carried out in the papers of R. Marris (1964;1998) and O. Williamson (1964;1970). All of them are characterized by a view of the firm as a vertically integrated complex entity consisting of many productive units, managed by salaried executives. Such a vertical hierarchy forms the structural framework of the internal organization (internalization) of the firm, the features of the use of funds and resources, and management decision-making. Together with the comparative advantages of the location, in general, this determines the specific benefits of the firm.

3.3. Family Tree of the Neoclassical FDI Models

During its existence, starting from the 1960s-70s, within the framework of IB, the Family tree of theoretical FDI models was developed, schematically presented in Fig. 2.

Figure 2. Family tree of major investment theories and models

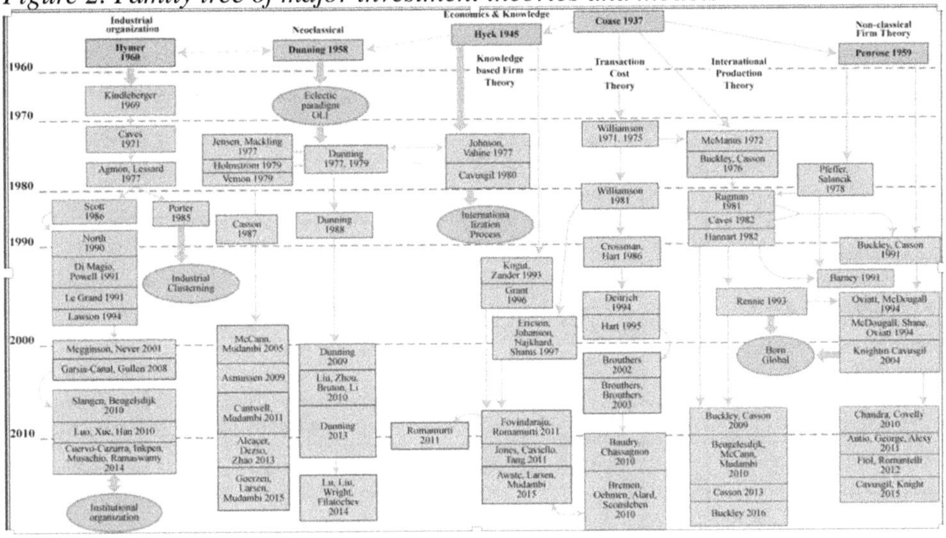

Source: authors

This whole motley palette of predominantly neoclassical theoretical models and approaches focuses attention on various aspects of a Complex Adaptive System (CAS) already in the case of a simple dyadic investment interaction of two firms in the Global Political Economy (GPE) space, not to mention more complex cases of multi-subject GVCs or GPNs. Of course, such diversity allows for a certain arbitrariness in the choice of the most suitable models for solving the tasks at hand. Some idea of the relative demand for different approaches can be obtained from the data in Table 6.

Table 6. Theoretical approaches to describing the investment expansion of the MNEs through OFDI into their subsidiaries abroad based on 645 theoretical and empirical articles

Theoretical approaches	Share of mentions Number of articles %		The main characteristics
Resource-based view	**144**	**22,3**	**FSAs* based on resource absorption, competence creation and technological and organizational capacities**
Behavioral theory of firm and MNE theory	70	10,8	FSAs based on global competitive advantages of the firm and multi-location configuration of the MNEs
Institutional-based perspective	99	15,3	FSAs and transformed **LSAs based on the global attractiveness and institutional advantages of the local innovation-oriented ecosystems as the complex adaptive systems of self-consistent interaction of the smart business entities
Network-based and Integration responsiveness approaches	86	13,4	DSAs and ***RSAs and transformed ****CSAs based on digital assets and digital resources
Other economic-based theories	86	13,4	
Other organizational and sociology-based theories	66	10,2	
No explicit theoretical anchoring	94	14,6	

Source: Meyer, Li&Schotter (2020), modified by the author
*FSAs-firm specific advantages
**LSAs-local specific advantages
***RSAs-region specific advantages
****CSAs-country specific advantages

As we can see from the data in this table, approximately a third of the articles are focused on a predominantly functional type of analysis in the resource-based and behavioral approach, and a little less than another third of the researchers' attention is paid to institutional and network approaches, and the last third cannot satisfactorily determine their initial theoretical and methodological basis. All this taken together shows that until the start of the COVID-19 pandemic, attempts to build a unified universal theory of the firm that can describe the dynamics of its economic growth, and even more development, due to the evolutionarily growing variety of factors to be taken into account, were not crowned with success. Although, to create theoretical and model tools for practical use, when MNCs developing their strategies for global investment expansion in the conditions of G3.0, and then G4.0, many models were developed that tried to take into account the multifaced nature of the multi-location enterprise. Perhaps the most typical and popular of them is the OLI model of J. Dunning, where the lack of a single, organic, and universal dynamic structure of the company is replaced by its Eclectic model, whose competitive advantages are constructed from three "building blocks": the benefits of Ownership, Location, and Internalization. From a methodological point of view, the totality of such models makes it possible to group objective, subjective, and motivational factors, respectively, determinants, drivers, and motives of an internationalizing MNC. However, mainly from the standpoint of an external observer and in the neoclassical phenomenological approach.

Meanwhile, there are several publications (see, for example, (Estola, 2014)) that pay attention to the logical inconsistency of the neoclassical theories of the firm, because the basic idea that a firm receives a constant profit while maximizing output does not leave room for its further economic growth and does not explain how the company finds its local, and even more global economic equilibrium, and attempts to mathematically build a dynamic model of the company conflict with its static versions. But even in this dynamic case, when mathematically modeling the individual economic behavior of a firm [Ibid], it is not possible to see the content to assess its potential and extract it from the depths of the tacit knowledge (Nonaka & Takeuchi, 1995). Meanwhile, the modern view of the firm and the management of its global competitiveness proceeds from the fact that "the primary task of managers consists in the conversation of tacit, human capital into explicit, structural capital" (Virtanen, 2011). However, this just implies not only the ability to mathematically describe the dynamic structure and features of the functioning of the company but also to understand the content. Only this kind of opportunity opens up a transition to the use of non-classical, quantum theoretical approaches, both to economics (see, for example: Rampling and Eddie, 2019) and management, which allowed "The Quantum Management Revolution", as it is for the first time, the Chinese company "HIER" demonstrated in practice (Zohar, 2022). At the same time, taking into account these deep-seated opportunities as sources of its inclusive innovative development are in itself insufficient for modeling its internationalization in the conditions of modern network-centric CAS (Chandra and Wilkinson,2017), where the trajectory of the firm's behavior is blurred, collective intelligence (CI) and norms of cooperative interactive interaction to achieve agreed goals.

Thus, we see that choosing an adequate theoretical and methodological basis for analyzing the current state, historical dynamics, and future needs of the Slovak economy for FDI and its own OFDI is indeed a non-trivial problem, both at the macro and micro levels. Of course, solving such a problem requires serious research efforts, especially taking into account the new opportunities of the DE, AI, and networks. One part of this problem is related to the need not only to expand the base of FDI models to a multilevel approach, capable of uniformly describing classical, non-classical, and post-non-classical cases of investment interactions, including multi-subject ones but also to make this description acceptable for AI.

The fundamental possibility for such solving is opened by the so-called 3x3 Matrix approach (Seniuk, 2023), the consideration of which is beyond the scope of this study. However, the second part, which is previously noted target of our approach, concerns a new mechanism for integrating a large complex of different knowledge for such TT, as well as the required new institutional and infrastructural means of such multi-level and multi-subject transformation within the framework of a holistic approach, without which sustainable inclusive development is hardly possible. This second part can be implemented by using the Triple Integration Model (TIM).

4. TRIPLE INTEGRATION MODEL AS A TRANSFORMATIVE KNOWLEDGE-BASED DIGITAL ENGINE FOR THE GLOBALLY INTEGRATED SUSTAINABLE DEVELOPMENT

As follows from the previous consideration, from a theoretical point of view, we are looking for a solution to a complex ESG transformation of a local CAS system capable of ensuring sustainable inclusive, and globally integrated development. Of course, this kind of approach requires the integration of relevant knowledge, competencies, and skills distributed in reality across subject-differentiated spheres of the education system, sector-oriented technology companies' sector-divided public administration, and local government. In addition, both general and specialized vocational education and knowledge are also distributed within the framework of a completely understandable vertical division into basic, secondary vocational, and higher levels (schools). Meanwhile, the modern cluster approach requires the integration of the entire complex of knowledge associated with its activities. Moreover, modern training of specialists at the level of secondary vocational education in the context of digitalization requires the involvement of knowledge from both the field of technological design and the field of IT and AI. At this level, it is necessary to obtain the required general knowledge (K) and Expertise (E), as well as acquire the necessary Skills (S). It is in this connection of K&E&S, and also the acquisition of practical experience (e), that the first integration within the framework of the general TI model, the basic diagram of which is shown in Fig. 3, consists.

Figure 3. The model of "triple integration" e-learning innovation education platform

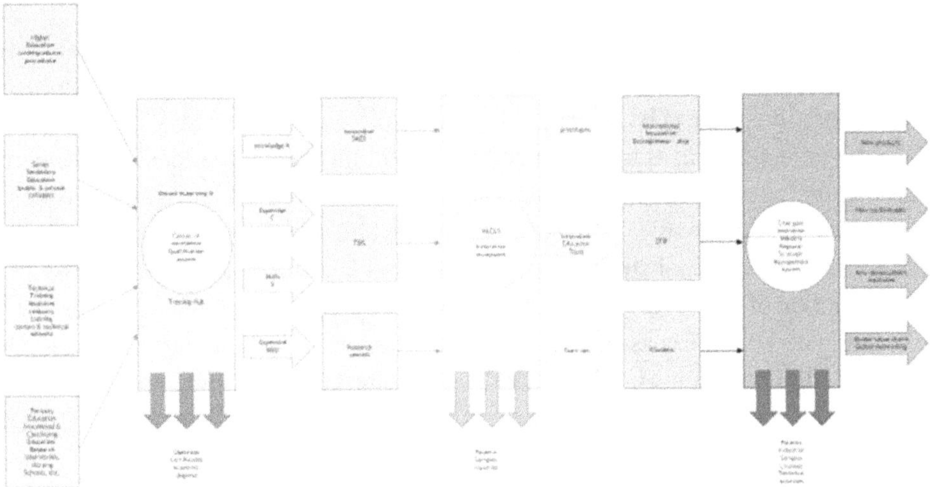

Here the left vertical row schematically shows the first K&E&S&e integration. In reality, this means the need for vertical integration of vocational training of workers based on secondary specialized education with elements of technological and ICT knowledge and skills from higher professional training. For example, training CNC (Computer Numerical Control) machine operators is no longer limited to pure operational aspects but require integration with knowledge and skills from process technology, software programming, and integration experience. The middle vertical row is intended for the integration of the codified external knowledge borrowed from the left row with the company's cultural-creative innovations originating from tacit knowledge (T), as well as contextual knowledge (C) extracted from the socio-cultural and cognitive sphere, integrated within the framework of an innovative startup project. Such a project is focused on the market commercialization of technological innovations and requires for its success a wider range of competencies and skills in social communication and managerial experience. From a fundamental point of view, it resembles the successful activities of a research university (U2.0) integrated with a technological business incubator (TBI). However, this kind of cooperation and integration can be organized in the form of a local PPP-based Digital Innovation Hub (DIH). Finally, the right vertical row represents the integration of complex K&E&S&T&C knowledge, skills, and experience (e) with strategic-oriented management (SM) and strategic DDM-based management (SG) within the framework of a holistic Global City (GS) or Global Region (GR). An entrepreneur university (U3.0), connected with the digital infrastructure for innovation industrialization within the framework of an SDG-driven regional strategy, can be considered as the globally integrated DIH and core of the ecosystem GS or GR.

In this case, U3.0 plays the role of an intelligence hub and integrator for innovation-driven MSMEs into GVCs. Being integrated with a full set of innovative development institutions, including TBI, science, and technological parks (SP&TP), such an SDG-driven ecosystem is transformed into U4.0, illustrating the ideal mechanism for TIM implementation. In combination with ESG-driven TT, such an ecosystem will be able to play the role of a global innovation hub (GS/GR), capable of not only transforming its regional structure of fixed capital and the efficiency of its use for the production of Gross Regional Product (GRP), but strategically managed process of creating new overseas assets through OFDI (and above all intangible and digital ones, including using own GIN and GPN), increasing Gross National Product (GNP) of the country. And of course, such a model can hardly work effectively without the use of AI.

5. DISCUSSION

The analysis of empirical trends carried out in Section 2 in the conceptual framework of Section 1, taking into consideration the theoretical and model approaches of Section 3 and in the context of the institutional construction TIM and TT from Section 4, allows us to generalize the results obtained as a platform for discussion.

1. As can be seen from Table 4, even the Czech Republic, which became a leader in V4 in terms of wealth per adult level ($82.2 thousand in 2021), during its membership in the EU was never able to reach the world average ($87.5 thousand), not to mention Slovakia with its $63.5 thousand. And this is even though in terms of the Economic Complexity Index Czechia ranks 6th in the world (E-CIGARETTES=1.75 in 2021) and Slovakia 12th (ECI=1.46), ahead of the USA (14th place) and China (18 places), and their ROWs are significantly higher than the world average (almost 2 times for the Czech Republic). This indicates that the underlying problem of insufficient economic dynamics of V4 economies is, at a minimum, structural in nature and cannot be solved only at the functional level using regulatory and investment policy. However, it is precisely the functional approach that is usually inherent in pragmatic policy.
2. This means that developing adequate responses to the global challenges of the time is impossible to do without the use of innovative model approaches, which are especially important in the context of interacting economies of different sizes and heterogeneous ESG environments, as in the case of Slovakia and China. Meanwhile, fairly high-quality analytical materials prepared, for example by the

National Bank of Slovakia (NBS), develop the traditional model approach for functional analysis, laid down at the beginning of the 21st century (see: Hoskova, 2001; Sabol and Hoskova, 2003). Modern Slovak analytics are presented in the same format (see, for example, the survey on Slovak FDI of Trading Economics 2024). Somewhat more detailed, but also in the spirit of macroeconomic analysis of empirical data, an in-depth review of Slovak economic dynamics was made by EC (2024), as well as in the study of the US Department of State (2024). In particular, the latter highlights 10 challenges facing Slovakia. Of these: Legacy dependence caused by diminishing Russian energy impact; High sensitivity to regional ED; weak public administration and ineffective judiciary; relatively limited rates of R&D; "Bran drain" and others. However, the formation of adequate responses to such challenges requires not only restructuring responses, but also institutional ones.

3. Given that Slovakia does not have its world-class MNEs, the situation with FDI into SMEs linkage is noteworthy (OECD 2022). The analysis shows that Slovak micro-enterprises are very weakly connected with innovations and R&D activity, while the share of innovative small-sized enterprises is 14% and reaches 24% for medium-sized ones, ahead of the European average (12% and 16%, respectively). Combined with a justified increase in attention to Slovakia's participation in GVC (Giorno 2019), especially taking into account the objective redetermination that condemns small economies to a low share of the added value created in the country (Banerjee and Zeman, 2020), this leaves no other choice than effective participation in these chains and GPNs of the innovation-driven SMEs. Moreover, the analysis suggests that prioritizing the intangible assets created there may play a leading role in improving Slovakia's position in GVCs (Durcova and Pekarcik, 2023), but this type of potential opportunities is primarily associated with high-tech startups and other innovative micro-enterprises. At the same time, the practical implementation of such potential requires high-quality national and regional innovation systems. Meanwhile, as the aforementioned OECD analysis showed, "the Slovak FDI-MSME policy system is fragmented".
4. From the above it follows that the traditional pragmatic response to the global innovative challenges facing Slovakia in the VUCA conditions is unlikely to change the direction of established trends. We need a different, asymmetrical, and non-trivial innovative model-based approach. In any case, the focus of this approach will one way or another be the effective participation of Slovak high-tech MSMEs in GVCs. However, such participation will require a special entity (like "Born Global") capable of consolidating potential participants and configuring innovation-oriented GVCs, as well as carrying out the necessary coordination/management functions for them. Typically, such functions, along

with investment ones, are performed by large, world-class MNEs. But since there are practically no such global players in Slovakia, a different path is needed. Fortunately, this hierarchical way of creating GVC under the control of MNE is only one of five possible ones (see, for example, Satoshi Inomata 2017, p.20). Fundamentally different prospect opens the so-called “market-type” of GVC, the configurator of which is a “lead company” as a new institutional subject corresponding to the U3.0 function, discussed in Section 4.

5. As has already been shown in Section 4, the lead company is primarily the operational modules within the framework of U3.0 as a core of an entire eco-system U4.0 built according to the TIM patterns. And it is clear that such a complex globally integrated SDG-driven inclusive firm-centric institutional construction is absent in the modern democratic society, and its creation will inevitably require PPP and ESG integration, then in this sense, the issues made in this section seem to form the framework of a platform for the discussion the proposed TIM-TT transition approach. Particularly important is the case of heterogeneous environments, usually observed on the border between countries from different civilizations and cultural areas and different regional integrative associations. In this spence, to a certain extent, a practical confirmation of the demand for this approach can be considered the project proposal of the Slovak Foreign Policy Association (SFPA) to create a cross-border Center SKUAC, connecting significantly different institutional and market spaces on both sides of the border with the EU (Duleba et el. 2024). A different and very promising opportunity for the practical implementation of the TIM-TT transition is opened by the European cross-border mechanism EGTC (European Groupings of Territorial Cooperation), which involves the creation of a joint managing entity as a configurator of such cooperation with legal powers in the territory of the EU (European Parliament 2006). Today such a mechanism as the European legal and organizational form can fully accommodate much of what was discussed in this research.

CONCLUSION

The analysis conducted in our study reveals that this research primarily addresses a problematic and staged character. Taking the Slovak Republic as an example, located on the Eastern border of the Eurozone, we uncover a serious issue regarding the post-industrial and post-pandemic restructuring of the economic landscape across the entire European continent. From the perspective of post-industrial transformation, since gaining membership in the European Union, Slovakia has unlike other partner countries, somewhat solidified its industrial priorities. It has slightly increased the share of manufacturing in its economy. This shift is largely attributed to a significant influx of Foreign Direct Investment (FDI), primarily from Germany, Czechia, and the USA, which has established Slovakia as the world's largest producer of cars per capita. However, despite entering the EU with the highest wealth per adult in the V4 group, Slovakia's economy has lagged behind the Czech Republic and Hungary over the past two decades. Current low economic growth, coupled with bleak prospects, has compelled the government to seek new methods and mechanisms for significantly improving the situation and achieving a sustainable development trajectory aligned with the 17 Sustainable Development Goals (SDGs).

As one of these alternatives, a strategic partnership with China is being considered, aimed mainly at further strengthening new industrial priorities, now associated with the production of electric vehicles. However, along with the great opportunities associated with attracting Chinese FDI, there are very serious potential risks of not so much improving as rather aggravating the trend of sliding to last place in the group ranking against the backdrop of Poland's growing economic pace. These risks are both objective in nature, associated with the influence of the Gravity Model (GM) on the distribution of added value as a result of trade and investment interaction between countries of different sizes in heterogeneous space, and subjective ones, caused by the shift in policy towards pragmatic interests with weakened scientific and methodological support necessary for funding non-trivial solutions and asymmetric innovative strategies. To a greater or lesser extent such problems, which are a consequence of serious differentiation of national capital and the uncertainty of the prospects for rapid growth of wealth per adult, are characteristic not only of Slovakia, but also of other V4 and CEE countries.

In this sense, our proposed conceptual firm-centric approach to the institutional designing of innovative SDG-driven and subject-oriented PPP-based local and regional ecosystems, implementing the TIM-TT transition, has a fairly universal significance. Intensively developing digitalization processes create the necessary tools for these, and the use of AI makes it possible to solve complex problems by taking into account the heterogeneity of different environments, which is especially important for cross-border cooperation. Ultimately, we are talking about opening up whole new layers of generating added value through the engagement of a huge number of MSMEs into innovative GVCs, focusing primarily on the industrialization of their technological innovations and thus transforming the quantitative and qualitative structure of distributed national capital, including the growth of its overseas components. Of course, on this path to implementing TT in the ESG space, there will be a lot of obstacles, including the previously noted weakness of the public administration, fragmentation of innovation policy and national and regional innovation systems, as well as the brain drain against the backdrop of the shares of innovative SMEs outpacing the EU's even, but simultaneously there are several key potential attractors, mainly related to the fact that in the case of creating such a cross-border TIM-based Digital Infrastructure for post-Industrial transformation, clustering, and networking are created, capable of ensuring inclusive and synchronized co-development of the participant, the growth rate of wealth per adult due to digital and intangible assets promises to record high. In this case, such cross-border DIHs can serve as a "reverse trap"; for once-escaped brains and capital. However, this refers to the future, and the road to its implementation has many steps, but like any road, it begins with the first step. For us, this step is the formulation of a scientific and methodological problem and its justification in conceptual completeness, to arouse interest in consolidating joint efforts to deepen and clarify their understanding and further cooperation in resolving them.

ACKNOWLEDGMENT

Funded by the EU NextGenerationEU through the Recovery and Resilience Plan for Slovakia under the project No. 09I03-03-V01-00084. As well scientific research project IGA BUEM Nr. 1/2023-M „A Study of the Motives, Drivers and Determinants of OFDI from China to the EU: the case of Chinese OFDI in Slovak Republic“

REFERENCES

Ahmad, N., & Primi, A. (2017). *From domestic to regional to global: Factory Africa and Factory Latin America?* In: Global Value Chain Development Report 2017. Measuring and Analyzing the Impact of GVCs on Economic Development. The World Bank. https://www.wto.or/english/res_/booksp_e/gvcs_report_2017. pdf

Ahmad, N., & Primi, A. (2017). *From domestic to regional to global: Factory Africa and Factory Latin America?* In: Global Value Chain Development Report 2017. Measuring and Analyzing the Impact of GVCs on Economic Development. The World Bank. https://www.wto.org/English/res_e/booksp_e/gvcs_report_report_2017.pdf

Ahn, J., Habib, A., Malacrino, D., & Presbitero, A. F. (2023, April 5). Fragmenting Foreign Direct Investment Hits Emerging Economies Hardest. https://www.imf.org/en/Blogs/Articles/2023/04/05/fragmenting-foreign-direct-investment-hits-emerging-economies-hardest

AList. (2022). PREDICTIONS 2022. Disruptive Forces Necessitate Bold Decisions. https://www.alistdaily.com/strategy/Forrester-2022-predictions-guid

Arthur, W. B. (1999). Complexity and the economy. *Science*, 284(5411), 107–109. DOI: 10.1126/science.284.5411.107 PMID: 10103172

Badarinza, C., Ramadorai, T., & Shimizu, C. (2022). Gravity, counterparties, and foreign investment. *Journal of Financial Economics*, 145(2, 2, part A), 132–152. DOI: 10.1016/j.jfineco.2021.09.011

Baier, S., & Standaert, S. (2024). Gravity, globalization and time-varying heterogeneity. *European Economic Review*, 163(April), 104679. DOI: 10.1016/j.euroecorev.2024.104679

Baumol, W. J. (1959). *Business Behavior, Value and Growth.* Macmillan.

Bhandari, K. R., Zamborsky, P., Ranta, M., & Salo, J. (2023, August). Digitalization, Internationalization and firm performance: A resource-orchestration perspective on new OLI advantages. *International Business Review*, 32(4), 102135. DOI: 10.1016/j.ibusrev.2023.102135

Byrne, D. M. (2022). The Digital Economy and Productivity. Finance and Economic Discussion Series 2022-038. Washington: Board of Governors of the Federal Reserve System. DOI: 10.17016/feds.2022.038

Cai, J., Yuan, L., Hong, G., & Chen, C. (2022). The approach of data factor participating in value creation- A general equilibrium analysis based on the general theory of value. *Journal of Management World*, 38(07), 108–121.

Can, H., & Paskaleva, M. (2017). Macroeconomic determinants of CDS: The case of Europe. New knowledge. *Journal of Science*, 6(3), 1080–1096.

CEIC Data. (2021). Chinal Capacity Utilization Rate. https://www.ceicdata.com/en/china/capacity-utilization-rate

Chandra, Y., & Wilkinson, I. F. (2017). Firm internationalization from a network-centric complex-systems perspective. *Journal of World Business*, 52(5), 691–701. DOI: 10.1016/j.jwb.2017.06.001

Chang, J., Lan, Q., Tan, W., Chen, H., Lou, J., & Duan, Y. (2023). Research on the Impact of Digital Economy of Manufacturing Total Factor Productivity. *Sustainability (Basel)*, 15(7), 5683. DOI: 10.3390/su15075683

Coase, R. H. (1937). The Nature of the Firm. *Economica*, 4(16), 386–405. DOI: 10.1111/j.1468-0335.1937.tb00002.x

Cong, L. W., Wei, W., Xie, D., & Xhang, L. (2022). Endogenous growth under multiple uses of data. *Journal of Economic Dynamics & Control*, 141(August), 104395. DOI: 10.1016/j.jedc.2022.104395

Cyert, R. M., & March, J. G. (1963). *A Behavioral Theory of the Firm.*

Degain, C., Meng, B., & Wang, Z. (2017). *Recent trends in global trade.* In: Global Value Chains Development Report 2017. Measuring and Analyzing the Impact of GVCs on Economic Development. The World Bank. https://www.wto.org/english/res_e/booksp_e/gves_report_2017.pdf

Delios, A. (2017). The Death and Rebitrh (?) of International Business Research. *Journal of Management Studies*, 54(3), 391–397. DOI: 10.1111/joms.12222

Dollar, D., & Thornton, J. L. (2017). *Executive summary.* In: Global Value Chain Development Report 2017. Measuring and Analyzing the Impact of GVCs on Economic Development, 1-36. https://www.wto.org/english/res_e/booksp_e/gvcs_report_2017.pdf

Duleba, A., Brezani, P., Oravcova, V. (2024). Slovak-Ukrainian Cross-Border Center (SKUAC). SFPA.

Dunning, J. H. (1981). Explaining the international direct investments position of countries: Toward a dynamic or development approach. *Weltwirtschaftliches Archiv*, 117(30), 30–64. DOI: 10.1007/BF02696577

Dunning, J.H., Narula, R. (1996). The Investment Development Path revisited. *Foreign Direct Investment and Governments: Catalysis for Economic Restructuring,* 1-41.

Durcova, J., & Pekarcik, M. (2023). Role intangible assets in global value chains: Evidence from the Slovak Republic. *Strategic Management*, 28(4), 31–40. DOI: 10.5937/StraMan2300036D

EC2023. Economic Commentary. (2023). How Has the Pandemic Impacted Inflation. https://blog.nationalwidefinancial.com/market-economy/how-has-the-pandemic-impacted-inflation

EC2024. (2024). *In-depth Review*. DOI: 10.2765/642448

Economics, T. (2024). Slovak Foreign Direct Investment. https://tradingeconomics.com/slovakia/foreign-direct-investment

Estola, M. (2014). The Neoclassical Theory of a Firm: Correction for its errors. *Hyperion International Journal of Econophisics & New Economy*, 7(1), 7–21.

European Commission. (2020). Support for SME Internalization beyond the EU-.https://evening.europe.eu/growth/smes/sme-strategy/assets-to-markets/internationalization/support-tools_en

European Parliament. (2006). European Groupings of Territorial Cooperation (EGTCs). Factsheets of the European Union. https://www.europarl.europa.eu/factsheets/en/sheet/94/Europa-groupings-of-territorial-cooperation-egtc

Fabuš, M., & Csabay, M. (2018). State aid and investment: Case of Slovakia. *Enterpreneurship and Sustainability Issues*, 6(1), 369–377. DOI: 10.9770/jesi.2018.6.1(23)

fDi Intelligence. (2023). Strategic Industries buck post-Covid Investment slump. https://www.fdiintelligence.com/content/data-trends/strategic-industries-buck-postcovid-investment-slump-82621?

fDi Intelligence. (2023). Wave of mega projects mounts in 2022. https://www.fdiintelligence.com/content/data-trends/wave-of-mega-projects-mounts-in-2022-82551

Fu, C. (2017). New structural economics - A way to unscramble via endogenous aggregate production function by PDE. *Economic Review (Kansas City, Mo.)*, 03, 81–103.

GFM. (2024). Largest Companies in the World. Global Finance Magazine, September 18, 2024. https://gfmag.com/data/biggest-companies-in-the-world

Global Times. (2023). China issue 15 measures to help SMEs stabilize growth, adjust structure. https://www.globaltimes.cn/page/202301/1283861.shtml

Grossman, G., & Helpman, E. (1991). *Innovation and Growth in the Global Economy*. MIT Press.

Hale, G., Leer, J. C., & Nechio, F. (2023). Inflationary effects of fiscal support to households and firms. National Bureau of Economic Research, 30906. https://www.nber.org/w30906

Holland, J. H. (2014). *Complexity: A very short introduction*. Oxford University Press. DOI: 10.1093/actrade/9780199662548.001.0001

Hulten, C. R. (2010). Growth Accounting. Handbook of the Economics of Innovation, 2, 987-1031.

IEA. (2022). Unlocking the Potential of Distributed Energy Resources. https://www.iea.org/reports/unlocking-the-potential-of-distributed-energy-resources

IEA. (2023). World Energy Investment 2023. https://iea.glob.core.windows.net/assets/8834d3af-af60-4df0-9643-72e2684f7221/WorldEnergyinvestment2023.pdf

IMF. (2021). Fiscal Monitor Database of Country Fiscal Measures in Response to the COVID-19 Pandemic. https://www.imf.org/en/Topics/inf-and-covid19/Fiscal-Policies-Database-in-Response-to-COVID-19

IMF. (2023). World Economic Outlook. https://www.imf.org/en/Publications/WEO

IMF. (2024). World Economic Outlook. Policy Pivot, Rising Threats.

Inomata, S. (2017). *Analytical framework for global value chains An Overview.* Global Value Chain Development Report 15-35. https://www.wto.org/english/res_e/booksp_e/gvcs_report_2017.pdf

Isard, W. (1956). *Location and Space-economy; a General Theory Relating to Industrial Location, Market, Land Use, Trade and Urban Structure.* Technology Press Massachusetts Institute of Technology and Wiley.

Jia, W., Collins, A., & Liu, W. (2023). Digitalization and Economic Growth in the new classical and new structural economics perspectives. Springer Link. *Digital Economy and Sustainable Development*, 1(1), 5. DOI: 10.1007/s44265-023-00007-0

Joint Statement. (2024). Joint Statement between the People's Republic of China and the Slovak Republic on the Establishment of a Strategic Partnership. November 1, 2024. https://www.fmprc.gov.cn/eng/zu/go/202411/f20241101_11520047.html

Korcok, I. (2022). Rules based international order at a time of great peril: Slovak foreign policy respinces. In *Yearbook of Slovak Foreign Policy 2021* (pp. 6–21). SFPA.

Korsita, B., Cania, L., Lazaj, A., & Pendi, L. (2024). An Application of the Gravity Model: Exploring Foreign Direct Investment in the Balkan Region. *Revue d'Economie Financiere*, 21, 2036–2041. DOI: 10.55365/1923.x2023.21.219

Li, Z., & Xizhen, Z. (2020). Political economic analysis of data participating in distribution as production function. *Study & Exploration*, 01, 109–115.

Lucas, R.Jr. (1988). On the mechanism of economic development. *Journal of Monetary Economics*, 22(1), 3–42. DOI: 10.1016/0304-3932(88)90168-7

Macrotrends. (2024). Trade to GDP ratio by country. https://www.macrotrends.net/global-metrics/countries/ranking/trade-gdp-ratio

March, J. G. (1958). A Behavioral Theory of Decision Making. *The Personnel Administrator*, 21(3), 8–10.

Marris, R. (1964). *The Economic Theory of 'Managerial' Capitalism.* Macmillan. DOI: 10.1007/978-1-349-81732-0

Marris, R. (1998). Managerial Theories of the Firm. In *Managerial Capitalism in Retrospect.* Palgrave Macmillan. DOI: 10.1057/9780230376168_5

Marshall, A. (1920). *Principal of Economics.* Macmillan.

MGI. 2020, October 13. Digital Challenges in the next normal in Central and Eastern Europe. McKinsey Report 2020. https://mckinsey.com/business-functions/McKinsey-digital/our-insights/digital-challenges-in-the-next-normal-in-Central-and-eastern-europe

Miroshnychenko, I., Kravchenko, T., & Drobyna, Y. (2021). Forecasting electricity generation from renewable sources in developing countries (on the case of Ukraine). *Neuro-Fuzzy Modeling Techniques in Economics*, 10(10), 164–198. DOI: 10.33111/nfmte.2021.164

Moody's Analytics. (2022). Global Fiscal Policy in the Pandemic. https://www.moodysanalytics.com/-/media/article/2022/global-fiscal-policy-in-the-pandemic.pdf

Narula, R., & Dunnung, J. H. (2010). Multinational enterprises, development and globalization: Some clarifications and a research agenda. *Oxford Development Studies*, 38(3), 263–287. DOI: 10.1080/13600818.2010.505684

Nonaka, I., & Takeuchi, H. (1995). *The Knowledge-Creating Company - How Japanese Companies Create the Dynamics of Innovation*. Oxford University Press. DOI: 10.1093/oso/9780195092691.001.0001

OECD. (2022). Strengthening FDI and SME linkage in the Slovak Republic. https://www.oecd.org/en/publications/strengthening-fdi-and-sme-linkages-in-the-slovak-republic_972946f5-en.html

Penrose, E. (1958). *The Theory of the Growth of the Firm. Oxford: Basil Blackwell.* John Wiley.

Radicic, D., Borovic, Z., & Trivic, J. (2023). Total factor productivity gap between the "New" and "Old" Europe: An industry-level perspective. *Post-Communist Economies*, 35(7), 770–795. DOI: 10.1080/14631377.2023.2236868

Ramsey, F. (1928). A mathematical theory of saving. *Economic Journal (London)*, 38(152), 543–559. DOI: 10.2307/2224098

Romer, P. (1986). Increasing returns and long-run growth. *Journal of Political Economy*, 94(5), 1002–1037. DOI: 10.1086/261420

Ruogu, L. (2008). *Institutional Suitability and Economic Development. Based on Practices in China*. China Economic Publishing House.

Sawitri, K. A., & Brennan, L. (2023). The investment development path literature: A review and research agenda. *Management Review Quarterly*, 73(4), 1825–1872. DOI: 10.1007/s11301-022-00287-4

Schumpeter, J. A. (1939). *Business Cycles. A theoretical, Historical and Statistical Analysis of the Capitalist Process*. McGraw-Hill Book Company.

Schumpeter, J. A. (2008). The Theory of Economic Development: As Inquiry into Profits, Capital, Credit, Interest and the Business Cycle. Transaction Publishers. (Original publication 1934)

Seniuk, N. (2022). Russian-Chinese trade: Current trends and prospects. *Baltic RIM Economies Review.*, (4), 48–49.

Seniuk, N., & Fabus, M. (2023). Theory of the firm, FDI, and development in the light of the global challenges: Modern firms in the era of digitalisation and green transition. Optimizing Energy Efficiency During a Global Energy Crisis, 307-326.

Seniuk, N., & Hudakova, M. (2023). Theory of foreign direct investment in light of the global innovation challenges. Public Administration and Regional Development.

Seniuk N.Y., Maltseva O.A., Schreiber N.H., & Hart A.K. (2022). Comparative analysis of the investment policy of Russia and China in Central Asia (2009-2020). International Business Magazine, 2(2).

Seniuk, Y. (2017). Transborder multi-level Digital interactive education-training Platform for Innovation-oriented co-development. Proceedings of the 15th International Conference on Emerging e-Learning Technologies and Applications ICETA2017. DOI: 10.1109/ICETA.2017.8102526

Shuyan, L., & Fabuš, M. (2019). Study on the spatial distribution of China's Outward Foreign Direct Investment in EU and its influencing factors. *Entrepreneurship and Sustainability Issues*, 6(3), 1080–1096. DOI: 10.9770/jesi.2019.6.3(16)

Shuyan, L., & Fabus, M. (2019). The impact of OFDI reverse technology spillover on China's technological progress: Analysis of provincial panel data. *Journal of International Students*, 12(4), 325–336. DOI: 10.14254/2071-8330.2019/12-4/21

Simon, H. A. (1947). *Administrative Behavior. A study of decision-making process in administrative organizations*. Macmillan.

Simon, H. A. (1957). *Models of Man*. John Wiley & Sons.

Solow, R. M. (1956). A Contribution to the Theory of Economic Growth. *The Quarterly Journal of Economics*, 70(1), 65–94. DOI: 10.2307/1884513

Statistsa. (2023). Global gross domestic product (GDP) at current prices from 1985 to 2028.https://www.statista.com/statistics/268750/global-gross-domestic-product-gdp

Strazay, T. (2022). The metamorphoses of Central Europe. In *Yearbook of Slovakia's Foreign Policy 2021* (pp. 108–122). SFPA.

Suszynski, C. (2013). *Business Enterprise. The Integration of Approaches*. Oficyna Wudawnicza Szkola Glowna Handlowa w Warszawie.

SYSR2024| Statistical Yearbook of the Slovak Republic. (2024). Statistical Office of the Slovak Republic. https://slovak.statistics.sk/wo's/portal

Tienbergen, J. (1962). An Analysis of World Trade Flows. In Tienbergen, J. (Ed.), *Shaping the World Economy*. Twentieth Century Fund.

Tinbergen, J. (1942). Zur Theorie der Langfristigen Wirtschaftsentwicklung. *Weltwirtschaftliches Archiv*, 55, 541–549.

UNCTAD. (2022). World Investment Report 2022. https://unctad.org/publication/world-investment-report-2022

UNCTAD. (2023). World Investment Report 2023. Investing in Sustainable Energy for All.https://unctad.org/system/files/official-document/wir2023_en.pdf

UNCTAD. (2023). Investment Trends Monitor (Issue 44, January 2023). https://unctad.org/system/files/official-document/diaeiainf2023d1_en.pdf

US Department of State. (2024). Investment Climate Statements: Slovakia. https://www.state.gov/reports/2024-investment-climate-statements/slovakia

Virtanen, I. (2011). Externalization of tacit knowledge implies a simplified theory of cognition. *Journal of Knowledge Management Practice*, 12(3), 139–145.

Walker, P. (2019). The Theory of the Firm. An overview of the economic mainstream.

Williamson, O. (1964). *The Economics of Discretionary Behavior: Managerial Objectives in a Theory of the Firm*. Prentice-Hall.

Williamson, O. (1970). *Corporate Control and Business Behavior*. Prentice-Hall.

Worldscience. (2023). Industrial Overcapacity and Duplicate Construction in China: Introduction. https://www.worldscience.com/doi/pdf/10.1142/9789813277281_0001.pdf

Xie, B., Yang, C., Song, W., Song, L., & Wang, H. (2023). The impact of environmental regulation on capacity utilization of China's manufacturing industry: An empirical research based on the sector level. *Ecological Indicators*, 148, 110085. DOI: 10.1016/j.ecolind.2023.110085

Xu, X., & Zhao, M. (2020). Data capital and economic growth path. *Economic Research Journal*, 55(10), 38–54.

Zohar, D., & Zohar, D. (2022). The Tao of Quantum Management. Zero Distance: Management in the Quantum Age, 71-80.

Chapter 8
Interconnection of Digital, Cultural, and Strategic Transformations on the Balkan Peninsula

Nikolay Todorov Dolchinkov
https://orcid.org/0000-0002-6171-6083
Vasil Levski National Military University, Veliko Tarnovo, Bulgaria

ABSTRACT

A brief overview and analysis of the digital, cultural, and strategic transformation and the relationship between each transformation is made. A SWOT analysis is made indicating positive and negative sides and how the gaps should be corrected. The advantages of each transformation, the method of implementation, and the role of state regulation in implementing the transformations are examined. An algorithm for implementing each of the three transformations is indicated and how they complement each other in their implementation. The implementation of the three transformations in Bulgaria and the countries of the Balkan Peninsula is described, and good practices and weaknesses are also indicated, as well as prospects for implementation in view of the specifics of the region.

DOI: 10.4018/979-8-3693-9435-9.ch008

INTRODUCTION

Digital transformation is a process of broader integration of existing digital technologies into all aspects of business activities and the economy, requiring fundamental changes in technology, culture, operations and principles for creating new products and services.

In order to maximize the use of new technologies and their rapid implementation not only in the economy, but also in all areas of human activity, enterprises must abandon their previous foundations and completely transform processes and work models, which, however, also carries certain risks.

This process means the gradual elimination of outdated technologies, the maintenance of which can be expensive for enterprises, as well as a change in culture, which must now support the acceleration of processes provided by digital transformation and technological revolution.

Digital transformation is a popular topic at the current moment of development of society and is a subject of discussion among technical experts, but if we have to talk more specifically, it has been talked about for several decades and we can say that its history is too short. However, in different cases the term digital transformation does not always mean the same thing and its different interpretations are possible. At the very beginning, a few decades ago, digital transformation was understood as the storage of traditional data forms in digital format. This is only one of the areas of digital transformation, but in the modern world this concept is much broader than the digital format and its content already has a completely different meaning (Wtat is, 2023).

It also includes the use of technologies such as cloud spaces, cloud computing, artificial intelligence and big data to improve the efficiency and competitiveness of enterprises. Digital transformation also changes the way companies interact with their customers, providing more personalized and efficient services and providing significantly greater opportunities.

Digital transformation brings significant benefits to the economy, business and society. Here are some of its main advantages:

1. Process optimization: New technologies allow the automation of routine tasks and the elimination of unnecessary steps, which leads to more efficient and flexible business processes and reduced production times.
2. Improved customer service: Digital technologies provide opportunities for more personalized and faster service, which increases customer satisfaction.

3. New revenue streams: The implementation of digital technologies opens up new business models and ways to generate revenue that were not previously possible. This generates new opportunities for implementing business ideas and expanding potential customers and their willingness to purchase our products.
4. Increased competitiveness: Companies that successfully implement digital transformation can better adapt to market changes and remain competitive. This significantly increases their flexibility and opportunities for restructuring production and the range of products offered.
5. Improved communication and collaboration: Digital tools facilitate communication and collaboration both within the organization and with external partners. This reduces the time for production and sales of products (B. Talin, 2023).

When most companies realized all the possibilities for using digitized data, they began to develop processes for these purposes. From that moment on, digital technologies began to develop rapidly, and the ability to quickly implement them directly determines the competitiveness of companies.

Businesses are rapidly replacing traditional interaction processes with digital ones, using the most advanced technologies. These processes are very dynamic and technologies are developing in a fairly short time. Very often, transformation occurs not because businesses want its application, but because they need it in order to survive and develop. Today, the market has increased the demand for effective digital technologies for businesses, and businesses that have not been able to adapt to the new model for digital consumers will most likely cease to exist (What is, 2023). Thus, those businesses that transform are significantly more viable than those that continue to work on old technologies and do not use digitalization.

Before the pandemic, Kazakhstan was one of the pioneers in Central Asia in the implementation of digital technologies – within the framework of the Digital Kazakhstan program, launched in December 2017. The country was also among the first in the region to launch e-government services back in 2008. As a result, in recent years, new laws on public services and new technologies have been adopted to legalize the electronic status, while the e-government system already provides more than 83% of public services (Zerde, 2020). In the recently published UN e-Government Development Index (EGDI), Kazakhstan is in 29th place, significantly up from 39th place in 2018. It is also among the countries with very high levels of e-participation and open government index (UN, 2020).

In 2019, Kyrgyzstan adopted the concept of the national digital transformation program "Digital Kyrgyzstan 2019-2023" and declared 2019 the "Year of Regional Development and Digitalization of Kyrgyzstan". Prior to this, in 2017, the government adopted the digital transformation program "Taza Koom", which also aimed to improve the national digital infrastructure. Although the country has problems with providing basic internet connections due to limited coverage and high prices, Kyrgyzstan's e-government system, e-kyzmat, has been steadily expanding its e-services to the population, planning to provide 80% of government services electronically by 2023 (Soltobaev, 2020). Currently, in the EGDI ranking, Kyrgyzstan ranks 83rd with a high EGDI and a high e-participation index, while the Open Government Data Index is rated as average (UN, 2020). Meanwhile, Uzbekistan is developing the "Digital Uzbekistan 2030" program. In his latest address to the nation, President Mirziyoyev outlined the transition to a digital economy for the next five years and called 2020 the "Year of Science, Education, and Development of the Digital Economy". While only 30% of government services are currently connected to e-government, a presidential decree from April 2020 envisages the integration of most services into the electronic system in the near future (Sputnik, 2020). In the EGDI ranking, the country ranks 87th with very high scores on e-participation and open government data (UN, 2020).

Tajikistan introduced its "Concept for the Formation of Electronic Government in the Republic of Tajikistan (2012-2020)" in 2011 and divided its implementation into three stages, yet the country is significantly behind schedule in providing e-government services. Low access to the Internet due to the inability to own electronic devices and high connection costs, including a 5% excise tax on the Internet, in addition to the lack of ICT infrastructure throughout the country, hinders the implementation of the program (Abdujaborov, 2019). In fact, as of 2020, only 26% of the population is connected to the internet (Data Portal, 2020). Accordingly, Tajikistan is ranked 133rd in the EGDI with an average EGDI and e-Participation index, and a low Open Government Data index.

Turkmenistan announced its "Concept for the Development of the Digital Economy until 2025" in 2019 and adopted a law on electronic document management and digital services in March 2020. The government intends to implement an electronic document management system in 2021, and President Gurbanguly Berdimuhamedov has instructed responsible officials to speed up the launch of the e-government system (CentralAsia.news, 2020). However, due to the low level of ICT infrastructure and connectivity issues, internet penetration in the country remains significantly low. Among the 193 UN member countries included in the EGDI, Turkmenistan ranks 158th with a low level of e-participation and open government data. In addition, according to Datareportal, only 1.2% of the population uses social media, indicating a low level of digital literacy among the population.

Thus, although the governments of Central Asian countries are developing their national digital strategies, it is difficult to implement the digital agenda without adequate ICT infrastructure. According to the World Bank, Central Asian states suffer from poor internet quality and expensive connectivity due to an incomplete regulatory framework, low levels of private investment, limited use of ICT, limited regional integration, and lack of connectivity to global internet traffic that bypasses Central Asian states (Navas-Sabater, 2019). As shown in the figure below, the level of internet penetration and the number of internet and mobile users in the region vary significantly across countries. According to Datareportal, as of January 2020, Kazakhstan has the highest internet penetration rate – 79%.

Digital transformation in China, South Korea, and Japan is a key factor in the economic and technological development of these countries.

China is focusing on radical changes in all spheres of life through the intensive implementation of digital, communication, and new manufacturing technologies. China's digital economy is growing at an average rate of 15.9% per year and accounts for a significant portion of the country's GDP1. Key technological trends include the development of new materials, the Industrial Internet of Things (IIoT), and 5G networks1.

South Korea is a leader in 5G technologies and artificial intelligence. The country is actively investing in smart cities and autonomous vehicles. South Korea is also developing digital platforms for healthcare and education, which is contributing to improving the quality of life of its citizens.

Japan is distinguished by innovations in robotics and automation. The country is also investing in IoT and artificial intelligence, aiming to create smart factories and smart homes. Japan is also developing digital solutions for its aging population, such as robots for elderly care.

Digital transformation in these countries is not only improving economic efficiency, but also creating new opportunities for innovation and sustainable development. If you have specific questions about any of these countries, don't hesitate to ask!

China's digital transformation is impressive, but it is not without its challenges. Here are some of the main difficulties the country faces:

Regulation and control: Chinese authorities are striving to strike a balance between promoting innovation and maintaining social stability. This has led to strict regulations that can sometimes limit the development of new technologies and business models.

Cybersecurity: With increasing digitalization, cybersecurity is becoming increasingly important. China must address the growing threats of cyberattacks and protect its digital infrastructures.

Inequality in access to technology: Despite significant progress, there are regions in China that still lag behind in terms of access to modern technology and the internet. This creates a digital divide between urban and rural areas.

Investment and innovation: Although China is a leader in many technological areas, maintaining a high level of investment and innovation is a constant challenge. Companies must continue to invest in research and development to remain competitive.

Global Competition: Chinese technology companies face intense competition in the global market. They must adapt to different regulatory environments and consumer preferences in different countries.

These challenges require coordinated efforts from the government, businesses, and society to ensure the sustainable development of China's digital economy.

Southeast Asia's digital transformation is a dynamic process that spans multiple countries and industries. Here are some key aspects and challenges in the region:

Key Trends

Artificial Intelligence (AI) and Cloud: Singapore is leading the way in the region with new initiatives such as HCLTech's AI/Cloud Native Lab, which will open in 2025. This lab will support the development of AI strategies and cloud technologies, while fostering collaboration with local educational institutions.

Smart Cities: Many countries in the region, including Malaysia and Thailand, are investing in smart cities that use IoT (Internet of Things) and other digital technologies to improve urban infrastructure and services.

E-Government: Countries such as Vietnam and Indonesia are actively developing e-government services to improve access to public services and increase the efficiency of administration.

Challenges

Infrastructure: Despite progress, many countries in the region still face challenges related to underdeveloped digital infrastructure, especially in rural areas2.

Cybersecurity: With increasing digitalization, cybersecurity is becoming increasingly important. The region needs to address the growing threats of cyberattacks and protect its digital infrastructures.

Technology Inequality: There are significant disparities in access to modern technologies across different social and economic groups, creating a digital divide.

Examples of Successful Initiatives

Singapore: Singapore's National AI Strategy is an example of successful integration of AI across sectors, including healthcare and transportation.

Malaysia: Kuala Lumpur's Smart Cities Program includes projects for intelligent traffic management and energy efficiency.

Southeast Asia's digital transformation continues to accelerate, creating new opportunities for economic growth and social development.

Digital transformation in India, Pakistan, and Iran is a key driver of economic and social development in these countries. Here are some key aspects and challenges for each:

India is a leader in digital transformation in the region, with the government actively supporting initiatives such as Digital India. Key highlights include:

E-Government: Developing platforms to deliver public services online.

FinTech: Expanding access to financial services through mobile applications and digital platforms1.

Education and Health: Implementing digital solutions to improve access and quality of education and health services.

Pakistan is also making significant strides in digital transformation, although it faces some challenges:

Infrastructure: Developing internet infrastructure and increasing access to high-speed internet.

Education: Implementing online education platforms to improve access to education in remote areas.

Cybersecurity: Strengthening measures to protect digital data and infrastructure.

Iran is also actively working on its digital transformation, despite international sanctions and other challenges:

E-government: Developing platforms to deliver public services online.

Telecommunications: Expanding internet infrastructure and increasing access to high-speed internet.

Startups: Supporting innovation and the development of start-ups in the technology sector.

Digital transformation in these countries is key to their future development and competitiveness in the global market.

Digital transformation in Africa is a key factor for the continent's economic and social development. Here are some key aspects and challenges:

Key Trends

Development of internet infrastructure: Many African countries are investing in expanding internet access, such as high-speed networks and mobile technologies. This is particularly important for improving connectivity in rural areas.

Financial technology (FinTech): Mobile payments and digital financial services are widespread in countries such as Kenya and Nigeria, making it easier for the population to access financial services.

E-government: Many governments in Africa are implementing e-services to improve access to public services and increase the efficiency of administration.

Challenges

Limited access to electricity: Many regions in Africa still have limited access to electricity, which hinders the adoption of digital technologies.

Low level of digital literacy: The lack of digital skills among the population is a significant challenge that requires investment in education and training.

Cybersecurity: With increasing digitalization, cybersecurity is becoming increasingly important. African countries need to address the growing threat of cyberattacks and protect their digital infrastructures.

Examples of Successful Initiatives

Kenya: M-Pesa, the mobile payment system, is an example of a successful FinTech initiative that has transformed the country's financial sector.

Rwanda: The country is known for its efforts to develop smart cities and implement digital technologies in governance.

Digital transformation in Africa continues to develop at a rapid pace, creating new opportunities for economic growth and social development.

Digital transformation in the Americas is a key factor for the economic and social development of these regions. Here are some key aspects and challenges:

North America

United States: The United States is a leader in digital technologies, with a focus on artificial intelligence (AI), cloud technologies, and cybersecurity. Companies such as Google, Amazon, and Microsoft are playing a leading role in the global digital transformation. The government is also actively supporting innovation through various initiatives and programs.

Canada: Canada is also an active participant in digital transformation, with a focus on AI and fintech. The country is investing in the development of digital skills and infrastructure, while also promoting innovation and start-ups.

South America

Brazil: Brazil is a leader in the region in terms of digital transformation, with a focus on e-government and fintech. The country is also investing in the development of internet infrastructure and the digital skills of the population.

Argentina and Chile: These countries are also making significant strides in digital transformation, with a focus on e-government and innovation in the technology sector.

Challenges

Infrastructure: Despite progress, many regions, especially in South America, still face challenges related to underdeveloped digital infrastructure.

Cybersecurity: With increasing digitalization, cybersecurity is becoming increasingly important. Countries must address the growing threats of cyberattacks and protect their digital infrastructures.

Inequality in access to technology: There are significant differences in access to modern technologies between different social and economic groups, creating digital inequality.

The digital transformation in the Americas continues to develop at a rapid pace, creating new opportunities for economic growth and social development.

Businesses that welcome change and are ready for it, as well as can adapt to more flexible work models, have greater potential for success than ever before and have the opportunity to expand their production and output. This is due to the fact that digital transformation covers all aspects of business and offers effective ways to improve them, along with the development of digital technologies.

New technologies allow enterprises to automate simpler processes and eliminate intermediate steps in more complex processes. This increases the flexibility of enterprises, which can now use their human resources much more efficiently, with a number of operations being shortened over time. In this way, they become much more flexible and can quickly reconfigure their production and implement completely new design solutions and products.

Cultural transformation, as another type of transformation observed in the development of society, is a process of profound changes in cultural values, norms, practices and identities within a given society or organization. It can be triggered by various factors, including technological innovations, social movements, globalization and political changes (S. Vassilev, 2024). It cannot be considered in isolation because it is linked to other processes that occur in the modern development of society.

The main aspects of cultural transformation at the modern stage of human development include:

1. Changing values and norms: New ideas and views can replace traditional beliefs and practices, which leads to changes in behavior and social expectations. However, at the same time, these changes must be accompanied by respect for the traditional values and norms of a given race, community, nationality, religion, because the forced imposition of values and norms is not always accepted as normal by different communities. Along with globalization, local cultural traditions must also be respected and respected, because they can also cause negative reactions.

2. Technological innovations: The introduction of new technologies can change the way people communicate, work and have fun, which in turn affects cultural practices (EU, 2023). Here too, innovations must be carefully implemented and taken into account the traditions and customs of local communities, and historical moments should not be ignored, especially in a region such as the Balkan Peninsula.
3. Globalization: Cultural globalization leads to the exchange of cultural elements between different peoples, which can lead to the hybridization of cultures and the creation of new cultural forms. At the same time, the customs and traditions of individual communities must be preserved, and not to impose a single culture on everyone without taking into account local characteristics. It is no coincidence that the motto of the European Union in its infancy was “United in Diversity”.
4. Social movements: Movements for social justice, equality and rights can cause significant cultural changes by changing public attitudes and policies. But here too, unregulated relations and the transfer of one culture to another nation or community should not be used. The minority should not impose its understandings on the entire society, but everyone should have the opportunity to profess their understandings and religions, in accordance with generally accepted norms and without imposing their views as the only correct ones.
5. Political changes: Changes in the political system or governance can lead to new cultural policies and initiatives that encourage or restrict certain cultural practices (D. Crane, 2016). Here too, a sensible approach should be taken and changes should not be forced by external forces, which usually have their own selfish or economic goals.

Cultural transformation, under certain conditions, can have a significant impact on business in several ways:

1. Improving the work environment: Changing cultural values and norms can create a more positive and supportive work environment, leading to increased employee motivation and satisfaction (Hou digital, 2024).
2. Increasing innovation: Cultural transformation often encourages openness to new ideas and experimentation, which can stimulate innovation and creativity in the organization (N. Mironova, 2020).
3. Increasing competitiveness: Companies that successfully adapt their cultural practices to changing market conditions can remain more competitive and respond more quickly to new opportunities and challenges (m. Slavova, 2016).
4. Improve communication and collaboration: Changing cultural norms can facilitate better communication and collaboration both within the organization and with external partners (Hou digital, 2024).

5. Attract and retain talent: Organizations with progressive and supportive cultures are more attractive to talented professionals, which can help attract and retain key personnel. In this way, currently strong and wealthy countries attract the minds of poorer nations, thereby becoming richer and weakening other nations.

Cultural transformation plays an important role in the development of societies around the world, influencing social, economic and political aspects of life. Here is how cultural transformation manifests itself in different regions:

Europe

In Europe, cultural transformation is closely linked to the processes of globalisation and integration in the European Union. Cultural diplomacy is an important tool for strengthening international relations and promoting cultural diversity. The European Commission develops cultural cooperation strategies that include social cohesion, economic development and international relations.

Asia

In Asia, cultural transformation is strongly influenced by rapid economic development and technological progress. Countries such as China, Japan and South Korea use their cultural identity to strengthen their position on the global stage. Cultural initiatives are often used to promote tourism and international cooperation.

Africa

In Africa, cultural transformation plays a key role in social and economic development. Many African countries use their cultural heritage to promote tourism and attract investment. Cultural projects often aim to strengthen national identity and social cohesion.

North America

In North America, cultural transformation is associated with diversity and innovation. The United States and Canada use their cultural power to promote democratic values and human rights. Cultural industries, such as cinema and music, play an important role in the economy and international relations.

South America

In South America, cultural transformation is associated with rich cultural heritage and social movements. Countries such as Brazil and Argentina use their cultural resources to promote social cohesion and economic development. Cultural initiatives often aim to strengthen national identity and international cooperation.

Cultural transformation is a dynamic process that continues to evolve and adapt to changing global conditions.

Globalization has had a significant impact on culture around the world, leading to a number of positive and negative effects. Here are some of the main ways in which globalization affects culture:

Positive Effects

Cultural exchange and diversity: Globalization facilitates the exchange of cultural ideas, customs, and traditions between different peoples. This leads to greater cultural diversity and mutual enrichment.

Access to information: Thanks to the Internet and the media, people have access to cultural products and information from all over the world. This makes it easier to understand and accept different cultures.

Economic benefits: Cultural globalization can stimulate economic growth through tourism and cultural industries, such as film, music, and the arts.

Negative Effects

Cultural homogenization: One of the main disadvantages of globalization is the tendency toward cultural homogenization, in which local cultures can be displaced by dominant global cultures. This can lead to the loss of unique cultural identities.

Commercialization of culture: Globalization often leads to the commercialization of cultural products, which can reduce their authenticity and value.

Social inequalities: Globalization can exacerbate social inequalities, with some cultures and groups receiving more attention and resources than others.

Examples of Cultural Globalization

Music and cinema: Hollywood films and Western music are popular around the world, leading to the global spread of American culture.

Gastronomy: Cuisine from different parts of the world, such as Italian, Chinese, and Mexican, are widespread and popular in many countries.

Globalization is a complex process that has both positive and negative aspects. It is important to find a balance between preserving local cultures and embracing global cultural influences.

Preserving indigenous cultures is an important process that requires coordinated efforts from governments, communities, and organizations. Here are some of the main ways in which this is achieved:

Education and Awareness

Educational programs: Incorporating indigenous culture into curricula helps younger generations learn about and appreciate their cultural heritage.

Cultural events and festivals: Organizing festivals and events that celebrate indigenous traditions and customs promotes cultural awareness and participation.

Support for Indigenous Artists and Artisans

Financial support: Providing grants and subsidies to indigenous artists and artisans helps preserve and develop traditional arts and crafts.

Platforms for expression: Creating platforms where indigenous artists can showcase their work encourages cultural diversity and innovation.

Legislation and Policies

Laws to protect cultural heritage: Enacting laws and regulations that protect cultural sites and traditions is a key factor in preserving indigenous cultures.

Cultural Diversity Policies: Developing policies that promote cultural diversity and integration helps preserve unique cultural identities.

Technology and Digitalization

Digital Archives: Creating digital archives and databases that store information about local cultures facilitates access to cultural heritage and its preservation.

Social Media and Platforms: Using social media and online platforms to promote local cultures helps reach a wider audience and fosters cultural exchange.

Examples of Successful Initiatives

Bulgaria: The Ministry of Agriculture and Food promotes the preservation of local vegetable and fruit varieties through interventions under the Strategic Plan for the Development of Agriculture and Rural Areas.

Heritage Gardening: The practice of heritage gardening preserves and recreates traditional gardening methods, which plays a crucial role in preserving local knowledge about plants and their uses.

The preservation of local cultures is a complex and multifaceted process that requires cooperation and commitment from all stakeholders.

The main threats to indigenous cultures are diverse and often interconnected. Here are some of the most significant:

Globalization and Cultural Homogenization

Globalization can lead to cultural homogenization, in which indigenous cultures are displaced by dominant global cultures. This can lead to the loss of unique cultural identities and traditions.

Urbanization and Migration

Rapid urbanization and migration to cities often lead to the weakening of traditional cultural practices and customs. People who move to cities can lose touch with indigenous cultures and traditions.

Economic Pressures

Economic pressures and the need for modernization can lead to the neglect of indigenous cultures in favor of more profitable activities. This may include the replacement of traditional crafts and practices with mass production.

Tourism

While tourism can be a source of income and promote cultural exchange, it can also lead to the commercialization and distortion of indigenous cultures. Tourism industries often adapt cultural practices to meet tourists' expectations, which can diminish their authenticity.

Climate Change and Environmental Threats

Climate change and environmental threats can affect indigenous cultures, especially those that are closely linked to the natural environment. Climate change can lead to the loss of traditional agricultural practices and resources.

Technological Advances

While technological advances can facilitate the preservation and dissemination of cultural heritage, they can also lead to the replacement of traditional cultural practices with modern technologies. This can lead to the loss of knowledge and skills passed down from generation to generation.

Preserving indigenous cultures requires coordinated efforts by governments, communities and organizations to address these threats and promote the sustainable development of cultural heritage.

Strategic transformation is a process of fundamental changes in the strategic direction of an organization in order to adapt to new market conditions, technologies, or competitive challenges. It involves rethinking and realigning the organization's mission, vision, goals, and core business models (Change, 2024).

Key aspects of strategic transformation include:

1. Rethinking mission and vision: Organizations often need to revisit their core goals and long-term visions to remain relevant and competitive (The 7 rs, 2023).
2. Adapting to new technologies: Implementing new technologies can require significant changes to an organization's operations and strategies.
3. Changing business models: Strategic transformation can involve developing new business models that better meet current market conditions and customer needs (The 7 rs, 2023).
4. Developing organizational culture: A change in strategic direction often requires a change in the organization's cultural norms and values to support the new goals and strategies.
5. Managing change: Effectively managing the change process is critical to successful strategic transformation. This includes clear communication, employee engagement, and managing resistance to change.

Strategic transformation planning is a complex process that requires careful consideration and coordination and is directly related to other transformations, and is not done in isolation. Here are the main steps that can be followed:

1. Analyzing the current state: It starts with assessing the current state of the organization, using tools such as SWOT analysis (strengths and weaknesses, opportunities and threats) and PEST analysis (political, economic, social and technological factors) to understand the internal and external factors that affect your business and make the optimal decision (J. Morales, 2016).
2. Defining a vision and goals: The key here is to formulate a clear vision for the future of the organization and set specific, measurable goals to be achieved. These goals should be consistent with the organization's long-term strategy and be tied to the environment in which it operates. When setting goals, all external and internal factors that may have an impact on the realization of the set goals should be carefully weighed.
3. Strategy Development: The working team should develop a strategy that includes specific actions and initiatives to achieve the set goals. This may include changes in business models, the implementation of new technologies, the use of the cultural traditions of the enterprise and the community, and improvements in operations.
4. Resource Allocation: The necessary financial, human, and technological resources are carefully determined and allocated effectively to support the implementation of the strategy and the set goals.
5. Strategy Implementation: HERE it is necessary for the team to implement the strategic plans into specific actions that will lead to the implementation of the set strategy. This includes developing an action plan, assigning responsibilities, and creating a monitoring and control system. Implementation should be broken down into stages and after each stage, an analysis of the results achieved and the weaknesses identified should be made.
6. Monitoring and Evaluation: It is necessary to continuously monitor progress and analyze and evaluate the effectiveness of the actions taken. When implementing the plan, it is necessary to use key performance indicators (KPIs) to measure progress and success and to make the necessary adjustments in the implementation of the set plan, goals and strategy.
7. Adaptation and improvement: In the implementation of the adopted plans and strategies, unforeseen situations arise and there must be a readiness to adapt the strategy in response to changing conditions and new challenges that arise during the implementation. It is necessary to regularly analyze what has been achieved and to review and update the strategic plan depending on the surrounding environment to ensure its relevance and effectiveness (A. Tran, 2024).

Strategic transformation has a significant impact on different regions of the world, changing economic, political and social structures. Here is how it manifests itself in Europe, Asia, Africa, North and South America:

Europe

In Europe, strategic transformation is closely linked to the integration processes in the European Union. Key highlights include:

Economic integration: Efforts to create a single market and currency (the euro) are key to economic stability and growth.

Political coordination: Cooperation in foreign policy and security is essential to maintaining stability in the region.

Asia

In Asia, strategic transformation is driven by rapid economic development and technological progress. Key highlights include:

Economic growth: Countries such as China, Japan and South Korea are leading the way in innovation and technology.

Geopolitical dynamics: The region is witnessing significant geopolitical changes, including the growing influence of China and India.

Africa

In Africa, strategic transformation is linked to efforts for economic development and social stability. Key highlights include:

Infrastructure projects: Investment in infrastructure is key to the continent's economic development.

Regional cooperation: The African Union plays an important role in promoting political and economic integration.

North America

In North America, strategic transformation is linked to innovation and technological advancement. Key highlights include:

Technological innovation: The United States and Canada are leaders in artificial intelligence and cloud technologies.

Economic power: The region is home to some of the largest and most influential companies in the world.

South America

In South America, strategic transformation is linked to efforts for economic development and social stability. Key highlights include:

Economic diversification: Countries in the region are seeking to diversify their economies and reduce their dependence on commodity exports.

Social reforms: Efforts to improve social justice and reduce poverty are key to the region's stability.

Strategic transformation in these regions continues to evolve, creating new opportunities and challenges.

Strategic transformation is a process that involves adapting and developing the economic, political, and social structures of countries. Some of the leading countries in this process are:

United States

The United States is a leader in technological innovation and strategic transformation. The country is investing significant resources in artificial intelligence, cybersecurity, and cloud technologies. The United States also plays a key role in global politics and economics.

China

China is another leading player in strategic transformation, with a focus on technological advancement and economic development. The country is actively investing in infrastructure, 5G networks, and artificial intelligence, while expanding its influence globally.

European Union

The European Union (EU) is also an important player in strategic transformation, focusing on economic integration and sustainable development. The EU is developing policies to promote innovation, the green transition, and digitalization.

Japan

Japan is known for its innovations in robotics and automation. The country is actively investing in research and development, while promoting sustainable development and digitalization.

South Korea

South Korea is a leader in 5G technology and artificial intelligence. The country is actively developing smart cities and autonomous vehicles, while investing in education and research.

India

India is also making significant strides in strategic transformation, with a focus on digitalization and innovation. The Digital India program is an example of the country's efforts to modernize its economic and social structures.

These countries play a key role in the global strategic transformation, creating new opportunities and challenges for the rest of the world.

In Europe and the Balkan Peninsula, some countries stand out for their efforts and successes in strategic transformation. Here are some of them:

Europe

Germany: Germany is a leader in the field of industrial automation and digitalization. The country is actively investing in artificial intelligence, green technologies and sustainable development.

France: France is also a leader in strategic transformation, with a focus on innovation and technological advancement. The country is developing strong policies to encourage start-ups and digital technologies.

Netherlands: The Netherlands is known for its innovations in the field of water management and sustainable development. The country is actively investing in green technologies and smart cities.

Balkan Peninsula

Slovenia: Slovenia is a leader in the Balkans in terms of innovation and sustainable development. The country is actively developing digital technologies and green initiatives.

Croatia: Croatia is also making significant steps in strategic transformation, with a focus on tourism and the digitalization of public services.

Greece: Greece is investing in the development of smart cities and digital technologies, while promoting sustainable development and tourism.

These countries play a key role in the strategic transformation of their regions, creating new opportunities for economic growth and social development.

The strategic transformations in the Balkans and South-Eastern Europe are diverse and encompass different aspects of economic, political and social development. Here are some key points for each of these countries:

Bulgaria

Bulgaria has made significant progress with its accession to the Schengen area, which is an important strategic goal for the country. This will facilitate trade and the movement of people, while strengthening economic ties with the rest of Europe. The country is also investing in infrastructure projects, such as motorways and railways, to improve its connectivity with the rest of the continent.

Romania

Romania also joined the Schengen area together with Bulgaria, which is a significant success for the country. Romania is actively working on modernising its infrastructure and promoting innovation and digitalisation. The country is also striving to improve its energy efficiency and sustainability.

Serbia

Serbia is in the process of joining the European Union and is actively working on reforms in various sectors, including justice, economy and administration. The country is also investing in infrastructure projects and promoting regional cooperation.

Greece

Greece focuses on sustainable development and modernization of its economy. The country is actively investing in green technologies and renewable energy sources. Greece is also working on improving its infrastructure and promoting tourism.

Turkey

Turkey is an important player in the region and is actively working on modernizing its economy and infrastructure. The country is investing in large infrastructure projects, such as new airports, bridges and highways. Turkey is also striving to improve its energy independence and sustainability.

Other Balkan countries

Albania: Albania is working on reforms in the judiciary and administration, while promoting economic development and investment.

North Macedonia: The country is striving to join the European Union and is actively working on reforms and modernization of its infrastructure.

Montenegro: Montenegro is also in the process of joining the EU and is investing in infrastructure projects and sustainable development.

These steps influence and help to plan and successfully implement the strategic transformation that will prepare the economic unit for future challenges and opportunities that were not foreseen in the initial planning.

Digital, cultural and strategic transformation are interrelated processes that together contribute to the overall development and adaptation of organizations in the modern world. They cannot be considered as independent activities, because there is a mutual relationship between them and their development and implementation. Here is how they are connected:

Digital transformation: This is the process of integrating digital technologies into all aspects of business and society. It includes the use of new technologies such as cloud computing, artificial intelligence and big data to improve efficiency and competitiveness.

Cultural transformation: For digital transformation to be successful, a change in the cultural values and norms of the organization is often also necessary. This includes encouraging innovation, openness to new ideas and creating a supportive work environment.

Strategic Transformation: It involves rethinking and realigning the organization's strategic goals and business models to adapt to new market conditions and technologies. Strategic transformation is often necessary to ensure long-term success and sustainability of digital and cultural changes.

The relationship between these three types of transformation is key to the successful adaptation of organizations to a rapidly changing environment. Digital transformation provides the necessary tools and technologies, cultural transformation creates the appropriate environment for their implementation, and strategic transformation provides a clear direction and goals for achieving sustainable success. In this way, we can briefly define the relationship between digital, cultural and strategic transformations, something characteristic of the modern development of humanity.

Successful digital, cultural and strategic transformation at the state level requires coordinated efforts and a clear vision. Without such a vision, it is impossible to implement transformations at the level of an enterprise, organization or other economic unit. State regulation is of utmost importance for the implementation of transformations. Here are some key steps that can help:

1. Develop a national strategy: Creating a comprehensive strategy that encompasses digital, cultural and strategic transformation is essential. This strategy should include specific goals and measures to achieve them. It should be tailored to national specificities and linked to universal human values, and it should be integrated into the global process, while preserving specific national characteristics.
2. Invest in infrastructure and technology: Providing a modern and reliable digital infrastructure is the basis for a successful transformation. This includes investments in broadband internet, cloud services, artificial intelligence and other new technologies (A. Tran, 2024). The construction of such infrastructure should be consistent with national and regional traditions and values. Such is, for example, the region that encompasses the countries of the Balkan Peninsula, where peoples with different beliefs, religions, and customs have coexisted for centuries, and when implemented, it is necessary to take these peculiarities into account, because it can be said that the Balkan Peninsula is a powder keg that can explode at the slightest spark.
3. Improving digital skills: Training and developing digital skills among the population and public sector employees is critical. This can be achieved through training programs, courses and upskilling initiatives (B. Talin, 2023). Here, the state should create regulators that encourage the education of the population and the use of digital technologies, taking them into account local customs, traditions, culture and religion.
4. Promoting cultural change: For digital transformation to be successful, it is necessary to change the culture of work and management. This includes encouraging innovation, openness to new ideas and creating a supportive environment for employees (What is, 2023). Here, too, state regulators must be skillfully used to achieve these changes.
5. Public-private cooperation: Partnerships between government, business and academia can accelerate the transformation process. This includes joint projects, knowledge and resource sharing (S. Vassilev, 2024). The opportunities here are very large and specific mechanisms that are traditional for the region can be relied on.
6. Monitoring and assessing progress: Continuous monitoring and assessing progress towards strategic goals is important for course correction and ensuring success. The use of key performance indicators (KPIs) can help measure results. This is noted when reporting the results of each stage and adapting the set goals, objectives and strategies to the changing environment.
7. Supporting innovation and entrepreneurship: Creating a favorable environment for innovation and entrepreneurship can stimulate economic growth and support transformation. This includes tax breaks, grants and other forms of support for start-ups and innovative projects (S. Vassilev, 2023).

These steps can help to successfully implement digital, cultural and strategic transformation at the state level, while ensuring sustainable development and competitiveness. Coordination of the state and the public and private sectors, their joint coordinated activity, is necessary in order to achieve the set goals at a specific level or stage of implementation (A. Tran, 2024).

Digital transformations have been successfully developing in this century and have already achieved significant results. Here are some examples of successful digital transformations in various industries around the world:

Amazon: Starting as an online bookstore, Amazon has transformed into the world's largest e-commerce platform. The company integrates technologies such as artificial intelligence and cloud computing to provide personalized services and optimize logistics processes.

Netflix: From a mail-order DVD rental company, Netflix has become a leader in streaming services. They use data analytics and artificial intelligence to recommend personalized content to their users.

Starbucks: It has implemented mobile apps and contactless payments to improve customer service. Loyalty programs and data analytics help them understand customer preferences and offer personalized benefits.

McDonald's: It uses artificial intelligence and interactive touchscreens for ordering in its restaurants. They have also developed a mobile app that makes it easier for customers to order and receive food.

Airbnb: It transformed the travel and hospitality industry by creating a platform for renting private homes. They use geolocation, online payments, and data analytics to provide quality services to their customers.

These few examples show how digital transformation can lead to significant improvements in efficiency, customer service, and competitiveness of companies.

On the other hand, a number of industries are also undergoing revolutionary changes and changing at an extremely rapid pace. Some of the industries that are transforming the fastest include:

Information Technology (IT): The technology sector is leading the way in digital transformation, constantly implementing new technologies such as artificial intelligence, cloud computing, and blockchain.

Financial Services: Fintech companies and traditional banks are investing significantly in digital technologies to improve customer service and optimize their operations.

Healthcare: The implementation of telemedicine, electronic health records, and big data analytics is transforming healthcare, making it more accessible and efficient. At the same time, when poorly administered, these processes become significantly more cumbersome and inaccessible.

Manufacturing: Industry 4.0 includes automation, the Internet of Things (IoT), and smart factories, which are significantly changing production processes. This has also led to the creation of completely new industries that were impossible to implement 50 years ago.

Retail: E-commerce and omnichannel strategies are changing the way consumers shop by providing more personalized and convenient services. Now almost everyone has at least tried to make online purchases, and for some it is an everyday occurrence. Here too, the customs, habits and culture of the population should not be overlooked. It is noticeable that people living in large cities use online shopping more often, as do people from the younger generation.

Energy: Renewable energy sources and smart grids are transforming the energy sector, making it more sustainable and efficient. But here again, we stumble into the other extremes, when their capabilities for continuous constant supply of electricity are overestimated and fertile fields are destroyed for the construction of photovoltaic parks. This is noticeable in many countries on the Balkan Peninsula, with perhaps the greatest irregularities being observed in Bulgaria.

These industries are leaders in adapting to new technologies and changing market conditions, which allows them to remain competitive and innovative. This is also related to the specifics of these sectors of the economy, because in other sectors this transformation occurs much more difficult.

In Bulgaria, digital, cultural and strategic transformation are interconnected processes that develop in parallel and complement each other. Here is how these transformations develop and what is the relationship between them:

The digital transformation in Bulgaria is aimed at integrating new technologies into all spheres of public and economic life. The National Strategy for Digital Transformation for the period 2024-2030 includes priorities such as developing digital infrastructure, improving digital skills and promoting innovation (B. Talin, 2023). This transformation aims to increase the competitiveness of the Bulgarian economy and improve the quality of public services.

Cultural transformation in Bulgaria focuses on adapting cultural values and practices to contemporary realities. This includes promoting cultural diversity, supporting creative industries, and developing cultural tourism (D. Crane, 2016). The country's cultural policy aims to create conditions for innovation and sustainable development through culture (S. Vassilev, 2023).

Strategic transformation in Bulgaria involves developing and implementing long-term development strategies that cover different sectors of the economy and society. The National Development Program "Bulgaria 2030" is a key document that sets out the country's strategic goals and priorities for the next decade. This program includes measures to improve education, healthcare, infrastructure, and innovation.

Digital, cultural, and strategic transformation are closely linked and mutually reinforcing in Bulgaria and the Balkan countries. Digital transformation provides the necessary technologies and tools, cultural transformation creates the appropriate environment for their implementation, and strategic transformation provides a clear direction and goals for achieving sustainable success. Together, these transformations support Bulgaria's development as a modern and competitive country.

The challenges facing digital, cultural and strategic transformation in Bulgaria and the Balkans are numerous and complex. Here are some of the main difficulties that are observed in their implementation in individual countries:

In Bulgaria

Insufficient digital infrastructure: Despite progress, there are still regions with limited access to high-speed internet, which makes it difficult to implement new technologies.

Lack of digital skills: Many people and organizations still do not have the necessary digital skills, which limits the opportunities for full use of new technologies.

Cultural barriers: Changing established cultural norms and practices can be resisted, especially in more conservative environments.

Financial constraints: The lack of sufficient investment in new technologies and infrastructure can slow down the transformation process. Many investors are leaving Bulgaria due to the unpredictability of the political situation and the lack of regulations.

In the Balkans

Political instability: The region is often affected by political conflicts and instability, which makes it difficult to plan and implement transformation projects in the long term. After the breakup of Yugoslavia, a number of new countries emerged, where there is political instability and unfavorable conditions for business.

Ethnic and religious conflicts: The diversity of ethnic and religious groups can lead to tensions and conflicts that make cooperation and integration difficult. These conflicts are sometimes fueled by external forces that are not familiar with the specifics of the region and foreign models cannot be automatically transferred. Tolerance and tolerance and respect for other opinions are necessary, which not everyone is able to do or finds external support for the realization of their ideas and views.

Economic inequalities: The significant differences in economic development between the different countries and regions in the Balkans can create additional challenges for coordinated transformation efforts. It is no coincidence that when integrating countries into the European Union and other organizations, they proceed in groups of 2 countries or independently, due to these differences. Different rates of development of individual countries and regions are also noticeable. For example, Northwestern Bulgaria is one of the poorest regions in all of Europe.

Energy dependency: Many countries in the Balkans are highly dependent on external energy sources, which can limit opportunities for sustainable development and transformation. There is a noticeable slowdown in energy development, which in the long term will lead to the region lagging behind. A positive example is Turkey, which is significantly developing its energy system and is becoming an unavoidable factor not only in the region, but also in Europe and the Middle East. In contrast, Bulgaria, which in November 2024 became a net importer of electricity for the first time in more than 50 years.

Solutions to the challenges of digital, cultural and strategic transformation in Bulgaria and the Balkan Peninsula require coordinated efforts and innovation. Here are some of the possible solutions and examples of countries that are doing well:

Solutions to the Challenges

Investment in infrastructure: Expanding and modernizing digital infrastructure, including high-speed internet and 5G networks, is key to a successful digital transformation.

Education and training: Developing training and upskilling programs in digital skills is essential. This includes both formal education and continuous professional development.

Supporting innovation: Creating a conducive environment for innovation through tax breaks, grants and other forms of support for start-ups and research projects can stimulate economic growth.

Political stability and cooperation: Promoting political stability and regional cooperation can facilitate the long-term planning and implementation of transformation projects.

Cultural change: Promoting cultural changes that support innovation and openness to new ideas is important for a successful transformation. This can include awareness-raising campaigns and changing public attitudes.

The biggest challenges facing transformations in the Balkan Peninsula can be formulated as follows:

Political instability: The Balkans are often affected by political conflicts and instability, which makes it difficult to plan and implement long-term transformation projects. There are many examples of this in historical terms, but the bad thing is that lessons are not always learned from the past.

Ethnic and religious conflicts: The diversity of ethnic and religious groups can lead to tensions and conflicts that make cooperation and integration difficult. There are many examples of this in historical terms, and hot spots continue to exist that make ongoing processes difficult.

Economic inequalities: The significant differences in economic development between different countries and regions in the Balkans create additional challenges for coordinated transformation efforts. It is not uncommon for large strategic investors to leave a particular country.

Corruption and weak institutions: High levels of corruption and weaknesses in the judicial and law enforcement systems undermine trust in state institutions and make it difficult to implement reforms.

Energy dependence: Many countries in the Balkans are highly dependent on external energy sources, which can limit opportunities for sustainable development and transformation.

National and local level decisions that need to be taken to accelerate the transformation, such as:

Strengthening institutions and fighting corruption: Introducing strict anti-corruption measures and strengthening institutions can increase trust in state structures and facilitate the implementation of reforms.

Promoting regional cooperation: Cooperation between the countries of the Balkans can help address common challenges and promote economic development. This includes joint projects and initiatives in the areas of infrastructure, energy and education. But there are insurmountable obstacles that limit the development of good inter-state relations and even damage relations with third countries.

Investing in education and training: Developing training and up-skilling programs in the field of digital skills and innovation is essential for a successful transformation. Continuous changes in educational programs and imitation of reforms lead to a deepening of problems in the education system. Funds are allocated for the development of STEM education and the promotion of innovative training, but they are not sufficient and do not always yield good results.

Support for innovation and entrepreneurship: Creating a favorable environment for innovation through tax breaks, grants and other forms of support for start-ups and research projects can stimulate economic growth. Although Bulgaria has one of the lowest tax rates in Europe, there is no noticeable influx of investors, and there is even a reverse trend towards a decrease in foreign investment.

Development of energy independence: Investments in renewable energy sources and smart grids can reduce dependence on external energy sources and support sustainable development. But this too must be regulated and countries must have the relevant regulators to properly conduct these transformations.

Here are a few examples of successful transformations in the countries of the Balkan Peninsula:

Slovenia is a leader in digital transformation in the Balkans. The country invests significantly in research and development, which supports economic growth. Slovenia is also known for its innovations in education and healthcare, using new technologies to improve services.

Croatia is making significant strides towards digital and strategic transformation. The country is investing in infrastructure and promoting innovation, while actively working to improve the digital skills of its population. Croatia is also developing its tourism sector by implementing new technologies.

Serbia is also making progress in digital transformation, especially in the area of e-government. The country is implementing e-services that facilitate citizens' access to administrative services and improve the efficiency of the public sector.

Romania is an example of a successful transformation in the field of information technology and communications. The country has one of the fastest growing IT industries in the region and is home to numerous start-ups and technology incubators.

Bulgaria is also making significant efforts towards digital transformation, investing in the development of digital infrastructure and improving digital skills. The country also promotes innovation and entrepreneurship through various programs and initiatives.

These examples show that with the right strategies and investments, Balkan countries can make significant progress in digital, cultural and strategic transformation, leading to sustainable development and increased competitiveness.

State aid plays an important role in supporting transformations in Balkan countries, but it often faces a number of challenges and limitations. Here are some of the main problems and bad practices related to state aid in the region:

Insufficient funding: Although there are various state aid programs, funds are often not sufficient to cover the needs of all sectors and regions.

Bureaucracy and complex procedures: The process of applying for and receiving state aid can be complex and bureaucratic, making access to finance difficult, especially for small and medium-sized enterprises.

Corruption and lack of transparency: High levels of corruption and lack of transparency in the allocation of state aid can lead to inefficient use of resources and unfair advantage for certain enterprises.

Inefficient resource management: Poor management and inefficient use of available resources can slow down or even defeat transformation efforts (B. Talin, 2023).

Bad practices observed in the countries of the Balkan Peninsula can be systematized as:

Lack of coordination: Insufficient coordination between different state institutions and levels of government can lead to duplication of efforts and inefficient use of resources.

Short-term thinking: Focusing on short-term political and economic goals instead of long-term strategies for sustainable development can lead to ineffective and inconsistent policies.

Insufficient citizen participation: The lack of active participation of citizens in decision-making processes and project implementation can lead to a lack of support and resistance to change.

The countries of the Balkan Peninsula are distinguished by unique historical, cultural and geopolitical characteristics that influence their transformations. Here are some of the main distinguishing features and recommendations for improving results in digital, cultural and strategic transformation:

Distinguishing Features

Historical heritage: The Balkan countries have a rich historical heritage that includes different cultures and civilizations. This creates a unique cultural identity, but can also lead to complex political and social relations.

Geopolitical location: Located at the crossroads between Europe and Asia, the Balkan countries are of strategic importance for international trade and politics. However, this location often leads to geopolitical tensions and conflicts.

Economic development: The economic development of the Balkans is uneven, with some countries being more advanced than others. This creates challenges for regional cooperation and integration.

Recommendations for Improving Results

Investment in infrastructure: Improving transport and digital infrastructure is key to the economic development and integration of the region. This includes building highways, railways and high-speed internet networks.

Promoting innovation: Investment in research and development, as well as support for start-ups, can stimulate innovation and technological progress. This includes the creation of innovation hubs and technology parks.

Education and training: Improving the education system and promoting digital skills are essential for a successful digital transformation. This includes training and retraining programmes for the workforce.

Cultural cooperation: Promoting cultural exchange and cooperation between countries in the region can strengthen cultural identity and foster social cohesion. This includes organising cultural events and festivals, as well as supporting cultural projects.

Regional cooperation: Strengthening regional cooperation and integration within the European Union and other international organisations can improve the political and economic stability of the region.

These recommendations can help the countries of the Balkan Peninsula achieve better results in implementing digital, cultural and strategic transformation, while preserving their unique cultural identity and historical heritage.

Examples of Successful Transformations

Slovenia: Slovenia is an example of successful transformation, especially in the field of innovation and sustainable development. The country is actively developing digital technologies and green initiatives, making it a leader in the region in terms of innovation.

Croatia: Croatia has made significant progress in tourism and the digitalization of public services. The country has successfully used its cultural heritage and natural resources to attract tourists and investments.

Greece: Greece is focused on sustainable development and modernization of its economy. The country is actively investing in green technologies and renewable energy sources, while working on improving infrastructure and promoting tourism.

Examples of Unsuccessful Transformations

Bosnia and Herzegovina: Despite reform efforts, the country continues to face political instability and ethnic tensions. This hinders economic development and integration into the European Union.

North Macedonia: Despite progress in some areas, the country still faces internal political conflicts and tensions between different ethnic groups. This hinders sustainable development and integration into international organizations.

Kosovo: Kosovo continues to face challenges related to international recognition and internal political stability. This hampers economic development and attracting investment.

Recommendations for Improving Performance

Investment in infrastructure: Improving transport and digital infrastructure is key to the economic development and integration of the region. This includes building highways, railways and high-speed internet networks.

Promoting innovation: Investment in research and development, as well as support for start-ups, can stimulate innovation and technological progress. This includes the creation of innovation hubs and technology parks.

Education and training: Improving the education system and promoting digital skills are essential for a successful digital transformation. This includes training and retraining programs for the workforce.

Cultural cooperation: Promoting cultural exchange and cooperation between countries in the region can strengthen cultural identity and promote social cohesion. This includes organizing cultural events and festivals, as well as supporting cultural projects.

Regional cooperation: Strengthening regional cooperation and integration within the European Union and other international organizations can improve the political and economic stability of the region.

These recommendations can help the countries of the Balkan Peninsula achieve better results in implementing digital, cultural and strategic transformation, while preserving their unique cultural identity and historical heritage.

These bad practices should not erase the achievements in implementing the digital, cultural and strategic transformation in the countries of the Balkan Peninsula, but only measures should be identified to overcome them. Good results have been achieved, but with the implementation of each specific task, an analysis of what has been achieved so far must be made and when setting further goals and tasks, they must be adapted to the situation in the specific country, region or enterprise. Only in this way can the countries of the Balkan region improve their indicators and catch up with the best in terms of results. The potential is there, the implementation remains.

REFERENCES

Businesses, H. D. T. H. (2024). https://www.tbmagazine.net/statia/kak-digitalnata-transformaciya-pomaga-na-biznesite.html

Diana Crane, N. K. (2016). *Global Culture: Media*. Arts, Politics and Globalization. DOI: 10.4324/9781315538792

Management, C. (2024). Strategies, Principles and Best Practices. https://nlpbulgaria.bg/news/upravlenie-na-promenite/

Mironova, N., & Galyarski, E. (2020). Effective Digitalization of Business and Increasing Competitiveness. Business Directions.

Morales, J. (2016). *What is Strategic Planning: Definition*. Meaning, Applications and Tools.

Slavova, M. (2016). Digital Transformation of Business. *Economic and Social Alternatives*, 2016(4), 142–149.

Strategic Framework for the EU Cultural Policy. (2023). https://culture.ec.europa.eu/bg/policies/strategic-framework-for-the-eus-cultural-policy

Talin, B. (2023). What is "Digital Transformation"? Definition and Explanation. https://morethandigital.info/bg/kakvo-e-digitalna-transformacia-opredelenie-i-obiasnenie/

The 7 Rs of Application Modernization: Your Strategic Roadmap to Digital Transformation. (2023). https://www.solix.com/bg/blog/learning/the-7rs-of-application-modernization-your-strategic-roadmap-to-digital-transformation/

Tran. (2024). Strategic Management Process.

Vassilev, S. (2024). Media, media culture, communications: processes and transformations. Rhetoric and Communications, 59, 7-27.

What is digital transformation and what are its benefits. (2023). https://ditech.bg/tsifrovata-transformatsiya/

Chapter 9
Strategies for Organizational Development in Modern Societies

Teodora Petrova
https://orcid.org/0000-0003-4672-1332
Trakia University, Stara Zagora, Bulgaria

Zhivo Petrov
National Defence College, Sofia, Bulgaria

Denis Solovev
Far Eastern Federal University, Vladivostok, Russia

ABSTRACT

This study provides a general overview of the organization and its basic structure, justifying opportunities for its development in the modern dynamic society. The main place in the study is occupied by corporate culture and personal management, as well as motivation. A different possibility for the development of medical tourism and the possibilities for the effective functioning of the organization are justified. In addition to theoretical models, practical opportunities for the implementation of the authors' ideas are also presented.

DOI: 10.4018/979-8-3693-9435-9.ch009

1. INTRODUCTION

Depending on the meaning, for which it is used, there are the following definitions for the organization: A social institute with a specific status. This includes enterprises, government bodies, non-governmental associations, etc.; A process involving the deliberate impact of organized people on an object (e.g., a product or service).; A characteristic or attribute of the object.

It is meant when it comes to organized and unorganized systems, political public organizations, effective and ineffective organizations, etc. There are numerous definitions of "organization," but two dominant views stand out: an organization as a rational system or as a system aimed at achieving specific goals. Based on these perspectives, four key definitions are often cited (Mladenov & Terziev, 2011a):

- In accordance with Bernard's theory, an organization is a cooperation of individuals distinguished from other social groups by consciousness, foresight, and goal orientation. The focus is on joint actions, cooperation, and achieving goals;
- March and Simon give another definition an organization is a society of interconnected individuals with a central coordination system. It resembles a complex biological organism. From the management point of view, the organization is a system of adopted and implemented management decisions;
- Blau and Scott give the third definition of an organization. An organization must be formalized and have a structured hierarchy to achieve specific goals effectively;
- In Etzioni's opinion, an organization is a consciously constructed and reconstructed social group aimed at achieving specific goals, with emphasis on members' conscious actions and involvement.

Key characteristics of organizations are (Mladenov & Terziev, 2011a):

- Presence of two or more individuals considered a group;
- Presence of compatible activities among these individuals;
- Presence of specific mechanisms or systems for coordinating their activities;
- Presence of a common goal shared and accepted by the majority.

Based on these features, a practical definition of an organization is: an organization is a group of people whose activities are consciously coordinated to achieve a common goal or set of goals (Terziev et al., 2018a; 2018b; Terziev & Can, 2018c; Terziev & Georgiev, 2018d; Terziev & Georgiev, 2017).

The social essence of an organization is reflected in fulfilling the aspirations and goals of its employees. People will join and contribute to organizations when their needs such as financial compensation, social interaction, professional growth, and self-realization are met.

Organizations often have diverse and interrelated goals, referred to as complex goals. All complex organizations share several common characteristics:

- availability, attraction and utilization of resources;
- dependence on the external environment;
- horizontal and vertical division of labor;
- separate divisions;
- need for management.

There are many approaches to building the typology of the organization in the literature.

Traditionally, they are divided into three types:

- Enterprises and organizations (production, trade, service);
- Institutions (financial, cultural, scientific, managerial, educational, medical);
- Public organizations (religious, trade unions and public).

The second approach is a division of organizations based on social relations: economic, social, cultural and administrative (state, political and public). In each of these types there is a certain similarity, which determines the proximity of the goals and functions of the organizations.

According to the American sociologist Etzioni, organizations are divided into three main groups (Mladenov & Terziev, 2011a):

- Voluntary – whose members unite on a voluntary basis (political parties, trade unions, clubs, etc.);
- Coercive – membership is enforced (e.g., prisons, the military);
- Practical (utilitarian) – members work together for mutual and individual goals (e.g., enterprises, financial firms).

Depending on the nature of internal relations, organizations are divided into formal and informal.

The formal organization is built on the basis of predefined relationships, hierarchical structures, regulated behaviors, and functional duties. They determine the attitude to power, the sphere of responsibility for the decisions and their implementation. They are registered in accordance with the established procedure (most often they are legal entities), led by designated heads. These organizations are the result of previously planned actions and efforts (Mladenov & Terziev, 2011a).

An informal arise spontaneously through interpersonal interactions within formal organizations. It exists within the formal one, most often supporting it. They often support the formal structure by fostering relationships and providing informal leadership. These organizations usually arise spontaneously.

Formal and informal organizations have very common features, such as: groups of people with common goals; they develop internal norms, standards and rules that regulate various aspects of people's behavior.

The German philosopher and sociologist Max Weber described the ideal model of a formal organization - bureaucracy (from the French bureau - office and the Greek kratos - power, domination, strength). This is an organization of public power, which consists of governing persons, holding positions and posts and forming a certain hierarchy. According to him, bureaucracy, which appeared at the beginning of the 19th century, contributed to the clarity of decisions made within the organization and required high professional qualities from officials. The main distinctive features of bureaucracy (Mladenov & Terziev, 2011a):

- People who are in the management bodies work only within the framework of the "impersonal" duties that exist in the organization;
- The hierarchy of positions and duties is clearly expressed;
- People are hired and continue to work on the basis of an employment contract;
- People holding a certain position receive a salary, the amount of which depends on the specific position on the hierarchical ladder;
- Bureaucracy is a career structure in which growth occurs by merit or seniority;
- The position held by a person is considered his only or main task;
- The activities of employees are based on strict official discipline and are subject to control.

The American sociologist Merton has identified some negative features of bureaucracy. First, narrow specialization can prevent the adoption of some progressive decisions, from which society as a whole may suffer. Second, the bureaucratic style of thinking, giving rise to routine and formalization, forms a special type of personality, which is usually conservative. Third, as a result, the ideology and interests of the bureaucracy become more significant than those of the people they serve. The interests of the bureaucracy predominate over the public interests, and it becomes a nuisance to social development.

One of the main approaches to analyzing the organization as an object of management is the mechanistic (rational) approach. Within the framework of the mechanistic (rational) approach, each part of the organization is separated and studied in isolation at a specific in time. The organization is presented as an “instrument”, a rational means for achieving clearly defined goals; as a set of separate independent parts, capable of changing and replacing one another, without disturbing the overall structure of the organization.

The creators of this approach, including Max Weber, neglect the importance of informal relations between members of the organization. The “organization – machine” model was created and developed by the French engineer and researcher, ideologist of the classical (administrative) school of management, Henri Fayol (Mladenov & Terziev, 2011a).

It plays an important role in the development of modern sociology of organization and management theory. In this concept, the organization is viewed as an impersonal mechanism in which formal-rational relations between workers and the hierarchical management structure prevail. Moreover, the task of the administration is to exercise control, coordination and planning of the work of the various units of the organization. A. Fayol believed that the work efficiency depends solely on management and the accurate distribution of labor. In this way, the organization is understood as an impersonal mechanism, an instrument for solving socially significant problems, and the person is a formal executor, an elementary cell in the general management system.

According to him, the operations that take place in the management of an enterprise are six separate groups (Mladenov & Terziev, 2011a):

- technical –production and processing;
- commercial – procurement and sales;
- financial – capital acquisition and management;
- security – protection of people and assets;
- accounting – inventory, balance sheets, maintenance and statistics;
- administrative – operations of forecasting, distribution, organization, coordination and control.

In one of his works, A. Fayol notes: “Management means planning, organization, command, coordination and control”:

- forecasting – studying the future and drawing up an action plan;
- organizing – establishing the material and social mechanisms of the enterprise;
- commanding – mobilizing people and personnel into action;
- coordination – connecting and uniting the efforts and actions of people;
- controlling – ensuring that everything proceeds according to established rules and orders.

Using his concept of management, A. Fayol formulated fourteen principles of management. These principles have not lost their relevance today, although they should not be accepted unconditionally and their use requires experience, reflection and responsibility (Mladenov & Terziev, 2011a):

– Division of labor. Leads to a clear specialization of functions and division of power in the enterprise. Execution of a large volume of work with higher quality;
– Authority and responsibility. Authority gives the right to give orders, and responsibility is its opposite. Where authority is given, there is also responsibility;
– Discipline. It implies the implementation of the agreements sealed between the company and the workers. It also implies the fair sanctions in case of its violation;
– Unity of command. The worker should receive orders only from his immediate superior;
– Compliance with the unity of leadership, i.e. one leader, as well as a common plan for the actions that are to be carried out in the name of a common goal for all;
– Subordination of personal interests to the general. The interests of one worker or group of workers should not prevail over those of the company;
– Remuneration of personnel. In order to ensure performance and support from workers, they should receive fair remuneration for their work;
– Centralization. The degree of centralization depends on the specific conditions. This gives rise to whatever proportion between centralization and decentralization. This gives good results in implementing the company's plan;
– Clarity in the hierarchy - a clear path along which messages pass "from top to bottom" and "bottom to top";
– Order. A place for everyone and everyone in their place;
– Fairness. This means benevolence with justice;
– Sustainability. Middle-level managers to be kept in the same position for a longer period of time;
– Initiative. Developing a plan and ensuring its successful implementation.

– Corporate spirit. It is created as a result of mutual understanding between the staff (Terziev & Georgiev, 2023; Georgiev & Terziev, 2023a; Terziev et al., 2023b; Terziev, 2023c; Vovchenko et al., 2023d; Vovchenko et al., 2022; Terziev et al., 2020a; Terziev et al., 2020b; Terziev et al., 2021a; Terziev et al., 2021b; Terziev et al., 2021c; Terziev and Lyubcheva, 2022a; Terziev et al., 2024).

2. CORPORATE CULTURE AND PERSONNEL MANAGEMENT IN "SMART FARM"

The general theoretical principles of corporate culture are applicable to the management of any manufacturing enterprise. However, the mechanisms for practical implementation should be tailored to the specific characteristics of a given economic sector. In agriculture, the organization and management processes differ somewhat from those in other industries. This distinction arises from the unique nature of the primary means of production: land, as well as the use of living organisms and plants as objects of labor (Petrova & Petrov, 2022b; Akbiyik & Can, 2023e; Dinçsoy & Can, 2023f; Ponomarev, 2014).

The concept of a "smart farm" aims to equip modern dairy farm owners with decision-support tools and advanced automation technologies. These technologies integrate equipment, services, and knowledge seamlessly to enhance milk quality, herd management, productivity, and overall profitability.

Based on this definition of the "smart farm", the following conditions are essential for its effective functioning:

- informatization of all farm processes through the inegration of Big Data elements;
- minimization of uncertainty, including the mitigation of the "human factor";
- maximum consideration of the natural-climatic and socio-economic characteristics of the region;
- availability of trained personnel to operate and manage the technologies effectively.

The development and adoption of new automated and robotic technologies, combined with the modernization and digitalization of existing machinery systems, can optimize costs, shorten project implementation timelines, and create favorable conditions for expanding the use of digital technologies in the dairy industry (Kibanov & Batkayeva, 2011b).

The concept of "culture" has been extensively analyzed across various scientific disciplines, including philosophy, sociology, and cultural studies. The term "culture" is commonly associated with the level of intellectual, spiritual, and aesthetic development of a society, its degree of civilization, the abstract state of a community during a specific historical period, and the forms and products of intellectual and artistic activity.

In the modern context, agrarian culture increasingly integrates into the global cultural system while retaining its distinct characteristics in all its specific forms, ranging from professional to individual (Dzhonson et al., 2015a). Corporate culture, as a subset of this broader cultural framework, is evident in all aspects of the activities of both individual entrepreneurs and entire enterprises. It encompasses elements such as staff appearance, clothing, attitudes toward clients, workplace cleanliness, the design and style of business interactions, and the creation of an atmosphere of trust or hostility.

The corporate culture of some organizations fosters a strong desire among individuals to collaborate with or work within such companies, while the culture of others can provoke contrasting feelings, such as rejection or antipathy. These external manifestations of corporate culture are rooted in the underlying values and attitudes that shape the organization's worldview.

A key responsibility of the general manager is to transform the company's employees into a cohesive team united by shared values, professional ethics, and a common culture. To achieve this, the company's leadership, including its owners and general manager, often establishes a "state within a state"-an internal identity that shapes how the organization is perceived by both its personnel and external stakeholders. This process involves developing distinct organizational attributes, such as a logo, slogan, corporate identity, colors, corporate code, and a set of rules, including sanctions or fines where necessary. Employees are encouraged to cultivate a sense of patriotism and loyalty toward the organization.

In essence, the leadership works to forge a unique identity and cohesive team spirit within the company by setting behavioral standards and introducing regulatory frameworks to uphold established norms. The practice of uniting individuals under a shared set of moral principles is deeply rooted in history. Religious, military, professional, and other organizations have long relied on this approach to foster ideological cohesion and a unified mindset. Examples include the Ten Commandments of the Old Testament, the Samurai Code of Bushido, the Hippocratic Oath, and professional codes of ethics for various disciplines. These frameworks illustrate the unification of like-minded individuals through formal or informal rules that establish shared norms and values (Aksakova, 2009; Petrova & Petrov, 2022b).

2.1. Formation and Analysis of the Organization's Corporate Culture

The formation of corporate culture is a complex and long-term systematic process. Applying a systems approach to this process enables the identification of the key components of corporate culture development within an organization (Petrova & Petrov, 2022b):

- Defining the mission of the organization;
- Establishing the organization's goals;

– Identifying core values;
– Developing behavioral standards for members of the organization based on these core values;
– Creating traditions and symbols that embody the organization's mission, goals, values, and behavioral standards.

These steps and their outcomes are typically documented in a corporate code. This document plays a crucial role in hiring and onboarding new employees by facilitating an assessment of how well potential hires align with the organization's values (Shatalova et al., 2003).

According to Kurt Lewin's model of strategic change, the formation of corporate culture unfolds sequentially through several stages:

– "thawing' the existing corporate culture to prepare for change;
– Conducting diagnostics and research to understand the current state;
– planning and implementation of the necessary changes;
– "movement";
– "freezing";
– consolidating and institutionalizing the achieved results.

There are various classifications of corporate culture. T. E. Deal and A. A. Kennedy identify four primary types of corporate culture based on two key parameters: the level of risk and the speed of feedback (Batkayeva et al., 2015b):

– High-risk, fast-feedback culture. This type of culture is characterized by individuals who are predominantly individualistic, frequently engage in risk-taking behavior, and receive rapid feedback on their actions, whether positive or negative;
– Low-risk, fast-feedback culture. In this culture, employees face minimal risk and are motivated to perform intensive tasks with relatively low uncertainty. Actions receive prompt feedback, primarily dictated by customer satisfaction. The central focus is on customer service and meeting client expectations. Unlike the emphasis on individual achievements, the collective efforts of the team are of primary importance;
– High-risk, slow-feedback culture. Organizations with this culture operate in high-risk environments with significant investments and long decision-making cycles. Feedback on actions is slow, often taking years. This culture emphasizes a long-term perspective and sustainability, as decisions require careful planning and patience;

– Low-risk, slow-feedback culture. This culture is characterized by low levels of risk and slow feedback processes. Both employees and management prioritize meticulous attention to detail, thorough risk assessment, and technical excellence. Significant importance is placed on maintaining documentation, archival records, notes, and continuous technical improvements.

William Ouchi, a prominent American management specialist, proposes a typology of corporate culture based on the regulation of relationships and interactions within organizations (Aksakova, 2009; Kibanov & Batkayeva, 2011b; Chemekov, 2000):

– Market culture. This type of culture is grounded in value-based relationships, where both management and employees are primarily focused on profitability. Efficiency is measured by cost indicators, which are directly linked to production expenses. The primary objective is to minimize production costs. The effectiveness of market mechanisms ensures the long-term sustainability of organizations operating within this cultural framework;
– Bureaucratic culture. Bureaucratic culture relies on a formal management system that regulates organizational activities through established rules, procedures, and instructions. Competence serves as the primary source of authority and power. This culture proves effective in stable, predictable environments; however, its efficiency diminishes as environmental uncertainty increases;
– Clan culture. Clan culture is often considered complementary to the market and bureaucratic cultures. It can coexist within the frameworks of either culture. The clan culture is built upon a shared system of values established by the organization. These values do not strictly regulate behavior but instead provide direction, creating flexibility and freedom of action. This adaptability allows organizations to respond effectively to dynamic and changing conditions.

Edgar Schein defines corporate culture as "...a set of core beliefs that are independently formed, learned, or developed by a particular group as it learns to solve problems of adaptation to the external environment and internal integration, that have proven effective enough to be considered valuable and are therefore passed on to new members as the correct way to perceive, think, and relate to specific problems." (Petrova & Petrov, 2022b)

The increasingly dynamic external environment compels organizations to adapt to societal changes and identify additional resources to maintain competitiveness. Corporate culture is one of the critical factors influencing an organization's ability to remain competitive.

Effective managers, particularly in the agricultural sector, utilize corporate culture as a strategic tool for personnel management, tailored to the specific conditions of farm operations. In farms with a strong corporate culture, employees exhibit heightened empathy, personal responsibility for the farm's success, and, consequently, strong loyalty to the organization. A robust culture also accelerates the integration of new employees, helping them adapt quickly to operational norms.

Corporate culture encompasses not only universal norms and rules but also business-specific practices and informal guidelines. It evolves organically, shaped by a combination of internal and external factors. The existence of numerous typologies reflects the multifaceted nature of corporate culture and highlights the challenges of selecting a singular framework to characterize an organization. In practice, the perception of corporate culture by management often leads to the creation of customized typologies, as no single model perfectly aligns with the specific conditions of every organization.

Despite these methodological complexities, the development of corporate culture remains highly relevant. Establishing a strong corporate culture has the potential to elevate farm operations to a new level of development, marked by the optimized use of both material and human resources.

Corporate culture is a formalized (code) or informalized system of values, communication norms, standards, traditions that exist in the organization. Corporate culture includes not only the working conditions of employees and the level of wages, but also corporate values on the farm, the employee information system, including the information exchange chain between the manager and the employee, the cultural recreation of the farm employees. Corporate culture can be formalized as a set of values or a corporate code.

Corporate (organizational) culture performs a number of functions Corporate culture refers to a formalized (as in a code) or informal system of values, communication norms, standards, and traditions that exist within an organization. It encompasses not only the working conditions and wage levels of employees but also the core values upheld on the farm, the employee information system (including the communication channels between management and staff), and the cultural activities available to farm employees. Corporate culture can be formalized in the form of a set of values or a corporate code.

Corporate (organizational) culture serves several key functions:

– The security function is to create a protective barrier, shielding the farm from undesirable external influences;
– Integrating function - strengthens the social stability of the farm, acting as a social glue that binds the organization together and ensures adherence to its established standards of behavior;

– Regulatory function - establishes and controls the appropriate forms of behavior and perceptions within the organization, guiding how employees should think and act.;
– The orienting function of corporate culture directs the activities of the organization and its members, ensuring alignment with its goals and values;
– Motivational function - fosters commitment to the organization's mission, promoting a sense of belonging and dedication among employees;
– The function of the organization's image - helps shape the organization's public image, distinguishing it from other entities in the sector.

The development of corporate culture on a farm is not an overnight process; it is labor-intensive and resource-demanding. However, it is a critical endeavor, as it significantly contributes to the effectiveness of the farm's motivation management system. This process can be refined with varying degrees of complexity. An expanded set of elements within the motivation management system is illustrated in Figure 1 (Petrova & Petrov, 2022b).

Figure 1. The structure of the elements of the motivation management system

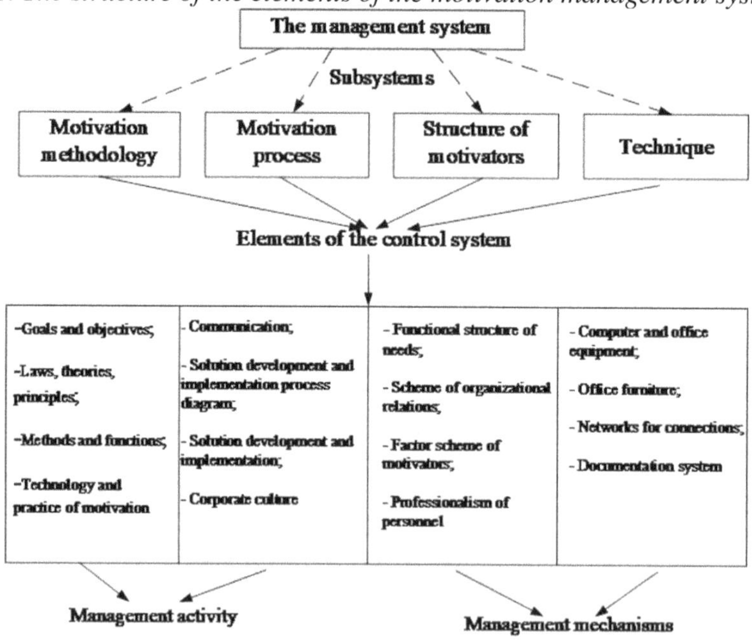

Source: authors

The methodology of motivation encompasses goals, principles, theories, functions, methods, technologies, and practical applications. The motivational process is a communication system involving the development and implementation of management decisions, as well as the provision of necessary information. The structure of motivators includes both functional and organizational frameworks, organizational relationship schemes, factor schemes of motivators, and the professionalism of the personnel. Management technology includes computer and organizational equipment, office furniture, communication networks (both internal and external, including the Internet), and document management systems.

In turn, the methodology and process of management shape management activities, while the structure and techniques of motivation form the management mechanism. The effectiveness of the employee motivation system directly impacts the overall performance and success of the organization (Petrova & Petrov, 2022b).

Creating favorable conditions for productive work is a highly beneficial business strategy. In addition to the positive effects associated with reducing staff turnover, such conditions contribute to increased average annual labor productivity and improved overall employee well-being. Another important factor in motivation is fostering a positive attitude toward work and its outcomes. This includes improving the socio-psychological climate, enhancing both material and moral incentives, cultivating value orientations, promoting responsible stewardship of company property, encouraging workers' active involvement in labor-related activities, increasing the prestige and attractiveness of farm labor, and providing opportunities for cultural recreation.

Numerous studies demonstrate the effectiveness of various factors on employee motivation. For instance, a positive socio-psychological climate within a team has been shown to increase production efficiency by 15-18%. Additionally, fostering a sense of thrift in relation to the means of production and enhancing workers' sense of responsibility for their labor outcomes contribute to increased farm profitability. The structure of external labor motivators is highly dynamic, with each factor manifesting at different levels and requiring corresponding management approaches.

The socio-psychological climate, for example, is primarily cultivated within the immediate team, while improving discipline involves efforts from both the workers and the farm as a whole. Furthermore, the creation of social conditions is a responsibility that extends beyond the farm to include the state. Therefore, for the effective application of motivational factors, a more detailed grouping is necessary, one that considers the specific characteristics of the sector, the degree to which each factor is utilized, and their situational combinations.

An increasing number of farm managers recognize that the integration of corporate culture into management practices significantly enhances the competitiveness of their organizations. This is particularly important for farms due to several factors:

– The farm workforce consists of individuals with varying levels of training and education, ranging from specialized experts to general laborers;
– The territorial fragmentation of farm divisions;
– The nature of the work, which involves direct interaction with animals.

The fundamental condition for the success of a corporate culture is the alignment of its values with those of the employees, fostering a unified direction. This alignment provides a competitive advantage in farm management and contributes to the overall efficiency of the farm's operations (Petrova & Petrov, 2022b).

3. MODERN THEORIES OF MOTIVATION

In contemporary organizational management science, it is widely acknowledged that the foundational assumptions underlying early motivational theories are flawed, although these concepts still warrant understanding. In previous eras, people's behavior and the customs they adhered to were often misunderstood as being highly effective. These methods proved successful for many years, but in recent decades, modern theories have emerged, requiring a cultural shift towards new, contemporary understandings of motivation (Mladenov & Terziev, 2011a).

Many managers may be inclined to adopt these traditional, simplistic, and pragmatic approaches, but such an approach is misguided. Employees in today's organizations are generally more educated than in the past, making their motivations more complex and challenging to influence. A clear understanding of motivation is essential in addressing these complexities. A brief historical overview helps to emphasize that effective motivation, like all aspects of management, is context-dependent.

The policy of reward and punishment remains central to motivating employees. Punishment may include the deprivation of bonuses, warnings, salary reductions, demotions, or dismissals, while encouragement typically involves promotions, financial rewards, and recognition.

When the "school of scientific management" emerged in the early 20th century, particularly in 1910, societal changes had not yet significantly advanced, despite technological progress. Frederick Taylor and his colleagues, who pioneered this approach, recognized the inefficiencies in production at the time. They emphasized the principle of "punishment and incentive", introducing the concept of "sufficient daily production" and proposing a payment system where wages were tied to output: the higher the quantity produced, the greater the compensation. The productivity gains achieved through this method, combined with more effective specialization and standardization, were remarkable for their era. The success of the "punishment and incentive" motivational framework has stood the test of time and continues to be utilized by organizational leaders today.

As companies increasingly capitalized on technological advancements and specialization, the quality of life for workers gradually improved. As living standards rose, managers began to recognize that simple incentives did not always drive increased effort. This realization prompted management scholars to explore new psychological approaches to motivation.

Attempts to use psychological methods in management. Although earlier attempts had been made to apply psychological principles in management, it was with the advent of Elton Mayo's work that the potential benefits of such approaches became clear. Moreover, it became evident that the traditional "punishment and reward" motivational framework was no longer sufficient.

Elton Mayo was one of the few scholars of his time who possessed a solid understanding of scientific management coupled with a strong background in psychology. He gained significant recognition for conducting an experiment in a textile factory during 1923-1924. The turnover rate in the spinning section of the factory had reached a staggering 250%, while turnover in other sections was only 5-6%. The material incentives proposed by efficiency experts were ineffective in reducing personnel turnover or increasing productivity in this particular section. As a result, the manager of the organization sought the assistance of Mayo and his colleagues to address the issue (Mladenov & Terziev, 2011a).

Upon conducting a thorough study of the situation, Mayo determined that the working conditions in the spinning section hindered communication among workers and failed to convey sufficient respect for their roles. He concluded that the solution to reducing turnover did not lie in increasing wages, but rather in improving the work environment. With the approval of management, he proposed granting workers two ten-minute breaks, which marked a key intervention in addressing the problem.

After carefully studying the situation, Mayo concluded that the working conditions in the spinning section hindered communication among workers and failed to convey adequate respect for their roles. He determined that the solution to reducing turnover lay in improving the working conditions, rather than increasing wages. With management's approval, Mayo proposed introducing two ten-minute breaks for the workers.

The results were striking. Employee turnover dropped significantly, and productivity increased. However, when the labor inspector later abolished these breaks, the situation reverted to its previous state, confirming that Mayo's intervention had indeed improved the working conditions of the department.

The "spinning wheel" experiment provided Mayo with valuable insight into the importance of considering workers' psychology, particularly the impact of seemingly minor behavioral "deviations". He concluded, "So far, social and industrial research has not sufficiently recognized that small deviations in the consciousness of the "average normal man" accumulate in his actions. While these deviations may not lead to a collapse in his psychology, they can result in a collapse in his work." However, Mayo himself did not fully grasp the significance of his discovery in this area, as psychology was still in its early stages of development at the time.

The first significant studies on worker behavior in the workplace were based on the Hawthorne experiments conducted by Elton Mayo and his associates in the late 1920s. The primary conclusion drawn from these experiments was that human factors, particularly social interaction and group dynamics, significantly influence individual labor productivity. These findings led to the development of a new management approach— the concept of "human relations", which dominated management theory until the mid-1950s (Mladenov & Terziev, 2011a).

However, while the Hawthorne experiments provided valuable insights, they did not yield comprehensive models of motivation that could fully explain the driving forces behind work behavior. Psychological theories of work motivation emerged much later, in the 1940s, and continue to evolve today.

The systematic study of motivation from a psychological perspective does not provide a definitive answer to what motivates an individual to work. However, research on human behavior in the workplace offers general explanations of motivation and enables the development of pragmatic models to understand and influence employee motivation.

Contemporary scholars in organizational management categorize motivation theories into two broad categories: content theories and process theories.

Content theories of motivation focus on identifying the internal drives (often referred to as needs) that compel individuals to behave in certain ways. Prominent content theories include those developed by Abraham Maslow, David McClelland, and Frederick Herzberg.

Process theories of motivation, which are more recent, focus on how individuals behave based on their perceptions. Key process theories include expectancy theory, equity theory, and the Porter-Lawler model of motivation.

Although these theories differ in various aspects, they are not mutually exclusive. The development of motivation theories follows an evolutionary, rather than a revolutionary, trajectory.

To fully understand the significance of content and process theories of motivation, it is essential to grasp the meaning of two fundamental concepts: needs and rewards.

Primary and secondary needs. Psychologists suggest that an individual experiences a need when they perceive physiological or psychological deficiencies. At any given moment, a person may not consciously feel the presence of such needs. Content theories of motivation aim to classify these universal human needs into distinct categories, although there is no universally accepted classification. However, most psychologists generally agree that needs can be broadly categorized as primary and secondary.

Primary needs are physiological in nature and are typically innate. Examples include the need for water, food, sleep, and sexual drive. Secondary needs, on the other hand, are psychological and encompass desires such as respect, affection, power, and the need for success. While primary needs are genetically determined, secondary needs are often shaped by individual experiences. As a result, secondary needs tend to vary more significantly among individuals compared to primary needs, given the diversity of personal experiences.

Needs and Motivational Behavior. Needs cannot be directly observed or measured; rather, their existence is inferred from individuals' behavior. Psychologists have determined that needs act as the driving force behind human actions.

When a person becomes aware of a need, it triggers a state of aspiration. This urge represents a feeling of deficiency and is directed toward fulfilling the need. It serves as a behavioral manifestation, focused on achieving specific goals that are perceived as means of satisfying the need. Upon reaching these goals, an individual's need may be fully satisfied, partially satisfied, or remain unsatisfied.

The degree of satisfaction derived from achieving a goal influences future behavior in similar situations. Generally, individuals are more likely to repeat behaviors that lead to the fulfillment of their needs and avoid behaviors that result in inadequate satisfaction. This phenomenon is known as the law of consequence.

To the extent that needs drive individuals to seek satisfaction, managers must create environments where employees feel that their actions can fulfill both personal and organizational goals. For instance, the introduction of new coal mining technology disrupted independent work groups and deprived miners of the close interpersonal relationships they once had. This example illustrates how the nature of the work environment and associated tasks can impact the satisfaction of individual needs. The new technology did not provide miners with a sense of accomplishment, as each worker only performed a small segment of the overall coal mining process. As a result, employees lacked the opportunity to demonstrate their full abilities. This led to deteriorating production discipline, increased downtime and labor turnover, and reduced labor productivity. These issues were resolved when management modified the production process to align with workers' needs, ensuring that the technology no longer conflicted with the workers' sense of fulfillment.

It is important to note that not all employees have a high need for achievement or independence. People possess a unique combination of traits, which implies that there are diverse human needs, different personal goals for satisfying these needs, and various types of behavior involved in achieving these goals.

Creating jobs with more complex tasks and greater responsibility can have a positive motivational effect for many employees, but this approach does not apply universally. Managers must recognize that there is no single optimal method for motivating employees. What proves effective for some individuals may be completely irrelevant for others. Moreover, the inherent structure of organizations complicates the application of motivation theories that are oriented toward individual differences.

The interdependence of work tasks, limited information about the performance of individual employees, and frequent changes in job responsibilities due to technological advancements all contribute to the complexity of motivation in the workplace (Mladenov & Terziev, 2011a).

4. MOTIVATIONAL MODEL FOR CONTEMPORARY MEDICAL TOURISM DEVELOPMENT

The economic potential of integrating the tourism industry with business interests in the field of public health holds strategic significance for both regional (local) governments and proactive business owners within these sectors. The primary motivations, which also serve as prerequisites for this assertion, can be described as follows: the development of tourism, along with health and medical services, leads to the achievement of:

– Enhancing the dynamics of regional financial flows, which consequently leads to an increase in financial resources. For example, tourists temporarily residing in a region contribute to the local economy by spending money, thereby supporting regional economic relations. In this context, the consumption of health and medical services by tourists during their stay directly contributes to economic profits, as tourists become active consumers of various goods and services within the region;

– Improving the economic stability of the region, which creates favorable conditions for: the employment of the local population and the reduction of unemployment among key demographic groups, such as youth and women; the growth of local income levels; the enhancement of the quality of life and living standards for the local population.

– The development of the tourism sector can significantly contribute to the economic prosperity of businesses in related industries, such as medical and health services. This impact is evident through several key outcomes, including: an increase in the number and diversity of social, health-improving, and cultural-educational events; the localization of medical tourism based on the availability of specific resource bases; the modernization of recreational and entertainment facilities; and improvements in infrastructure and transportation quality;

– Improving the quality of life for the population in areas where the health and tourism industries are simultaneously developed, as well as enhancing the state of the medical, ecological, and socio-cultural environment, are key outcomes of such development. This improvement is particularly evident in the increased public attention to maintaining the infrastructure of modernized medical facilities, protecting the environment, preserving architectural monuments, and developing convenient and accessible transportation infrastructure;

– Increasing the recognition, popularity, and integration of the region by developing its competitive advantages, and expanding opportunities for regional growth through the implementation of large-scale social, health, and economic development projects and programs;

– Enhancing the stability and sustainable development of the region while mitigating the risks associated with living in unhealthy conditions, a health-risk environment, and environmental insecurity;

– Improving regional competitiveness, which is reflected in the health tourist's assessment of the competitive advantages of a destination. This assessment determines whether the tourist considers the destination 'worthy' of meeting their needs or not.

Regions are therefore motivated to enhance the attractiveness of their territorial tourist and medical-health improvement zones, which are defined by the effective integration of medical and tourism infrastructure, along with the availability of conditions conducive to socio-cultural and health-improvement adaptation. It is important to emphasize that recreational resources, as objects of tourist interest, are primarily successful marketing products. These products are presented with 'appealing and attractive packaging,' with a promotional focus on medical tourism. Moreover, such initiatives should receive funding from regional and national budgets.

4.1. Development of Modern Medical Tourism

Prior to the COVID-19 pandemic, in the context of the dynamic progress of the global economy, tourism experienced not only a significant increase in tourist flows but also a notable expansion in the number of destinations, types of tourism, and tourist profiles. This reflects the ongoing segmentation of the tourism market. These developments manifest in the increasing diversification of tourism demand, which is met by a corresponding diversification in tourism supply. Some destinations have become multidisciplinary, others have reoriented their offerings to target new markets, and some have revived previously diminished market positions. These trends have affected resort destinations worldwide.

In the contemporary global tourism landscape, resort destinations are characterized by a wide diversity and unique historical development. These destinations specialize in various types and forms of medical tourism, offering different service types and technologies, and cater to distinct target markets. Additionally, they vary in terms of the scope of their target audience and emerging development trends. Health tourism, as a segment of the broader tourism market, constitutes a relatively small share of global tourist flows. A key challenge is the difficulty in processing statistical data, primarily due to the large number of subtypes and forms of health tourism across different countries and regions. Many of these forms remain unstudied due to their nationally specific characteristics, and there is a lack of comprehensive research on the variety of medical and health services offered within different states. These factors complicate the study and management of resort destinations, while simultaneously highlighting the relevance of scientific inquiry and research in the field of resort management and health tourism.

An increasing number of experts from various countries are focusing their research on the sustainable development of resort destinations and medical tourism. This trend is driven by both the diverse opportunities presented by contemporary conditions for the development of the tourism market and the emerging challenges in the modern management of resort towns. However, scholars worldwide have observed that the rapid growth of health tourism is outpacing the existing body of literature, with recent publications on its development struggling to keep up with the speed and diversity of its expansion (Kuvshinova, 2014a).

Throughout the history of tourism, people have traveled for health and wellness purposes. While the exact origins of health tourism remain uncertain due to the lack of written evidence, scholars generally agree that "health tourism is as old as ancient history and as modern as the future" (Suchitra, 2015c). Health tourism is both a historically established practice that defines the purpose of travel and a contemporary, global industry. It encompasses a broad range of opportunities and services, facilitated by new technologies arising from medical advancements and the development of social communications. Modern medical tourism is primarily aimed at maintaining or improving health and is focused on destinations and facilities specializing in the provision of medical and health services. These include sea climate resorts, balneological or balneoclimatic resorts, thermal resorts by warm lakes, sanatoriums and hospitals offering mineral waters and mud treatments, thermal springs, as well as mountain climate and ski resorts.

Experts identify three main forms of health tourism:

– treatment or medical tourism – this form involves travel to specific medical facilities or specialists to receive highly specialized treatments or to access medical services of a higher quality than those available in the tourist's home region);
– recovery – also referred to as fitness & wellness or spa & wellness, this includes trips to specialized facilities such as mud or hydrotherapy clinics, weight loss centers, cosmetology clinics, or fitness and health resorts aimed at promoting general well-being and health recovery.;
– rehabilitation – this form of tourism involves travel to destinations or facilities offering specialized care or located in regions that are particularly conducive to health recovery or rehabilitation (Han Team, 2009a).

Health tourism is becoming increasingly diversified, reflecting the niche segmentation within this type of travel. Over the past decade, medical tourism has emerged as a rapidly growing segment and a significant industry, attracting millions of travelers annually (Dokuchaev, 2015d). Once considered a niche market within the tourism industry, it has now become mainstream. For many countries, medical tourism represents a rapidly expanding global industry, generating substantial revenues and attracting a growing number of specialists from various medical fields. This trend reflects the increasing demand for a wide array of medical services. A key characteristic of health tourism is its diversification, which mirrors the evolving preferences of travelers and the corresponding segmentation of the market for health services. This segmented approach has led to the development and consolidation of categories such as "curative", "clinical", "medical", "restorative", "thermal", "spa", and "wellness tourism", among others.

Modern health tourists visit the same destinations and often for the same reasons as in previous centuries. However, advancements in technology and shifts in tourism trends, including the diversification of demand and patterns of tourist consumption, have introduced new destinations, opportunities, and challenges to the health tourism industry. Tourists who once frequented Mediterranean resorts are now seeking treatment in Turkish hospitals, which are equipped with cutting-edge medical technology and staffed by specialized professionals. Similarly, tourists are traveling to India for high-tech heart surgeries. France has established a healthcare system that is ranked as the best in the world by the World Health Organization (2011), and global demand for the services provided by French clinics continues to rise.

The development of health tourism is marked by an increasing number of countries and regions emerging as destinations for health-related travel. For instance, China has become a prominent destination for experimental stem cell therapy. Even the cruise industry is expanding its services by incorporating medical tourism offerings aboard its ships.

These evolving conditions and trends are prompting significant changes that modern entrepreneurs, particularly those with interests in combining tourism and healthcare, must consider. One such change is the need to incorporate and account for several new characteristics that are now integral to the development and growth of health tourism:

– Age demographics: The aging populations in many affluent countries have significantly increased the demand for healthcare services. Older tourists are increasingly seeking treatment options that offer shorter wait times and more affordable prices for services addressing chronic conditions in health tourism destinations;

– Increasing emphasis on "youth culture": In Western countries, particularly the United States, a "youth culture" is emerging. This concept and ideology emphasize the importance of maintaining a youthful appearance and health at any age, with individuals striving to project physical health, beauty, strength, endurance, and vitality. This trend manifests in people's growing desire to delay the aging process, both in terms of their appearance and overall well-being. As a result, spending on health-related services, including cosmetic procedures and anti-aging therapies, has become a significant part of personal expenditures, alongside spending on vacations, real estate, and luxury goods;

– Cost of Health Services (An Important Factor for Medical Tourism): The cost of healthcare is a critical factor for many medical tourists, especially for those who lack health insurance in their home country, have limited insurance coverage, or face high deductibles for medical care. For these individuals, medical tourism offers a cost-effective alternative, enabling them to receive more attentive services at lower costs. In many cases, tourists can access well-equipped accommodation facilities for themselves and their companions, often surpassing the level of care and amenities available in their home countries;

– Increased Media Attention to Medical Tourism: Media coverage of medical tourism has contributed to increased public awareness of its benefits and opportunities. In 1990, there were no reports on medical tourism in the English-language media. By 1992, there were eight reports, and by 2007, this number had grown to over 2,300. Online, a Google search for "medical tourism" yielded 1,100,000 results on July 29, 2007. Within two months, this number had surged to 300,000,000, and by mid-January 2012, it had reached 7,370,000. As of 2020, the number of search results had risen to 21,800,000. This dramatic increase in media attention highlights the growing global interest in medical tourism.

– Increased Accessibility to Tourism: The global reduction in airfares, coupled with the introduction of low-cost airlines, has significantly enhanced the accessibility of tourism for mass travelers, including those seeking medical care. As a result, greater awareness of available medical and health services has become a reality. More individuals now have both the desire and the opportunity to travel for medical purposes, further expanding the reach of medical tourism.

A significant trend in the development of health tourism is its increasing positive impact on the economy of the destination. This growth is associated with the enhancement of medical services and overall healthcare standards, leading to an improvement in the quality of life for local residents in communities hosting tourists. Tourists benefit from high-quality medical care at competitive prices, while the expenditure they incur supports other sectors of tourism, stimulates the healthcare industry, and bolsters local economies. Additionally, the influx of health tourists contributes to the improvement of public health in countries that serve as tourist destinations.

Modern medical tourism presents a number of challenges, including concerns related to the responsibility of healthcare providers, the reliability of services, medical confidentiality, financial accountability, and security. In some countries, medical services may involve experimental or even dangerous procedures that are prohibited elsewhere. A particularly serious issue is the increasing commodification of health, where tourists may purchase illegal medical supplies, such as organs for transplantation.

A notable trend in the development of health tourism is the rapid growth of the spa tourism segment. Experts suggest that spa tourism not only plays a role in preventing and treating chronic diseases but also contributes to an individual's overall well-being and personal harmony. The expectations of tourists participating in spa tourism can be classified into several categories: spending time in a tranquil environment, relaxation and recreation in comfort and quality, benefits for personal health and self-esteem through water therapies, a sense of security and care, access to professional and qualified staff, and a price-to-quality balance (Erfurt-Cooper & Cooper, 2009b).

4.2. Motivational Model for Forming a Tourist Image in a Regional Aspect

The concept of tourism marketing is closely tied to the development of a positive regional image in the eyes of stakeholders. The primary objective of tourism marketing is to increase profits by selling more tourism products. A well-developed tourist infrastructure and abundant tourist resources allow visitors to form a positive perception of a given region, which, in turn, can enhance its attractiveness and overall image. This positive image not only contributes to regional profitability but also improves the socio-economic situation. The competitiveness and investment attractiveness of a region are largely influenced by the prevailing social and economic conditions within the country. However, the key determinant of a region's investment attractiveness is its image, as it is perceived by society. In the process of establishing a brand for a tourist destination, the same principles apply as in any other business: strengthening the competitive advantages of the region and minimizing its imperfections (Fig. 2) (Suchitra, 2015c).

Figure 2. The regional process of moving towards the tourism branding concept

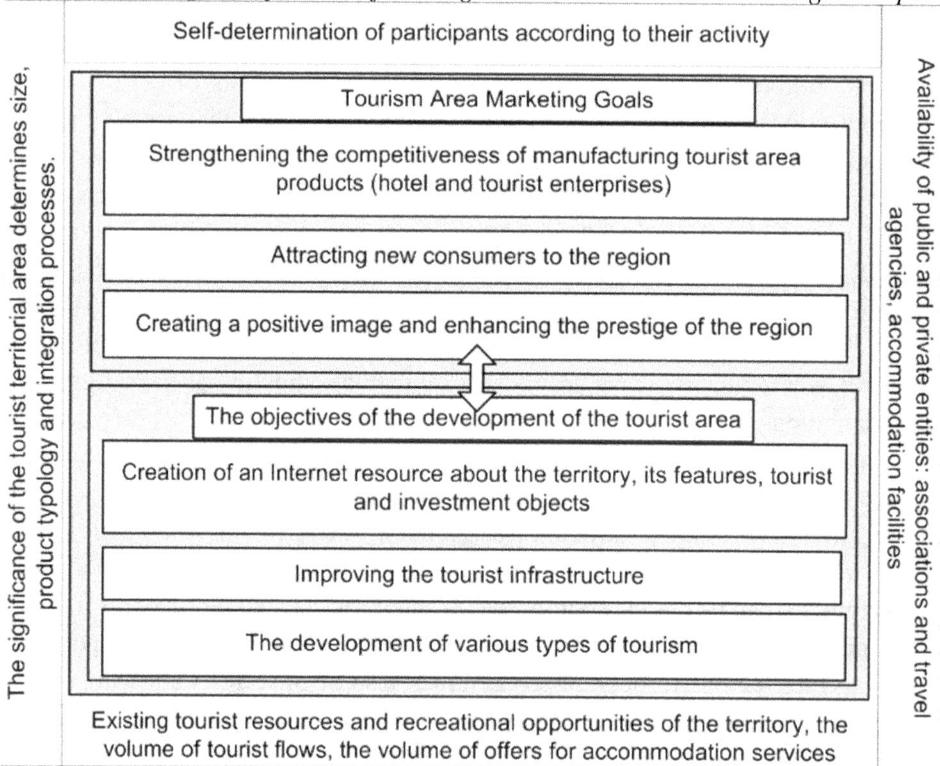

Source: authors

Theoretical and practical research on territory marketing as a tool for developing a medical tourism destination brand forms the foundation for creating a model that shapes the image of a region's tourist territory. This model involves the application of various marketing tools aimed at enhancing the attractiveness of the region's tourist area (Fig. 3) (Han Team, 2009a; Lambier, 2014b; Stolley, 2012).

The tourist image of a region reflects the current state of its economy, the standard of living of its population, climatic factors, and the distinctive features of its history, religion, culture, social life, and education. It also encapsulates the overall level of development and progress within the region. The significance of creating a tourist brand for a territory is twofold: first, it offers substantial potential for attracting additional financial resources, and second, it leads to an increase in the number of tourists and an expansion of the range of tourist services within the region.

Figure 3. Processing of a regional model for image formation of the key indicators of the tourist territory

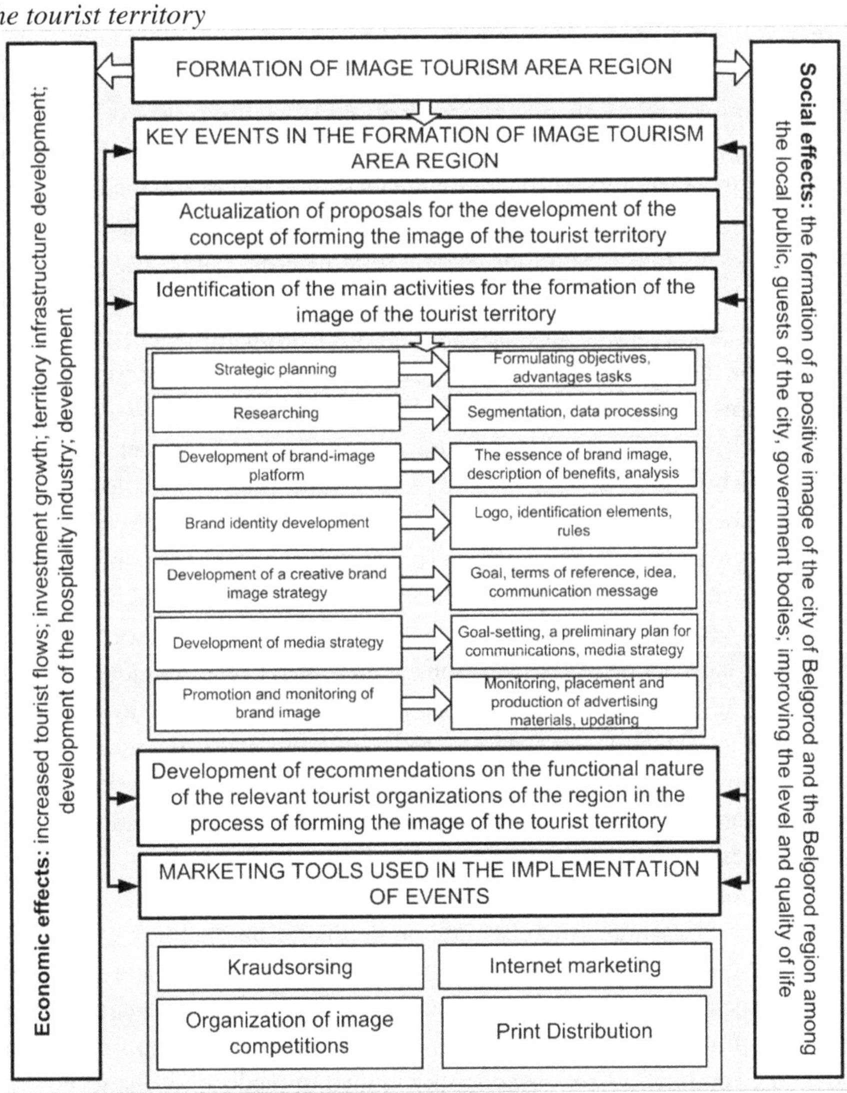

Source: authors

4.3. Trends in the Development of Health and Medical Tourism

Health tourism, and in particular medical tourism, plays a dual role in contributing significantly to the sustainable development of society while also serving as a strategically important source of steadily increasing revenue for the state. Medical tourism is one of the fastest-growing sectors of global tourism. According to forecasts by the World Health Organization (WHO), by 2026, tourism, in conjunction with the healthcare sector, will become one of the most critical areas for the development of national economies.

Health and medical tourism involves visits to clinics and resorts for medical and preventive purposes by both citizens and non-residents staying temporarily in the country for periods ranging from 24 hours to six months. In addition to natural healing resources, factors such as the availability of well-developed tourist infrastructure, the application of innovative technologies, and highly qualified personnel are becoming increasingly significant for the growth of health and medical tourism.

There is currently no unified classification of terms related to health and medical tourism, as various definitions exist across different countries. For example, terms such as health tourism, medical tourism, wellness, spa, and medical wellness are commonly used. Health and medical tourism is typically understood as travel undertaken for the purpose of recreation and health promotion within specialized health programs. According to the WHO, health is defined not only as the absence of disease or physical ailments but as a state of complete physical, mental, and social well-being (Horowitz et al., 2007). The term "health tourism" is most frequently used to describe stays in specialized health facilities. It is advisable to distinguish between medical and health tourism based on the "degree of the medical component" in a patient's overall treatment plan. Treatment may be the primary purpose of the trip, or it may serve as an adjunct to recreational or wellness activities.

Health tourism encompasses at least one of three primary categories of programs: prevention, diagnostic and treatment, and rehabilitation. It offers tourists various medical services (including prevention, rehabilitation, and drug and/or non-drug treatments) provided either in medical facilities (medical tourism) or in specialized accommodations, such as sanatoriums, dispensaries, and other recreational facilities (sanatorium-resort tourism).

Medical tourism typically involves medical interventions conducted in medical institutions, covering areas such as surgery, dentistry, ophthalmology, and more. Accommodation for medical tourists may be provided either at the medical institution itself or at associated facilities, such as hotels, boarding houses, or sanatoriums. Due to this overlap in accommodation types, it is often challenging to obtain distinct statistical data on tourist flows specifically related to medical tourism.

Medical tourism can be defined as the provision of medical services coupled with the relocation of a patient-tourist to a region or country other than their place of permanent residence. This combination inherently involves varying expectations – expectations regarding the treatment outcome, as well as the anticipation of new experiences associated with exploring new destinations. Medical tourism can serve not only as the primary motive or premise for a trip but also as an internal factor driving the journey.

From a service provision perspective, medical tourism introduces a level of complexity to the range of services typically offered by travel agencies. In addition to the usual services – such as accommodation, meals, air and train tickets, and transfers – it is essential to coordinate the timing of medical services with the health facility and to arrange for special conditions related to accommodation and meals.

Currently, there is no standardized approach to the terminology associated with medical tourism. There is no consensus on whether to refer to the client as a "patient" or a "tourist", nor is there clarity on who should provide these services – whether it be a "travel agency" or an "intermediary agent". When travel agencies act as intermediaries in medical tourism, it is advisable to employ specialists with medical qualifications within their staff to offer competent services for selecting health and medical tours. Alternatively, these services could be provided by intermediary companies specializing in medical and health tourism. These companies – medical tourism tour operators – can work directly with individual clients as well as with corporate clients, such as employer organizations, and collaborate with insurance companies and visa centers (Fig. 4).

Figure 4. Medical tourism

Source: authors

Given that the results and consequences of medical procedures can be unpredictable, and the duration of the rehabilitation period varies depending on the individual characteristics of the patient, it is advisable for tourists and patients to obtain a special medical visa to stay in the country of treatment for the required duration.

Under current legislation, employers are permitted to enter into voluntary medical insurance contracts for the benefit of their employees. Contributions made to insurance companies for covering medical expenses and spa treatments for insured employees are considered deductible for the purpose of business taxation (Zhuravleva, 2014c). Furthermore, individuals can receive social deductions for diagnostic, preventive, treatment, and medical rehabilitation services, including those provided by sanatorium-resort organizations (Petkova-Georgieva et al., 2021d; Petrova & Petkova-Georgieva, 2020c).

One of the key priorities in healthcare is the continued development and expansion of high-tech medical care, with a focus on improving accessibility. High-tech medical care encompasses advanced, complex, and scientific technologies that utilize modern equipment and materials, as well as non-invasive and minimally invasive surgical procedures. These procedures are characterized by minimal blood loss, reduced complications, and shorter hospital stays. The advancement of high-tech medical care requires the establishment of innovative medical infrastructure, the identification of priority areas and technologies for development, and the creation of specialized practices for high-tech medical services within the healthcare sector. Additionally, it involves the development of supportive systems to maintain high standards in high-tech medical care, including research, personnel, medical-clinical and technological aspects, as well as industries related to medicine, such as pharmaceuticals, chemical industries, medical instrument manufacturing, optical equipment production, control and measurement instruments, and information technology. Beyond supporting high-tech medicine, other crucial elements for the development of medical tourism in regions include the establishment of specialized medical technology parks, collective use centers, prototyping facilities, business incubators, and clusters.

To attract additional inflows of health tourism, it is essential to promote medical institutions within the international market for medical and health services. To achieve this, it is important to identify priority areas in the field of medical and health services at the state level, such as ophthalmology, cardiac surgery, and in vitro procedures, among others. State-targeted programs should support research and experimental developments in these areas, as the growth of health and, particularly, medical tourism, is largely driven by innovations within the healthcare sector.

Additionally, it is crucial to establish a system of insurance guarantees and implement marketing strategies to promote health services in the international market. At the state level, visa support for foreign medical tourists must be organized.

Regionally, it is important to establish information and consultation centers for foreign patients and to foster cooperation between regional medical associations and medical organizations in other countries (Petkova-Georgieva et al., 2021d; Petrova & Petkova-Georgieva, 2020c; Terziev et al., 2019; Terziev et al., 2021e; Terziev & Georgiev, 2024a; 2024b; 2024c; 2024d; Terziev & Petkova- Georgieva, 2019a; 2019b; 2019c; 2019d; 2019e; 2019f; 2019g; 2020d; 2020e; 2020f; Terziev et al., 2020g).

5. CONCLUSION

A key component of the motivational model for the development of modern medical tourism is effective marketing of the medical tourism product. This encompasses all stages of the process supporting the primary product, including the creation of optimal conditions for stay, provision of additional services, and the organized travel experience. A thorough analysis of each stage is necessary to ensure the medical tourist's objectives are accurately and fully met. The outer layer of the "product framework" consists of positioning and promoting tourist products aimed at generating high-quality demand. Positioning efforts focus on establishing competitive product offerings, with the cost of these efforts influencing the competitive positioning and branding strategies.

It is more effective to promote not just individual tourist products but to position the service and destination as a whole. This involves shaping the image of the destination, the quality of the stay, and the overall concept of the medical services provided, which collectively form the experiences that a tourist can expect from this type of tourism. Key ideas such as creating an unforgettable experience, offering pleasant memories, and fostering a desire to return or recommend the destination and medical facility should guide the advertising campaign for promoting medical tourism in the region. Building the image of a given tourist region as suitable for medical tourism should be a collaborative effort within a cluster of stakeholders, including both tourism and medical sectors. Unlike individual travel agencies, such a cluster has the necessary scale and resources to effectively address the challenges associated with large-scale projects (Petkova-Georgieva et al., 2021d; Petrova & Petkova-Georgieva, 2020c; Dincsoy et al., 2024e).

REFERENCES

Akbiyik, S., & Can, H. (2023e). Structural and Qualitative Defects in Adaptation to Digital Transformation in Local Governments. In Okur Dinçsoy, M., & Can, H. (Eds.), *Optimizing Energy Efficiency During a Global Energy Crisis* (pp. 327–340). IGI Global Scientific Publishing. DOI: 10.4018/979-8-3693-0400-6.ch018

Aksakova, A.N. (2009). Organizational culture of corporate standards: concept, structure, features. Personnel Management, 13 215), 53-56.

Batkayeva, I.A., & Mitrofanova, E.A. (2015b). Personnel management. Theory and practice. Organization of compensation of personnel.

Chemekov, V.P. (2000). Corporate culture and those who form it.

Dincsoy, M., Can, H., Dincsoy, E., & Terziev, V. (2024e). The impact of property rights and government integrity on the economic freedom: the case of the European region, the Brics countries, and the USA. 107th International Scientific Conference on Economic and Social Development – Economic and Social Survival in Global Changes – Zagreb, 16-17 February, 2024, Economic and Social Development (Book of Proceedings), 265-275.

Dinçsoy, M. O., & Can, H. (2023f). The Relationship of Renewable Energy Generation, Renewable Energy Consumption, and Economic Growth: The Case of Türkiye. In Okur Dinçsoy, M., & Can, H. (Eds.), *Optimizing Energy Efficiency During a Global Energy Crisis* (pp. 65–74). IGI Global Scientific Publishing. DOI: 10.4018/979-8-3693-0400-6.ch005

Dokuchaev, D. S. (2015d). Regional identty in the Ivanovo region and politcs of constructon area image: A factor of tourism. *Services and Tourism: Current Challenges*, 9(3), 76–82. DOI: 10.12737/12885

Erfurt-Cooper, P., & Cooper, M. (2009b). *Health and Wellness Tourism: Spas and Hot Springs*. Channel View Publications. DOI: 10.21832/9781845411138

Georgiev, M. P., & Terziev, V. K. (2023a). The Labor Market Policies and Social Development in Bulgaria. In Okur Dinçsoy, M., & Can, H. (Eds.), *Optimizing Energy Efficiency During a Global Energy Crisis* (pp. 239–281). IGI Global Scientific Publishing. DOI: 10.4018/979-8-3693-0400-6.ch015

Han Team. (2009a). Medical Tourism and Global Healthcare: Where Are You Going? Health WorldNet Inc. http: healthworldnet.com/articles/heads-or-tails/medicaltourism-and-global-healthcare-where-are-yougoing.html

Horowitz, M. D., Rosensweig, J. A., & Jones, Ch. A. (2007). Medical Tourism: Globalization of the Healthcare Marketplace. Medscape General Medicine, 9(4), 33. http://www.ncbi.nlm. nih.gov/pmc/articles/PMC2234298/

Kibanov, A. Ya., & Batkayeva, I. A. (2011b). Motivation and stimulation of labor activity.

Kuvshinova, I. A. (2014a). The formaton of the tourist potental of the area, Cultural and health services in educatonal and leisure insttutons: Experience, problems, prospects: Coll. artcles on the materials of VII all-Russian scientfc-practcal conference. Magnitogorsk: Nosov Magnitogorsk State Technical University.

Lambier, C. (2014b). Smooth Sailing: Cruise Lines and Medical Tourism Magazine. http://www.Medicaltourismmag. com/article/Smooth-Sailing-cruise-lines-andmedical-tourism-a-budding-relationship.html

Mladenov, Y., & Terziev, V. (2011a). *Management Fundamentals.*

Petkova-Georgieva, S., Petrova, T., & Petrov, Zh. (2021d). The medical tourism social and public_benefits in the development of tourist services. *Annual of Assen Zlatarov University, Burgas, Bulgaria*, L(2), 31–36.

Petrova, T., & Petkova-Georgieva, S. (2020c). Motivational model for contemporary medical tourism development. Scientific Atlas.

Petrova, T., & Petrov, Zh. (2022b). Corporate culture and personnel management in "Smart farm". Intelligent Animal Husbandry. DOI: 10.15547/joiah.2022.01.005

Ponomarev, I. P. (2014). Motivation work in the organization.

Shatalova, N. I., & Alexandrova, N. A. (2003). Personnel management on production: textbook.

Stolley, K. S. (2012). *Watson S. Medical Tourism: A Reference Book.* ABCCLIO.

Suchitra, P. (2015c). Tourism branding and its relevance in today's marketng scenario. *Internatonal Journal of Business and General Management*, 4(3), 21–28.

Terziev, V., & Petkova-Georgieva, S. (2019a). The Bulgarian health care system practical research on the usefulness of the performance measurement system. Proceedings of ADVED 2019 - 5th International Conference on Advances in Education and Social Sciences, 21-23 October 2019, International Organization Center of Academic Research, 369 - 375.

Terziev, V., & Petkova-Georgieva, S. (2019b). The pesticides toxic impact on the human health condition and the ecosystem. Proceedings of ADVED 2019 - 5th International Conference on Advances in Education and Social Sciences, 376 - 382.

Terziev, V., & Petkova-Georgieva, S. (2019c). Human health problems and the classification of the most toxic pesticides. Proceedings of ADVED 2019 - 5th International Conference on Advances in Education and Social Sciences, 383 - 390.

Terziev, V., & Petkova-Georgieva, S. (2019d). Organo-phosphonate, organo-halogenated, cyanides and arsenic toxic impact on the human health care condition. Proceedings of ADVED 2019 - 5th International Conference on Advances in Education and Social Sciences, 426 - 431.

Terziev, V., & Petkova-Georgieva, S. (2019e). Human health prevention by detection and quantification of toxic chemical compounds. Proceedings of ADVED 2019 - 5th International Conference on Advances in Education and Social Sciences, 443 - 449.

Terziev, V., & Petkova-Georgieva, S. (2019f). Toxic chemical compounds detection for the society social health care prevention. Proceedings of ADVED 2019 - 5th International Conference on Advances in Education and Social Sciences, 432 - 442.

Terziev, V., & Petkova-Georgieva, S. (2019g). The level of decentralization impact on the Bulgarian social health care competitiveness. Proceedings of ADVED 2019 - 5th International Conference on Advances in Education and Social Sciences, 361 - 368.

Terziev, V., & Petkova-Georgieva, S. (2020d). Testing the cost assessment methods application at a hospital for the decision "make or buy". Proceedings of INTCESS 2020- 7th International Conference on Education and Social Sciences, 789-796.

Terziev, V., & Petkova-Georgieva, S. (2020e). Bulgarian health system cost assessment methods application for the decision "make or buy". Proceedings of INTCESS 2020- 7th International Conference on Education and Social Sciences, 797-801.

Terziev, V., & Petkova - Georgieva, S. (2020f). Basic conditions for implementation of an effective strategic decision support system at a hospital. Proceedings of INTCESS 2020- 7th International Conference on Education and Social Sciences, 739-745.

Terziev, V., Banabakova, V., & Georgiev, M. (2018a). Possibilities for Determining Customer's Profitability. Proceedings of INTCESS2018- 5th International Conference on Education and Social Sciences, 438-444.

Terziev, V., Banabakova, V., & Georgiev, M. (2018b). Customer service standards. Proceedings of INTCESS2018- 5th International Conference on Education and Social Sciences, 431-437.

Terziev, V., Bencheva, N., Stoeva, T., & Georgiev, M. (2020g). Developing social entrepreneurship in the EU: a cross-country analysis. Proceedings of INTCESS 2020- 7th International Conference on Education and Social Sciences, 746-753.

Terziev, V., Bogdanova, M., Kanev, D., Georgiev, M., & Simeonov, S. (2019). The social assistance system in Bulgaria. Proceedings of ADVED 2019 - 5th International Conference on Advances in Education and Social Sciences, 391-397. DOI: 10.2139/ssrn.3477129

Terziev, V., & Can, H. (2018c). The relation between the migration, population aging, labor force productivity and economic growth: an analysis for Bulgaria. Proceedings of INTCESS2018- 5th International Conference on Education and Social Sciences, 445-451.

Terziev, V., & Georgiev, M. (2017). Highlights of the evolution of the „balanced scorecard" idea as a model for managing strategy development and control. Proceedings of SOCIOINT 2017- 4th International Conference on Education, Social Sciences and Humanities, 607-610.

Terziev, V., & Georgiev, M. (2018d). Efficient management as optimization of the organization. Proceedings of INTCESS2018- 5th International Conference on Education and Social Sciences, 452-461.

Terziev, V., & Georgiev, M. (2023). *Challenges to active social policies in Bulgaria, gabriell-e-lit.*

Terziev, V., & Georgiev, M. (2024a). New social transformations and changes in societies. 112th International Scientific Conference on Economic and Social Development – "Creating a unified foundation for Sustainable Development: Interdisciplinarity in Research and Education", 24-25.

Terziev, V., & Georgiev, M. (2024b). Social development and the contribution of science. 112th International Scientific Conference on Economic and Social Development – "Creating a unified foundation for Sustainable Development: Interdisciplinarity in Research and Education" – Varazdin, 4-5 June, 2024, Economic and Social Development (Book of Proceedings), 209-231.

Terziev, V., & Georgiev, M. (2024c). Social transformations and social programming. 112th International Scientific Conference on Economic and Social Development – "Creating a unified foundation for Sustainable Development: Interdisciplinarity in Research and Education" – Varazdin, 4-5 June, 2024, Economic and Social Development (Book of Proceedings), 251-256.

Terziev, V., & Georgiev, M. (2024d). New social transformations and changes in societies. 112th International Scientific Conference on Economic and Social Development – "Creating a unified foundation for Sustainable Development: Interdisciplinarity in Research and Education" – Varazdin, 4-5 June, 2024, Economic and Social Development (Book of Proceedings), 311-329.

Terziev, V., Georgiev, M., Simeonov, S., & Ivanov, I. (2021e). Knowledge in the context of strategic management of the military education system. 23rd RSEP International Economics, Finance & Business Conference, 136-141.

Terziev, V., & Lyubcheva, M. (2022a). Shared knowledge and changes in the higher education system in Bulgaria. 79th International Scientific Conference on Economic and Social Development, 228-237.

Terziev, V., Lyubcheva, M., Andreeva, O., & Georgiev, M. (2020b). Revolution in industry and evolution in education or development of intelligence. 63rd International Scientific Conference on Economic and Social Development – "Building Resilient Society" - Zagreb, 11-12 December, 2020, Economic and Social Development (Book of Proceedings), 133-142.

Terziev, V., Lyubcheva, M., & Georgiev, M. (2021b). Domestic and international challenges in higher education. 7th ITEM Conference – "Innovation, Technology, Education and Management" and 67th International Scientific Conference on Economic and Social Development – Sveti Martin na Muri, 29-30 April, 2021, Economic and Social Development (Book of Proceedings), 88-97.

Terziev, V., Lyubcheva, M., & Georgiev, M. (2021c). The contemporary strategic challenges facing higher education. Proceedings of SOCIOINT 2021 8th International Conference on Education and Education of Social Sciences, 134-141.

Terziev, V., Lyubcheva, M., & Mihailova, M. (2021a). The necessity of changes in the higher education in Bulgaria. Proceedings of INTCESS 2021 8th International Conference on Education and Education of Social Sciences, 646-657. DOI: 10.51508/intcess.202104

Terziev, V., Lyubcheva, M., & Solovev, D. (2020a). The interaction: business-education- investment for development. Proceedings of INTCESS 2020- 7th International Conference on Education and Social Sciences, 865-869.

Terziev, V. K. (2023c). Innovation Development of Industrial Business Organizations. In Okur Dinçsoy, M., & Can, H. (Eds.), *Optimizing Energy Efficiency During a Global Energy Crisis* (pp. 282–306). IGI Global. DOI: 10.4018/979-8-3693-0400-6.ch016

Terziev, V. K., Lyubcheva, M. I., & Georgiev, M. P. (2023b). Vocational education in Bulgaria: Professionalism, compliance and challenges. *Social Entrepreneurship and Corporate Social Responsibility*, 4(1), 41–58. DOI: 10.18334/social.4.1.116942

Terziev, V.K., Lyubcheva, M.I., Andreeva, O.V., & Simeonov, S.V. (2024) Creating an analytical model for the study of social entrepreneurship. Economics & Society: Contemporary Models of Development, 14(2), 91–112. .DOI: 10.18334/ecsoc.14.2.121514

Vovchenko, N. G., Andreeva, O. V., Dmitrieva, V. D., Galazova, S. S., & Terziev, V. K. (2022). Modelling of Economic Clusters in the Russian Regions in the Context of Formation of the Industry 4.0. In Trifonov, P. V., & Charaeva, M. V. (Eds.), *Strategies and Trends in Organizational and Project Management. DITEM 2021. Lecture Notes in Networks and Systems* (Vol. 380). Springer. DOI: 10.1007/978-3-030-94245-8_91

Vovchenko, N. G., Andreeva, O. V., Dmitrieva, V. D., Kaptsova, V. S., & Terziev, V. K. (2023d). Technological, Economic, and Social Changes: The Role of End-to-End Technologies. In Makarenko, E. N., Vovchenko, N. G., & Tishchenko, E. N. (Eds.), *Technological Trends in the AI Economy. Smart Innovation, Systems and Technologies* (Vol. 625). Springer. DOI: 10.1007/978-981-19-7411-3_2

Zhuravleva, I.V. (2014c). Marketing technologies in creatng the image of Sevastopol tourist territory. Bulletn of Kemerovo State University, 2–7(62), 172–176.

Chapter 10
Exploring Social Inequalities and Social Entrepreneurship Opportunities

Venelin Terziev
https://orcid.org/0000-0003-1115-8877
Black Sea Institute, Bourgas, Bulgaria

Marusya Lyubcheva
Black Sea Institute, Bourgas, Bulgaria

Olga Valentinovna Andreeva
Rostov State University of Economics, Rostov-on-Don, Russia

Marin Georgiev
https://orcid.org/0000-0002-4530-6471
Black Sea Institute, Bourgas, Bulgaria

Simeon Simeonov
https://orcid.org/0009-0007-1433-0931
University Hospital Kaneff, Rousse, Bulgaria

Milen Dimitrov
https://orcid.org/0009-0003-6499-3742
Black Sea Institute, Bourgas, Bulgaria

ABSTRACT

We live in dynamic times, with increasing social problems. Social entrepreneurship is a mechanism that could successfully solve some of the problems accompanying society. Perspectives and opinions on social entrepreneurship are sometimes opposed. A set of factors and different understandings make them so – some are positive, others extremely negative. The topic of the emergence, development, and various substantive features of social entrepreneurship is considered to gain an adequate idea of the essential characteristics of this "phenomenon". The ambition is to create a clear perspective to point out directions in which involvement in social entrepreneurial initiatives will be effective and efficient. The interweaving of economic theories in

DOI: 10.4018/979-8-3693-9435-9.ch010

socially entrepreneurial and purely entrepreneurial initiatives is inevitable. There are differences between "business entrepreneurship" and "social entrepreneurship" and they are in a substantive aspect, but mostly in a result-oriented direction. Entrepreneurship is defined as the process by which motivated individuals recognize and exploit business opportunities regardless of the resources available to them. Social entrepreneurship is a form of entrepreneurial activity that has an orientation towards social problems. Ambiguities still exist regarding the definition of social entrepreneurship, which is why it is considered easier to describe than to define.

1. INTRODUCTION

The ongoing social processes in modern societies are of particular interest, not least because they directly or indirectly affect a large part of the planet's population. Similar processes, accompanied by global social transformations, have occurred in various historical periods of humanity's existence. They have a kind of cyclicity, but also a high specificity. Their study, as well as the behavior of the formation of new social leaders, is essential for the strategic management of these processes.

According to the respondents, the reasons for starting a social entrepreneurship are mainly Social systems have their characteristics and cannot exist by themselves. Although there are different definitions and different interpretations in the scientific and popular literature, they are the ones that form the social attitudes of the individuals (people) in the environment. Countries can be seen as social systems, and even the world can be seen as one social system.

Social systems function under the organization of certain rules. These rules are created to satisfy certain needs of the individuals who participate in a given social system. The development of social systems leads to a distortion of the set of existing rules, which becomes unacceptable to individuals. This is one of the prerequisites for implementing change in social systems or their destruction. The period of transformation of one social system into another is usually accompanied by cataclysms that societies experience.

Historians speak of cyclicality in the change of social systems, which has only some accuracy in such logic. However, it should be emphasized that the changes that occur in social systems are caused by certain circumstances and factors that have an impact on the system itself. The turbulence that precedes certain transformations in the social system is a signal that the period of system change is in the near term.

Signals of changing social systems are a large set of events and actions that occur in a certain sequence. Such can be frequent regional military conflicts, tensions in certain communities that create discomfort in the coexistence of a certain group of people, and some other manifestations.

A significant problem is the divergence in action between those who manage social systems and those who participate in social systems. When the expectations of one and the other are in different directions, the rupture in this social system is completely predictable and expectedly possible.

All the elements of a state of tension of existing social systems are present. The internal and external environments function in a series of defect processes. This, in addition to creating a sense of failure of their existence, also foreshadows many transformations to come. The rules created for the normal functioning of these social systems have exhausted their essence and must be replaced by other rules that satisfy the existence of the new social systems.

Even a basic overview of the behavior of the leaders of the existing social societies speaks emphatically that a dramatic change is ahead, in which all participants will be subjected to certain loads, even tensions during this period of active transformations.

The changes that individuals participating in these new public social systems will have to accept may prove overwhelming for some of them, unacceptable for others, and for others an objective impossibility to physically survive this transformation.

Approaches and models are being sought for the creation of new social systems, which will condition new rules of interaction in them, which in turn will lead to the formation of new types of social relations. Undoubtedly, the newly formed social leaders will play a key role in these transformations.

This process of active and preferential influence of social leaders is known historically. The dominant influence of strong social leaders was also evident after the end of the two world wars. Their decisions affect both large and small social systems. The rules of functioning of the transformed social systems are set and partially shaped by the new social leaders of the historical moment.

The inevitability of such a process is almost impossible to predict with absolute accuracy, but considering that such processes take approximately several years, it can be said that we are already in a stage of the period of active social transformations.

The lack of research in this direction and the possibility of planning and forecasting these processes is puzzling. Even if we assume that some of them are under the guise of protecting national security, the deepening of research in this direction must happen quickly enough and, if possible, with the participation of researchers with high expertise in various fields.

2. SOCIAL SYSTEMS AND SOCIAL INEQUALITIES

Social inequalities in societies continue to deepen and create prerequisites for changes in existing social systems. Processes that remain unchanged towards deepening disparities are deeply troubling, for all involved. Regardless of improving the economic indicators of the respective societies, and development opportunities, as well as observing the positive trends in the labor market, the social problems are so strong and difficult to overcome. Mechanically overcoming them is not possible, even with the creation of good opportunities for the environment. This raises important questions about the nature of their occurrence and the impossibility of their successful regulation.

For example, in Bulgaria in the second quarter of 2024, the unemployment rate was 4.3% of the country's economically active population between the ages of 15 and 64 based on the national census in 2021.

These are relatively low levels, according to global trends. This circumstance should provide positive information for overcoming existing social inequalities. Regardless of these positive levels, social inequalities in Bulgarian society exist and have deepened in recent years. The Bulgarian National Employment Service has defined several groups of unemployed persons, which, following their average monthly dynamics, can be found to have a permanent tendency to remain in an unequal position in the labor market and society in general. These are persons with primary and lower education, long-term unemployed persons who have been out of work for more than 12 months, persons who have not acquired a professional qualification, persons with a certain reduced ability to work, and those who are under 29 years of age.

Bulgaria conducts an active promotion policy, helping employers to hire persons from these vulnerable groups. In this regard, a National Action Plan in the field of employment is adopted annually by the government. Some of these measures are defined in the special law for the promotion of employment.

Regardless of the institutional support, the actions taken, and the conditions created, social inequalities remain a permanent trend that cannot be overcome.

The existing social system fails to meet the requirements of all its participants on the one hand, and on the other hand to influence or support those who have permanent problems to be included in this system. Some scientists and researchers believe that in every society there is a certain minimum of people who fail to join the social system and remain excluded from it. This is observed in almost all social systems and recorded over a long period and can be taken as a relatively true statement. Regardless of this condition, the presence of such groups of people who constantly experience problems with their social inclusion is a problem for the social system itself and its functioning.

The set of impacts is well-known and used in different countries with varying success rates. Part of the measures that are applied are called a complex of active labor market policies. They are usually combined with so-called passive labor market policies. Passive policies are related to financial support through monetary benefits to certain groups of persons according to certain criteria. The two sets of policies in different social situations are reinforced to quell certain social tensions that are caused by social inequalities.

This to a certain extent shows the defects of the existing social systems and their crises. Determining these defects is not always an easy task, and this leads to a certain cyclicality and repetition of the critical situations that arise.

Undoubtedly, social systems experience difficulties in overcoming a series of critical situations, and from there all participants in social systems are to one degree or another exposed to certain negative impacts.

3. DYSFUNCTIONS OF SOCIAL SYSTEMS

Social systems have their own characteristics and they cannot exist by themselves. Regardless of the fact that different definitions and different interpretations are found in the scientific and popular literature, they are those that form the social attitudes of the individuals (people) in the environment. Countries can be seen as social systems, even the world can be seen as one social system.

A welfare state is a form of government in which the state (or a well-established network of social institutions) protects and promotes the economic and social well-being of its citizens, based upon the principles of equal opportunity, equitable distribution of wealth, and public responsibility for citizens unable to avail themselves of the minimal provisions for a good life (2024).

There is substantial variability in the form and trajectory of the welfare state across countries and regions (Béland et al., 2021). All welfare states entail some degree of private–public partnerships wherein the administration and delivery of at least some welfare programs occur through private entities (Béland and Morgan, 2021a). Welfare state services are also provided at varying territorial levels of government (Béland and Morgan, 2021a).

Early features of the welfare state, such as public pensions and social insurance, developed from the 1880s onwards in industrializing Western countries (Skocpol, 1995; Béland et al., 2021; Koehler–Derrick and Lee, 2023). World War I, the Great Depression, and World War II have been characterized as important events that ushered in the expansion of the welfare state (Skocpol, 1995; O'Hara, 1999). The fullest forms of the welfare state were developed after World War II (Béland et al., 2021).

The German term sozialstaat ("social state") has been used since 1870 to describe state support programs devised by German sozialpolitiker ("social politicians") and implemented as part of Otto von Bismarck's conservative reforms (Fay, 1950).

The literal English equivalent "social state" did not catch on in Anglophone countries (Smith, 1901). However, during the Second World War, Anglican Archbishop William Temple, author of the book Christianity and the Social Order (1942), popularized the concept using the phrase "welfare state" (Gough, 1989) Bishop Temple's use of "welfare state" has been connected to Benjamin Disraeli's 1845 novel Sybil: or the Two Nations (in other words, the rich and the poor), where he writes "power has only one duty – to secure the social welfare of the PEOPLE" (Disraeli, 2024a). At the time he wrote Sybil, Disraeli (later a prime minister) belonged to Young England, a conservative group of youthful Tories who disagreed with how the Whigs dealt with the conditions of the industrial poor. Members of Young England attempted to garner support among the privileged classes to assist the less fortunate and to recognize the dignity of labor that they imagined had characterized England during the Feudal Middle Ages (Alexander: Medievalism).

Before looking in detail at the ongoing processes in social systems, it is good to clarify the concept of social structure.

Social structure is a term used in sociology and the social sciences to denote characteristically constructed social formations that make society as a whole and that determine to some extent the actions of individuals socialized in that structure.

The meaning of the term social structure has different applicability. In macro sociology, it is a system of socioeconomic stratification, social institutions, or certain relations between large social groups. In meso-sociology, it is a social network structure that creates connections between individuals or organizations. In macro sociology, it can also be how norms determine the behavior of individuals in a social system.

Social systems function under the organization of certain rules. These rules are created to satisfy certain needs of the individuals who participate in a given social system. The development of social systems leads to a distortion of the set of existing rules, which becomes unacceptable to individuals. This is one of the prerequisites for implementing change in social systems or their destruction. The period of transformation of one social system into another is usually accompanied by cataclysms that societies experience.

Historians speak of cyclicality in the change of social systems, which has only some accuracy in such logic. However, it should be emphasized that the changes that occur in social systems are caused by certain circumstances and factors that have an impact on the system itself. The turbulence that precedes certain transformations in the social system is a signal that the period of system change is soon.

Signals of changing social systems are a large set of events and actions that occur in a certain sequence. Such can be the frequent regional military conflicts and tensions in certain communities that create discomfort in the coexistence of a certain group of people and many others.

A significant problem is the divergence in action between those who manage social systems and those who participate in social systems. When the expectations of the one and the other are in different directions, the rupture in this social system is completely predictable and expectedly possible.

All the elements of a state of tension of existing social systems are present. The internal and external environments function in a series of defect processes. This not only creates a sense of failure in their existence but also foreshadows many transformations to come. The rules created for the normal functioning of these social systems have exhausted their essence and must be replaced by other rules that satisfy the existence of the new social systems.

Even a basic survey of the behavior of the leaders of the existing social societies speaks unequivocally that a dramatic change is coming, in which all participants will be subjected to certain loads, even tensions during this period of active transformations.

The changes that will have to be accepted by the individuals participating in these new public social systems may turn out to be overwhelming for some of them, for others - unacceptable, and for others - an objective impossibility to physically survive this transformation.

They are looking for the creation of new social systems, which will condition new rules of interaction in them, which will also form new types of social relations. Undoubtedly, the newly formed social leaders will play a key role in these transformations.

This process of active and preferential influence of social leaders is known historically. The dominant influence of strong social leaders was also evident after the end of the two world wars. Their decisions affect both large and small social systems. The rules of functioning of the transformed social systems are set and partially shaped by the new social leaders of the historical moment.

The inevitability of such a process is almost impossible to predict with absolute accuracy, but considering that such processes take approximately several years, it can be said that we are already in a stage of the period of active social transformations.

The lack of research in this direction and the possibility of planning and forecasting these processes is puzzling. Even if we assume that some of them are under the guise of protecting national security, the deepening of research in this direction must happen quickly enough and with the possibility of the participation of researchers with high expertise in various fields.

The changes that are taking place of a geopolitical nature also imply social changes in social systems. Many analysts predict drastic changes in social relations, which will lead to the formation of new spheres of influence. Whether this will happen and especially when it will happen is a question from the point of view of a specific strategic analysis. Despite the impossibility of analyzing with a certain precision the multidirectional information in this plane, it can be concluded with a great deal of objectivity that several main centers of influence. These centers have the economic, financial, military, political, and cultural capacity to influence social systems. They have a high power of influence that they can even model them. To a certain extent, this gives us an objective possibility of predictability, and on the other hand, it also predicts uncertainty in the direction of development of these processes.

Social systems function according to certain rules and have their internal dependencies. Their main purpose is to serve the requirements of the participating individuals in these social systems. Tensions in social systems create an objective danger to their existence. This leads to significant discrepancies between the expectations and needs of those participating in social systems and their objective reality. All this can be caused by the new expectations or new needs that have arisen as a result of the social development of the systems, but it can also be a result of the internal tensions that have arisen in the systems themselves. These stresses can be classified in different ways and according to different criteria, but this is not the subject of the present analysis. Rather, it is important that the tensions in social systems that occur or are created by crises cause changes. These changes can be both desired and undesired. They will ensure the further existence or transformations of a social system. The impossibility of preserving their functioning in this form is more than obvious. Attempts to preserve them in this form will continue, but this is unlikely to be possible. The elites of the societies have raised new claims, which must be realized in some kind of social development, which will lead to serious transformations and changes in the social systems.

The objective prerequisites for significant changes in social systems are present. New paradigms and new social claims are announced, numerous crises of different natures arise, as well as the fact that the leading social leaders create expectations for changes through their behavior.

Social leaders in their communication in the social environment use the full range of means to impose their emerging desires. They do not always directly correspond with the wishes and expectations of those participating in a certain system. The environment in the social system becomes unstable and this further leads to the creation of future expectations of change.

Objective scientific and research approaches provide only a small part of the answers for managing change in social systems, and they can even be misleading and even wrong in some cases.

Social systems begin to obey the managerial views and specific decisions of social leaders who have a dominant influence. Historical retrospect provides some answers to these new expectations. They are not always related to the logic and correctness of the subsequent decisions, but rather to objectification in some reality of the strategic decisions of the dominant social leaders. Dominant social leaders begin to create social systems according to new rules and new requirements. If objectively possible, they try to transform them, or rather adapt them to their views, demands and intentions. In other extreme situations, they try to destroy them and recreate them. This version of the existence of social systems is the most critical from the point of view of the individuals participating in them, but sometimes the most pragmatic from the point of view of the dominant social leaders. Naturally, during the transformations or the creation of new social systems, various factors of the environment will have a significant and undetermined influence. They will be carriers of both progressive and regressive ideas. Support for both will change and gain different importance over time. It will be illusory to claim that the sustainability of the newly created or transforming systems will pass into an acceptable conditionality for all participants. The emergence of new demands and new conditions will put them to trials that they have not experienced at any other time in their human existence. Objectively, a larger part of the participants in the social systems will try to adapt to the new social conditions, but a significant part will find it impossible to do so. Here it is perhaps correct to divide them into two groups - those who have a complete or partial disagreement with the imposed new social rules and others who, due to their social nature, will be unsuitable for the new social conditions. This mass of individuals, however, will be appreciably small to withstand the forward movement of social systems. Rather, change will only register the occurrence of such fluctuations, and new social systems will attempt to extinguish or ignore their existence.

4. SOCIAL ENTREPRENEURSHIP AND ITS SOCIAL MISSION

Social entrepreneurship creates a good opportunity for positive intervention in social systems. This impact can be expected to have a lasting and positive effect.

The Law on Enterprises of the Social and Solidarity Economy in Bulgaria was adopted in 2018 (2024b) It regulates public relations related to the social and solidarity economy, the types of entities and measures for their promotion, as well as the terms and conditions for the activity of social enterprises and has as its main objective to promote the development of the social and solidarity economy as an economic branch with special rules with the following objectives:

- Improving access to employment and training for acquiring or improving professional qualifications to raise the standard of living of people from vulnerable groups;
- Creating conditions for providing support to persons from vulnerable groups for social inclusion and an independent lifestyle;

– Reduction of social inequality and sustainable territorial development.

With the adoption of this law, conditions are created for increasing the recognition of social enterprises, increasing consumer demand for their goods and services, creating a Register of Social Enterprises in Bulgaria, and a special certification mark denoting the goods and services produced and provided by social enterprises. The law also includes a specially created Methodology for assessing the social impact of the activities of social enterprises, which measures the achieved social contribution and impact:

– enterprises that employ persons from vulnerable groups and provide them with employment and social inclusion;
– enterprises whose financial result (realized profit), the greater part of which (after taxation) is redistributed to achieve social goals.

The Report on the Ex-post Impact Assessment of the Law on Social and Solidarity Economy Enterprises (2023a) defines several main groups of problems, namely (Terziev and Georgiev, 2024c; 2024d; 2024e):

Problem 1: As a concept, the social economy is similar to others such as solidarity, and cooperative economy based on the social and public interest, characteristic of them. The presence of diverse practices in the field of social economy and their unification in a single framework necessitates their regulation through a legal instrument, such as The Law on Enterprises of the Social and Solidarity Economy. In this context, one of the essential challenges is the creation of a single, comprehensive system of rules, related and consistent with the principles of the social and solidarity economy, defining the conditions, organization, and order in which social enterprises as its main subjects function and interact with the state and the municipalities. The legal framework provides the legal grounds to separate the social economy sector as an independent one, functioning according to rules.

Problem 2: At the time of the adoption of the law, there was no explicit legislative regulation of social entrepreneurship and social enterprise as a separate entity of the social economy.

In 2012, the Council of Ministers adopted a National Concept of Social Economy, which indicates the characteristics of social enterprises that distinguish them from other economic entities as a different type of business, but they are not legally enshrined, which gives rise to opportunities for "misuse" of the meaning and significance of social entrepreneurship and social enterprises, with consequences for misdirecting resources for their development and promotion in society as creating, in addition to economic and social added value. To overcome this unregulated approach to social entrepreneurship and social enterprises, as well as to the existing regulatory deficit, the Law introduces formal criteria and procedural rules that are the basis for the objective identification of the main subjects of the social and solidarity economy, especially concerning social enterprises. The criteria are in line with current European practice and the practice of the Organization for Economic Cooperation and Development.

Problem 3: Adequate statistical information is required for analytical purposes and to provide periodic and accurate information about the subjects of social and solidarity. Its content and adequacy for justifying political decisions and for a better description of specific measures require a rethinking of the way of collecting data and reference to clearly defined criteria for distinguishing social enterprises from other economic enterprises, as well as from other subjects of the social and solidarity economy. In this regard, actions have been taken to create a Register of Social Enterprises at the Ministry of Labor and Social Policy, in which social enterprises are entered according to previously, legally prescribed procedures and criteria.

Problem 4: Social enterprises implement a hybrid business model that combines economic and social goals. The identification of the social added value of their activity is related to distinguishing their social contribution. The draft law provides that the measurement of the social added value will be carried out using a methodology that is also one of the conditions for entering the enterprise in the national register of social enterprises, thus emphasizing the importance of social enterprises in achieving an additional, in addition to the economic, social value added. For the first time in the practice of the social economy in Bulgaria, through the draft law, a method for measuring the added social value is legally introduced, and in this way, the social change that occurs in the target group can be tracked. This is necessary for the better market positioning of social enterprises.

The upcoming changes in social systems will force all participants in them to adapt to the new conditions. Knowing the reasons for the changes occurring, as well as the ongoing processes, will enable adequate and accurate corrective actions to be taken. This is a challenge both to scientists and researchers and to those who are actively involved in the management of social systems.

It finds innovative solutions to significant social problems to which society has no adequate answer, through entrepreneurial behavior, and financially independent and sustainable organization.

Social entrepreneurship is not just a management goal. It seeks a balance between economic goals and the needs of society. And this makes it necessary for a well-developed nation, social entrepreneurship is defined as an activity through which social problems are solved in various areas - education, social security, environment, poverty reduction, human rights, etc.

Social entrepreneurship is a means of social change using entrepreneurial practices. Social entrepreneurs are aware of social problems in their community and find solutions to these problems.

Table 1. Analytical model for studying social entrepreneurship

Social entrepreneurship – regulation and practice				
1. Theory of social entrepreneurship	**2. Social entrepreneurship as a phenomenon**	**3. The social environment of social entrepreneurship**	**4. Support for social entrepreneurship**	**5. Does social entrepreneurship have a future?**
1.1. Models of social entrepreneurship	2.1. Is social entrepreneurship social?	3.1. What do young people think about social entrepreneurship	4.1. Social economy	5.1. Best practices
1.2. Legal regulation	2.2. A look at the development of social entrepreneurship	3.2. What do young people do for social entrepreneurship	4.2. Social entrepreneurship in the financial system	5.2. The future of social entrepreneurship

Source: authors

To understand the details, we look for a logical sequence in information bases and build an analytical model for studying social entrepreneurship. It is necessary to clarify the existing legal framework through an analysis of policies and measures for participation in initiatives. Does this give an idea of real circumstances and do they fit into the patterns created by government agencies?

Is social entrepreneurship social? Can entrepreneurship be social?

- Social entrepreneurship builds innovative business models that are fully subordinated to the ultimate goal of creating value by solving a socially significant problem;
- Social entrepreneurship is carried out without seeking profit or emphasizing the profit they can get.

Is social entrepreneurship entrepreneurship. Can social problems be solved through entrepreneurship?

- Entrepreneurship is a key factor in economic development and improving the welfare of society;
- Entrepreneurship solves important economic and social problems, such as reducing unemployment, increasing innovation activity, accelerating structural changes in the economy, regional development, etc.;

– Entrepreneurial activity leads to the emergence of new business models that increase the productivity of economic agents in particular and the competitiveness of the economy in general.

Who do we want to attract to social entrepreneurship? Why is it important?

– What are the reasons? Where are the young people? What are the theories? What are the practices? (Table 1-2)

Table 2. Analytical model for the study of social entrepreneurship and its application to practice

MARKETING		**CRITICAL COMPARISON**		**MEASURES**	
Goal setting		**Research**		**Conclusions**	
Search	**Observation**	**Analysis**	**Decomposition**	**Good practices**	**New reading**
Relationship Management in Social Entrepreneurship					
Theory of social entrepreneurship	Social entrepreneurship as a phenomenon	Social environment of social entrepreneurship	What do young people think?	Does social entrepreneurship have a future?	Can social entrepreneurship have great potential to mobilize young people?

Source: authors

The genesis of the term "social entrepreneurship" is difficult to trace. Opinions about its first appearance in economic literature date back to 1830. Then the French liberal economist Charles Dunauer published "Treatise on Social Economy", in which he advocated a more moral approach to the economy. In the period 1820-1860, a core of social economists formed in France. They began a structural reorientation under the influence of John Stuart Mill and Leon Walras and provided an alternative to the changes (inequality, poverty) brought by the Industrial Revolution in the 18th and 19th centuries. The practical foundations were laid in the 1970s when French cooperatives were in full bloom and received the collective name – "social economy". Economist Peter Drucker sees the mission of this "social sector" as a response to social challenges. He believes that in modern society, social entrepreneurship is as important as economic entrepreneurship. Today, Ken O'Neill analyzes the nature and characteristics of the social economy. According to him, it works to achieve social goals by building mutual relationships between people and organizations. Social economy is created by organizations that primarily seek to reinvest all their profits back into the implementation of the organization's social goals. The latter should not contradict social principles, since they are mutually exclusive.

There are two trends in social economics: - “European”, developing the concept of collective entrepreneurship (cooperatives, mutually supportive companies); and “American”, which is more closely associated with services and an individual approach (foundations, charities, and trusts). In search of the place and role of the business model on which the social economy is built, Dees analyzes the ideas of Say, Schumpeter, Drucker, and Stevenson. According to him, they can easily be applied both in the social sphere and in business. Dees insists that the understanding of social entrepreneurship should be based on a strong tradition of entrepreneurship theory and research.

Social entrepreneurship is currently developing in Bulgaria. However, entrepreneurs rarely take into account the specific features of the Bulgarian context. From a theoretical point of view, the problem of “social entrepreneurship” has been poorly studied in the context of Bulgarian reality. This makes it difficult to form trends or forecast prospects. Insufficient commitment from the state and local government is also a factor limiting the spread of entrepreneurial practice. A significant problem is the lack of highly qualified entrepreneurs willing to develop such initiatives. Large businesses are also not actively involved in such initiatives. Researchers in this sector come to the conclusion that social enterprises need additional opportunities, both in developing projects to attract additional funding and in developing organizational capacity, and strategic and business planning. There is a need for additional training in business planning, accounting, financial management, marketing, building partnerships and coalitions, fundraising, etc. Not least of all, this is a misunderstanding of this form, coupled with the activities of potential social entrepreneurs is also located.

The current Bulgarian legislation regulating relations in the social sphere does not provide a legal definition of a social enterprise. However, definitions can be found in a number of strategic European and Bulgarian documents. The preamble to the draft Regulation on European Funds for Social Entrepreneurship contains the following wording: “Social enterprises cover a wide range of enterprises with different legal forms that provide social services or goods to vulnerable or marginalized persons. These services include access to housing, health care, assistance to the elderly or disabled, childcare, access to employment and training, and the fight against addiction. Social enterprises also include enterprises that use a method of producing goods or services for a social purpose, but whose activities may go beyond the provision of social goods or services. These activities include social and professional integration through access to employment for people in a disadvantaged situation, in particular, due to insufficient qualifications or social or professional problems leading to exclusion and marginalization”.

A number of studies report that many social enterprises in Europe have achieved greater impact through development strategies based on the expansion of social capital and the implementation of social change strategies. In this respect, social enterprise development strategies are relevant for Europe but still have unproven effectiveness in the Bulgarian context. It is clear that connectivity and social capital are key factors in the development of social enterprises. It specifies that effective combinations of business strategies and strategies based on social approaches should be linked to the strengths and capabilities of social enterprises. At the same time, each social entrepreneur should also be aware of the possible risks in the implementation of various strategies, especially strategies related to new products and markets, as well as strategies based on the use of information and communication technologies, which require a lot of initial resources, and insufficient planning can lead to serious financial risks.

A serious problem of social entrepreneurship is its almost restrictive connection with people with disabilities. This deprives it of a much larger idea of implementing the mission of social orientation of economic entities outside specific social groups /disabled, marginalized, etc./. Particular attention is drawn to the limitation of the law in that a social enterprise arises in the form of a commercial legal entity created on the basis of the Commercial Law or the Law on Cooperatives. Thus, an enterprise can exist in the form of a joint-stock company, a limited liability company, a limited partnership, a limited partnership with shares, and a general partnership, as well as a cooperative. In practice, more common forms are joint-stock companies and limited liability companies, since they are commercial capital companies with a clear delineation of the scope of liability. Another possibility for registering a social enterprise in accordance with a special law is a cooperative of people with disabilities, regulated by the Law on Cooperatives. To establish it, it is sufficient to express the will of at least seven individuals. The second requirement is that the social enterprise is engaged in the production of goods or provision of services, which makes it an active participant in the economy. In addition, quantitative measurements of the employed personnel have been introduced.

Who are the users of social entrepreneurship? Socially weak, marginalized groups? Can social entrepreneurship be equated with social economy, i.e. in the economy, which, along with making a profit, also solves social problems? Despite the diversity of business strategies that are used to achieve business growth and competitive advantages, they are of particular importance in social enterprises - this is the use of tools that guarantee the fulfillment of the social mission. The use of heterogeneous business strategies to ensure the economic growth of social enterprises largely depends on the level of development and the phase of the life cycle they are in. According to Marina Stefanova, the most popular business strategy is the development of a new market. This can be a completely new geographic area or an expansion of the territorial coverage of services.

The main product strategy of a social enterprise is the differentiation of products or services. In the main practice of most social enterprises, there are a number of ways to differentiate a product or service against the backdrop of growing competition. One of the ways to develop such a new market for social enterprises is to educate the audience. This is a longer-term public relations strategy than a one-time advertising campaign. One of the popular tools used in marketing when making strategic choices about products and markets to work in is the so-called Ansoff matrix. This approach can also be used to launch social entrepreneurial initiatives.

An important and key characteristic of social entrepreneurship innovation is its flexibility, informality, and adaptability to changes in the environment. A deep look at social enterprises suggests that they operate as an intersection of talent and entrepreneurial drive, combined with informal communication and a long-term vision for development. Recently, rapidly developing information and communication technologies have dramatically changed the environment in which social enterprises operate. These technologies allow social enterprises to expand their market beyond the geographic region in which they operate. Additional social impact is created by providing services in underdeveloped regions at an acceptable cost level. Social enterprises can use new technologies to improve traditional business practices, thereby creating new opportunities and challenges. A serious issue related to financial independence can be discussed here. Many proponents of the concept of generating income in the social sphere speak of it as a form of financial independence, and of other sources of funding as a form of "dependency".

Financial independence is understood as something that can only be achieved when a person relies entirely on the income they receive. This can be seen as the ultimate goal of the most ambitious social entrepreneurs. When we talk about financial strategies in social entrepreneurship, it is useful to clarify the terms used, especially the understanding of "income generation". For those unfamiliar with this economic term, it is income that comes from the sale of goods or services. This is in stark contrast to the widely popular methods of raising funds in the non-governmental sector through charity, donations, or government grants, and is one of the most widely discussed concepts in social entrepreneurship. In addition, many researchers view income generation strategies as a powerful tool for social entrepreneurship.

The most common financial strategy for social enterprises, or one that can ensure their financial sustainability over time while taking advantage of the dual nature of these structures, is to diversify their revenue sources, i.e., move away from or reduce their reliance on free funding and donations. When a social enterprise is focused on generating revenue to become less dependent, it must understand that generating revenue depends on customers choosing its products and services over others in the market. In addition, this type of social enterprise is often dependent on key suppliers, specific expertise and labor markets, and access to capital, which may require other types of business strategies. The financial independence, freedom, and flexibility of a social enterprise are only important if they lead to achieving greater positive social impact. Focusing on the financial aspects of social entrepreneurship should not be done at the expense of social impact. Instead, when applying financial strategies to generate revenue, follow the so-called dual track, which focuses on both financial and social impact. Regardless of the outcome of the debate on this topic, one thing is clear and indisputable: the main indicator of the difference between a "market" and a "social" economy is the degree of "social added value".

Social added value can be defined as achieving a social effect for the target group as a result of the social enterprise's activities as a whole - its positive and negative changes, and collateral effects as a result of other actions or inactions. On the part of the social enterprise. Theories of social-added value offer a way to recognize the role of social entrepreneurs in society and their contribution to social change. Jed Emerson, a researcher on the topic of the added value of social entrepreneurs, notes that social benefit cannot be easily decomposed into separate elements - social, economic, and public benefits, but, on the contrary, it is necessary to consider the overall combined effect. Social added value can also be characterized as the benefit of the activities of an organization or enterprise in terms of the achieved social and/or environmental effect.

In Bulgaria, with the adoption of the Regulation on the Implementation of the Law on Social and Solidarity Economy Enterprises, a methodology for assessing social added value was created. It is a mechanism for studying the effects of the activities of social and solidarity economy enterprises in terms of costs, benefits, and effects for a wide range of stakeholders, as well as in terms of direct benefits for society and communities in which social enterprises operate. The additional provisions of the law define "Social Added Value" as the achieved social effect for the target group as a result of the activities carried out by a social enterprise. After all, regardless of the choice of strategy, the achievement of added social value is mainly realized by "social capital" in all its meanings.

The characteristics of social enterprises and their strong connection with people and social problems, that is, their focus on achieving social impact and social change, in most cases predetermine the need to implement strategies related to social capital. According to one of the leading researchers of social capital, R. Putnam, there are four main components of social capital, namely:

– Networks (groups of people connected by many and different types of connections);

– Values, norms, and sanctions (common standards of behavior and expectations); This may include beliefs, traditions, rituals, and laws;
– Reciprocity (people helping each other, with a clear awareness and conviction that this will contribute to the development of the group or someone in the future will respond in kind);
– Trust (the expectation that other members of the community will be honest and willing to cooperate).

Social capital helps entrepreneurs to "get their foot in the door." This provides broad access to investment capital and potential customers. The relationship between social capital and social entrepreneurship has been explored by several authors, who have concluded that social entrepreneurs create their social capital. This is believed to be one of the reasons why some social entrepreneurs are more successful than others who do not invest enough in social capital. Gregory Dees believes that a social entrepreneur should also focus on social relationships, as they are essential to the operational potential of a social enterprise and are the basis for innovative solutions to social problems. Social capital can also be defined as resources that are embedded in social networks and can be accessed or mobilized through relationships in existing networks. In general, through such social relationships or social networks, an entrepreneur can access or use the resources of other partners. Networks and sharing as components of social capital can stimulate innovation while facilitating the process of knowledge dissemination in social enterprises.

Several studies in the social economy sector show that social enterprises have an advantage in using informal networks as an element of social capital – through networks and industry partnerships they can achieve a greater competitive advantage than through business skills or specialized business support. Very often, social enterprises operate in a particular territorial community, which provides many opportunities for the development of their activities, while simultaneously representing a major market for the products and services of social enterprises. This is a successful strategy for the development of social enterprises linked to the local community: on the one hand, the social economy sector brings its benefits to the community, and on the other hand, the community creates a market for the sale of the products and services of social enterprises. Social capital is a particularly important element of social entrepreneurship. Its importance increases in the context of achieving specified social change. Social change itself can be characterized as a systematic transformation of modes of action, behavior, social relations, and social structures over a long period. Businesses can change the behavior of individuals and groups in various areas, for example, those related to the environment, health, social exclusion, and civic participation. Social enterprises typically commit to achieving social change that may be linked to long-term social impact in a particular area.

Many researchers point to four main areas for achieving social change: environmental behavior; healthy behavior; social and economic inclusion; trade participation. The social benefits of social enterprises vary widely, with a number of studies of social enterprises in Bulgaria showing a preference for the following social areas and/or goals: supporting low-income individuals; improving health and quality of life; creating employment opportunities and integration in the labor market; addressing social exclusion; integrating children and young people in vulnerable situations; improving services in underdeveloped rural areas. A key prerequisite for the implementation of this type of goals is the existence of clearly defined principles and measurable indicators for assessing the social impact, as well as adopted approaches and methodologies for assessing the social added value.

Recently, there has been activity in Bulgarian academic circles on this issue. In her analysis, Maria Ilcheva examines a diagnostic tool for social entrepreneurship policy. The data obtained by the author show the following: social effect, as well as the adopted approaches and methods for assessing social added value (Ilcheva, 2019). Recently, there has been activity in Bulgarian academic circles on this issue. In her analysis, Maria Ilcheva examines a diagnostic tool for social entrepreneurship policy. The data obtained by the author show the following (Ilcheva, 2019)

– The areas with the lowest scores are entrepreneurship culture and – access to finance. This is due to the insufficient activity of social entrepreneurship entities in Bulgaria. Including civil society organizations and educational institutions to promote the sector as an effective tool for employment and social inclusion;
– "Access to finance" – there is no single source of information on funding programs and financial instruments. Insufficient number of specialized countries with private funding actively targeting social enterprises. This is also reported in a number of strategic documents on the social economy of Bulgaria. There is a need for specialized sources of financial support in combination with business consulting or technical assistance;
– The highest score was obtained for "Institutional framework". The result is based on serious steps taken to approve and implement the national strategy for the social economy, linked to two-year action plans;
– "Legal framework" has a high rating and the reason for this is the special law on social economy enterprises adopted in 2018. It is being prepared with the active participation of all stakeholders;
– With a good title – "Impact Management, Measurement, and Reporting". This is due to the availability of social impact assessment indicators. For example, an adopted methodology for measuring social added value and the development of awareness-raising initiatives on impact measurement and reporting of social enterprises;

– Another important component is "Skills and Business Development". Its assessment shows the lack of specialized structures to support the development of social enterprises' businesses. Lack of resources for broad support and limited access to support networks and coaching programs. The main conclusion for the future development of the sector is related to expanding opportunities for participation in European networks, clusters, and consortia, which can facilitate the exchange of experience and best practices, having a direct impact on improving business skills and implementing successful strategies;
– "Access to Markets" is rated low, since there are no regulated social provisions when concluding public contracts. Insufficient support for submitting competitive offers and qualified participation in tenders and assignments; A positive step in addressing this deficit is the introduction of a certified brand "Social Entrepreneurship Product". Each social enterprise registered in the register of social enterprises will receive it.

It has been established that the term "social economy" arose in connection with the flourishing of French cooperatives. The mission of this "social sector" is a response to social challenges. A detailed analysis, supported by various opinions of our and foreign researchers, shows that the ideas of the business sector can easily be applied in the field of social entrepreneurship.

5. STRATEGIES USED IN BUSINESS ARE ALSO APPLICABLE TO SOCIAL ENTREPRENEURSHIP

This means that marketing strategies are relevant to social entrepreneurship. A successful strategy at the European level, as revealed by a number of studies, is that many social enterprises in Europe have achieved greater impact through a development strategy based on the expansion of social capital, as well as the implementation of social change strategies. These social enterprise development strategies are relevant for Europe but still have unproven effectiveness in the Bulgarian context.

One of the main indicators of the difference between the "market" and "social" economy is the degree of "social added value". Social added value can be described as the benefit of the activities of an organization or enterprise in terms of the achieved social and environmental effect. The goal is social change. Social change itself can be described as a systematic transformation of modes of action, behavior, social relations, and social structures over a long period. The Bulgarian reality of social entrepreneurship is still unclear. Some of the reasons for this situation are low entrepreneurial culture; lack of a single source of information on funding programs and financial instruments; lack of specialized structures to support the development of social enterprises' businesses; lack of resources for broad support and limited access to support networks and coaching programs. Lack of clearly regulated social provisions when concluding public contracts. There are also positive steps, for example: serious steps have been taken to approve and implement a national strategy for social economy, linked to two-year action plans; a special law on social economy enterprises has been adopted; the presence of social impact assessment indicators.

In our opinion, the biggest problem remains with public attitudes. For the attitude of a successful person, "it is extremely or very important that he or she has good health, is ambitious, has a good (high) education, works hard for his or her success, has connections and, if possible, is younger." At the same time, in the public space, through the images of certain groups, such as people in need of social assistance, disseminated by print and electronic media, their initiative is harmed. Thus, certain groups of people are stigmatized. Bulgaria is still working on solving these problems. It is envisaged to introduce various tools (job search seminars, work with psychologists and curators, training, etc.). Reaching inactive and unemployed youth through a comprehensive approach and combining the efforts of intermediaries, institutions, social partners, and local authorities. Improving data exchange, holding information days, using modern information channels, and developing electronic services. It is expected that the focus will be on counseling oriented towards the needs of individuals, their strengths and potential, motivation, career guidance, and consideration of the status of the entire family of the long-term unemployed person. Stimulation and outreach to individuals include inclusion in labor exchanges, subsidized employment, and support at the workplace. A corresponding mechanism for the involvement and outreach of young people is the launch of the services "Family Consultant" and "Counseling and Mentoring after Return to Work".:

Based on the analysis of the topic, the following areas can be identified that require intervention for the favorable development of social entrepreneurship. The social entrepreneurship initiative expands the scope of positive solutions and at the same time can give meaning to the life of a small local community. Unfortunately, there is no specific mechanism for promoting this form, and the consolidation of policies and funding mechanisms is lagging. There is also a lack of resources aimed at supporting social entrepreneurship initiatives. The problems can be solved if specific and targeted initiatives are taken. Urgent measures are needed:

– Policy development – based on the deficit in the systemic aspect of social entrepreneurship initiatives;
– It is necessary to create a flexible financial mechanism following the needs of financing such initiatives;
– There is a need to develop specific resources to support the process of social entrepreneurship from start-up to sustainable development;

– It is necessary to set up an active and accessible information flow on the topic.

To take measures, a large-scale and targeted media campaign is needed, aimed at:

– Changing public opinion;
– Implementation of an accessible physical and media environment;
– Promoting the possibilities of social entrepreneurship initiatives;
– Policy development – based on the deficit in the systemic aspect of social entrepreneurship initiatives;
– It is necessary to create a flexible financial mechanism in accordance with the needs of financing such initiatives;
– There is a need to develop specific resources to support the process of social entrepreneurship from start-up to sustainable development;
– It is necessary to set up an active and accessible information flow on the topic.

A large-scale and targeted media campaign aimed at:

– Changing public opinion;
– Implementing an accessible physical and media environment;
– Promoting the possibilities of social entrepreneurial initiatives.

6. CONCLUSION

Social entrepreneurship is a philosophy that can help solve many problems in the social environment, focusing primarily on those problems that are the most significant and most acute for society. The accumulated set of problems and the identification of various, most vulnerable groups of the population require specific approaches and the search for adequate and correct solutions. Social entrepreneurship is a good opportunity to implement various social policies aimed at at-risk groups.

The implementation of this opportunity for the successful implementation and implementation of the idea of social entrepreneurship is a long and difficult process, but it is expected to give good and effective results. Approaches to its implementation should be well analyzed and understood, and the use of the methodology of its practical implementation should be well-tested on various social problems (Terziev et al., 2020; Terziev et al., 2020a; Terziev et al., 2021b; Terziev et al., 2021c; Terziev and Lyubcheva, 2022; Terziev et al., 2024f).

REFERENCES

Béland, D., & Morgan, K. J. (2021a). *Governance, The Oxford Handbook of the Welfare State*. Oxford University Press. DOI: 10.1093/oxfordhb/9780198828389.001.0001

Béland, D., Morgan, K. J., Obinger, H., & Pierson, C. (2021). *Introduction, The Oxford Handbook of the Welfare State*. Oxford University Press. DOI: 10.1093/oxfordhb/9780198828389.001.0001

Disraeli, B. (2024a). *Chapter 14. Sybil. Vol. Book 4*, https://www.gutenberg.org/files/3760/3760-h/3760-h.htm

Fay, S. B. (1950). Bismarck's Welfare State. *Current History (New York, N.Y.)*, XVIII(101), 1–7. DOI: 10.1525/curh.1950.18.101.1

Gough, I. (1989). *The Welfare State, The New Palgrave Social Economics*. W.W. Norton.

Ilcheva, M. (2019). Social economy and social entrepreneurship – views and fragmentary approbations. *Publishing house Faber.*

Koehler–Derrick, G., & Lee, M. M. (2023). War and Welfare in Colonial Algeria. *International Organization*, 77(2), 263–293. DOI: 10.1017/S0020818322000376

Law on Enterprises of the Social and Solidarity Economy. (2024b), *Pub. DV. No. 91 of November 2, 2018, amended DV. No. 17 of February 26, 2019, amended and add. DV. No. 24 of March 22, 2019, add. DV. No. 17 of February 25*, 2020, https://lex.bg/bg/laws/ldoc/2137187968

O'Hara, P. A. (Ed.). (1999). *Welfare state. Encyclopedia of Political Economy* (p. 1247). Routledge. DOI: 10.4324/9780203443217

Report on the follow-up assessment of the impact of the Law on Enterprises, Social and Solidarity Economy, MLSP, (2023a), https://www.mlsp.government.bg/posledvashchi-otsenki-na-vzdeystvieto

Skocpol, T. (1995). Protecting Soldiers and Mothers. *Belknap Press.* https://www.hup.harvard.edu/books/9780674717664

Smith, M. (1901). Four German Jurists. IV. *Political Science Quarterly*, 16(4), 641–679. DOI: 10.2307/2140421

Terziev, V., & Georgiev, M. (2024c). Social development and the contribution of science. *112th International Scientific Conference on Economic and Social Development – "Creating a unified foundation for Sustainable Development: Interdisciplinarity in Research and Education" – Varazdin, 4-5 June, 2024, Economic and Social Development (Book of Proceedings),* 209-231.

Terziev, V., & Georgiev, M. (2024d). Social transformations and social programming. *112th International Scientific Conference on Economic and Social Development – "Creating a unified foundation for Sustainable Development: Interdisciplinarity in Research and Education" – Varazdin, 4-5 June, 2024, Economic and Social Development (Book of Proceedings),* 251-256.

Terziev, V., & Lyubcheva, M. (2022). Shared knowledge and changes in the higher education system in Bulgaria. *79th International Scientific Conference on Economic and Social Development – Rabat, 25-26 March, 2022, Economic and Social Development (Book of Proceedings),* 228-237.

Terziev, V., Lyubcheva, M., Andreeva, O., & Georgiev, M. (2020a). Revolution in industry and evolution in education or development of intelligence. *63rd International Scientific Conference on Economic and Social Development – "Building Resilient Society" - Zagreb, 11-12 December, 2020, Economic and Social Development (Book of Proceedings),* 133-142.

Terziev, V., Lyubcheva, M., & Georgiev, M. (2021b). Domestic and international challenges in higher education. *7 th ITEM Conference – "Innovation, Technology, Education and Management" and 67th International Scientific Conference on Economic and Social Development – Sveti Martin na Muri, 29-30 April,* 2021, *Economic and Social Development (Book of Proceedings),* 88-97.

Terziev, V., Lyubcheva, M., & Georgiev, M. (2021c). The contemporary strategic challenges facing higher education. *Proceedings of SOCIOINT 2021 8th International Conference on Education and Education of Social Sciences 14-15 June,* 134-141.

Terziev, V., Lyubcheva, M., & Solovev, D. (2020). The interaction: business-education- investment for development. *Proceedings of INTCESS 2020- 7th International Conference on Education and Social Sciences 20-22 January, 2020 - DUBAI (UAE)*, 865-869.

Terziev, V. K., Lyubcheva, M. I., Andreeva, O. V., & Simeonov, S. V. (2024f). Creating an analytical model for the study of social entrepreneurship. *Economics & Society: Contemporary Models of Development*, 14(2), 91–112. DOI: 10.18334/ecsoc.14.2.121514

Terziev, V. & Georgiev, M. (2024e). New social transformations and changes in societies. 112th International Scientific Conference on Economic and Social Development – "Creating a unified foundation for Sustainable Development: Interdisciplinarity in Research and Education" – Varazdin, 4-5 June, 2024, Economic and Social Development (Book of Proceedings), 311-319.

Chapter 11
The Absorption of Environmentalism in the Modes for Business Transformation:
Theoretical and Practical Insights

Elizabeth Yoneva
https://orcid.org/0000-0003-3911-063X
University of National and World Economy, Sofia, Bulgaria

ABSTRACT

The chapter explores the principal dimensions of the integration of environmental directions in business strategy and culture in order to evaluate their repercussions for specific shifts in the economic realm. Especially interesting are the motivational factors for the absorption of environmentalism in the modes for business transformation, so delving into the multiple benefits of being a purpose-driven company is a crucial task of the analysis. The research showcases the main vectors in the development of the theoretical fundament of the environmental trajectories regarding the pursuit of business transformation. The author discusses explicit aspects of the evolving role of businesses as part of society from the perspective of the advancements in the last years, outlining the conceptual frame of the efforts to solidify the distinction between shareholders and stakeholders, beneficial to the conversion of the companies into prominent factors, empowered to induce large-scale change through value-driven approaches.

DOI: 10.4018/979-8-3693-9435-9.ch011

INTRODUCTION

Presently, the pressing issues of facing the multiple challenges, generated by environmental degradation, are dictating the solidification of the dominant narrative of preserving the natural capital. The burning need to protect the biosphere stimulated a crucial shift in global political and economic agenda, amalgamated with the expansive efforts to change public perceptions about the attitudes and the models in which humanity manages the use of resources. The echoing debate on the introduction of the practices for reducing our ecological footprint pushed to the forefront the ideas for broadly constructed paradigm, involving a synthesis of international regulations, governmental action, business involvement, and societies' engagement. Emphasizing the necessity of acute environmental reforms that should be both long-term and systemic in orientation, experts underline that we should primo rethink the prevailing development mode based on the worship of growth and the addiction to profits. Not only on macroeconomic, but also on microeconomic level, growth is obeyed as a No.1 task. The rush to advance and expand conventionally stimulates rapid absorption of natural resources, materials, and energy, along with the dumping of escalating wastes into the environment – hence adding to ecological degradation.

Undoubtedly, the anthropocentric mold of the last centuries, flourishing in the era of the industrialization obsession, planted an exploitative attitude towards nature and speeded up the loss of biodiversity. However, the present ecological crisis is energizing a raising disenchantment with growth. The new goal is to form a resource and energy efficient, and environmentally friendly structure of industries and businesses, inflaming a metamorphosis in the modes of production and consumption, and the general development model, but also a fundamental changeover of worldview, lifestyle and values. Furthermore, this should be not only the ambition of the international institutions, the states and the people, but synchronously a mission for the business as well. Nevertheless, the absorption of environmentalism in the firm strategies and practices is not an easy task at all. Nowadays, companies must cope with an unprecedented acceleration of the endogenous and exogenous dynamics of the developments in their ambiance. The speed and the magnitude of the unfolding phenomena serves as a catalyst for an emerging situation of fluidity and unpredictability, making the businesses more exposed to numerous risks. In the era of complexity and uncertainty, it is easier to deviate from the right course and crash into underwater reefs, so the priority of every company is to be faster, smarter, and more creative, in order to adapt to change.

On the other hand, the recipes to make your business model more resilient and competitive are not always universally valid or serving as a cure-all. Regardless of the scope of their activities (local, national or international in nature), the companies operate in specific setting and are subjected to different regulations and cultural specifics. Therefore, considering the characteristics of the social context is a significant task for establishing a productive and efficient modus operandi. Moreover, the rapid technological development forces all businesses to maneuver in a shrinking world, where the spill-over waves of particular events flood the globe in seconds. In consequence, modifications in the geopolitical landscape could touch and disturb every business activity. The impact of global events and trends should not be underestimated with regard to their reframing power, as it urges the firms to recheck and to amend their strategy and business models in pursuance of survival, thus contributing to the impetus to mature and to evolve.

In the light of these challenges, business transformation is described as the buzzword of today. Overcoming the perplexity in solving the rebus, how to pilot your company in the jungle of an extremely competitive and highly volatile business environment, requires embracing a holistic approach to transformation that integrates different compounds. Only through the medium of comprehensive techniques is possible not only to achieve endurance, but also to reach business excellence and advancement. In times, when humanity has reached a moment of crisis in its relationship with nature, one of the essential elements of business strategy is to incorporate tools and measures to deliver sustainable growth. In order to complete this quest, the companies must accommodate eco-ethics and devote to environmental responsibility. The clangorous slogan of sustainability is especially associated with businesses, as they are the largest contributors to ecological degradation. The debate, how to implement adequate stratagems and actions to reduce their carbon footprint, has bloomed in prescriptions of identifying the points of intersection, where the competing interest of society, business and environment could be reconciled. Seeking synergy means that the companies should learn, how to position themselves as a part of society, so to be able to make money and do good at the same time. Namely the business sector holds the keys to driving positive change, as the fruitful and rewarding rearrangement of business models could prove that profitability, progress, social responsibility and sustainability could be blended. The consolidation of "doing good" and "doing well" corresponds with the process of creating shared value.

The resounding call for sustainability has set, and will continue to set, a numerous parameters in the scientific discussions in the field of exploring business transformation, and this is precisely the reason for the orientation of the current research work towards this topic. The paper explores the principal dimensions of the integration of environmental directions in business strategy and culture, in order to evaluate their repercussions for specific shifts in the economic realm. Especially interesting are the motivational factors for the absorption of environmentalism in the modes for business transformation, so to delve into the multiple benefits of being a purpose-driven company is a crucial task of the analysis. The research showcases the main vectors in the development of the theoretical fundament of the environmental trajectories regarding the pursuit of business transformation. The emphasis lies on contemporary metamorphoses in the context of the impact of the 2020 pandemic, the 2021 energy crisis and the ongoing wars in Ukraine and the Middle East, resulting in a miscellaneous disruptions in the global economic landscape.

The author discusses explicit aspects of the evolving role of businesses as part of society from the perspective of the advancements in the last years, outlining the conceptual frame of the efforts to solidify the distinction between shareholders and stakeholders, beneficial to the conversion of the companies into prominent factors, empowered to induce large-scale change through value-driven approaches. Special attention is paid to the significant focus on the energy challenges for the business and the plans to switch to new energy models. In view of the current global dilemmas, the aim of the study is to discuss the main environmental dimensions of the crusade of business transformation not only through the theoretical lens, but also per using practical optics with the help of distinguishing cases.

1. Many Theories, Same Problems

In the last decades, the attempts to find novel explanations about the changing essence of business and to define the factors for its progress within the framework of the global economic transformations succeeded in generating several theoretical contributions. They were promoted as appropriate models to reflect the new realities in the context of the globalization processes, the rapid development of information and communication technologies, and the latest editions of the industrial revolutions. These visions offered alternative tools for measuring and analyzing business advancement. This redefinition of the forces that influence the prosperity of companies brought up modern ideas, how to upgrade the traditional fundament of profits and to urge the organizations to adopt avant-garde approached for achieving business excellence, where the center of gravity shifts towards the role of firms as drivers for modifying the broader social and economic landscape.

In the light of the pressing global challenges, it was quite necessary to recognize the importance of business in effectively addressing them. The acceleration of industrial production demonstrated that the depletion of resources is an imminent threat and they can no longer be taken for granted. The concept for "resource wars" promoted the idea that resource flows draw the most important dividing lines on the world map, far more important than ideological and political ones. The picture of rising competition for control over scarce and unevenly distributed resources (Sharp, 2007) was quite not futuristic, as the alarming signs for its start stimulated the demand for rethinking the nature or resource security (Humphreys, 2012). Evidently, securing supplies from definite importers or gaining access to undeveloped or hard-to-reach resources was associated with corresponding geopolitical influence (Le Billon, 2004), whereby the ball was thrown into the broader field of international configurations.

Synchronically, as another important topic emerged the ecological footprint of human activities. The concerns about our impact on the environment induced growing attention towards ecological degradation, climate change, global warming and greenhouse gas emissions. They served as catalysts for starting the search for alternatives to traditional fossil fuels and for measures for more efficient use of energy. Furthermore, the pattern of global issues was marked by another important vector – the one of social deformities such as poverty and inequality (Ruhana et al., 2024), opening the Pandora's box of evils in several underdeveloped regions. They assisted in the boost of disproportionate burdens, social exclusion, unrest, and political instability, thus contributing to deepening development gaps. From this perspective, the need for comprehensive strategies and sustainable approaches for achieving social cohesion and inclusive progress became axiomatic, as it is mandatory not only to target directly these complications but also to address the root causes for them.

However, within this context of pressing global challenges, it seemed to be quite difficult to get people out of the scheme of their daily problems, so that they could change their perceptions of the complications in the bigger picture and to engage in pro-active actions. Nevertheless, experiencing different types of crises activated modifications in their mindset, which had their repercussions in the business realm. However, what are we ultimately most concerned about today? The results of the 2023 research (Fairtrade America, 2024a) on the development of the Fairtrade system in the United States show that in the rankings of the most important challenges facing the world in 2023 to be addressed, 61% of the respondents pointed to inflation, followed by poverty and economic justice (44%), climate change and environmental causes (42%), supply chain challenges (29%), health-related causes (28%), political polarization (25%), racial justice and diversity (22%), women's causes (19%), and children's causes (17%). Ultimately, this arrangement indicates that people are mostly concerned with the economic problems, and place less importance on political issues and even on justice and human rights. Furthermore, climate change is still not fully prioritized.

In the light of recent developments, as important question in the business sphere emerges the examination, how to achieve sustainable growth and long-term success in this turbulent environment. One of the most popular concepts in the field is the so-called Triple Bottom Line, which is decomposed into "three P's"- Profit, People, and the Planet. It goes beyond the vision for favoring simply the financial gain, but to consider the broader context of business activities, in order to incorporate their effect on the environment and their societal impact. This approach was introduced by John Elkington (the founder of a British consultancy called "Sustainability") in

1994 for the purpose of inducing a shift in perspective and establishing a new setting in measuring success through economic, social and environmental performance. By applying the Triple Bottom Line Concept, business performance is not oriented solely towards traditional metrics such as net income, profit margins, and cash flow. Additionally, "it also includes considerations like ethical income and social responsibility" (Emerick, 2024). The accomplishments of the company should not be limited to maximizing profits – they have to be expanded in the relevant vector of creating value in sustainable way.

Generally, the concept emphasizes the minor role of economic growth to that of benefiting people and the planet. It highlights the need to distinguish between shareholders and stakeholders. Definitely, business decisions have repercussions on multiple levels, as they affect customers, employees, suppliers, and communities. All of them are stakeholders, which should be considered by the firms in their business strategies, as creating value for them is an essential element. However, the social impact should be not reduced to the answer to the regular question, how the companies treat their employees. Undeniably, providing fair wages and safe and healthy work environment for them is a paramount issue. Nevertheless, businesses should also take into account how they interact with the communities in the realm, where they operate. According to the guidelines of the Triple Bottom Line concept, the companies should be oriented towards making a positive contribution to the society. For example, business commitment to the welfare of human beings could be advanced through the support of different initiatives in fields such as health care and education.

Beyond the social aspect, companies should also consider their environmental responsibility. Their efforts to make positive impact on the planet could be demonstrated in actions, intended to:

a) regulating energy consumption (including reducing it especially with regard to fossil fuels), shifting towards the use of renewable energy, introducing measures and innovations for improving energy efficiency;
b) relying on sustainable resources and recycled (or at least partially recycled) materials instead of single-use plastics;
c) reducing water consumption;
d) minimizing the waste, produced during the manufacturing processes and its eco-friendly disposal;
e) decreasing greenhouse gas emissions and pollution;
f) avoiding practices harmful to the environment;
g) supporting eco initiatives for planting trees, cleaning up polluted areas, etc., as well as funding research, and donating to environmental causes.

By taking such steps in the context of the third component of the Triple Bottom Line approach, companies will contribute to scale down the ecological footprint, to safeguard biodiversity, and diminish the depletion of natural resources. Considering their social and environmental performance means that the companies should be also proactive in limiting their negative impact in both dimensions, in order to prove their loyalty and backing for enforcing sustainable development. Achieving more beneficial cumulative effect would be possible only through collective actions and aggregate devotion to the transformative business course. Redefining and upgrading the vision for measuring success, this influential concept accentuates on the extra, that creating value for all stakeholders impacted by business decisions adds to the company's own value.

Although it seemingly neglects profits, this approach actually seeks a way out of ignoring the traditionally favored financial bottom line. The main idea is how to find the opportunities for profit by contributing to the environmental and social good. By embracing sustainable practices, the companies could save some of their costs in the long term and to draw the attention of new customers with mindset, favoring such values. Maximizing profits is regarded as a goal compatible with sustainability in serving as drivers for the businessmen.

The Triple Bottom Line approach is perceived as an upgrade of the concept for Corporate Social Responsibility (CSR). It emerged in the latter part of the 20th century and was defined by Archie B. Carroll. He visualized it in the form of pyramid, illustrating the obligations of the companies in four key areas: profitability, legality, ethics, and philanthropy. According to Carroll's model, these obligations were not all equal, because economic drivers have priority, so they form the base of the pyramid. Putting profitability in the foundations, he placed upon it (in decreasing order with regard to the significance) the need to obey the law, promote proper business ethics, and become a moral member of the community making local contributions. With the business evolution, the model was adapted to the new environment. Nowadays, its main postulate refers to the idea that the business has the society as its surrounding ambience, so the firms' activities should be guided by the principle to show engagement to this broader public context and to arrange a duty-bound and respectful attitude towards the community in their operating style. CSR could be decomposed into several types, but usually a differentiation into four categories is applied: environmental, philanthropic, ethical, and economic responsibility:

a) **Environmental responsibility** is described as one of the standard and most common forms of CSR. As an alternative, in the scientific literature and in the business practices is used the term "environmental stewardship". Apparently, all of them are bound to the obligation to protect the natural capital and to avoid destructive and harmful to the biosphere ways of production and functioning.

b) **Ethical responsibility** promotes the moral dimension of business codes. It urges the companies to adopt a fair, just, humane and high-principled modes, methods and routines. According to the experts, "organizations that embrace ethical responsibility aim to practice ethical behavior through fair treatment of all stakeholders, including leadership, investors, employees, suppliers, and customers" (Stobierski, 2021b). There are various articulations of ethical responsibility. For example, the firms could pay extra attention to their suppliers and ensure that ingredients, components, materials, or products are properly sourced.

c) In addition to the ethical and environmental dimension, **Philanthropic Responsibility** is another crucial component of CSR. It is tied to the aim of being active in supporting the efforts to address different challenges for the world and for the communities. The firms could dedicate a portion of their profits to donate to charities and nonprofits that align with their missions or contribute to other worthy causes. In the extra case, philanthropic responsibility could be expressed in creating own charitable trust or organization, in order to return part of the earnings to the society and have a positive impact in explicit field. They represent long-standing form of charitable giving that distributes its proceeds and assets based on specific instructions. Charitable trusts could be used for some tax benefits as well.

d) **Economic Responsibility** is explained through the postulate that the companies should base their financial decisions on the commitment to do good. Once more, this brings to the forefront the idea about the main focus of the business that should not have as a supreme goal to maximize profits. The firms have to center their operations on the positive impact on the environment, people, and society. Once again, the essence of this component displays the web structure of the different types of CSR, where no single element could endure separately.

2. The Ethical Responsibility on Practical Ground

The ethical component of CSR is a multidimensional one. One of its most crucial manifestations is the concept of ethical sourcing which is applicable to the whole supply chain. Not only the products, but also the services in each segment of the supply chain should be obtained in a fair way. Such model includes as a prerequisite a complex of safe working conditions, labor rights, and general business ethics. In other words, companies should consider the impact of their decisions on the people and the communities of their supply chains. Definitely, this is not an easy process for monitoring as well, because the visibility over ethical risks decreases in the lower sections of the supply chains. In this regard, the companies should sidestep from problematic suppliers and refrain from contributing to the advance of discriminatory practices such as poor working conditions, low safety standards, poverty wages, forced or child labor, slavery, etc.

In the scientific literature, the terms "responsible sourcing" and "sustainable sourcing" are also applied alongside "ethical sourcing". There is no absolutely clear distinction between them, so in several cases they are used interchangeably. According to an explanation provided by Sedex, "the term "ethical sourcing" focuses on social concerns and working conditions within supply chains, and may not include environmental areas. Sustainable sourcing tends to focus on the environmental impacts of a supply chain. Responsible sourcing is an umbrella term that usually refers to aspects of both ethical and sustainable sourcing" (Sedex, 2024).

Experts underline, that promoting ethical responsibility could turn your business into more resilient and prosperous. There are several benefits in this regard such as reducing supply chain risks and generally social ones; achieve operational efficiencies and productivity savings; increase the resilience of the supply chains; safeguard the company's reputation and improve its prestige among customers, investors, and employees; avoid violation of the legislation and thus the payment of fines and penalties. The last one is especially important, as many countries have adopted laws, in order to promote ethical business models. For instance, there are legal measures against corruption, slavery (like the Modern Slavery Act, introduced in the United Kingdom in 2015), and import of goods produced with forced labor. They foresee severe penalties for offenders, as seen in the case of Germany, where under the Supply Chain Due Diligence Act the firms could be fined up to 2% of their annual global turnover. Along the EU, in the group of the leading countries with regard to legislation for ethical sourcing are also UK, Norway, Switzerland, and as examples outside Europe - Australia, and India. In the United States, California was the first state with such measures, adopting the Transparency in Supply Chains Act in 2010 with the requirement for annual reports from manufacturers and large retailers.

Noticeably, with regard to these modern trends, there is a rush in labelling products and services as ethically sourced. However, specific problems arise from this fashionable praxis, because it also opens the door for abuses, as there is no small probability to exploit such label just as marketing trick. This represents a considerable risk in the case of the "ethically sourced" classification, as there is no clear-cut and explicit set of standards and no official institution supervising the use of this mark. Consequently, such label could cover a broad spectrum of ethical dimensions.

In contrast, other labels such as "Fairtrade" are bound to global certification system and its use is permitted only if the production process and the supply chain of the companies comply with the standards in economic, social and environmental plan. The Fairtrade International System is based on extensive network that spans across over 70 countries, connecting over 2 million farmers and workers, and more than 2,000 brands, which are Fairtrade certified. The aim of the system is not only to label products as ethical, but also to modify the way trade works, trying to "create real sustainable change by more equitably distributing resources to the beginning of the supply chain, leveraging local and regional agricultural expertise and creating standards that protect people and the environment" (Fairtrade America, 2024b). The systems postulates that "current global trading models are built on an imbalance of power where it is socially acceptable to sacrifice people for profit". On the contrary, the fair trade is a way of doing business and shopping differently, because by choosing certified products, the customers are investing into a global pattern, oriented towards introducing new norms. The standards of the system are described as a blend of social, economic and environmental criteria that support the sustainable development of small producer organizations and agricultural workers in low- and middle-income countries. The system has its standards library, with the popular ones being such as those for tea, cocoa, coffee, cane sugar, honey, flowers and plants, vegetables, oilseeds and oleaginous fruit, cereals, nuts, herbs and spices, gold and associated precious metals for artisanal and small-scale mining, textile, climate, etc. Fairtrade offers a specific certification procedure, backed up by standards compliance check. Its key element is the review of the recipe and supply chains of the products, so to make sure that they were sourced from certified farms and meet the ingredient thresholds. After going through the registration and labeling phase, the client enters into a licensing agreement with Fairtrade and is able to use the mark. The company also gets help in the form of training for correctly position and exploit it, including how to update its marketing materials.

The results of the 2023 research (Fairtrade America, 2024a), conducted on a biannual basis by the firm GlobeScan, in order to explore the achievements of the system in the United States, show that 61% of the customers in the country recognize the Fairtrade mark (in 2021 the recognition was 41%). For the period 2019-2023, the label awareness has increased by 118%. The visibility of Fairtrade products has advanced for nearly all major product categories in the country, and buyers claim that they have seen the label mostly on products such as coffee, chocolate and cocoa, tea, bananas and avocados. On a global level, 71% of the customers recognize the Fairtrade mark. Two in three US customers, familiar with the mark, prefer retailers that carry certified products and 80% of the Fairtrade shoppers declare that they would pay more to ensure a fairer price for producers, and 67% said they would pay more for certified products, despite inflation. Millennials appear as the most enthusiastic purchasers. Among the 25-34 years olds, who know the label, 63% confirmed that they buy Fairtrade products regularly, and 35% occasionally. By comparison, the regular purchases reach 49% for the age group (35-54 years), 38% for Generation Z (18-24), and only 26% for the age group 55+ years. When exploring the motivation of the buyers to purchase such products, most of all with regard to the potential impact areas, stand out the safer or reduced use of artificial pesticides, chemicals or genetically modified products (33%), ensuring no child labor (30%), helping tackle poverty and improve living standards for farmers and workers (28%), ensuring no forced labor or modern slavery (26%), protecting again deforestation and improving land management (25%), and ensuring decent and safe working conditions for farmers and workers (24%). Especially interesting is also the picture with regard to the effect of the mark on brand perceptions. 85% of US shoppers confirm that carrying the Fairtrade label would make a positive impact on their impressions of a brand.

Along Fairtrade, another important term is “Cruelty-free”, but it does not deal with factors such as labor conditions. Such a label indicates that the product and its ingredients were not tested on animals. Usually, it is used in the cosmetic industry. For instance, the US have no regulatory system for the “cruelty-free” identification. The United States Food And Drug Administration underlines, that the lack of legal definitions for the term results in its unrestricted use by cosmetic companies. It also draws attention to the fact, that “many raw materials, used in cosmetics, were tested on animals years ago when they were first introduced. A cosmetic manufacturer might only use those raw materials and base their “cruelty-free” claims on the fact that the materials or products are not “currently” tested on animals” (USFDA, 2000). By contrast, the EU had experienced a long evolution of regulations in this sphere. In 2004, the cosmetic products tested on animals were forbidden on its territory. This represented the first step in this quest, as it took into account only the final cosmetic product, and not the ingredients. In 2009, tests on ingredients and final products were blocked, except the ones measuring long term toxicity effects. As a final step, in 2013, the EU introduced a ban on “any cosmetic product whose final product and ingredients have been tested on animals” (Eco Mundo, 2018). The new law affected imported products as well. With the latest regulations, the label “cruelty-free” is not a necessary one within the EU.

Another label is “Organic”, but it is similarly not affiliated with labor rights and working conditions. It is oriented towards criteria for growing and processing foods, so it is used mainly in the agricultural sector and in the livestock farming. This label encompasses various elements such as soil quality, seed sources, crop health, pest and weed control, water systems, use of additives, contamination and commingling risks and prevention, animal raising methods, etc. The United States regulate its use through the Department of Agriculture (USDA). The certified organic foods should be grown and processed according to federal guidelines. The producers have to “rely on natural substances and physical, mechanical, or biologically based farming methods to the fullest extent possible” (McEvoy, 2012). None of the organic foods should be grown or handled using genetically modified organisms. The USDA organic seal is presented as a tool, helping the shoppers to make informed choices. The EU has also specific standards for this label, as it has introduced its own organic logo that provides a coherent visual identity to organic products produced in the member-countries. The logo helps the customers to distinguish organic products and assists the farmers in marketing them across the EU. The certification is achievable by fulfilling strict conditions in the segments of producing, processing, transportation and storage. According to the definition of the European Commission, “the logo can only be used on products when they contain at least 95% organic ingredients and additionally, respect further strict conditions for the remaining 5%” (European Commission, 2024).

Apparently, the categories of ethical responsibility and sourcing are substantial ones for industries with recorded troublesome experiences of problematic practices and indigent or pauperized working conditions, as such are observed in the cases of diamonds, coffee, palm oil, clothing, etc. For companies, operating in specific sectors, it is extremely important to have an ethical sourcing policy. Pointedly, for every firm is of consequence to examine each segment of the supply chain and to provide satisfying visibility of it, in order to guide in optimal way its procurement activities. The organizations could use several tools for such purposes like risk assessments, supplier self-assessment questionnaires, on-site social audits like SMETA, or generally using consultancy or other supporting services in this field. As an important mechanism, SMETA is oriented towards the standards of labor, health and safety, environmental performance, and ethics not only within the company but also for the suppliers. The auditors provide Corrective Action Plan reports, in order to assist in boosting performance in these fields.

Based on its specifics, every company could find its own instruments for upgrading its ethical responsibility. Certainly, as the most significant problem emerges the protection of the workers from unsafe conditions, low pay, overwork, discrimination, and forced labor. As a meaningful measure, experts recommend to the firms to considering the option to set their own, higher minimum wage if the one fixed by the public authorities is not considered as one at a livable level. Likewise, as a result of the pandemic crisis companies should also consider wider health and safety implications and modify its practices. Finding the best tools for maintaining ethical standards would be pivotal for long-term success, because they help in building trust with all stakeholders and maintain a reputable public image. Thus, ethical organizations enhance their social license to operate and build a competitive advantage in a world of numerous choices.

Remarkably, ethical responsibility is intertwined with other terms such as “business ethics” and “organizational ethics”. According to promoted definitions, “business ethics refer to an essential system of policies and practices that uphold a corporation’s legal and moral responsibilities” and should address among others the principles of corporate, community and environmental responsibility (University of York, 2024). Generally, business ethics is perceived as a broader concept, including corporate social responsibility. According to some authors, "if you were trying to re-create a pyramid of CSR with the understanding that profitability cannot be the base, business ethics might be a suitable replacement. When ethics inform everything else up the pyramid, businesses create more consistent approaches to modern CSR, from profits to corporate environmentalism" (Bartel, 2022). Additionally, "organizational ethics" is described as encompassing "a wide range of practices and policies that govern how a business operates, how it treats its employees, customers, and the wider community, and how it handles issues of legality and morality" (Business Ethics Network, 2023). The pillars of this concept are the principles of integrity, fairness, respect, and responsibility. However, they should not be treated as abstract ideals, but as practical guidelines, shaping the way the firms conduct their business. Clearly, the use of so many terms on a scientific and practical level indicates that they form a complex tangle of interwoven issues and challenges. This demonstrates that the most desirable business strategy and practice should incorporate all dimensions – environmental, social and ethical.

3. The Benefits of Embracing Corporate Social Responsibility

In the light of the new realities, many companies are implementing currently extensive CSR programs. Some of them add in their organizational structure C-level executives and entire departments for social and environmental initiatives. These executives are commonly referred to as chief officers of corporate social responsibility or chief sustainability officers (CSO) (Gavin, 2019b). Certainly, practicing CSR may produce different models, reflecting the specifics of the firm, but their final goal is the same – doing well by doing good. In several countries, CSR standards are embedded in law, but in the most cases, it is mainly a self-regulated endeavor and such business practices are adopted as an element of the firm's culture.

Positive messages for embracing CSR come also from indications for shifts in the corporate mindset. In a study by Deloitte, 93% of business leaders revealed that they believe companies are not just employers, but stewards of society. Furthermore, 95% reported their plans to take bigger stances on societal-impact issues in the coming year and to devote substantial resources to socially responsible initiatives. Evidently, business leaders have embraced the new role of companies, because 59% of the respondents confirmed that between 1 and 5% of their revenues is dedicated to programs with a purpose (Deloitte, 2019). Besides these conclusions, Deloitte's 2019 Global Human Capital Trends survey displayed that, for the first time ever, CEOs named societal impact as the top success factor for annual performance (Evans & Siesfeld, 2020). The consulting firm also tries to measure business value, added from corporate social activities, outlining six drivers - brand differentiation, talent attraction and retention, innovation, operational efficiency, risk mitigation, and capital access and market valuation.

There are also several rankings or honoree lists with reference to CSR. For example, Ethisphere launched in 2006 the World's Most Ethical Companies recognition program to measure and showcase the superior achievements of organizations in the field. It evaluates a company's a) ethics and compliance program, b) culture of ethics, c) corporate citizenship and responsibility, d) governance, and e) third party management. In 2024, 136 organizations from 20 countries and 44 industries were included in the World's Most Ethical Companies Honoree List as recognized for their commitment to business integrity (Ethisphere, 2024).

Turning to corporate social responsibility is not only an issue of conviction. Generally, embracing this concept produces several benefits. Beyond its role as serving as moral creed, it could be exploited as a mighty marketing tool, helping in gaining favorable positions in the markets. The evolution of this construct is driven by exceptional dynamics, having its multifold manifestations on theoretical and practical ground. One of them is related to the modes for identification of the organizations as socially responsible. Currently, there are diverse designations or seals such as B Corporations (B Corps), Social Purpose Corporations (SPCs), and Low-Profit Limited Liability Companies (L3Cs).

B Corps are for-profit companies, proved their compliance with specific social and environmental criteria. They receive such certification from the international nonprofit network B Lab, founded in 2006 and based in the United States. The applying companies go through an assessment process of their practices across five categories - governance, workers, community, environment, and customers. The period of validity is three years, and after its expiry, a recertification is needed. B Lab presents an annual "Best for the World" list, praising the top performers in each category and for specific region. B Lab describes its mission as building a movement to change the economic system, in order to "shift the behavior, structure, and culture of capitalism" and to create "an inclusive, equitable, and regenerative economy" (B Lab, 2024). As of August 2024, there are 9,140 certified B corporations across 162 industries in 102 countries worldwide. B corps are often confused with another label – benefit corporations that are companies of specific type, operating for the benefit not only of its shareholders, but also of all stakeholders and the society. The two types of firms have similar accountability and transparency requirements, but "the performance of a benefit corporation is self-reported, whereas a B corp must "pass" the B Lab Impact Assessment" (Daugherty, 2024).

The Social Purpose Corporation was previously known as Flexible Purpose Corporation, designed as a hybrid corporate form and as alternative to both traditional corporation and benefit corporation (Chiodini, 2014). SPC is a for-profit entity with a special mission to pursue a public purpose like nonprofit organizations. This purpose should be articulated in the Articles or Certificate of the corporation. As, SPCs are able to distribute profits to shareholders, they have no tax-exempt status.

The Low-Profit Limited Liability Company is a hybrid as well, representing a "private organization that does earn profits, but only so that it can conduct business to help a certain cause" (Muslic, 2017). Therefore, it combines characteristics of for-profit and non-profit entities. The requirement for a L3C is to have as its primary objective a socially beneficial mission. For instance, it could further a charitable or educational purpose. An additional requirement postulates that L3C cannot have political purposes. According to the experts, "L3Cs are best for business entities that operate in industries with a social mission, such as environmental sustainability, and expect to generate some profits as well as conduct some nonprofit activities such as accepting contributions" (Tarver, 2024).

Beyond categorization issues, another important topic with regard to CSR relates to the communication of the company's efforts in the field to external and internal stakeholders. Preparing a corporate social responsibility reports is one of the common instruments for such transmission. CSR reports serve for articulation of the mission, actions, and outcomes of the organization towards employees, shareholders, customers, local communities, and the general public. Such documents should reflect the impact of the firm's operations on the environment and the society and draw attention to the achievements of the company. A special recommendation highlights the significance of releasing a CSR report on an annual basis, in order to create accountability and use it for integrating the image of responsibility into the brand's identity. Therefore, the presentation and dissemination of this type of document is described as a marketing and public relations event as well.

However, the regulations for releasing CSR reports are quite different around the world. In several countries, it is mandatory for corporations to publish such documents annually. In the cases of the lack of such obligation, there is growing interest towards the use of this communication tool. For example, according to research results, 90% of companies on the S&P 500 index published CSR reports in 2019 — up from 86% in 2018, 75% in 2014, and only 20% in 2011 (Cote, 2021b). In 2024, the Governance & Accountability Institute presented the 13th annual edition of its research series, tracking the sustainability reporting trends of the largest U.S. publicly-traded companies. It showed its record levels at a moment, when public companies in the country prepared for mandated disclosure, as the U.S. regulatory framework followed the steps of Europe in this sphere. In 2023, 93% of Russell 1000 companies published a sustainability report - an increase from 90% in 2022 (Governance & Accountability Institute, 2024a).

Obviously, this new requirements open the door for the development of a whole supporting sector, as several organizations began to offer services in helping companies to publish their first sustainability report or for firms looking to improve the quality of their developed reports. The goal of this kind of assistance is to tell the company's story in a way that maximizes return on investment by moving its scores and ratings with environmental, social, and governance (ESG) data providers such as Bloomberg, MSCI, Sustainalytics, ISS, S&P Global, etc. Currently, there are numerous reporting frameworks and standards, and the most popular include the Global Reporting Initiative (GRI) Standards, Sustainability Accounting Standards Board (SASB) Standards, International Integrated Reporting Council (IIRC), recommendations from the Task Force on Climate-related Financial Disclosures (TCFD), the United Nations' Sustainable Development Goals (SDGs), and emerging standards such as the European Sustainability Reporting Standards (ESRS) and the disclosure standards of the International Sustainability Standards Board (ISSB) (Governance & Accountability Institute, 2024b).

Additionally, more investors have started to consider ESG metrics in taking their investment decisions. Typically, they use ESG metrics to analyze the sustainability practices and the ethical impact of companies, examining factors such as carbon footprint, water usage, community development efforts, and board diversity. A 2021 IBG study shows that 83% of personal investors stress that, in the next 12 months, they will invest, divest, or lobby fund managers to change investment mixes based on social responsibility and/or environmental sustainability factors (Orrell et al., 2021).

With regard to investments, another important indicator is the social return on investment (SROI), which reflects the measurement of social, environmental, and economic outcomes, calculating them in monetary values. A prominent institution, engaged with developing the principles for assessing SROI and social value in general, is Social Value International. Its mission is to embed a mindset, where impact and social value are integrated into decision-making and are part of an organization's culture.

However, all indicators, classifications and accountability actions are of little importance for the customers. As experts underline, "no one has ever fallen in love with a brand because it complies with regulations or publishes a report" (Allegrini, 2024). To turn this endeavor into a real opportunity, it is necessary to construct a compelling narrative and display the company's efforts in an efficient and inspiring way that resonates with the target audiences. Only in this case, it would be possible to spark brand preference and loyalty. This conclusion draws the spotlight to the communicating aspects of the activities, which will help the firms to use the social and environmental causes to differentiate.

Furthermore, as a specific problem in the sphere emerges the so-called greenwashing behavior (GWB) of the companies. GSBs are described as the primary obstacle of ESG disclosure (Liu et al, 2024). As methods for effective regulation of GWB's in ESG are still unclear, many firms use the option to deceptively offer information that does not reflect their real environmental performance. Clearly, ESG disclosure brings competitive advantages and is beneficial to the organizations, because it offers better access to finance, lower cost of capital, and higher risk resilience. Therefore, greenwashing should be treated as fraud. Moreover, the inconsistency of ESG disclosure standards opens the gate for GWBs, as the differences in the ESG ratings facilitates such actions. The responsibility for regulating greenwashing is hold primarily by the governments. Nevertheless, the investors relying on ESG ratings are also interested in monitoring processes.

4. Sustainable Business Practices – Adding New Components to the Familiar Picture

The theoretical contributions of CSR and the Triple Bottom Line are intertwined with the concept of sustainable development. It is also a multifaceted one and gradually turned into the leading functional paradigm for offering a path for attacking the challenges, generated by the structural economic and societal changes worldwide. It was designed to find a modus of achieving harmony between the accelerating technological progress, the push for economic growth and the environmental degradation. The pursuit of economic prosperity brought to the forefront the problem with the depletion of natural resources and urgency of the preservation of the biosphere for the next generations. Alongside these complications, there were also no efficient answers to the call for solving the puzzle of social shortcomings and deformities, characterized by poverty, inequality, unemployment, malnutrition and food insecurity, poor access to healthcare and education, etc. Therefore, the paradigm of sustainable development promoted the idea of new order based on the trinity - environment, economy and social justice. Such modern mode of development would enable to meet the current needs of the population without compromising the ability of future generations to do the same. This theory emerged in the 1980s as a contribution in the framework of neoclassical economics, considering the role of natural resources in economic development.

Sustainable development is linked to the concept of green economy, where important elements are the green transition and the green growth. All of the "green" terms are focused on the idea, how to prosper in environmentally sustainable and socially inclusive way. Especially "the broader concept of "inclusive" green growth or sustainable development incorporates fully the social sustainability aspects" (Green Growth Knowledge Platform, 2013). In 2012, in order to promote the transition to a green economy, the Green Growth Knowledge Platform (GGKP) was established as a global partnership of international organizations (such as the Organization for Economic Co-operation and Development (OECD), the United Nations Environment Programme (UNEP), and the World Bank), research institutes, think tanks, and experts. It is oriented towards supporting policymakers, practitioners and experts with data, analysis, guidance and best practices. It has specific sectors for green policy, green finance, green industry, etc. They serve as an important tool, assisting the business to become more competitive by going green.

The application of the concept of sustainable development became an ongoing process of changing attitudes towards the environment. It has its own manifestations on the business level as well. Especially valuable one refers to incorporating sustainability into business culture and strategy. The research on the topic of sustainable business practices puts in the spotlight valuable ones such as: 1) partnering with nonprofit organizations; 2) educating the company's employees; 3) encouraging volunteerism; 4) rethinking of the supply chain (Stobierski, 2021). Another model suggests focusing on the following actions for introducing sustainability in business: 1) using sustainable materials in the manufacturing process; 2) optimizing supply chains to reduce greenhouse gas emissions; 3) relying on renewable energy sources to power facilities; 4) sponsoring education funds for youth in the local community (Spiliakos, 2018). Similar concept favors the emphasis on business strategies for social change. As examples for such the experts point out: 1) engaging in and promoting ethical business practices; 2) forming strategic partnerships with nonprofit organizations; 3) encouraging employees to volunteer; 4) inspiring action with corporate platforms (Gavin, 2019a).

According to a popular definition, "the general goal of a sustainable business strategy is to positively impact the environment and society" (Miller, 2020). Principally, it should go beyond the classical strategic planning centered around maximizing profits, reducing costs, and mitigating risk. While not underestimating hampering financial performance or underestimating success, a sustainable business strategy should also address the global pressing challenges and effect positive change in the world. Moreover, experts underline the importance for business professionals of developing sustainability and social responsibility knowledge and skills (Cote, 2021a). Firstly, they should collect foundational information about the impact of their company's activities in both spheres. In this phase, it is advisable to conduct a formal sustainability audit, in order to considering elements such as carbon emission levels; waste produced annually; toxins used in the manufacturing process; waste and toxins created in the product life cycle; employees' satisfaction, rights, representation, and quality of life; volunteerism and civic engagement, required infrastructure to support sustainable practices, etc. The second skill refers to strong leadership, expressed in delegating tasks and empowering employees to work on them, communicating organizational change effectively, etc. As third and fourth skills are praised the ability to identify strategic opportunities and demonstrate a forward-thinking. The fifth one represents the creative problem-solving, needed for cultivating innovation within the organization. The sixth skill is oriented towards calculating the potential value of project ideas. As a seventh one is identified the collecting, analyzing, and reporting on data. Lastly, the eight skill in this model is the effective communication of purpose.

Obviously, when analyzing the role businesses play in driving social change, the leading interpretation refers to taking into consideration not only the firms as an inanimate objects, but also as a circle of individuals, interested in taking actions to address the problems in their communities. In this regard, the initiatives to involve the employees in practical endeavors is especially important, as engaging the staff with different social campaigns or encouraging them to volunteer will not only support specific causes, but also serve as a soldering ingredient for the collective. Furthermore, a modern trend in the psychological research underscores how giving a purpose of their job could boost employee motivation, productivity, and creativity. Thus, engaging and empowering the staff could have a growing in size or effect multiplication of advancements. Another relevant suggestion highlights the portrayal of the companies as capable and powerful agents pushing for transformation, as they could serve as role models and deliver strong messages and persuasive calls. Specifically, they could mobilize particular instruments such as modern digital channels (like using blogs and social media platforms) for advocating for different causes.

Many authors discuss the advantages for a company that adopts an orientation towards incorporating sustainability into its business strategy. For example, as benefits of sustainability in business are considered: 1) protecting the firm's brand and mitigating risks; 2) being purpose-driven is a competitive advantage; 3) profit from the growing market for sustainable goods; 4) cooperative action can drive change (Chladek, 2019).

Especially salient is the human dimension of these advantages that could be found in the face of workforce and customers. A purpose-driven company could attract more skilled and motivated employees, demonstrating outstanding loyalty and strong devotion in their work. On the other side, such approach could lure and captivate new groups of customers, which will be intrigued and tempted to buy the products of the company or support its sustainable practices. Increasing sales and gaining biggest market share seems lucrative enough as results, in order to magnetize the business to convert to such modern strategy. In the marketing studies, there are also several confirmations for the unfolding of a flourishing interest in sustainable products and ingredients, and for such branded with the mark of social duty and responsibility. Principally, millennials are considered as a sustainability-minded generation, inclined to buy and to pay larger sums for such goods.

Different studies support the validity of these trends. A report of Pew Research Center, presenting the results of a survey in 17 advanced economies from North America, Europe and the Asia-Pacific region, found that 72% of the respondents are concerned that they will be personally harmed by climate change in their lifetimes (Bell at al., 2021). Additionally, 80% declare that they are willing to make at least some changes to their lives to help reduce the effects of ecological degradation. Moreover, only 46% of the people are confident that actions of the international community will significantly reduce the impact of climate change. Evidently, these results show that there is a need for another type of actions in this direction, involving the business and the societies.

As Edelman Trust Barometer for 2022 shows, business is the most trusted institution (with 61% of the statements of over 36,000 respondents in 28 countries), and it is ahead of NGOs, governments and media. The public authorities are also not seen as able to solve social problems (by 44% of the people), so the business is viewed as the factor to take the leadership role in this direction. Simultaneously, social fears are on the rise - 85% of the respondents said they worry about job loss, 75% about climate change, and 71% about hackers and cyber-attacks (Edelman, 2022). The results of the survey demonstrate that the citizens are seeing the business as competent and effective driver of positive change, and therefore it should act as a stabilizing force. Additionally, they await form the business sector to prefer long-term thinking over short-term gain. Clearly, the trend of rising ethical consumerism proves that firms can no longer afford to ignore CSR.

CSR is also a factor talent attraction and retention. An IBV report found out that talent advantage have namely the sustainability-focused companies - 68% of the employees confirm that they are keener to apply for jobs in such firms, with 48% willing to accept a lower salary (Orrell et al., 2021). A previous survey in 2019, presenting the results of conversations with 1,000 employees at large U.S. companies, showed that over 70% of the respondents are more likely to choose to work at a company with a strong environmental agenda. More than a third stressed that they have devoted more time and effort to their work because of their employer's sustainability commitment. Nearly 40% of millennials have chosen a job because of company sustainability. Less than a quarter of generation X respondents said the same, and only 17% of baby boomers (Peters, 2019).

5. The Marketing Pattern of Incorporating Sustainability Into Business Practices

The consumer behavior and the global consumption patterns are constantly evolving, triggering transformation of the markets and acceleration of the dynamics of people's interaction with goods and services. Generally, consumer behavior is tied to psychological and emotional processes, but we should not underestimate the role of the social ones as well, because all of them influence human decisions to buy and use goods and services. On the other hand, the aggregate outcome of their behaviors forms the consumption design that reflects the broader economic, cultural and societal models of purchasing goods and services. Henceforth, the consumption represents a form of communication that serves individuals as a channel for expressing identity, attachment, association, belonging and values. In that matter, a resourceful explaining capacity contains the consumer culture theory (CCT) that attempts to explain how consumption is embedded in the comprehensive social and cultural context (Arnould et al., 2019). It further expands our understanding of how the blossoming values of favoring sustainability and community support are forcing marketing communications to change, in order to align with the new trends. These new-fashioned preferences pressurize the brands to embrace environmental practices or back specific initiatives, so they could resonate with the consumers' inclination that is increasingly leaning towards social responsibility. These developments suggest that the modification is not just about meeting immediate needs, but also about adjusting consumption to the wider cultural shift towards ethical and responsible living.

On analytical level, another ideational insight could be found in the social identity theory (McGowana et al., 2016). It underlines that consumption is positioned as an extension of social identification and inclusion that are stimulating consumers to view their purchasing choices as meaningful contributions to a larger group or community cause. Therefore, they seek to coordinate their picks with collective identity and distinctiveness or social values. Consumers' selection could be oriented towards expressing solidarity with specific social group, in particular a vulnerable one, or towards supporting different campaigns or missions with positive impact on the population. This concept provides also an explanation about the favorable treatment of products from brands that demonstrated concern about global problems, because such preferment could be rooted in the established public perceptions. Surely, the intense gravity of sustainable consumption could be driven by the expanding awareness of environmental issues. However, its significance could be reinforced by the dominating mental attitude or mainstream sentiments. Obviously, the current trend towards sustainability reflects a shift in consumer values, but engineering and forging such changes refer ones more to the issue of the role of specific agents (not only on the level of political elites or influential international structures, but also with regard to the mission of the business) that are capable of inducing and enforcing these transformations by implementing constructivist approaches.

Nevertheless, both theories imply that alongside traditional factors such as price and quality apparently new ones should be considered as well, as the social, cultural and ecological components have exclusive impact on consumption. Thereupon, the study of clients' behavior should not be limited to personal needs, but on the contrary – be more comprehensive, because in order to find what makes consumers tick or what products impress or captivate them, we have to explore the resound on both a rational and emotional layers. Understanding consumption is crucial for the marketing stratum, as it assists in predicting buyers' behavior, creating better products, and delivering productive and convincing communication strategies. For their part, the companies must continuously adapt by correcting and refitting their approaches or by integrating new tactics into their modus operandi to effectively engage purchasers, foster consumer loyalty and drive business growth in an increasingly complex markets.

Additionally, the metamorphoses in the greater economic landscape could also have their repercussions for consumption patterns. For instance, economic crises or pandemic ones (as we have experienced recently) have their long-term consequences for the business. These include changes in industries' structure, market dynamics, consumer behavior and companies' strategies. In the case of the pandemic of 2020, it raised people's awareness of the global interconnectedness and showed how fragile and vulnerable are the social systems. This realization raised the sensibility towards ecological degradation and the further recognition of the need for sustainability. The reduction of transport and industrial activities had its positive effect on the environment, visible in the decrease of the greenhouse gas emissions (especially these of carbon dioxide). The pandemics proved the significance of the attentiveness towards the impact of our daily activities on the biosphere. To turn this trend into a constant, it is required to accentuate on the demand for modification of personal mindset and habits, corporate strategies and public policies. For a reason, a peculiar product of the pandemics and the following economic disturbances was the call for sustainable recovery.

Synchronically with the ascending environmental concerns, the people became more interested in donating funds in charitable campaigns or purchasing products with social impact. This suggests that brands demonstrating a commitment to such issues and causes, and integrate sustainable practices into their business models will be more likely to stand out and attract attention in the markets, and dazzle the customers. At the same time, the companies should also adapt their marketing strategies to meet the new consumer demands. In this context, the communications should focus on ethics and social responsibility and provide transparency.

Several studies provide valuable evidences of the commented trends. The signs of the start of an era of empathy, where consumers are personally invested in a wide variety of sustainability and social responsibility issues, are visible in a report about their perceptions after the pandemics. It shows that 93% of the consumers (based on a poll of 14,000 adults from 9 countries) declare that COVID-19 influenced their views on sustainability (Orrell et al., 2021). A similar portion of people are focused on social responsibility, with roughly 3 in 4 consumers highlighting as important for them access to education and ensuring good health and well-being.

An IBV consumer report, based on conducted global survey of more than 19,000 respondents across 28 countries in September 2021, shows that 50% of consumers are willing to pay a premium for sustainable brands that align with their priorities

(Haller et al., 2022). They are ready to pay extra mainly for products with non-toxic ingredients (62%), greater health and wellness benefits (60%), organic ingredients (50%), and environmental responsibility (50%). These results are considered as an element of larger consumer mindset shift, as people are "thinking about their own environmental impact more holistically, considering sustainability when shopping, investing, choosing employment, and selecting modes of transportation". Furthermore, 62% of consumers declare that they are willing to change their purchasing habits to reduce environmental impact. However, having in mind the so called "intention-action gap", clients underline that price and quality appear as the two major barriers for them in buying more sustainable products. This opens the door for the business to step up on sustainability and find solutions for overcoming these barriers. Another interesting result of IBM's report is that purpose-driven consumers have overtaken value-driven consumers as the largest segment of the population with 44%. They prioritize brands that align with their values and lifestyles with regard to their care about sustainability. Additionally, their strong engagement offers a potential to serve as brand ambassadors.

More evidences for the changed perceptions provides a report of Kantar. It shows that, over a 12-year period, brands with a perceived positive sustainability impact have grown in brand value at a faster rate compared to those with a low perceived impact (Kyriakidi, 2021). Kantar's BrandZ data and their series of brand ranking reports are based on the largest global brand equity study, encompassing 4.3 million consumers and 21,000 brands across 54 markets, so their conclusions are quite promising. In order to fit into the sustainable cluster, brands should focus not simply on profit or purpose, but on purpose with profit.

6. Embracing Transformation as the New Constant

Obviously, the new realities institute fresh types of challenges for business people and especially for executives. They are facing the urgency firstly to alter their strategy and business model and secondly – to modify the role of their companies within the social realm. Simultaneously, as a third task, they should be able to comprehend and take into consideration the reframing repercussions of global events and trends. The notion of experiencing transformation is certainly not an unknown or modish one. In order to survive in a competitive business environment, firms unable to adapt, are doomed to failure. Therefore, dealing with modification is not a theoretical abstraction, but an everyday struggle. However, the recent brainchildren of management philosophy suggest not only to perceive transformation as a perpetual process and a nonstop practice, but also to raise it to the level of business ideology, predeterming the creed and the modus of planning and proceeding. Experts underline that nowadays the business setting is profoundly different, because three major factors are influencing it as explosive forces. This specific vision highlights the significance of asymmetry, complexity and uncertainty as defining for our era (Ito & Howe, 2016a). Asymmetry is accentuated as the mightiest in the lineup, as the most massive threat could come from the smallest players or from the most unpredictable of trends. Complexity, as based on the definition by Scott E. Page, represents a combination of the key components of interdependence, connectedness, diversity, and adaptation/learning (Page, 2009). Undoubtedly, rising complexity is related to a lack of predictability (Page, 2010). This brings us to the third factor of uncertainty, which brings predicting of future processes almost beyond the bounds of possibility. Unforeseen and speedy developments in technology, biosphere, and the geopolitical realm will affect economies and people. They will reshape perceptions and values, so strategy would be not the most powerful tool for guaranteeing success - it should be replaced by business culture.

According to the authors of this concept, "the tools of our modern existence are getting faster, cheaper, and smaller at an exponential rate, just as billions of strangers around the world are suddenly just one click or tweet or post away from each other". Usually, "such periods of dramatic change have always produced winners and losers" (Ito & Howe, 2016b). However, the logic of the faster future, which will run on an entirely new operating system, will force us not to rely of the accumulated wisdom of the past, but to obey new "rules" for surviving and advancing such as emphasizing "disobedience over compliance," "resilience over strength," and "diversity over ability". The authors suggest going beyond the limits of formal education, which fosters our inclination to accepting established and proven ideas. As an alternative, we should stimulate our ability to create new ones and question the status quo through solidifying the spirit of learning, which as a self-initiating process will vitalize more innovative brainwork. In this context, "disobedience" is associated with defending your unique point of view and challenging norms, in order to create originative solutions for the existing complications. Furthermore, energizing diversity could steam up productivity, as having a wide range of contrasting perspectives and experiences will trigger inventiveness. Therefore, it is "not only that diversity is healthy and gratifying - it's necessary for us to prosper, perhaps now more than ever" (Gibson, 2017).

Another prominent work also unpacks in detail the conceptualization of transformation. It highlights the capacity of disruption as the principal challenge for business leaders. In such volatile conditions, they should turn to "dual transformation", driving two parallel courses of shift – primarily comes the need to reposition their core businesses (transformation A), and the next step is consisting of unlock new growth in a new market (transformation B). Transformation A will provide the capital for funding transformation B, which in the initial phase will not generate large profits, but over time the new growth business, if successful, could become more lucrative. The researchers underline that "transformations A and B should share a capabilities link of difficult-to-replicate assets that give businesses a competitive advantage" (Anthony et al., 2017). For example, these assets include proprietary technology, stores, brands, patents, or a company's client network. The essence of transformation A is to solve an old problem in a new way, while the constitution of transformation B is to solve a new but related problem in a new way. Namely, the second vector of modification could capitalize on disruptive trends and shock waves by finding originative and avant-garde fixes to alarming complications. Apparently, making your current business model more resilient and competitive is not a satisfactory praxis anymore. In the interim, executives should explore and pursue alternative channels and create new markets.

Clearly, transformation is a painful and tormenting endeavor. Therefore, understanding its complexity is a crucial task for business strategists. As Derek Freely points out, "all transformation is change, but not all change is transformation". Thereupon, he speaks of Triple Aim Transformation, based on five elements, or the five Ps (Freeley, 2019). The first one is the need of paradigm shift, as executing a line of small adaptations would not generate transformation – a fundamental revision of the dominating mindset is required to break the traditional structures. The second element is related to designing a plan, how to reach the envisaged target or destination. Moreover, the tactical apparatus should be also clarified, in order to have precise and effective tools for constructing the desirable future state. For this reason, it is advisable to engage in organizing and sequencing new approaches. The third P is focused on proactive action, as reactive "fixing" does not mean to take control over the shift. The fourth element is referring to people, because change may need one person, but transformation is driven by a critical mass of people. Consequently, business leaders should seek engaging all stakeholders in the process. The fifth P is identified with purpose, which could cultivate the motivation to transform. Having a shared purpose would give meaning to people's efforts. Henceforth, the transformation is not the goal, but the instrument for reaching it.

Taking into account the unprecedented challenges of our time and the urgency of navigating the complexity, another vision to re-evaluate and re-align business strategy proposes a framework for triple transformation (Roland Berger, 2020). As its fundament serve the three dimensions – position, perform and progress. "Position" means to rethink and correct the course of company's strategy, reassess partnerships and investments, and develop a business model, focused on long-term success. "Perform" is related to the value creation and the optimization of company's activities, in order to ensure competitive performance. The dimension of "Progress" is oriented towards the renewal of the organization, so it would be able to meet the expectations of customers, employees, and general public. It encompasses the moves of improving environmental and social sustainability, and building a more resilient firm.

Many researchers, international institutions and structures have their own contributions to the visions of transition. The "twin transition" is often described as a key to sustainable growth. With regard to future action on climate change, there are expectations that the digitalization has a crucial role to play in this sphere. The twin transition approach calls for abandoning the treatment of digital and green shift in isolation, because their combination will generate more efficient and productive outcomes (Blüm, 2022). Digitization should become sustainable, and modern technologies and digital tools offer valuable opportunities to drive more sustainable mindset. In this context, Royal Schiphol Group and PA Consulting have partnered in co-producing the Twin Transition Playbook as a practical guide to help business leader to join digital and sustainability roadmaps and provide them with guidance and instruments to build a successful transition strategy (PA Consulting, 2022).

The European Green Deal is supporting this understanding of a twin transition as well. It is based on the same postulate, that digital and green transitions should not be tackled separately but simultaneously, so they could reinforce each other. Nevertheless, the EU goes further in its vision by adding the social dimension of transformation. As experts underline, that "the social transition aims to ensure that everyone is included in the process towards a more sustainable and competitive economy" (Schmerber, 2024). The added social dimension leads to launching the concept of a triple transition, integrating digital, green and social aspects of development. This model should serve in reaching the EU goals for achieving climate neutrality and circularity by 2050, building a more competitive and resilient European industry, and upgrading cohesion within the Union. The EU adopted its Corporate Sustainability Reporting Directive (CSRD), serving as a replacement of the Non-Financial Reporting Directive (NFRD). The European Commission introduces the European Sustainability Reporting Standard that should take effect by 2026 at the latest. It envisages new reporting obligations for the business. This new regulatory framework will force companies to reshape their business models and practices, in order to meet the standards for data collection and reporting. Apparently, the tightening regulations are inspired by several complications and turbulences that member states had to face in several sectors. These efforts are seemingly in harmony with European aspirations to keep the environmental leadership.

7. The Energy Imperative of Business Transformation

Clearly, the energy challenges serve as an additional motivational factor for embracing sustainability not only on political level, but also in business strategies. The complicated global energy landscape is a result of the complex processes that have taken place in the sector in the last decades. The intensified competition between the buyers of energy resources was attributed to the newly industrialized countries, emerging as more and more resource-hungry as a result of their progressing economic development. For the largest importers, the topics how to secure supplies and how to minimize the risks of import dependency emerged as intricate ones. Having in mind, that energy is essential for industrial and commercial activities, transport, communications, etc., its role in driving socio-economic development is undeniable. In the domain of international relations, energy is considered as a "currency of power" (Heinberg, 2021). In the greater framework of the resource conflicts, the growing trend toward militarization of energy security should be not underestimated as well. Therefore, the promoted green vector of development seems to be extremely beneficial. Gradually, renewables have grown outside the limits of the schematization of being suitable only for local applications. Despite being characterized as a fashion, they proved their qualities not only in the developed, but also in the developing countries. The successful experiences of using them as a growth generating tool after the 2008 economic crisis induce hopes for further exploitation of their capacity for the same purposes.

Undoubtedly, with regard to recent developments, as the greatest energy challenge of this decade emerged the crisis processes in the sector. After the complications in the energy realm, generated by the COVID-19 pandemics, the energy crisis in Europe and other regions showed several internal deficiencies in the blueprint for green transformation. With the start of the war in Ukraine in 2022 began the new wave of modifications, resulting in the redrawing of the world energy map. The current episode of the war in the Middle East demonstrates again the importance of the geopolitics of energy. After experiencing so many energy crises with regard to the evolutions in the framework of the different industrial revolutions, the world should be equipped with the tools to reduce their negative effects, but it seems that the new specifics of expanding interconnectedness of energy markets left us unprepared once again to deal adequately with the far-reaching disruptions.

The advertised recipe for dealing with the complications included the spell of "green growth" and "sustainable recovery". In collaboration with the International Monetary Fund, the International Energy Agency released its "Sustainable Recovery Plan" (International Energy Agency, 2020), in order to call for taking the path to energy transition. The EU upgraded the adopted before the pandemics Green Deal (European Commission, 2019), as with the start of the war in Ukraine energy issues were pushed once more on the top of the political agenda. In 2022, the European Commission presented its new ideas for enlarging renewable energy capacity and improving energy efficiency with the RePowerEU plan (European Commission, 2022). According to the commitments, the share of renewable energy is to rise to

45% by 2030. The plan instructed an obligation to install solar panels on all public and commercial buildings by 2025 and on all residential buildings by 2029.

In contrast to the trends in the department of fossil fuels, renewables proved as the most resilient in the face of different crises such as the pandemic one or the turbulences, provoked by the wars in Ukraine and the Middle East. However, the specific energy crisis in 2021 demonstrated that when the energy systems go through a process of cardinal modification, they are especially vulnerable to shocks. Some researchers pleaded for a more balanced approach for energy transition, because the swift embrace of renewable energy technologies could lead to multiple complications (Dewan, 2021). The concentration of funds dominantly in the green energy industry is seen also as a problematic aspect at this stage of the transformation (Baker et al., 2021). Especially resounding were the alarming voices, indicating that we need a more adequately and wisely managed energy transition (Nuttall, 2021).

However, with the start of the war in Ukraine in 2022, the repercussions for the energy markets generated new forms of pressure with regard to the supply disruptions. Europe was compelled to search for alternatives and rearrange its energy partnerships. The crisis stimulated the efforts for accelerating the green transition, but they were limited by the arising new dilemmas. Additionally, with reference to the rising energy bills, several countries had to implement measures for reducing the negative effects of the crisis for businesses and households. Nevertheless, these measures were often met with reservation. For example, OECD criticized the broad-based support as costly and limiting "the incentives to save energy and transition away from fossil fuels" (OECD, 2023). Another vector of remedies could be found in the receipt for improving energy efficiency. The 7th Annual Global Conference on Energy Efficiency, organized by IEA in 2022, produced a joint statement (Danish Ministry of Climate, Energy and Utilities, 2022), issued by 26 countries, calling on governments, industry, and stakeholders to bolster their action on energy efficiency under the motto: "The cleanest energy is the energy we don't use".

In these turbulent times, many businesses took the path to adaptation and development of green practices. It is quite normal for every company to strive for a better positioning in the current and future energy landscape. The measures for reducing energy consumption and improving energy efficiency are crucial for every organization. Clearly, achieving energy autonomy or self-sufficiency is an almost impossible quest, especially in the globalized world. However, finding the best energy solutions for the single firm would be beneficial for the whole green transition process.

CONCLUSION

In the last decades, different signals indicate that the essence of business has slowly changed. Nowadays, the companies have to consider the growing importance of value-driven trends, the increasing demand for transparency in their activities, the command to become prominent contributors within the communities, and the need to demonstrate responsibility towards a vast assortment of stakeholders. Perhaps the business is overloaded with expectations. The transformation of its role in the social domain means that the firms should position themselves not only against the competition, but also as a part of the society. Companies have to find their own answers to the question, where to find the intersection between "doing good" and "doing well" in the process of creating shared value. Whether they will accomplish this mission or they will fail and get entangled in the trap of greenwashing, depends on their preparedness to integrate environmental and social goals in their activities.

Having in mind the ecological degradation, transformation looks not so much as an overused buzzword, but as an imperative. The pressing environmental problems make it not possible to take the nature for granted anymore. Its protection lies in the vital interests of the people. Ultimately, the business in not a virtual construct, because its backbone is formed namely by human beings. Logically, this means that businesses are integral part not only of the society, but also of the biosphere, so they have responsibilities in both dimensions. The endurance of business is not meaningful or possible without the survival of the people. In this context, embracing sustainability in business models is a rational move. Currently, sustainability is perceived as a competitive advantage, but in the future, it should become the usual business mold.

The current metamorphoses are undoubtedly paradigmatic in nature. The transformative power of global events turns adaptation into a constant. Definitely, transformation in itself is not a recent or fashionable phenomenon. Nevertheless, the growing global volatility, fluidity and uncertainty put their stamp on the rapidly evolving business landscape. Clearly, there is no universal tool for all companies, helping them in become profitable, purpose-driven, and future ready at the same time. Achieving business excellence in the 21st century is not an easy task at all, considering the shrunken global realm. The world is no more analog, but digital and it reacts instantly to events. Therefore, the timeslot for reaction is also limiting. The speedy developments often require not only tactical adjustments, but also changes in the business strategies. Undoubtedly, the business solutions are always faster than public ones, so the calculations of businesses leading the way in resolving the global problems are accurate. According to a Chinese proverb, "The business is a war without swords". However, this does not mean that companies should not be equipped with other instruments for winning the battle. Probably, in the new realities, the champions will be the ones, armed with sustainable business strategies.

REFERENCES

Allegrini, M. (2024). SEC Reporting – So What? - PRWeek, 08 April 2024, available at: https://www.prweek.com/article/1868046/sec-reporting-%E2%80%94-so-what

America, F. (2024a). Fairtrade & the Sustainable Shopper – 2023 US Consumer Insights. - Fairtrade America Online, available at: https://www.fairtradeamerica.org/app/uploads/2023/09/2023-Fairtrade-America-Consumer-Insights.pdf

America, F. (2024b). More than a Label. - Fairtrade America Online, available at: https://www.fairtradeamerica.org/why-fairtrade/the-fairtrade-difference/for-businesses/

Anthony, S. (2017). *Dual Transformation - How to Reposition Today's Business While Creating the Future*. Harvard Business Press.

Arnould, E. (2019). Consumer Culture Theory: Development, Critique, Application and Prospects. - Foundations and Trends in Marketin, available at: https://www.researchgate.net/publication/332647213_Consumer_Culture_Theory_Development_Critique_Application_and_Prospects

Baker, D. (2021). Today's global energy crisis is just the first in the "clean power" era. - World Oil, 5 October 2021, available at: https://www.worldoil.com/news/2021/10/5/today-s-global-energy-crisis-is-just-the-first-in-the-clean-power-era

Bartel, J. (2022, June). Corporate Social Responsibility and Business Ethics. *Forbes*, 27. https://www.forbes.com/councils/forbesfinancecouncil/2022/06/27/corporate-social-responsibility-and-business-ethics/

Bell, J. (2021). In Response to Climate Change, Citizens in Advanced Economies Are Willing To Alter How They Live and Work. Pew Research Center. https://www.pewresearch.org/global/wp-content/uploads/sites/2/2021/09/PG_2021.09.14_Climate_FINAL.pdf

Berger, R. (2020). Triple Transformation: A Framework for the Auto Industry in the 2020s. – Roland Berger.com. https://www.rolandberger.com/en/Insights/Publications/Triple-Transformation-A-framework-for-the-auto-industry-in-the-2020s.html

Blüm, S. (2022). What is the "Twin Transition" - And Why Is It key to Sustainable Growth? - World Economic Forum. https://www.weforum.org/stories/2022/10/twin-transition-playbook-3-phases-to-accelerate-sustainable-digitization/

Business Ethics Network. (2023). Organizational Ethics: Building a Culture of Integrity and Responsibility. https://www.businessethicsnetwork.org/organizational-ethics-building-a-culture-of-integrity-and-responsibility/

Chiodini, S. (2014). Goodbye Flexible Purpose Corporation, Hello Social Purpose Corporation: Governor Brown Signs S.B. 1301. https://www.adlercolvin.com/blog/2014/10/06/goodbye-flexible-purpose-corporation-hello-social-purpose-corporation-governor-brown-signs-s-b-1301/

Chladek, N. (2019). Why You Need Sustainability in Your Business Strategy. – Harvard Business School Online's Business Insights. https://online.hbs.edu/blog/post/business-sustainability-strategies

Consulting, P. A. (2022). Twin Transition Playbook 2.0. https://www2.paconsulting.com/the-twin-transition-playbook-request.html

Cote, C. (2021a). 8 Sustainability Skills for Working Professionals. – Harvard Business School Online's Business Insights. https://online.hbs.edu/blog/post/sustainability-skills

Cote, C. (2021b). What Is a CSR Report & Why Is It Important? – Harvard Business School Online's Business Insights. https://online.hbs.edu/blog/post/what-is-a-csr-report

Danish Ministry of Climate, Energy and Utilities. (2022). Joint Statement: Urgent Action on Energy Efficiency, No. 2022 – 85. https://en.kefm.dk/Media/637904431073034736/joint%20statement.pdf

Daugherty, G. (2024). B Corp: Definition, Advantages, Disadvantages, and Examples. – Investopedia. https://www.investopedia.com/b-corp-7488828

Deloitte. (2019). The Rise of the Socially Responsible Business - Deloitte Global's Societal Impact Survey. https://www.deloitte.com/global/en/about/story/impact/societal-impact-survey-deloitte-global.html

Dewan, A. (2021). Europe's gas crisis is also a renewables crisis, but there are ready solutions. – CNN. https://edition.cnn.com/2021/09/22/business/europe-energy-gas-renewables-climate-cmd-intl/index.html

Edelman. (2022), Trust Barometer 2022. https://www.edelman.com/sites/g/files/aatuss191/files/2022-01/2022%20Edelman%20Trust%20Barometer_FullReport.pdf

Emerick, D. (2024). What is the Triple Bottom Line Approach? The 3Ps of Corporate Impact. – ESG – The Report. https://esgthereport.com/what-is-esg/the-g-in-esg/what-are-the-3-components-of-the-triple-bottom-line-approach/

Ethisphere. (2024). The 2024 World's Most Ethical Companies Honoree List. https://worldsmostethicalcompanies.com/honorees/

European Commission. (2019). The European Green Deal, Brussels, 11.12.2019, COM(2019) 640 final.

European Commission. (2022). REPowerEU: Joint European Action for more affordable, secure and sustainable energy, Strasbourg, 8.3.2022, COM(2022) 108 final.

European Commission. (2024). The Organic Logo. – Section Common Agricultural Policy - Agriculture and Rural Development. https://agriculture.ec.europa.eu/farming/organic-farming/organic-logo_en

Evans, R., & Siesfeld, T. (2020). Measuring the Business Value of Corporate Social Impact. – Deloitte. https://www2.deloitte.com/us/en/insights/topics/social-impact/business-value-of-improving-your-csr-scorecard.html

Feeley, D. (2019). The Five Ps of Triple Aim Transformation. – Institute for Healthcare Improvement. https://www.ihi.org/insights/five-ps-triple-aim-transformation

Gavin, M. (2019a). How to Create Social Change: 4 Business Strategies. – Harvard Business School Online's Business Insights. https://online.hbs.edu/blog/post/how-can-business-drive-social-change

Gavin, M. (2019b). 6 Examples of Corporate Social Responsibility That Were Successful. - Harvard Business School Online's Business Insights. https://online.hbs.edu/blog/post/corporate-social-responsibility-examples

Gibson, L. (2017). Joi Ito and Jeff Howe's New Rules for Our Faster, Tech-driven World. Ford Foundation. https://www.fordfoundation.org/news-and-stories/stories/joi-ito-and-jeff-howes-new-rules-for-our-faster-tech-driven-world/

Governance & Accountability Institute. (2024a). 2024 Sustainability Reporting In Focus. https://www.ga-institute.com/research/ga-research-directory/sustainability-reporting-trends/2024-sustainability-reporting-in-focus/

Governance & Accountability Institute. (2024b). Full Suite Corporate Sustainability Reporting. https://www.ga-institute.com/services/our-portfolio-of-services/sustainability-esg-reporting-disclosure/full-suite-corporate-sustainability-reporting/

Green, G. K. P. (2013). Moving towards a Common Approach on Green Growth Indicators - A GGKP Scoping Paper. https://www.greenpolicyplatform.org/sites/default/files/downloads/resource//GGKP%20Moving%20towards%20a%20Common%20Approach%20on%20Green%20Growth%20Indicators.pdf

Haller, K. (2022). Consumers Want It All: Hybrid Shopping, Sustainability, and Purpose-driven Brands. IBM Institute for Business Value. https://www.ibm.com/downloads/documents/us-en/10c31775c8540243

Heinberg, R. (2021). Understanding Power. Post Carbon Institute. https://www.postcarbon.org/understanding-power/

Humphreys, J. (2012). *Resource Wars: Searching for a New Definition. - International Affairs 88: 5.* The Royal Institute of International Affairs. https://ciaotest.cc.columbia.edu/journals/riia/v88i5/f_0026234_21492.pdf

International Energy Agency. (2020), Sustainable Recovery. https://www.iea.org/reports/sustainable-recovery

Ito, J., & Howe, J. (2016a). *Whiplash: How to Survive Our Faster Future*. Grand Central Publishing.

Ito, J., & Howe, J. (2016b). Whiplash: How to Survive Our Faster Future. Abstract. MIT Media Lab. https://www.media.mit.edu/publications/whiplash-how-to-survive-our-faster-future/

Kyriakidi, M. (2021). Finding Your Sweet Spot for Sustainable Brand Growth. Kantar. https://www.kantar.com/inspiration/brands/%20finding-your-sweet-spot-for-sustainable-brand-growth

Lab, B. (2024). Building the Movement. https://www.bcorporation.net/en-us/movement/

Le Billon, P. (2004). *The Geopolitics of Resource Wars*. Routledge.

Liu, C., Gong, W., Dong, G., & Ji, Q. (2024, July). Regulation of Environmental, Social and Governance Disclosure Greenwashing Behaviors Considering the Risk Preference of Enterprises. -. *Energy Economics*, 135, 107637. DOI: 10.1016/j.eneco.2024.107637

McEvoy, M. (2012). Organic 101: What the USDA Organic Label Means. - United States Department of Agriculture. https://www.usda.gov/media/blog/2012/03/22/organic-101-what-usda-organic-label-means

McGowana, M. (2016, November). The Influence of Social Identity on Value Perceptions and Intention. *Journal of Consumer Behaviour*, 16(3). https://www.researchgate.net/publication/310790712_The_influence_of_social_identity_on_value_perceptions_and_intention_Social_identity_and_value_perceptions

Miller, K. (2020). The Triple Bottom Line: What It Is & Why It's Important. - Harvard Business School Online's Business Insights. https://online.hbs.edu/blog/post/what-is-the-triple-bottom-line

Mundo, E. (2018). Using the "Cruelty-Free" logo in Europe. Eco Mundo Online. https://www.ecomundo.eu/en/blog/cruelty-free-regulations-cosmetics-europe

Muslic, H. (2017). A Jargon-Free Guide to Low-Profit Limited Liability Companies. Nonprofit Hub. https://nonprofithub.org/jargon-free-guide-l3c/

Nuttall, P. (2021, September). The power trap: Why the energy crisis is a crisis of politics. *New Statesman (London, England)*, 28. https://www.newstatesman.com/international-politics/climate-international-politics/2021/09/the-power-trap-why-the-energy-crisis-is-a-crisis-of-politics

OECD. (2023). Aiming Better: Government Support for Households and Firms during the Energy Crisis. OECD Economic Policy Paper No. 32. https://www.oecd-ilibrary.org/docserver/839e3ae1-en.pdf?expires=1692914306&id=id&accname=guest&checksum=0341DA666836280BAC460A99A84531BE

Orrell, G. (2021). Sustainability at a Turning Point: Consumers Are Pushing Companies to Pivot. - IBM Institute for Business Value. https://www.ibm.com/downloads/documents/us-en/10a99803f92fda61

Page, S. (2009). *Understanding Complexity*. The Teaching Company.

Page, S. (2010). Complexity in Social, Political, and Economic Systems. - American Economic Association, Ten Years and Beyond: Economists Answer NSF's Call for Long-Term Research Agendas. Available at: https://ssrn.com/abstract=1889359

Peters, A. (2019). Most Millennials Would Take a Pay Cut to Work at an Environmentally Responsible Company. Fast Company. https://www.fastcompany.com/90306556/most-millennials-would-take-a-pay-cut-to-work-at-a-sustainable-company

Ruhana, F. (2024). Combating Poverty and Social Inequality in 2023 - a Global Imperative for Equitable Development and Social Justice. International Journal of Science and Society. https://ijsoc.goacademica.com/index.php/ijsoc/article/view/1081/946

Schmerber, L. (2024). Triple Transition and Corporate Responsibility – A New Framework for Businesses. Interreg Europe. https://www.interregeurope.eu/policy-learning-platform/news/triple-transition-and-corporate-responsibility-a-new-framework-for-businesses#:~:text=This%20is%20the%20core%20of%20the%20concept%20of,process%20towards%20a%20more%20sustainable%20and%20competitive%20economy

Sedex. (2024). What does "Ethically Sourced" Mean? https://www.sedex.com/blog/what-does-ethically-sourced-mean/

Sharp, T. (2007). Resource Conflict in the Twenty-First Century. Peace Review: A Journal of Social Justice, 19(3), 323–330.

Spiliakos, A. (2018). What Does "Sustainability" Mean in Business? Harvard Business School Online's Business Insights. https://online.hbs.edu/blog/post/what-is-sustainability-in-business

Stobierski, T. (2021a). 4 Impactful Sustainable Business Practices That Can Make a Difference. Harvard Business School Online's Business Insights. https://online.hbs.edu/blog/post/sustainable-business-practices

Stobierski, T. (2021b). What Is Corporate Social Responsibility? 4 Types. Harvard Business School Online's Business Insights. https://online.hbs.edu/blog/post/types-of-corporate-social-responsibility

Tarver, E. (2024). 8 Types of LLCs Explained & Compared. Forbes. https://www.forbes.com/advisor/business/llc-types/

University of York. (2024). What are business ethics, and why do they matter? https://online.york.ac.uk/what-are-business-ethics-and-why-do-they-matter/

USFDA. (2000). "Cruelty Free"/"Not Tested on Animals". United States Food And Drug Administration. https://www.fda.gov/cosmetics/cosmetics-labeling-claims/cruelty-freenot-tested-animals

Compilation of References

Abbas, J., Mahmood, S., Ali, H., Ali, R., Aman, J., Bano, S., & Nurunnabi, M. (2024). The effects of corporate social responsibility practices and environmental factors through a moderating role of social media marketing on sustainable performance of business firms. *Sustainability*, 13(18), 10463. DOI: 10.3390/su131810463

Abdalla, S., Mushtaha, E., Rashid, M., Opoku, A., Hamad, R., Dweiri, F., & El-mualim, A. (2023). Pre-design CSFs (critical success factors) of building projects for Dubai's development boom. *Built Environment Project and Asset Management*, 13(3), 359–374. DOI: 10.1108/BEPAM-09-2022-0144

Abdelfattah, L., Bazzoni, F., & Choubassi, R. (2021). The redemptive potential of the street. a multi-angular analysis of dubai's pedestrian infrastructure. *The Journal of Public Space*, 6(1), 67–94. DOI: 10.32891/jps.v6i1.1326

Abdelrady, H. (2023). Exploring the effectiveness of using digital tourism platforms in egyptian tourist destination. *Journal of Association of Arab Universities for Tourism and Hospitality*, 24(1), 389–405. DOI: 10.21608/jaauth.2023.235547.1499

Acemoglu, D., & Restrepo, P. (2020). The Race Between Man and Machine: Implications of Technology for Growth, Factor Shares, and Employment. *The American Economic Review*, 108(6), 1488–1542. DOI: 10.1257/aer.20160696

Adekuajo, I. (2023). The digital evolution in hospitality: A global review and its potential transformative impact on u.s. tourism. *International Journal of Applied Research in Social Sciences*, 5(10), 440–462. DOI: 10.51594/ijarss.v5i10.633

Aguerrebere, P. (2023). Dubai expo 2020's impact on the united arab emirates brand: A quantitative analysis of american and european media companies. *Journal of Advanced Research in Social Sciences*, 6(4), 16–29. DOI: 10.33422/jarss.v6i4.1122

Ahmad, N., & Primi, A. (2017). *From domestic to regional to global: Factory Africa and Factory Latin America?* In: Global Value Chain Development Report 2017. Measuring and Analyzing the Impact of GVCs on Economic Development. The World Bank. https://www.wto.or/english/res_/booksp_e/gvcs_report_2017.pdf

Ahmad, N., & Primi, A. (2017). *From domestic to regional to global: Factory Africa and Factory Latin America?* In: Global Value Chain Development Report 2017. Measuring and Analyzing the Impact of GVCs on Economic Development. The World Bank. https://www.wto.org/English/res_e/booksp_e/gvcs_report_report_2017.pdf

Ahn, J., Habib, A., Malacrino, D., & Presbitero, A. F. (2023, April 5). Fragmenting Foreign Direct Investment Hits Emerging Economies Hardest. https://www.imf.org/en/Blogs/Articles/2023/04/05/fragmenting-foreign-direct-investment-hits-emerging-economies-hardest

Akbiyik, S., & Can, H. (2023). Structural and Qualitative Defects in Adaptation to Digital Transformation in Local Governments. In Okur Dinçsoy, M., & Can, H. (Eds.), *Optimizing Energy Efficiency During a Global Energy Crisis* (pp. 327–340). IGI Global. DOI: 10.4018/979-8-3693-0400-6.ch018

Aksakova, A.N. (2009). Organizational culture of corporate standards: concept, structure, features. Personnel Management, 13 215), 53-56.

Alarefi, A. H., Ameerbakhsh, O., Ab Ghani, M. K., & Zidan, Y. A. (2024). Energy efficiency in the GCC region: Prospects, challenges and opportunities. *International Journal of Thermofluids*, 21, 1000511. DOI: 10.1016/j.ijft.2023.100511

Alawadi, K. (2016). Place attachment as a motivation for community preservation: The demise of an old, bustling, dubai community. *Urban Studies (Edinburgh, Scotland)*, 54(13), 2973–2997. DOI: 10.1177/0042098016664690

Alawadi, K., & Benkraouda, O. (2017). The debate over neighborhood density in dubai: Between theory and practicality. *Journal of Planning Education and Research*, 39(1), 18–34. DOI: 10.1177/0739456X17720490

Alexis-Thomas, C. (2020). An examination of issues related to tourism and health and well-being as a sustainable development goal by tourism providers in tobago. *Worldwide Hospitality and Tourism Themes*, 12(3), 293–303. DOI: 10.1108/WHATT-02-2020-0006

Alford, P., & Jones, R. (2020). The lone digital tourism entrepreneur: Knowledge acquisition and collaborative transfer. *Tourism Management*, 81, 104–139. DOI: 10.1016/j.tourman.2020.104139

AList. (2022). PREDICTIONS 2022. Disruptive Forces Necessitate Bold Decisions. https://www.alistdaily.com/strategy/Forrester-2022-predictions-guid

Allegrini, M. (2024). SEC Reporting – So What? - PRWeek, 08 April 2024, available at: https://www.prweek.com/article/1868046/sec-reporting-%E2%80%94-so-what

AlNuaimi, B. K., Singh, S. K., Ren, S., Budhwar, P., & Vorobyev, D. (2022). Mastering Digital Transformation: The Nexus Between Leadership, Agility, and Digital Strategy. *Journal of Business Research*, 145, 636–648. DOI: 10.1016/j.jbusres.2022.03.038

Alrawadieh, Z., Alrawadıeh, Z., & Çetin, G. (2020). Digital transformation and revenue management: Evidence from the hotel industry. *Tourism Economics*, 27(2), 328–345. DOI: 10.1177/1354816620901928

Al-Saidi, M., & Elagib, N. (2018). Ecological modernization and responses for a low-carbon future in the Gulf Cooperation Council countries. *Wiley Interdisciplinary Reviews: Climate Change*, 9(4), e528. DOI: 10.1002/wcc.528

Al-Saidi, M., Zaidan, E., & Hammad, S. (2019). Participation modes and diplomacy of Gulf Cooperation Council (GCC) countries towards the global sustainability agenda. *Development in Practice*, 29(5), 545–558. DOI: 10.1080/09614524.2019.1597017

Al-Shihabi, S., Aydin, R., Hadj-Alouane, A., & Alshanasi, A. (2023). Sustainable technologies, mega-events, and environmental awareness—Lessons from expo 2020 dubai. *Frontiers in Sustainable Cities*, 5, 1192295. Advance online publication. DOI: 10.3389/frsc.2023.1192295

Aman, E., & Papp-Váry, A. (2022). Digital marketing as a driver for sustainable tourism development. *Multidiszciplináris Kihívások Sokszínű Válaszok*, 2(2), 3–33. DOI: 10.33565/MKSV.2022.02.01

America, F. (2024a). Fairtrade & the Sustainable Shopper – 2023 US Consumer Insights. - Fairtrade America Online, available at: https://www.fairtradeamerica.org/app/uploads/2023/09/2023-Fairtrade-America-Consumer-Insights.pdf

America, F. (2024b). More than a Label. - Fairtrade America Online, available at: https://www.fairtradeamerica.org/why-fairtrade/the-fairtrade-difference/for-businesses/

Amrousi, M., Elhakeem, M., Paleologos, E., & Misuri, M. (2019). Engineered landscapes: The new dubai canal and emerging public spaces. *International Review for Spatial Planning and Sustainable Development*, 7(3), 33–34. DOI: 10.14246/irspsd.7.3_33

Andreeva, O. V., Vovchenko, N. G., Galazova, S. S., Sukhoveeva, A. A., & Kravchenko, E. V. (2023). Benefits and Risks of Digitalization of Providing Social Services by the State. In Popkova, E. G., & Sergi, B. S. (Eds.), *Anti-Crisis Approach to the Provision of the Environmental Sustainability of Economy. Approaches to Global Sustainability, Markets, and Governance*. Springer. DOI: 10.1007/978-981-99-2198-0_14

Anthonisz, A., & Mason, G. (2019). Reinventing tourism: The dubai phenomenon. *Worldwide Hospitality and Tourism Themes*, 11(3), 279–286. DOI: 10.1108/WHATT-01-2019-0004

Anthony, S. (2017). *Dual Transformation - How to Reposition Today's Business While Creating the Future*. Harvard Business Press.

Archi, Y., Benbba, B., Zhu, K., Andaloussi, Z., Pataki, L., & David, L. (2023). Mapping the nexus between sustainability and digitalization in tourist destinations: A bibliometric analysis. *Sustainability (Basel)*, 15(12), 9717. DOI: 10.3390/su15129717

Armijos-Orellana, A., González, M., Maldonado-Matute, J., & Guerrero, P. (2023). Un acercamiento teórico a la economía digital. *Estudios de la Gestión*, 14, 78-90. https://revistas.uasb.edu.ec/index.php/eg/article/download/4116/3999/16300

Arnould, E. (2019). Consumer Culture Theory: Development, Critique, Application and Prospects. - Foundations and Trends in Marketin, available at: https://www.researchgate.net/publication/332647213_Consumer_Culture_Theory_Development_Critique_Application_and_Prospects

Arthur, W. B. (1999). Complexity and the economy. *Science*, 284(5411), 107–109. DOI: 10.1126/science.284.5411.107 PMID: 10103172

Arviana, N., & Wibisono, M. (2023). The Effect Of Fundamental Factors On Triple Bottom Line And Firm Value. *JRAK*, 15(1), 12–18. DOI: 10.23969/jrak.v15i1.5474

Asian Development Bank. (2024, Jul 15). *Leveraging Fintech for Women Entrepreneurs in Indonesia, the Philippines, and Viet Nam*. https://www.adb.org/publications/leveraging-fintech-women-entrepreneurs

Athapaththu, K., & Karunasena, G. (2018). Framework for sustainable construction practices in sri lanka. *Built Environment Project and Asset Management*, 8(1), 51–63. DOI: 10.1108/BEPAM-11-2016-0060

Athey, S. (2017). Beyond prediction: Using big data for policy problems. *Science*, 355(6324), 483–485. DOI: 10.1126/science.aal4321 PMID: 28154050

Autor, D., Dorn, D., Katz, L., Patterson, C., & Van Reenen, J. (2020). The Fall of the Labor Share and the Rise of Superstar Firms. *The Quarterly Journal of Economics*, 135(2), 645–709. DOI: 10.1093/qje/qjaa004

AWS. (2023). *¿Qué es la transformación digital?* Recuperado de https://aws.amazon.com/es/what-is/digital-transformation/

Aydın, Ö., & Öztürk, A. (2022). Pazarlamada Yeni Trend Fijital Pazarlama. M. Kısa (Dü.) içinde, *Sosyal. Beşeri ve İdari Birimler Alanında Uluslararası Araştırmalar.*, 4, 155–168.

Ayoub, E., & Freeman, B. (2023). People, Planet, and Profits: Comparing Media Treatment of Dubai Sustainable City. *SAGE Open*, 13(3). DOI: 10.1177/21582440231190299

Badarinza, C., Ramadorai, T., & Shimizu, C. (2022). Gravity, counterparties, and foreign investment. *Journal of Financial Economics*, 145(2, 2, part A), 132–152. DOI: 10.1016/j.jfineco.2021.09.011

Baggio, R., Micera, R., & Chiappa, G. (2020). Smart tourism destinations: A critical reflection. *Journal of Hospitality and Tourism Technology*, 11(3), 407–423. DOI: 10.1108/JHTT-01-2019-0011

Baier, S., & Standaert, S. (2024). Gravity, globalization and time-varying heterogeneity. *European Economic Review*, 163(April), 104679. DOI: 10.1016/j.euroecorev.2024.104679

Baker, D. (2021). Today's global energy crisis is just the first in the "clean power" era. - World Oil, 5 October 2021, available at: https://www.worldoil.com/news/2021/10/5/today-s-global-energy-crisis-is-just-the-first-in-the-clean-power-era

Balakrishnan, R., & Das, S. (2020). How do Firms Reorganize to Implement Digital Transformation? *Strategic Change*, 29(5), 531–541. DOI: 10.1002/jsc.2362

Baldwin, R. (2016). *The great convergence: Information technology and the new globalization*. Harvard University Press. DOI: 10.2307/j.ctv24w655w

Balkan, H., & Aydın, M. (2021). Neobank: Kavram, Gelişim ve İş Modelleri. *Bankacılar Dergisi*, (116), 104–126.

Bartel, J. (2022, June). Corporate Social Responsibility and Business Ethics. *Forbes*, 27. https://www.forbes.com/councils/forbesfinancecouncil/2022/06/27/corporate-social-responsibility-and-business-ethics/

Batkayeva, I.A., & Mitrofanova, E.A. (2015b). Personnel management. Theory and practice. Organization of compensation of personnel.

Baumol, W. J. (1959). *Business Behavior, Value and Growth.* Macmillan.

Bddk.gov.tr. (2022, Jun 01). Regulation on the Operating Principles of Digital Banks and Banking As a Service Model: https://www.bddk.org.tr/Mevzuat/DokumanGetir/1128

Bddk.gov.tr. (2024, Sept 15). Digital Banks Establishment and Operation Permits: https://www.bddk.org.tr/Mevzuat/Liste/55

Béland, D., & Morgan, K. J. (2021a). *Governance, The Oxford Handbook of the Welfare State.* Oxford University Press. DOI: 10.1093/oxfordhb/9780198828389.001.0001

Bell, J. (2021). In Response to Climate Change, Citizens in Advanced Economies Are Willing To Alter How They Live and Work. Pew Research Center. https://www.pewresearch.org/global/wp-content/uploads/sites/2/2021/09/PG_2021.09.14_Climate_FINAL.pdf

Berger, R. (2020). Triple Transformation: A Framework for the Auto Industry in the 2020s. – Roland Berger.com. https://www.rolandberger.com/en/Insights/Publications/Triple-Transformation-A-framework-for-the-auto-industry-in-the-2020s.html

Bhandari, K. R., Zamborsky, P., Ranta, M., & Salo, J. (2023, August). Digitalization, Internationalization and firm performance: A resource-orchestration perspective on new OLI advantages. *International Business Review*, 32(4), 102135. DOI: 10.1016/j.ibusrev.2023.102135

Bharadwaj, A., El Sawy, O. A., Pavlou, P. A., & Venkatraman, N. (2013). Digital business strategy: Toward a next generation of insights. *Management Information Systems Quarterly*, 37(2), 471–482. DOI: 10.25300/MISQ/2013/37:2.3

Binshakir, O., AlGhanim, L., Fathaq, A., AlHarith, A. M., Ahmed, S., & El-Sayegh, S. (2023). Factors affecting the bidding decision in sustainable construction. *Sustainability (Basel)*, 15(19), 14225. DOI: 10.3390/su151914225

Blanco, F., Eaton, B., & Bawden, D. (2001). La información y el conocimiento: factores de producción en la actividad económica. *Revista Base*, 2(1), 186-200. https://www.redalyc.org/pdf/3372/337228632009.pdf

Blüm, S. (2022). What is the "Twin Transition" - And Why Is It key to Sustainable Growth? - World Economic Forum. https://www.weforum.org/stories/2022/10/twin-transition-playbook-3-phases-to-accelerate-sustainable-digitization/

Botsman, R., & Rogers, R. (2010). *What's Mine Is Yours: The Rise of Collaborative Consumption.* HarperBusiness.

Bower, J. L., & Christensen, C. M. (1995). Disruptive Technologies: Catching the Wave. *Harvard Business Review*.

Brynjolfsson, E., & Hitt, L. M. (2000). Beyond computation: Information technology, organizational transformation, and business performance. *The Journal of Economic Perspectives*, 14(4), 23–48. DOI: 10.1257/jep.14.4.23

Brynjolfsson, E., & McAfee, A. (2014). *The second machine age: Work, progress, and prosperity in a time of brilliant technologies*. W.W. Norton & Company.

Buckley, M., & Hanieh, A. (2013). Diversification by urbanization: Tracing the property-finance nexus in dubai and the gulf. *International Journal of Urban and Regional Research*, 38(1), 155–175. DOI: 10.1111/1468-2427.12084

Buhalis, D. (2019). Technology in tourism-from information communication technologies to etourism and smart tourism towards ambient intelligence tourism: A perspective article. *Tourism Review*, 75(1), 267–272. DOI: 10.1108/TR-06-2019-0258

Bukht, R., & Heeks, R. (2017). Defining, Conceptualising and Measuring the Digital Economy (2017). *Development Informatics Working Paper no. 68*. DOI: 10.2139/ssrn.3431732

Burritt, R., & Christ, K. (2016). Industry 4.0 and environmental accounting: A new revolution? *Asian Journal of Sustainability and Social Responsibility*, 1(1), 23–38. DOI: 10.1186/s41180-016-0007-y

Business Ethics Network. (2023). Organizational Ethics: Building a Culture of Integrity and Responsibility. https://www.businessethicsnetwork.org/organizational-ethics-building-a-culture-of-integrity-and-responsibility/

Businesses, H. D. T. H. (2024). https://www.tbmagazine.net/statia/kak-digitalnata-transformaciya-pomaga-na-biznesite.html

Byrne, D. (2022). The Digital Economy and Productivity. *Finance and Economics Discussion Series (FEDS)* DOI: 10.17016/feds.2022.038

Cai, J., Yuan, L., Hong, G., & Chen, C. (2022). The approach of data factor participining in value creation- A general equilibrium analysis based on the general theory of value. *Journal of Management World*, 38(07), 108–121.

Çakın, Ö., & Yaman, D. (2020). Fijital (Phygital) Pazarlama Uygulamaları Üzerine Bir İnceleme: Amazon Go Örneği. *Middle Black Sea Journal of Communication Studies*, 5(1), 1–10.

Can, H., & Minkovska, D. (2020). Current Status and Future of Artifical Inteligence, XXIX ISTC "ADP-2020", Sozopol, Bulgaria, ISSN 2682-9584, 162-165, https://mf.tu-sofia.bg/ADP%20Magazine%20site/index.html

Can, H., & Terziev, V. (2017, October). Climate Change Effect on Energy Production Index. In *Сборник Доклади от Научна Конференция „Актуални Проблеми на Сигурността", Електронно издание Велико Търново* (pp. 292-297). DOI: 10.2139/ssrn.3383943

Can, H., Minkovska, D., & Stoyanova, L. (2020, October). Estimation of Energy Performance Classes of Concrete Structures with Artificial Intelligence Models. In *2020 III International Conference on High Technology for Sustainable Development (HiTech)* (pp. 1-3). IEEE. DOI: 10.1109/HiTech51434.2020.9364003

Can, H., & Paskaleva, M. (2017). Macroeconomic determinants of CDS: The case of Europe. New knowledge. *Journal of Science*, 6(3), 1080–1096.

Can, H., & Terziev, V. (2016). The relationship economic growth and information technologies. Retrieved from *SSRN*: https://ssrn.com/abstract=3383899 or DOI: 10.2139/ssrn.3383899

Cao, D., Teng, X., Chen, Y., Tan, D., & Wang, G. (2023). Digital transformation strategies of project-based firms: Case study of a large-scale construction company in China. *Asia Pacific Journal of Innovation and Entrepreneurship*, 17(2), 82–98. DOI: 10.1108/APJIE-02-2023-0027

Castells, M. (1996). *The Rise of the Network Society*. Blackwell.

CEIC Data. (2021). Chinal Capacity Utilization Rate. https://www.ceicdata.com/en/china/capacity-utilization-rate

Çelik, Z. (2021). *Fijital (Phygital) Pazarlama. Dijitalleşen Dünyada Pazarlama*. Nobel Yayınevi.

CEPAL. (2013). *La economía digital: Un motor para el desarrollo sostenible*. Retrieved from https://www.cepal.org/es/publicaciones/25756-economia-digital-motor-desarrollo-sostenible

Chandra, Y., & Wilkinson, I. F. (2017). Firm internationalization from a network-centric complex-systems perspective. *Journal of World Business*, 52(5), 691–701. DOI: 10.1016/j.jwb.2017.06.001

Chang, J., Lan, Q., Tan, W., Chen, H., Lou, J., & Duan, Y. (2023). Research on the Impact of Digital Economy of Manufacturing Total Factor Productivity. *Sustainability (Basel)*, 15(7), 5683. DOI: 10.3390/su15075683

Chanias, S., Myers, M. D., & Hess, T. (2019). Digital transformation strategy making in pre-digital organizations: The case of a financial services provider. *The Journal of Strategic Information Systems*, 28(1), 17–33. DOI: 10.1016/j.jsis.2018.11.003

Chaudhary, R., & Nalwaya, N. (2021). Hybrid Banking: The Convergence of Physical with Digital Banking - An Evolving Transformation. *International Journal of Scientific Research*, 10(6), 101–105.

Chemekov, V.P. (2000). Corporate culture and those who form it.

Cheng, X., Xue, T., Yang, B., & Ma, B. (2023). A digital transformation approach in hospitality and tourism research. *International Journal of Contemporary Hospitality Management*, 35(8), 2944–2967. DOI: 10.1108/IJCHM-06-2022-0679

Chen, L., Jiang, S., Pu, R., Li, L., & Hong-mei, Y. (2022). Knowledge map of digital tourism: A bibliometric approach using citespace. *Problems and Perspectives in Management*, 20(4), 573–587. DOI: 10.21511/ppm.20(4).2022.43

Chesbrough, H. (2006) *Open Innovation: A New Paradigm for Understanding Industrial Innovation. 10th Anniversary Summer Conference on Dynamics of Industry and Innovation: Organizations, Networks and Systems*, 1-12. DOI: 10.1093/oso/9780199290727.003.0001

Chesbrough, H. W. (2007). Business Model Innovation: It's Not Just About Technology Anymore. *Strategy and Leadership*, 35(6), 12–17. DOI: 10.1108/10878570710833714

Chiang, C. (2020). Developing an emarketing model for tourism and hospitality: A keyword analysis. *International Journal of Contemporary Hospitality Management*, 32(10), 3091–3114. DOI: 10.1108/IJCHM-03-2020-0230

Chiodini, S. (2014). Goodbye Flexible Purpose Corporation, Hello Social Purpose Corporation: Governor Brown Signs S.B. 1301. https://www.adlercolvin.com/blog/2014/10/06/goodbye-flexible-purpose-corporation-hello-social-purpose-corporation-governor-brown-signs-s-b-1301/

Chladek, N. (2019). Why You Need Sustainability in Your Business Strategy. – Harvard Business School Online's Business Insights. https://online.hbs.edu/blog/post/business-sustainability-strategies

Christensen, C. M. (1997). *The innovator's dilemma: When new technologies cause great firms to fail.* Harvard Business Review Press.

Christensen, C. M. (2006). The Ongoing Process of Building a Theory of Disruption. *Journal of Product Innovation Management*, 23(1), 39–55. DOI: 10.1111/j.1540-5885.2005.00180.x

Coase, R. H. (1937). The nature of the firm. *Economica*, 4(16), 386–405. DOI: 10.1111/j.1468-0335.1937.tb00002.x

Cohen, M., & Sundararajan, A. (2015). Self-regulation and innovation in the peer-to-peer sharing economy. *University of Chicago Law Review Online*, 82.

Cohen, S., de Long, D., & Zysman, J. (2000). *The New Economy: A New Perspective on the Economic Landscape*.

Cong, L. W., Wei, W., Xie, D., & Xhang, L. (2022). Endogenous growth under multiple uses of data. *Journal of Economic Dynamics & Control*, 141(August), 104395. DOI: 10.1016/j.jedc.2022.104395

Consulting, P. A. (2022). Twin Transition Playbook 2.0. https://www2.paconsulting.com/the-twin-transition-playbook-request.html

Contini, G., & Peruzzini, M. (2022). Sustainability and industry 4.0: Definition of a set of key performance indicators for manufacturing companies. *Sustainability (Basel)*, 14(17), 11004. DOI: 10.3390/su141711004

Costa, V. B. F., Capaz, R. S., Silva, P. F., Doyle, G., Aquila, G., Coelho, É. O., de Lorenci, E., Pereira, L. C., Maciel, L. B., Balestrassi, P. P., Bonatto, B. D., & da Silva, L. C. (2022). Socioeconomic and Environmental Consequences of a New Law for Regulating Distributed Generation in Brazil: A Holistic Assessment. *Energy Policy*, 169, 113176. DOI: 10.1016/j.enpol.2022.113176

Cote, C. (2021a). 8 Sustainability Skills for Working Professionals. – Harvard Business School Online's Business Insights. https://online.hbs.edu/blog/post/sustainability-skills

Cote, C. (2021b). What Is a CSR Report & Why Is It Important? – Harvard Business School Online's Business Insights. https://online.hbs.edu/blog/post/what-is-a-csr-report

Cyert, R. M., & March, J. G. (1963). *A Behavioral Theory of the Firm*.

Dąbrowska, J., Al-Mawali, H., Wilson, R., & Gore, T. (2024). The role of digital social identity in the stakeholder engagement process. *Journal of Business Research*, 172, 114442. DOI: 10.1016/j.jbusres.2023.114442

Dang-Pham, D., Hoang, A. P., Vo, D. T., & Kautz, K. (2022). Digital Kaizen: An Approach to Digital Transformation. *AJIS. Australasian Journal of Information Systems*, 26, 1–28. DOI: 10.3127/ajis.v26i0.3851

Danish Ministry of Climate, Energy and Utilities. (2022). Joint Statement: Urgent Action on Energy Efficiency, No. 2022 – 85. https://en.kefm.dk/Media/637904431073034736/joint%20statement.pdf

Das, M. (2024). Impact of Social and Environmental Practices on SME Business Performance, *Authorea Preprints*.

Daugherty, G. (2024). B Corp: Definition, Advantages, Disadvantages, and Examples. – Investopedia. https://www.investopedia.com/b-corp-7488828

Davenport, T. H., & Beck, J. C. (2001). *The attention economy: Understanding the new currency of business*. Harvard Business Review Press.

Davis, F. D. (1989). Perceived Usefulness, Perceived Ease of Use, and User Acceptance of Information Technology. *Management Information Systems Quarterly*, 13(3), 319–340. DOI: 10.2307/249008

De Stefano, V. (2016). The rise of the "just-in-time workforce": On-demand work, crowdwork, and labor protection in the gig-economy. *Comparative Labor Law & Policy Journal*, 37, 471–504.

Degain, C., Meng, B., & Wang, Z. (2017). *Recent trends in global trade.* In: Global Value Chains Development Report 2017. Measuring and Analyzing the Impact of GVCs on Economic Development. The World Bank. https://www.wto.org/english/res_e/booksp_e/gves_report_2017.pdf

Delios, A. (2017). The Death and Rebitrh (?) of International Business Research. *Journal of Management Studies*, 54(3), 391–397. DOI: 10.1111/joms.12222

Deloitte. (2019). The Rise of the Socially Responsible Business - Deloitte Global's Societal Impact Survey. https://www.deloitte.com/global/en/about/story/impact/societal-impact-survey-deloitte-global.html

Demirel, E., Karagöz Zeren, S., & Hakan, K. (2022). Smart contracts in tourism industry: A model with blockchain integration for post pandemic economy. *Current Issues in Tourism*, 25(12), 1895–1909. DOI: 10.1080/13683500.2021.1960280

Denicol, J., Davies, A., & Pryke, S. (2021). The organisational architecture of megaprojects. *International Journal of Project Management*, 39(4), 339–350. DOI: 10.1016/j.ijproman.2021.02.002

Dessouky, N., Wheeler, S., & Salama, A. (2023). The five controversies of market-driven sustainable neighborhoods: An alternative approach to post-occupancy evaluation. *Social Sciences (Basel, Switzerland)*, 12(7), 367. DOI: 10.3390/socsci12070367

Deusto, O. (2017). *Por qué la Economía Digital.* Retrieved from https://www.orkestra.deusto.es/euskadi-economia-digital/2017/por-que-economia-digital.phtml

Dewan, A. (2021). Europe's gas crisis is also a renewables crisis, but there are ready solutions. – CNN. https://edition.cnn.com/2021/09/22/business/europe-energy-gas-renewables-climate-cmd-intl/index.html

Diana Crane, N. K. (2016). *Global Culture: Media.* Arts, Politics and Globalization. DOI: 10.4324/9781315538792

Dias, A. M., Carvalho, A. M., & Sampaio, P. (2022). Quality 4.0: Literature Review Analysis, Definition and Impacts of the Digital Transformation Process on Quality. *International Journal of Quality & Reliability Management*, 39(6), 1312–1335. DOI: 10.1108/IJQRM-07-2021-0247

Dincsoy, M., Can, H., Dincsoy, E., & Terziev, V. (2024e). The impact of property rights and government integrity on the economic freedom: the case of the European region, the Brics countries, and the USA. 107th International Scientific Conference on Economic and Social Development – Economic and Social Survival in Global Changes – Zagreb, 16-17 February, 2024, Economic and Social Development (Book of Proceedings), 265-275.

Dinçsoy, E. E. (2023). *Dijital Dünyanın Paradigmaları. Geleceği İnşa Etmek: Metaverse ve Yapay Zeka ile İşletmelerde Dijital Dönüşüm.* Paradigma Akademi.

Dinçsoy, E. E. (2023). Dijital Dünyanın Paradigmaları. In Kayapınar, Ö., & Yürük Kayapınar, P. (Eds.), *Geleceği İnşa Etmek: Metaverse ve Yapay Zeka ile İşletmelerde Dijital Dönüşüm* (pp. 1–28). Paradigma Akademi.

Disraeli, B. (2024a). *Chapter 14. Sybil. Vol. Book 4*, https://www.gutenberg.org/files/3760/3760-h/3760-h.htm

Dokuchaev, D. S. (2015d). Regional identty in the Ivanovo region and politcs of constructon area image: A factor of tourism. *Services and Tourism: Current Challenges*, 9(3), 76–82. DOI: 10.12737/12885

Dollar, D., & Thornton, J. L. (2017). *Executive summary.* In: Global Value Chain Development Report 2017. Measuring and Analyzing the Impact of GVCs on Economic Development, 1-36. https://www.wto.org/english/res_e/booksp_e/gvcs_report_2017.pdf

Dubai Creek Harbour. (2024). Retrieved from https://properties.emaar.com/en/our-communities/dubai-creek-harbour/

Duğru, M. (2023). Bankacılık Sektöründe Dijitalleşme. In Kayapınar, Ö., & Yürük Kayapınar, P. (Eds.), *Metaverse, Yapay Zeka Ve Robotik Süreç Otomasyonlarinin Önemi* (pp. 273–297). Paradigma Academy.

Duğru, M. (2024). Innovation in the Banking World. In Abdelkader, M. S. D. (Ed.), *Social and Ethical Implications of AI in Finance for Sustainability* (pp. 228–246). IGI Global. DOI: 10.4018/979-8-3693-2881-1.ch010

Duğru, M., & Dinçsoy, E. E. (2014). Bankacılık Hizmetlerinin Pazarlanmasında Bölgesel Müşteri Profilinin Önemi Üzerine Bir Alan Çalışması. *Trakya Üniversitesi İktisadi ve İdari Bilimler Fakültesi E-Dergi*, 3(2), 46–72.

Duleba, A., Brezani, P., Oravcova, V. (2024). Slovak-Ukrainian Cross-Border Center (SKUAC). SFPA.

Dunning, J.H., Narula, R. (1996). The Investment Development Path revisited. *Foreign Direct Investment and Governments: Catalysis for Economic Restructuring,* 1-41.

Dunning, J. H. (1981). Explaining the international direct investments position of countries: Toward a dynamic or development approach. *Weltwirtschaftliches Archiv*, 117(30), 30–64. DOI: 10.1007/BF02696577

Durcova, J., & Pekarcik, M. (2023). Role intangible assets in global value chains: Evidence from the Slovak Republic. *Strategic Management*, 28(4), 31–40. DOI: 10.5937/StraMan2300036D

Dwivedi, Y. K., Hughes, D. L., Coombs, C., Constantiou, I., Duan, Y., Edwards, J. S., Gupta, B., Lal, B., Misra, S., Prashant, P., Raman, R., Rana, N. P., Sharma, S. K., & Upadhyay, N. (2020). Impact of COVID-19 pandemic on information management research and practice: Transforming education, work and life. *International Journal of Information Management*, 55, 102211. DOI: 10.1016/j.ijinfomgt.2020.102211

EC2023. Economic Commentary. (2023). How Has the Pandemic Impacted Inflation. https://blog.nationalwidefinancial.com/market-economy/how-has-the-pandemic-impacted-inflation

EC2024. (2024). *In-depth Review*. DOI: 10.2765/642448

Economics, T. (2024). Slovak Foreign Direct Investment. https://tradingeconomics.com/slovakia/foreign-direct-investment

Edelman. (2022), Trust Barometer 2022. https://www.edelman.com/sites/g/files/aatuss191/files/2022-01/2022%20Edelman%20Trust%20Barometer_FullReport.pdf

Eichelberger, S., Eller, R., Kallmuenzer, A., & Peters, M. (2023). Organisational learning and sustainable tourism: The enabling role of digital transformation. *Journal of Knowledge Management*, 27(11), 82–100. DOI: 10.1108/JKM-06-2022-0434

Einav, L., & Levin, J. (2014). Economics in the age of big data. *Science*, 346(6210), 1243089. DOI: 10.1126/science.1243089 PMID: 25378629

Ejjami, R. (2024). The digital evolution: Strategies for overcoming cybersecurity and adoption challenges in French SMEs. International Journal For Multidisciplinary Research, 6(3).

El-khateeb, S. (2019). Sustainable neighborhoods in arab world; a path towards sustainability. *The Academic Research Community Publication*, 3(1), 153–166. DOI: 10.21625/archive.v3i1.437

Eller, R., Alford, P., Kallmünzer, A., & Peters, M. (2020). Antecedents, consequences, and challenges of small and medium-sized enterprise digitalization. *Journal of Business Research*, 112, 119–127. DOI: 10.1016/j.jbusres.2020.03.004

Eltoum, A., Yatiban, A., Omar, R., & Islam, M. (2022). Sustainability awareness in society and its impact on the level of responsible business adoption in the business sector of dubai. *Problems and Perspectives in Management*, 20(3), 540–551. DOI: 10.21511/ppm.20(3).2022.43

Emerick, D. (2024). What is the Triple Bottom Line Approach? The 3Ps of Corporate Impact. – ESG – The Report. https://esgthereport.com/what-is-esg/the-g-in-esg/what-are-the-3-components-of-the-triple-bottom-line-approach/

Erfurt-Cooper, P., & Cooper, M. (2009b). *Health and Wellness Tourism: Spas and Hot Springs*. Channel View Publications. DOI: 10.21832/9781845411138

Ergen, A., Girginkaya Akdağ, S., & Ekin, G. (2024). Rethinking The Servicescapes of New Generation Banks: Evidence From Türkiye. *New Design Ideas*, 8(1), 97–115. DOI: 10.62476/ndi.8197

Estola, M. (2014). The Neoclassical Theory of a Firm: Correction for its errors. *Hyperion International Journal of Econophisics & New Economy*, 7(1), 7–21.

Ethisphere. (2024). The 2024 World's Most Ethical Companies Honoree List. https://worldsmostethicalcompanies.com/honorees/

European Commission. (2019). The European Green Deal, Brussels, 11.12.2019, COM(2019) 640 final.

European Commission. (2020). *Digital Economy and Society Index 2020.*

European Commission. (2020). Support for SME Internalization beyond the EU-.https://evening.europe.eu/growth/smes/sme-strategy/assets-to-markets/internation alization/support-tools_en

European Commission. (2022). REPowerEU: Joint European Action for more affordable, secure and sustainable energy, Strasbourg, 8.3.2022, COM(2022) 108 final.

European Commission. (2024). The Organic Logo. – Section Common Agricultural Policy - Agriculture and Rural Development. https://agriculture.ec.europa.eu/farming/organic-farming/organic-logo_en

European Parliament. (2006). European Groupings of Territorial Cooperation (EGTCs). Factsheets of the European Union. https://www.europarl.europa.eu/factsheets/en/sheet/94/Europa-groupings-of-territorial-cooperation-egtc

Evans, R., & Siesfeld, T. (2020). Measuring the Business Value of Corporate Social Impact. – Deloitte. https://www2.deloitte.com/us/en/insights/topics/social-impact/business-value-of-improving-your-csr-scorecard.html

Evans, D., & Schmalensee, R. (2016). *Matchmakers: The New Economics of Multisided Platforms*. Harvard Business Review Press.

EXPO 2020 Dubai UAE. (2024). Retrieved from Our commitment to sustainability: https://www.expo2020dubai.com/en/understanding-expo/expo-initiatives/sustainability-at-expo

EXPO 2020 Dubai UAE. (26.10.2024). Retrieved from https://www.expo2020dubai.com/

Fabuš, M., & Csabay, M. (2018). State aid and investment: Case of Slovakia. *Entrepreneurship and Sustainability Issues*, 6(1), 369–377. DOI: 10.9770/jesi.2018.6.1(23)

Fay, S. B. (1950). Bismarck's Welfare State. *Current History (New York, N.Y.)*, XVIII(101), 1–7. DOI: 10.1525/curh.1950.18.101.1

fDi Intelligence. (2023). Strategic Industries buck post-Covid Investment slump. https://www.fdiintelligence.com/content/data-trends/strategic-industries-buck-postcovid-investment-slump-82621?

fDi Intelligence. (2023). Wave of mega projects mounts in 2022. https://www.fdiintelligence.com/content/data-trends/wave-of-mega-projects-mounts-in-2022-82551

Feeley, D. (2019). The Five Ps of Triple Aim Transformation. – Institute for Healthcare Improvement. https://www.ihi.org/insights/five-ps-triple-aim-transformation

Fernández, A., Gómez, B., Binjaku, K., & Meçe, E. K. (2023). Digital Transformation Initiatives in Higher Education Institutions: A Multivocal Literature Review. *Education and Information Technologies*, 28(10), 12351–12382. DOI: 10.1007/s10639-022-11544-0 PMID: 37361743

Fetting, C. (2020). The European Green Deal. In *ESDN Report, December 2020*. ESDN Office.

Firdausi, F. (2023). Digital activism for sustainable tourism: management of social media instagram @travelxism through voluntrip activities. *Symposium of Literature Culture and Communication (Sylection) 2022, 3*(1), 106.

Fond-Harmant, L., Philippart, A., Megherbi, S., Pereaux, P., & Gavrila-Ardelean, M. (2023). Digitalization of the European society: Challenges for social work. *Social Work Research*, 1, 141–155.

Forbes. (2020). Bernard Marr-How the covid-19 pandemic is fast-tracking digital transformation in companies. https://www.forbes.com/sites/bernardmarr/2020/03/17/how-thecovid-19-pandemic-is-fast-tracking-digital-transformation-incompanies/#449f9158a8ee/

Fu, C. (2017). New structural economics - A way to unscramble via endogenous aggregate production function by PDE. *Economic Review (Kansas City, Mo.)*, 03, 81–103.

Garg, M., & Kumar, P. (2024). Harnessing Digital Technologies for Triple Bottom Line Sustainability in the Banking Industry: A Bibliometric Review. *Future Business Journal*, 10(62), 1–23. DOI: 10.1186/s43093-024-00336-2

Gavin, M. (2019a). How to Create Social Change: 4 Business Strategies. – Harvard Business School Online's Business Insights. https://online.hbs.edu/blog/post/how-can-business-drive-social-change

Gavin, M. (2019b). 6 Examples of Corporate Social Responsibility That Were Successful. - Harvard Business School Online's Business Insights. https://online.hbs.edu/blog/post/corporate-social-responsibility-examples

Gedik, Y. (2021). Pazarlamada Yeni Bir Dönem: Fijital Pazarlama. *Hacettepe University Journal of Social Sciences*, 3(2), 99–131.

Geels, F. W. (2022). Conflicts between economic and low-carbon reorientation processes: Insights from a contextual analysis of evolving company strategies in the United Kingdom petrochemical industry (1970–2021). *Energy Research & Social Science*, 91, 102729. DOI: 10.1016/j.erss.2022.102729

Gegenhuber, T., Logue, D., Hinings, B. C., & Barrett, M. (2020). Digital transformation and institutional theorizing: Consequences, opportunities and challenges. Research in the Sociology of Organizations. Call for papers.

Generis Global. (2024). Retrieved 05.08.2023, from The Growing Role of AI in Dubai's Tourism Sector: https://generisonline.com/the-growing-role-of-ai-in-dubais-tourism-sector/

GFM. (2024). Largest Companies in the World. Global Finance Magazine, September 18, 2024. https://gfmag.com/data/biggest-companies-in-the-world

Ghazal, T. M., Hasan, M. K., Alshurideh, M. T., Alzoubi, H. M., Ahmad, M., Akbar, S. S., Al Kurdi, B., & Akour, I. A. (2024). IoT for smart cities: Machine learning approaches in smart healthcare—A review. *Future Internet*, 13(8), 218. DOI: 10.3390/fi13080218

Giardina, G. (2019). Expo 2020 and sustainability: Luxury hotel properties challenges and future outlook. *Worldwide Hospitality and Tourism Themes*, 11(3), 314–326. DOI: 10.1108/WHATT-01-2019-0005

Gibson, L. (2017). Joi Ito and Jeff Howe's New Rules for Our Faster, Tech-driven World. Ford Foundation. https://www.fordfoundation.org/news-and-stories/stories/joi-ito-and-jeff-howes-new-rules-for-our-faster-tech-driven-world/

Global Times. (2023). China issue 15 measures to help SMEs stabilize growth, adjust structure. https://www.globaltimes.cn/page/202301/1283861.shtml

Gomes, S., Lopes, J., & Ferreira, L. The impact of the digital economy on economic growth: The case of OECD countries. *RAM Revista de Administração Mackenzie* https://doi.org/DOI: 10.1590/1678-6971/eRAMD220029.en

Goos, M., Manning, A., & Salomons, A. (2014). Explaining job polarization: Routine-biased technological change and offshoring. *The American Economic Review*, 104(8), 2509–2526. DOI: 10.1257/aer.104.8.2509

GoTyme Bank. (2024, Jul 0). https://www.gotyme.com.ph/media/news/gotyme-bank-2-million/

Gough, I. (1989). *The Welfare State, The New Palgrave Social Economics*. W.W. Norton.

Governance & Accountability Institute. (2024a). 2024 Sustainability Reporting In Focus. https://www.ga-institute.com/research/ga-research-directory/sustainability-reporting-trends/2024-sustainability-reporting-in-focus/

Governance & Accountability Institute. (2024b). Full Suite Corporate Sustainability Reporting. https://www.ga-institute.com/services/our-portfolio-of-services/sustainability-esg-reporting-disclosure/full-suite-corporate-sustainability-reporting/

Granovetter, M. (1973). The Strength of Weak Ties. *American Journal of Sociology*, 78(6), 1360–1380. DOI: 10.1086/225469

Green, G. K. P. (2013). Moving towards a Common Approach on Green Growth Indicators - A GGKP Scoping Paper. https://www.greenpolicyplatform.org/sites/default/files/downloads/resource//GGKP%20Moving%20towards%20a%20Common%20Approach%20on%20Green%20Growth%20Indicators.pdf

Greenwood, R., Hinings, C. R., & Whetten, D. (2014). Rethinking institutions and organizations. *Journal of Management Studies*, 51(7), 1206–1220. DOI: 10.1111/joms.12070

Grossman, G., & Helpman, E. (1991). *Innovation and Growth in the Global Economy*. MIT Press.

Hale, G., Leer, J. C., & Nechio, F. (2023). Inflationary effects of fiscal support to households and firms. National Bureau of Economic Research, 30906. https://www.nber.org/w30906

Hallaq, A., Ninov, I., & Dutt, C. (2020). The perceptions of host-city residents of the impact of mega-events and their support: The expo 2020 in dubai. *Journal of Policy Research in Tourism, Leisure & Events*, 13(3), 374–396. DOI: 10.1080/19407963.2020.1839088

Haller, K. (2022). Consumers Want It All: Hybrid Shopping, Sustainability, and Purpose-driven Brands. IBM Institute for Business Value. https://www.ibm.com/downloads/documents/us-en/10c31775c8540243

Han Team. (2009a). Medical Tourism and Global Healthcare: Where Are You Going? Health WorldNet Inc. http: healthworldnet.com/articles/heads-or-tails/medicaltourism-and-global-healthcare-where-are-yougoing.html

Han, D., Weber, J., Bastiaansen, M., Mitas, O., & Lub, X. (2019). Virtual and augmented reality technologies to enhance the visitor experience in cultural tourism. *Augmented reality and virtual reality: The power of AR and VR for business*, 113-128.

Haneef, S., Ansari, Z., & Bhavani, G. (2019). Attractions of dubai and expo 2020: An exploratory study. *Worldwide Hospitality and Tourism Themes*, 11(3), 266–278. DOI: 10.1108/WHATT-01-2019-0007

Han, Y., Li, Y., & Wang, Q. (2023). Digital finance, environmental regulation, and green development efficiency of China. *Frontiers in Environmental Science*, 11, 1131058. DOI: 10.3389/fenvs.2023.1131058

Heinberg, R. (2021). Understanding Power. Post Carbon Institute. https://www.postcarbon.org/understanding-power/

Hess, T., Matt, C., Benlian, A., & Wiesböck, F. (2016). Options for formulating a digital transformation strategy. *MIS Quarterly Executive*, 15(2), 123–139.

He, X., & Chen, W. (2024). Digital Transformation and Environmental, Social, and Governance Performance from a Human Capital Perspective. *Sustainability (Basel)*, 16(11), 4737. DOI: 10.3390/su16114737

Holland, J. H. (1995). *Hidden Order: How Adaptation Builds Complexity*. Addison-Wesley.

Holland, J. H. (2014). *Complexity: A very short introduction*. Oxford University Press. DOI: 10.1093/actrade/9780199662548.001.0001

Horowitz, M. D., Rosensweig, J. A., & Jones, Ch. A. (2007). Medical Tourism: Globalization of the Healthcare Marketplace. Medscape General Medicine, 9(4), 33. http://www.ncbi.nlm. nih.gov/pmc/articles/PMC2234298/

Horváth, D., & Szabó, R. Z. (2019). Driving forces and barriers of Industry 4.0: Do multinational and small and medium-sized companies have equal opportunities? *Technological Forecasting and Social Change*, 146, 119–132. DOI: 10.1016/j.techfore.2019.05.021

HubSpot. (2023). *Qué es la transformación digital: características, proceso y ejemplos*. Recuperado de https://blog.hubspot.es/sales/transformacion-digital

Hulten, C. R. (2010). Growth Accounting. Handbook of the Economics of Innovation, 2, 987-1031.

Humphreys, J. (2012). *Resource Wars: Searching for a New Definition. - International Affairs 88: 5*. The Royal Institute of International Affairs. https://ciaotest.cc.columbia.edu/journals/riia/v88i5/f_0026234_21492.pdf

Hürriyet Gazetesi. (2024, Apr 4). www.hurriyet.com.tr: https://www.hurriyet.com.tr/ekonomi/turk-sanayiini-kumbaralar-kurdu-39100486

Huseynov, N., & Dinçsoy, M. O. (2023). Döngüsel Ekonomi ve COVID-19 Pandemisinin Etkileri. *Balkan and Near Eastern Journal of Social Sciences*, 9(Special Issue), 262–279.

Idris, S. H., Chang, L. W., Prihandono, I., & Rasidi, S. A. (2024). Green financing and climate change: Challenges and regulatory mechanisms in Malaysia and Indonesia. *Clean Technologies and Environmental Policy*, 26(12), 1–12. DOI: 10.1007/s10098-024-02829-8

IEA. (2022). Unlocking the Potential of Distributed Energy Resources. https://www.iea.org/reports/unlocking-the-potential-of-distributed-energy-resources

IEA. (2023). World Energy Investment 2023. https://iea.glob.core.windows.net/assets/8834d3af-af60-4df0-9643-72e2684f7221/WorldEnergyinvestment2023.pdf

Ilcheva, M. (2019). Social economy and social entrepreneurship – views and fragmentary approbations. *Publishing house Faber.*

IMF. (2021). Fiscal Monitor Database of Country Fiscal Measures in Response to the COVID-19 Pandemic. https://www.imf.org/en/Topics/inf-and-covid19/Fiscal-Policies-Database-in-Response-to-COVID-19

IMF. (2023). World Economic Outlook. https://www.imf.org/en/Publications/WEO

IMF. (2024). World Economic Outlook. Policy Pivot, Rising Threats.

Im, K. S., Pesaran, M. H., & Shin, Y. (2003). Testing for unit roots in heterogeneous panels. *Journal of Econometrics*, 115(1), 53–74. DOI: 10.1016/S0304-4076(03)00092-7

Inomata, S. (2017). *Analytical framework for global value chains An Overview.* Global Value Chain Development Report 15-35. https://www.wto.org/english/res_e/booksp_e/gvcs_report_2017.pdf

International Energy Agency. (2020), Sustainable Recovery. https://www.iea.org/reports/sustainable-recovery

Ioannou, A., Tussyadiah, I., & Miller, G. (2021). That's private! Understanding travelers' privacy concerns and online data disclosure. *Journal of Travel Research*, 60(7), 1510–1526. DOI: 10.1177/0047287520951642

Isard, W. (1956). *Location and Space-economy; a General Theory Relating to Industrial Location, Market, Land Use, Trade and Urban Structure.* Technology Press Massachusetts Institute of Technology and Wiley.

Ito, J., & Howe, J. (2016b). Whiplash: How to Survive Our Faster Future. Abstract. MIT Media Lab. https://www.media.mit.edu/publications/whiplash-how-to-survive-our-faster-future/

Ito, J., & Howe, J. (2016a). *Whiplash: How to Survive Our Faster Future*. Grand Central Publishing.

Ivančić, L., Vukšić, V. B., & Spremić, M. (2019). Mastering the Digital Transformation Process: Business Practices and Lessons Learned. *Technology Innovation Management Review*, 9(2), 36–50. DOI: 10.22215/timreview/1217

Ivanova, O. B., Vovchenko, N. G., Andreeva, O. V., Chernobay, O. S., & Kostoglodova, E. D. (2023c). Innovative Green Finance Tools. In Popkova, E. G. (Ed.), *Smart Green Innovations in Industry 4.0 for Climate Change Risk Management. Environmental Footprints and Eco-design of Products and Processes*. Springer. DOI: 10.1007/978-3-031-28457-1_52

Jacobides, M. G., Cennamo, C., & Gawer, A. (2018). Towards a theory of ecosystems. *Strategic Management Journal*, 39(8), 2255–2276. DOI: 10.1002/smj.2904

Jia, W., Collins, A., & Liu, W. (2023). Digitalization and Economic Growth in the new classical and new structural economics perspectives. Springer Link. *Digital Economy and Sustainable Development*, 1(1), 5. DOI: 10.1007/s44265-023-00007-0

Johnson, M., & Barlow, R. (2021). Defining the Phygital Marketing Advantage. *Journal of Theoretical and Applied Electronic Commerce Research*, 16(6), 2365–2385. DOI: 10.3390/jtaer16060130

Joint Statement. (2024). Joint Statement between the People's Republic of China and the Slovak Republic on the Establishment of a Strategic Partnership. November 1, 2024. https://www.fmprc.gov.cn/eng/zu/go/202411/f20241101_11520047.html

Jong, M., Hoppe, T., & Alawadi, N. (2019). City branding, sustainable urban development and the rentier state. how do qatar, abu dhabi and dubai present themselves in the age of post oil and global warming? *Energies*, 12(9), 1657. DOI: 10.3390/en12091657

Jung, C., Awad, J., & Al Qassimi, N. (2021). Analyzing the users' satisfaction levels and perceptions of the dubai water canal for future waterfront development in uae. *Future Cities and Environment, 7*(1).

Jung, C., Abdelaziz Mahmoud, N. S., & Alqassimi, N. (2023). Enhancing indoor air quality and sustainable living in newly constructed apartments: Insights from dubai. *Frontiers in Built Environment*, 9, 1292531. Advance online publication. DOI: 10.3389/fbuil.2023.1292531

Kallou, S., & Kikilia, A. (2021). A transformative educational framework in tourism higher education through digital technologies during the covid-19 pandemic. *Advances in Mobile Learning Educational Research*, 1(2), 37–47. DOI: 10.25082/AMLER.2021.01.005

Kamble, S., Kaushik, D., Bhat, I. A., & Alfalou, A. (2024). The role of big data analytics and artificial intelligence in sustainable supply chain management: A survey. *Global Transitions*, 6, 100151. DOI: 10.1016/j.glt

Kao, C. (1999). Spurious regression and residual-based tests for cointegration in panel data. *Journal of Econometrics*, 90(1), 1–44. DOI: 10.1016/S0304-4076(98)00023-2

Kapoor, K., Bigdeli, A. Z., Schroeder, A., & Baines, T. (2022). A platform ecosystem view of servitization in manufacturing. *Technovation*, 118(102248), 1–12. DOI: 10.1016/j.technovation.2021.102248

Kashmanian, R. M. (2022). Scaling Up Transformational Change: Facing Up to Global Megatrends and Their Environmental Impacts. *Environmental Management and Sustainable Development*, 11(3), 13–60. DOI: 10.5296/emsd.v11i3.19875

Kässi, O., & Lehdonvirta, V. (2020). Digital labor and the pandemic: The case of platform work. *Socio-economic Review*, 18(4), 1001–1025.

Kazaz, D., Okur Dinçsoy, M., & Şenalp, U. E. (2023). Doğrudan Yabanci Yatirim, Ekonomik Büyüme Ve Karbon Emisyonu İlişkisinin Yeşil ve Kahverengi Alan Yatirimlari Açisindan Analizi. Trakya Üniversitesi Sosyal Bilimler Dergisi, 25(Özel Sayı), 429-446.

Kenney, M., & Zysman, J. (2016). The rise of the platform economy. *Issues in Science and Technology*, 32(3), 61–69.

Khasanova, S. S., & Saydulgerieva, M. A. (2024). Green economy as a tool for sustainable development and a factor contributing to the formation of a low-carbon economy. In BIO Web of Conferences, 82(04003), 1-8. DOI: 10.1051/bioconf/20248204003

Khitskov, E., Veretekhina, S., Medvedeva, A., Mnatsakanyan, O., Shmakova, E., & Koteney, A. (2017). Digital transformation of society: Problems entering in the digital economy. *Eurasian Journal of Analytical Chemistry*, 12(5b, 5B), 855–873. DOI: 10.12973/ejac.2017.00216a

Kibanov, A. Ya., & Batkayeva, I. A. (2011b). Motivation and stimulation of labor activity.

Kim, J. W., Rhee, J. H., & Park, C. H. (2024). How Does Digital Transformation Improve Supply Chain Performance: A Manufacturer's Perspective. *Sustainability (Basel)*, 16(7), 3046. DOI: 10.3390/su16073046

Klaus, P. (2021). Viewpoint: Phygital – The Emperor's new clothes? *Journal of Strategic Marketing*, (September), 1–8.

Koehler–Derrick, G., & Lee, M. M. (2023). War and Welfare in Colonial Algeria. *International Organization*, 77(2), 263–293. DOI: 10.1017/S0020818322000376

Koenker, R. (2004). Quantile Regression for Longitudinal Data. *Journal of Multivariate Analysis*, 91(1), 74–89. DOI: 10.1016/j.jmva.2004.05.006

Kogut, B., & Zander, U. (1992). Knowledge of the firm, combinative capabilities, and the replication of technology. *Organization Science*, 3(3), 383–397. DOI: 10.1287/orsc.3.3.383

Kohli, R., & Melville, N. P. (2019). Digital innovation: A review and synthesis. *Information Systems Journal*, 29(1), 200–223. DOI: 10.1111/isj.12193

Korcok, I. (2022). Rules based international order at a time of great peril: Slovak foreign policy respinces. In *Yearbook of Slovak Foreign Policy 2021* (pp. 6–21). SFPA.

Korsita, B., Cania, L., Lazaj, A., & Pendi, L. (2024). An Application of the Gravity Model: Exploring Foreign Direct Investment in the Balkan Region. *Revue d'Economie Financiere*, 21, 2036–2041. DOI: 10.55365/1923.x2023.21.219

Köse, N., & Yengin, D. (2018). Dijital Pazarlamadan Fijital Pazarlamaya Geçişe Örnek Olarak Artırılmış Gerçeklik ve Sanal Gerçeklik Uygulamalarının Pazarlama Üzerindeki Katkılarının İncelenmesi. *İstanbul Aydın Üniversitesi Dergisi, 10*(1), 77-111.

Kotler, P. (1997). *Marketing Management.* Prentice Hall.

Kotter, J. P. (1996). *Leading Change*. Harvard Business Review Press.

Kumar, S., Kumar, V., Bhatt, I., Kumar, S., & Attri, K. (2023). Digital transformation in tourism sector: Trends and future perspectives from a bibliometric-content analysis. *Journal of Hospitality and Tourism Insights*, 7(3), 1553–1576. DOI: 10.1108/JHTI-10-2022-0472

Kuriyan, R., Bailur, S., Gigler, S., & Park, K. R. (2011). *Technologies for Transparency and Accountability: Implications for ICT policy and Implementation. Open Development Technology Alliance*. World Bank.

Kuvshinova, I. A. (2014a). The formaton of the tourist potental of the area, Cultural and health services in educatonal and leisure insttutons: Experience, problems, prospects: Coll. artcles on the materials of VII all-Russian scientfc-practcal conference. Magnitogorsk: Nosov Magnitogorsk State Technical University.

Kyriakidi, M. (2021). Finding Your Sweet Spot for Sustainable Brand Growth. Kantar. https://www.kantar.com/inspiration/brands/%20finding-your-sweet-spot-for-sustainable-brand-growth

Lab, B. (2024). Building the Movement. https://www.bcorporation.net/en-us/movement/

Lambier, C. (2014b). Smooth Sailing: Cruise Lines and Medical Tourism Magazine. http://www.Medicaltourismmag. com/article/Smooth-Sailing-cruise-lines-andmedical-tourism-a-budding-relationship.html

Latour, B. (2005). *Reassembling the social: An introduction to actor-network-theory*. Oxford University Press. DOI: 10.1093/oso/9780199256044.001.0001

Law on Enterprises of the Social and Solidarity Economy. (2024b), *Pub. DV. No. 91 of November 2, 2018, amended DV. No. 17 of February 26, 2019, amended and add. DV. No. 24 of March 22, 2019, add. DV. No. 17 of February 25*, 2020, https://lex.bg/bg/laws/ldoc/2137187968

Le Billon, P. (2004). *The Geopolitics of Resource Wars*. Routledge.

Le, D. N., & Nguien, S. H. (2024). Unveiling the impact of artificial intelligence adoption intention on green innovation and new venture performance: The mediating effect of green dynamic capability. *Journal of Innovation & Knowledge*, 100504. Advance online publication. DOI: 10.1016/j.jik.2024.100504

Lei, J., Indiran, L., & Kohar, U. (2023). Barriers to digital transformation among msme in tourism industry: Cases studies from bali. *International Journal of Academic Research in Business & Social Sciences*, 13(3), 844–858. DOI: 10.6007/IJARBSS/v13-i3/16575

Lei, Y., Liang, Z., & Ruan, P. (2023). Evaluation on the impact of digital transformation on the economic resilience of the energy industry in the context of artificial intelligence. *Energy Reports*, 9, 785–792. DOI: 10.1016/j.egyr.2022.12.019

Li, K., Kim, D. J., Lang, K. R., Kauffman, R. J., & Naldi, M. (2020). How should we understand the digital economy in Asia? Critical assessment and research agenda. *Electronic Commerce Research and Applications*, 44, 101004. DOI: 10.1016/j.elerap.2020.101004 PMID: 32922241

Li, N., Liu, Z., & Zhang, X. (2022). A study on the impact of dynamic visitor demand on the digital transformation of enterprises—Considerations based on the regional innovation environment and the level of big data. *Sustainability (Basel)*, 15(1), 261. DOI: 10.3390/su15010261

Liu, C., Gong, W., Dong, G., & Ji, Q. (2024, July). Regulation of Environmental, Social and Governance Disclosure Greenwashing Behaviors Considering the Risk Preference of Enterprises. -. *Energy Economics*, 135, 107637. DOI: 10.1016/j.eneco.2024.107637

Li, Z., & Xizhen, Z. (2020). Political economic analysis of data participating in distribution as production function. *Study & Exploration*, 01, 109–115.

Lucas, R.Jr. (1988). On the mechanism of economic development. *Journal of Monetary Economics*, 22(1), 3–42. DOI: 10.1016/0304-3932(88)90168-7

Ly, B. (2023). The Interplay of Digital Transformational Leadership, Organizational Agility, and Digital Transformation. *Journal of the Knowledge Economy*. Advance online publication. DOI: 10.1007/s13132-023-01377-8

Machado, J. A. F., & Santos Silva, J. M. C. (2019). Quantiles via Moments. *Journal of Econometrics*, 213(1), 145–173. DOI: 10.1016/j.jeconom.2019.04.009

Macrotrends. (2024). Trade to GDP ratio by country. https://www.macrotrends.net/global-metrics/countries/ranking/trade-gdp-ratio

Majeed, S., Zhou, Z., Lu, C., & Ramkissoon, H. (2020). Online tourism information and tourist behavior: A structural equation modeling analysis based on a self-administered survey. *Frontiers in Psychology*, 599, 11. DOI: 10.3389/fpsyg.2020.00599 PMID: 32373008

Management, C. (2024). Strategies, Principles and Best Practices. https://nlpbulgaria.bg/news/upravlenie-na-promenite/

Manikas, I., Sundarakani, B., Madmoune, A., & Alvares, R. (2022). Integrated supply chain sustainability for mega-events: An empirical study of dubai expo 2020. *Event Management*, 26(6), 1409–1432. DOI: 10.3727/152599522X16419948391032

March, J. G. (1958). A Behavioral Theory of Decision Making. *The Personnel Administrator*, 21(3), 8–10.

Margherio, C. (1998). *The Emerging Digital Economy*. U.S. Department of Commerce.

Marino, A., & Pariso, P. (2021). Digital government platforms: Issues and actions in europe during pandemic time. *Journal of Entrepreneurship and Sustainability Issues*, 9(1), 462–485. DOI: 10.9770/jesi.2021.9.1(29)

Marris, R. (1964). *The Economic Theory of 'Managerial' Capitalism*. Macmillan. DOI: 10.1007/978-1-349-81732-0

Marris, R. (1998). Managerial Theories of the Firm. In *Managerial Capitalism in Retrospect*. Palgrave Macmillan. DOI: 10.1057/9780230376168_5

Marshall, A. (1920). *Principal of Economics*. Macmillan.

McEvoy, M. (2012). Organic 101: What the USDA Organic Label Means. - United States Department of Agriculture. https://www.usda.gov/media/blog/2012/03/22/organic-101-what-usda-organic-label-means

McGowana, M. (2016, November). The Influence of Social Identity on Value Perceptions and Intention. *Journal of Consumer Behaviour*, 16(3). https://www.researchgate.net/publication/310790712_The_influence_of_social_identity_on_value_perceptions_and_intention_Social_identity_and_value_perceptions

McNaughton, M., Rao, L., & Verma, S. (2020). Building smart communities for sustainable development. *Worldwide Hospitality and Tourism Themes*, 12(3), 337–352. DOI: 10.1108/WHATT-02-2020-0008

Mehraliyev, F., Choi, Y., & Köseoğlu, M. (2019). Progress on smart tourism research. *Journal of Hospitality and Tourism Technology*, 10(4), 522–538. DOI: 10.1108/JHTT-08-2018-0076

Mesenbourg, T. L. (2001). *Measuring the Digital Economy*. U.S. Bureau of the Census.

MGI. 2020, October 13. Digital Challenges in the next normal in Central and Eastern Europe. McKinsey Report 2020. https://mckinsey.com/business-functions/McKinsey-digital/our-insights/digital-challenges-in-the-next-normal-in-Central-and-eastern-europe

Miller, K. (2020). The Triple Bottom Line: What It Is & Why It's Important. - Harvard Business School Online's Business Insights. https://online.hbs.edu/blog/post/what-is-the-triple-bottom-line

Mironova, N., & Galyarski, E. (2020). Effective Digitalization of Business and Increasing Competitiveness. Business Directions.

Miroshnychenko, I., Kravchenko, T., & Drobyna, Y. (2021). Forecasting electricity generation from renewable sources in developing countries (on the case of Ukraine). *Neuro-Fuzzy Modeling Techniques in Economics*, 10(10), 164–198. DOI: 10.33111/nfmte.2021.164

Mladenov, Y., & Terziev, V. (2011a). *Management Fundamentals*.

Mohammad, N., & Rahmat, M. K. (2024). Exploring the potential of artificial intelligence in augmenting tourism and hospitality industry in United Arab Emirates (UAE). *SHS Web of Conferences. 189*, p. 03007. EDP Sciences.

Mohsin, M., Taghizadeh-Hesary, F., Iqbal, N., & Saydaliev, H. (2024). The role of digitalization and public-private partnerships in sustainable economic development: Evidence from selected Asian economies. *Journal of Risk and Financial Management*, 16(9), 397. DOI: 10.3390/jrfm16090397

Mondal, S., & Samaddar, K. (2020). Issues and challenges in implementing sharing economy in tourism: A triangulation study. *Management of Environmental Quality*, 32(1), 64–81. DOI: 10.1108/MEQ-03-2020-0054

Moody's Analytics. (2022). Global Fiscal Policy in the Pandemic. https://www.moodysanalytics.com/-/media/article/2022/global-fiscal-policy-in-the-pandemic.pdf

Morais, E., Cunha, C., & Mendonça, V. (2022, September). Tourism and Internet of Things: A bibliometric analysis of scientific production from the Scopus database. In *International Conference on Advanced Research in Technologies, Information, Innovation and Sustainability* (pp. 244-255). Cham: Springer Nature Switzerland. DOI: 10.1007/978-3-031-20316-9_19

Morales, J. (2016). *What is Strategic Planning: Definition*. Meaning, Applications and Tools.

Moravcikova, D., & Kliestikova, J. (2017). Brand Building with Using Phygital Marketing Communication. *Journal of Economics, Business and Management, 5*(3).

Muduli, A., & Choudhury, A. (2024). Exploring the Role of Workforce Agility on Digital Transformation: A Systematic Literature Review. *Benchmarking*. Advance online publication. DOI: 10.1108/BIJ-02-2023-0108

Mumford, E. (2006). The story of sociotechnical design: Reflections on its successes, failures and potential. *Information Systems Journal*, 16(4), 317–342. DOI: 10.1111/j.1365-2575.2006.00221.x

Mundo, E. (2018). Using the "Cruelty-Free" logo in Europe. Eco Mundo Online. https://www.ecomundo.eu/en/blog/cruelty-free-regulations-cosmetics-europe

Muñiz, D., Vila, N., & Brea, J. (2021). Changes in consumption patterns and tourist promotion after the covid-19 pandemic. *Journal of Theoretical and Applied Electronic Commerce Research*, 16(5), 1332–1352. DOI: 10.3390/jtaer16050075

Muratova, E., Muratov, D., Kravchenko, E., Sukhoveeva, A., & Andreeva, O. (2023b). Forecasting the Technical and Economic Parameters of the Combine Harvester Operation Using Pneumatic and Inertia Separator. In *XV International Scientific Conference "INTERAGROMASH 2022". INTERAGROMASH 2022. Lecture Notes in Networks and Systems, vol 575*. Springer, Cham. DOI: 10.1007/978-3-031-21219-2_154

Museum Of The Future. (2024). Retrieved from https://museumofthefuture.ae/en)

Museum Of The Future. (2024). Retrieved from Inhabit The Skies: https://museumofthefuture.ae/en/experience

Muslic, H. (2017). A Jargon-Free Guide to Low-Profit Limited Liability Companies. Nonprofit Hub. https://nonprofithub.org/jargon-free-guide-l3c/

Nadkarni, S. (2019). Conclusions: Expo 2020 and its impact on Dubai. *Worldwide Hospitality and Tourism Themes*, 11(3), 341–345. DOI: 10.1108/WHATT-02-2019-0011

Nadkarni, S. (2019). The pre- and post-event planning roadmap for expo 2020: Dubai's coming-out-party. *Worldwide Hospitality and Tourism Themes*, 11(3), 259–265. DOI: 10.1108/WHATT-02-2019-0009

Nadkarni, S., & Morris, S. (2019). Innovation-centric courses in hospitality management education in dubai. *Worldwide Hospitality and Tourism Themes*, 2(2), 166–172. DOI: 10.1108/WHATT-12-2018-0084

Narula, R., & Dunnung, J. H. (2010). Multinational enterprises, development and globalization: Some clarifications and a research agenda. *Oxford Development Studies*, 38(3), 263–287. DOI: 10.1080/13600818.2010.505684

Nawaz, M., Dinc, M. S., Qureshi, M. B., & Magda, R. (2024). Metaverse and tourism in the digital age: A bibliometric analysis. *Technological Forecasting and Social Change*, 202, 123298. DOI: 10.1016/j.techfore.2024.123298

Nazare, A., Moldoveanu, A., & Moldoveanu, F. (2023). Virtual Journeys, Real Engagement: Analyzing User Experience in a Virtual Traveling Social Platform. *Information 2024, 15*, 396.

Nitlarp, T., & Mayakul, T. (2023). The Implications of Triple Transformation on ESG in the Energy Sector: Fuzzy-Set Qualitative Comparative Analysis (fsQCA) and Structural Equation Modeling (SEM) Findings. *Energies*, 16(5), 1–26. DOI: 10.3390/en16052090

Nnaomah, U. I., Aderemi, S., Olutimehin, D. O., Orieno, O. H., & Ogundipe, D. O. (2024). Digital Banking and Financial Inclusion: A Review of Practices In The Usa And Nigeria. *Finance & Accounting Research Journal*, 3(6), 463–490. DOI: 10.51594/farj.v6i3.971

Nonaka, I., & Takeuchi, H. (1995). *The Knowledge-Creating Company - How Japanese Companies Create the Dynamics of Innovation*. Oxford University Press. DOI: 10.1093/oso/9780195092691.001.0001

Noori, N., Hoppe, T., & Jong, M. (2020). Classifying pathways for smart city development: Comparing design, governance and implementation in amsterdam, barcelona, dubai, and abu dhabi. *Sustainability (Basel)*, 12(10), 4030. DOI: 10.3390/su12104030

North, D. C. (1990). *Institutions, Institutional Change and Economic Performance*. Cambridge University Press. DOI: 10.1017/CBO9780511808678

Nur, A., Niswaty, R., Mustafa, D., & Guntur, M. (2021, September). The role of technology in development policy in the era of globalization in south sulawesi indonesia. *3rd Annual International Conference on Public and Business Administration (AICoBPA 2020)* (pp. 126-132). Atlantis Press. Retrieved from DOI: 10.2991/aebmr.k.210928.026

Nuttall, P. (2021, September). The power trap: Why the energy crisis is a crisis of politics. *New Statesman (London, England)*, 28. https://www.newstatesman.com/international-politics/climate-international-politics/2021/09/the-power-trap-why-the-energy-crisis-is-a-crisis-of-politics

O'Hara, P. A. (Ed.). (1999). *Welfare state. Encyclopedia of Political Economy* (p. 1247). Routledge. DOI: 10.4324/9780203443217

OECD. (2022). Strengthening FDI and SME linkage in the Slovak Republic. https://www.oecd.org/en/publications/strengthening-fdi-and-sme-linkages-in-the-slovak-republic_972946f5-en.html

OECD. (2023). Aiming Better: Government Support for Households and Firms during the Energy Crisis. OECD Economic Policy Paper No. 32. https://www.oecd-ilibrary.org/docserver/839e3ae1-en.pdf?expires=1692914306&id=id&accname=guest&checksum=0341DA666836280BAC460A99A84531BE

OIT/Cinterfor. (2020). *Digitalización en las organizaciones*. Recuperado de https://www.oitcinterfor.org/digitalizacion/digitalizacion-organizaciones

Okumus, F., Buhalis, D., & Taheri, B. (2024). The transformative power of technological advancements on service delivery, experiences and value co-creation in tourism, hospitality, leisure, and events. *Journal of Service Management*. Advance online publication. DOI: 10.1108/JOSM-11-2023-0496

Okur Dincsoy, M. (2009). Can ICT Economically Catalyze a Regional GDP Per Capita Convergence? A Case Study of Major East Asian Countries. , 7(1), 45-64.

Okur Dinçsoy, M. (2020). Sustainable Development and Industry Revolutions. In New Approaches to CSR, Sustainability and Accountability, Volume I. Accounting, Finance, Sustainability, Governance & Fraud: Theory and Application (pp. 61-79). Singapore: Springer.

Omarini, A. E. (2018). Banks and Fintechs: How to Develop a Digital Open Banking Approach for the Bank's Future. *International Business Research*, 11(9), 23–36. DOI: 10.5539/ibr.v11n9p23

Orrell, G. (2021). Sustainability at a Turning Point: Consumers Are Pushing Companies to Pivot. - IBM Institute for Business Value. https://www.ibm.com/downloads/documents/us-en/10a99803f92fda61

Page, S. (2009). *Understanding Complexity*. The Teaching Company.

Page, S. (2010). Complexity in Social, Political, and Economic Systems. - American Economic Association, Ten Years and Beyond: Economists Answer NSF's Call for Long-Term Research Agendas. Available at: https://ssrn.com/abstract=1889359

Pan, S., Yang, M., Li, Y., & Gao, M. (2024). Digitalization for sustainable development: A systematic literature review of evolving trends and practices. *Heliyon*, 24974. Advance online publication. DOI: 10.1016/j.heliyon.2024.e24974

Paramita, A., Winarso, H., Hudalah, D., & Syabri, I. (2023). Path dependency and development impacts of megaproject: A case study of north jakarta bay reclamation. *International Journal of Sustainable Development and Planning*, 18(11), 3477–3490. DOI: 10.18280/ijsdp.181113

Parker, G. G., Van Alstyne, M. W., & Choudary, S. P. (2016). *Platform revolution: How networked markets are transforming the economy and how to make them work for you*. W.W. Norton & Company.

Participation Banks Association of Türkiye. (2024, Apr 10). Digital Banking Statistics: https://veripetegi.tkbb.org.tr/

Paus, E. (2018). *Confronting Dystopia: The New Technological Revolution and the Future of Work*. Cornell University Press. DOI: 10.7591/9781501719868

Pedroni, P. (1999). Critical values for cointegration tests in heterogeneous panels with multiple regressors. *Oxford Bulletin of Economics and Statistics*, 61(s1, S1), 653–670. DOI: 10.1111/1468-0084.61.s1.14

Pedroni, P. (2004). Panel cointegration: Asymptotic and finite sample properties of pooled time series tests with an application to the PPP hypothesis. *Econometric Theory*, 20(3), 597–625. DOI: 10.1017/S0266466604203073

Penrose, E. (1958). *The Theory of the Growth of the Firm. Oxford: Basil Blackwell.* John Wiley.

Pérez, A., & Guzmán, M. (2015). Los estudios organizacionales como programa de investigación. *Revista Latinoamericana de Estudios Organizacionales*, 2(1), 1-20. https://www.scielo.cl/scielo.php?pid=S0717-554X2015000200001&script=sci_arttext

Peters, A. (2019). Most Millennials Would Take a Pay Cut to Work at an Environmentally Responsible Company. Fast Company. https://www.fastcompany.com/90306556/most-millennials-would-take-a-pay-cut-to-work-at-a-sustainable-company

Petkova-Georgieva, S., Petrova, T., & Petrov, Zh. (2021d). The medical tourism social and public_benefits in the development of tourist services. *Annual of Assen Zlatarov University, Burgas, Bulgaria*, L(2), 31–36.

Petrova, T., & Petkova-Georgieva, S. (2020c). Motivational model for contemporary medical tourism development. Scientific Atlas.

Petrova, T., & Petrov, Zh. (2022b). Corporate culture and personnel management in “Smart farm”. Intelligent Animal Husbandry. DOI: 10.15547/joiah.2022.01.005

Pickard, S., & Lemma, A. (2023). In search of nexus triple wins: Planning for and evidence of economic transformation, social inclusion and ecological sustainability in Sri Lanka, Thailand and the Dominican Republic. *The Journal of Poverty and Social Justice : Research, Policy, Practice*, 31(3), 351–371. DOI: 10.1332/175982721X16916833771132

Plekhanov, D., Franke, H., & Netland, T. H. (2023). Digital Transformation: A Review and Research Agenda. *European Management Journal*, 41(6), 821–844. DOI: 10.1016/j.emj.2022.09.007

Ponomarev, I. P. (2014). Motivation work in the organization.

PowerData. (2023). *Transformación digital: Qué es y su importancia*. Recuperado de https://www.powerdata.es/transformacion-digital

Prakash, O., Solanki, P., Shekhawat, R. S., & Dhiman, G. (2024). Revolutionizing Industries With Blockchain-Based Internet of Things and Artificial Intelligence Based Applications. *Computers & Electrical Engineering*, 115, 109287.

Prensky, M. (2001). Digital Natives, Digital Immigrants Part 1. *On the Horizon*, 9(5), 1–6. DOI: 10.1108/10748120110424816

Prihandono, D., Wijaya, A. P., Wiratama, B., Prananta, W., & Widia, S. (2024). Digital transformation to enhance Indonesian SME performance: Exploring the impact of market competition and digital strategy. *Problems and Perspectives in Management*, 22(2), 103–113. DOI: 10.21511/ppm.22(2).2024.09

Putnam, R. D. (2000). *Bowling Alone: The Collapse and Revival of American Community*. Simon & Schuster.

Qatawneh, D., Adnan, A., AlZoughool, S., & AlQudah, T. (2020). A study of the leading factors that induced confidence in the foreign investors for investing in real estate business for the period 1970- 2019. *Scholars Journal of Economics Business and Management*, 07(01), 39–43. DOI: 10.36347/sjebm.2020.v07i01.007

Rabadán, A., González-Moreno, Á., & Sáez-Martínez, F. J. (2019). Improving Firms' Performance and Sustainability: The Case of Eco-Innovation in the Agri-Food Industry. Sustainability, 11(20), 5590, 1-13

Radicic, D., Borovic, Z., & Trivic, J. (2023). Total factor productivity gap between the "New" and "Old" Europe: An industry-level perspective. *Post-Communist Economies*, 35(7), 770–795. DOI: 10.1080/14631377.2023.2236868

Raj, A., Dwivedi, G., Sharma, A., de Sousa Jabbour, A. B. L., & Rajak, S. (2020). Barriers to the adoption of industry 4.0 technologies in the manufacturing sector: An inter-country comparative perspective. *International Journal of Production Economics*, 224, 107546. DOI: 10.1016/j.ijpe.2019.107546

Ramsey, F. (1928). A mathematical theory of saving. *Economic Journal (London)*, 38(152), 543–559. DOI: 10.2307/2224098

Rani, P., Sharma, P., & Gupta, I. (2024). Toward a greener future: A survey on sustainable blockchain applications and impact. *Journal of Environmental Management*, 120273, 354. DOI: 10.1016/j.jenvman.2024.120273 PMID: 38350276

Rasheed, K. A. (2023). Enabling Financial Inclusion in Rural India Through a Phygital Model. 06 10, 2024 tarihinde iimk.ac.in/uploads/publications/IIMKWPS569FIN202303.pdf

Report on the follow-up assessment of the impact of the Law on Enterprises, Social and Solidarity Economy, MLSP, (2023a), https://www.mlsp.government.bg/posledvashchi-otsenki-na-vzdeystvieto

Rethinking The Future. (2024). Retrieved from Smart Cities: Exploring how technology is being integrated into urban infrastructure and services: https://www.re-thinkingthefuture.com/architectural-community/a10783-smart-cities-exploring-how-technology-is-being-integrated-into-urban-infrastructure-and-services/

Rochet, J. C., & Tirole, J. (2003). Platform competition in two-sided markets. *Journal of the European Economic Association*, 1(4), 990–1029. DOI: 10.1162/154247603322493212

Romer, P. (1986). Increasing returns and long-run growth. *Journal of Political Economy*, 94(5), 1002–1037. DOI: 10.1086/261420

Rozak, H. A., Adhiatma, A., Fachrunnisa, O., & Rahayu, T. (2021). Social Media Engagement, Organizational Agility and Digitalization Strategic Plan to Improve SMEs' Performance. *IEEE Transactions on Engineering Management*, 70(11), 3766–3775. DOI: 10.1109/TEM.2021.3085977

Ruhana, F. (2024). Combating Poverty and Social Inequality in 2023 - a Global Imperative for Equitable Development and Social Justice. International Journal of Science and Society. https://ijsoc.goacademica.com/index.php/ijsoc/article/view/1081/946

Ruogu, L. (2008). *Institutional Suitability and Economic Development. Based on Practices in China*. China Economic Publishing House.

Saarikko, T., Westergren, U. H., & Blomquist, T. (2020). Digital Transformation: Five Recommendations for the Digitally Conscious Firm. *Business Horizons*, 63(6), 825–839. DOI: 10.1016/j.bushor.2020.07.005

Saarinen, J. (2020). Tourism and sustainable development goals: Research on sustainable tourism geographies. In *Tourism and Sustainable Development Goals* (pp. 1–10). Routledge. DOI: 10.1201/9780429324253-1

Saleh, A., Bassil, C., & Safari, A. (2021). Tourism research for the gcc region: Current status and future research directions. *Tourism Economics*, 28(6), 1626–1646. DOI: 10.1177/1354816621999968

Samuel, G., Lucivero, F., & Croxatto, L. (2022). The environmental sustainability of digital technologies: Stakeholder practices and perspectives. *Sustainability (Basel)*, 14(7), 3791. DOI: 10.3390/su14073791

Sang, Y., & Han, E. (2023). A win-win way for corporate and stakeholders to achieve sustainable development: Corporate social responsibility value co-creation scale development and validation. *Corporate Social Responsibility and Environmental Management*, 30(3), 1177–1190. DOI: 10.1002/csr.2412

Santosh, K. (2019). Phygital Banking – A Game Changer In Indian Banking Sector. *International Journal of Innovative Technology and Exploring Engineering*, 8(9), 289–292. DOI: 10.35940/ijitee.H7283.078919

SAP. (2023). *¿Qué es la Transformación Digital? | Importancia y Beneficios*. Recuperado de https://www.sap.com/latinamerica/insights/what-is-digital-transformation.html

Sawitri, K. A., & Brennan, L. (2023). The investment development path literature: A review and research agenda. *Management Review Quarterly*, 73(4), 1825–1872. DOI: 10.1007/s11301-022-00287-4

Schallmo, D., Williams, C. A., & Lohse, J. (2019). Digital strategy—Integrated approach and generic options. *International Journal of Innovation Management*, 23(08), 1940005. DOI: 10.1142/S136391961940005X

Schmerber, L. (2024). Triple Transition and Corporate Responsibility – A New Framework for Businesses. Interreg Europe. https://www.interregeurope.eu/policy-learning-platform/news/triple-transition-and-corporate-responsibility-a-new-framework-for-businesses#:~:text=This%20is%20the%20core%20of%20the%20concept%20of,process%20towards%20a%20more%20sustainable%20and%20competitive%20economy

Schumpeter, J. A. (2008). The Theory of Economic Development: As Inquiry into Profits, Capital, Credit, Interest and the Business Cycle. Transaction Publishers. (Original publication 1934)

Schumpeter, J. A. (1939). *Business Cycles. A theoretical, Historical and Statistical Analysis of the Capitalist Process*. McGraw-Hill Book Company.

Schwab, K. (2016). The Fourth Industrial Revolution: What It Means, How to Respond. World Economic Forum, January 16.

Sedex. (2024). What does "Ethically Sourced" Mean? https://www.sedex.com/blog/what-does-ethically-sourced-mean/

Seniuk N.Y., Maltseva O.A., Schreiber N.H., & Hart A.K. (2022). Comparative analysis of the investment policy of Russia and China in Central Asia (2009-2020). International Business Magazine, 2(2).

Seniuk, N., & Fabus, M. (2023). Theory of the firm, FDI, and development in the light of the global challenges: Modern firms in the era of digitalisation and green transition. Optimizing Energy Efficiency During a Global Energy Crisis, 307-326.

Seniuk, N., & Hudakova, M. (2023). Theory of foreign direct investment in light of the global innovation challenges. Public Administration and Regional Development.

Seniuk, Y. (2017). Transborder multi-level Digital interactive education-training Platform for Innovation-oriented co-development. Proceedings of the 15th International Conference on Emerging e-Learning Technologies and Applications ICETA2017. DOI: 10.1109/ICETA.2017.8102526

Seniuk, N. (2022). Russian-Chinese trade: Current trends and prospects. *Baltic RIM Economies Review.*, (4), 48–49.

Sharma, S., Stranjančević, A., & Kleber, D. (2019). The effects of hosting events on destination branding: Dubai expo 2020. *Kinerja*, 23(2), 91–102. DOI: 10.24002/kinerja.v23i2.2390

Sharp, T. (2007). Resource Conflict in the Twenty-First Century. Peace Review: A Journal of Social Justice, 19(3), 323–330.

Shatalova, N. I., & Alexandrova, N. A. (2003). Personnel management on production: textbook.

Shehade, M., & Stylianou-Lambert, T. (2020). Revisiting authenticity in the age of the digital transformation of cultural tourism. *Cultural and tourism innovation in the digital era: Sixth international IACuDiT conference* (pp. 3-16). Springer International Publishing.

Sheikh Mohammed bin Rashid Al Maktoum. (2024). Retrieved from Mohammed bin Rashid Launches Digital Wealth Initiative and Dubai IoT Strategy: https://sheikhmohammed.ae/en-us/news/details?nid=25236&cid=

Shevchenko, H., & Petrushenko, M. (2021). Rural tourism within the sustainable development goals: the case of ukraine. *SHS Web of Conferences, 95*. DOI: 10.1051/shsconf/20219501004

Shuyan, L., & Fabuš, M. (2019). Study on the spatial distribution of China's Outward Foreign Direct Investment in EU and its influencing factors. *Entrepreneurship and Sustainability Issues*, 6(3), 1080–1096. DOI: 10.9770/jesi.2019.6.3(16)

Shuyan, L., & Fabus, M. (2019). The impact of OFDI reverse technology spillover on China's technological progress: Analysis of provincial panel data. *Journal of International Students*, 12(4), 325–336. DOI: 10.14254/2071-8330.2019/12-4/21

Sieglin, V. (2014). Economía de conocimiento y culturas organizacionales en la academia. *Ciencia UANL*, 17(69), 45-60. https://cienciauanl.uanl.mx/?p=2590

Simbolon, A. N. (2024). Innovative Trends in Economic Development: Towards a New Era of Creativity and Productivity. *Innovative Economics Journal*, 1(1), 16–24.

Simon, H. A. (1947). *Administrative Behavior. A study of decision-making process in administrative organizations*. Macmillan.

Simon, H. A. (1957). *Models of Man*. John Wiley & Sons.

Singh, S., Sharma, M., & Dhir, S. (2021). Modeling the Effects of Digital Transformation in Indian Manufacturing Industry. *Technology in Society*, 67, 101763. DOI: 10.1016/j.techsoc.2021.101763

Skocpol, T. (1995). Protecting Soldiers and Mothers. *Belknap Press*. https://www.hup.harvard.edu/books/9780674717664

Slavova, M. (2016). Digital Transformation of Business. *Economic and Social Alternatives*, 2016(4), 142–149.

Smith, M. (1901). Four German Jurists. IV. *Political Science Quarterly*, 16(4), 641–679. DOI: 10.2307/2140421

Soloviov, E., & Danilov, A. (2020). The beginning of phygital world. *South Asian Journal of Engineering and Technology*, 10(2), 1–4. DOI: 10.26524/sajet.2020.2.7

Solow, R. M. (1956). A Contribution to the Theory of Economic Growth. *The Quarterly Journal of Economics*, 70(1), 65–94. DOI: 10.2307/1884513

Spiliakos, A. (2018). What Does "Sustainability" Mean in Business? Harvard Business School Online's Business Insights. https://online.hbs.edu/blog/post/what-is-sustainability-in-business

Srnicek, N. (2016). *Platform Capitalism*. Polity Press.

Srnicek, N. (2017). *Platform capitalism*. Polity Press.

Starnawska, S. E. (2021). *Sustainability in the Banking Industry Through Technological Transformation. The Palgrave Handbook of Corporate Sustainability in the Digital Era*. Palgrave Macmillan.

Statistsa. (2023). Global gross domestic product (GDP) at current prices from 1985 to 2028.https://www.statista.com/statistics/268750/global-gross-domestic-product-gdp

Stobierski, T. (2021a). 4 Impactful Sustainable Business Practices That Can Make a Difference. Harvard Business School Online's Business Insights. https://online.hbs.edu/blog/post/sustainable-business-practices

Stobierski, T. (2021b). What Is Corporate Social Responsibility? 4 Types. Harvard Business School Online's Business Insights. https://online.hbs.edu/blog/post/types-of-corporate-social-responsibility

Stolley, K. S. (2012). *Watson S. Medical Tourism: A Reference Book*. ABCCLIO.

Strategic Framework for the EU Cultural Policy. (2023). https://culture.ec.europa.eu/bg/policies/strategic-framework-for-the-eus-cultural-policy

Strazay, T. (2022). The metamorphoses of Central Europe. In *Yearbook of Slovakia's Foreign Policy 2021* (pp. 108–122). SFPA.

Suchitra, P. (2015c). Tourism branding and its relevance in today's marketng scenario. *Internatonal Journal of Business and General Management*, 4(3), 21–28.

Sula Averbek, G., & Aysuna Türkyılmaz, C. (2021). *Sanal evrende markaların geleceği: yeni internet dünyası metaverse ve marka uygulamaları. Sosyal Bilimlerde Multi Disipliner Çalışmalar: Teori, Uygulama ve Analizler*. İstanbul Efe Akademi.

Sultan, M., Sharmin, F., Bădulescu, A., Ştiubea, E., & Xue, K. (2020). Travelers' responsible environmental behavior towards sustainable coastal tourism: An empirical investigation on social media user-generated content. *Sustainability (Basel)*, 13(1), 56. DOI: 10.3390/su13010056

Sundararajan, A. (2016). *The sharing economy: The end of employment and the rise of crowd-based capitalism*. MIT Press., DOI: 10.7551/mitpress/10425.001.0001

Suszynski, C. (2013). *Business Enterprise. The Integration of Approaches*. Oficyna Wudawnicza Szkola Glowna Handlowa w Warszawie.

SYSR2024| Statistical Yearbook of the Slovak Republic. (2024). Statistical Office of the Slovak Republic. https://slovak.statistics.sk/wo's/portal

Taha, B., & Allan, A. (2022). Planning for Legacy–A Cost Effective and Sustainable Approach. Case Study: Dubai Expo 2020. *ISPRS Annals of the Photogrammetry, Remote Sensing and Spatial Information Sciences*, 10, 237–244. DOI: 10.5194/isprs-annals-X-4-W3-2022-237-2022

Talattov, A. P., Wibowo, M. R., & Kallman, M. (2021). Corporate Transformation Towards Sustainability: The case of the Indonesian pulp and papers industry. *Sustainability Science and Resources*, 1(1), 107–134. DOI: 10.55168/ssr2809-6029.2021.1005

Talin, B. (2023). What is "Digital Transformation"? Definition and Explanation. https://morethandigital.info/bg/kakvo-e-digitalna-transformacia-opredelenie-i-obiasnenie/

Tapscott, D. (1996). *The Digital Economy: Promise and Peril in the Age of Networked Intelligence*. McGraw-Hill.

Tapscott, D. (2016). *Blockchain Revolution: How the Technology Behind Bitcoin is Changing Money, Business, and the World*. Penguin.

Tarver, E. (2024). 8 Types of LLCs Explained & Compared. Forbes. https://www.forbes.com/advisor/business/llc-types/

Terziev, V. & Georgiev, M. (2024e). New social transformations and changes in societies. 112th International Scientific Conference on Economic and Social Development – "Creating a unified foundation for Sustainable Development: Interdisciplinarity in Research and Education" – Varazdin, 4-5 June, 2024, Economic and Social Development (Book of Proceedings), 311-319.

Terziev, V., & Can, H. (2018c). The relation between the migration, population aging, labor force productivity and economic growth: an analysis for Bulgaria. Proceedings of INTCESS2018- 5th International Conference on Education and Social Sciences, 445-451.

Terziev, V., & Georgiev, M. (2017). Highlights of the evolution of the „balanced scorecard" idea as a model for managing strategy development and control. Proceedings of SOCIOINT 2017- 4th International Conference on Education, Social Sciences and Humanities, 607-610.

Terziev, V., & Georgiev, M. (2018d). Efficient management as optimization of the organization. Proceedings of INTCESS2018- 5th International Conference on Education and Social Sciences, 452-461.

Terziev, V., & Georgiev, M. (2024a). New social transformations and changes in societies. 112th International Scientific Conference on Economic and Social Development – "Creating a unified foundation for Sustainable Development: Interdisciplinarity in Research and Education", 24-25.

Terziev, V., & Georgiev, M. (2024b). Social development and the contribution of science. 112th International Scientific Conference on Economic and Social Development – "Creating a unified foundation for Sustainable Development: Interdisciplinarity in Research and Education" – Varazdin, 4-5 June, 2024, Economic and Social Development (Book of Proceedings), 209-231.

Terziev, V., & Georgiev, M. (2024c). Social development and the contribution of science. *112th International Scientific Conference on Economic and Social Development – "Creating a unified foundation for Sustainable Development: Interdisciplinarity in Research and Education" – Varazdin, 4-5 June, 2024, Economic and Social Development (Book of Proceedings),* 209-231.

Terziev, V., & Georgiev, M. (2024c). Social transformations and social programming. 112th International Scientific Conference on Economic and Social Development – "Creating a unified foundation for Sustainable Development: Interdisciplinarity in Research and Education" – Varazdin, 4-5 June, 2024, Economic and Social Development (Book of Proceedings), 251-256.

Terziev, V., & Georgiev, M. (2024d). New social transformations and changes in societies. 112th International Scientific Conference on Economic and Social Development – "Creating a unified foundation for Sustainable Development: Interdisciplinarity in Research and Education" – Varazdin, 4-5 June, 2024, Economic and Social Development (Book of Proceedings), 311-329.

Terziev, V., & Georgiev, M. (2024d). Social transformations and social programming. *112th International Scientific Conference on Economic and Social Development – "Creating a unified foundation for Sustainable Development: Interdisciplinarity in Research and Education" – Varazdin, 4-5 June, 2024, Economic and Social Development (Book of Proceedings),* 251-256.

Terziev, V., & Lyubcheva, M. (2022). Shared knowledge and changes in the higher education system in Bulgaria. *79th International Scientific Conference on Economic and Social Development – Rabat, 25-26 March, 2022, Economic and Social Development (Book of Proceedings),* 228-237.

Terziev, V., & Lyubcheva, M. (2022a). Shared knowledge and changes in the higher education system in Bulgaria. *79th International Scientific Conference on Economic and Social Development – Rabat, 25-26 March, 2022, Economic and Social Development (Book of Proceedings),* 228-237.

Terziev, V., & Lyubcheva, M. (2022a). Shared knowledge and changes in the higher education system in Bulgaria. 79th International Scientific Conference on Economic and Social Development, 228-237.

Terziev, V., & Petkova - Georgieva, S. (2020f). Basic conditions for implementation of an effective strategic decision support system at a hospital. Proceedings of INTCESS 2020- 7th International Conference on Education and Social Sciences, 739-745.

Terziev, V., & Petkova-Georgieva, S. (2019a). The Bulgarian health care system practical research on the usefulness of the performance measurement system. Proceedings of ADVED 2019 - 5th International Conference on Advances in Education and Social Sciences, 21-23 October 2019, International Organization Center of Academic Research, 369 - 375.

Terziev, V., & Petkova-Georgieva, S. (2019b). The pesticides toxic impact on the human health condition and the ecosystem. Proceedings of ADVED 2019 - 5th International Conference on Advances in Education and Social Sciences, 376 - 382.

Terziev, V., & Petkova-Georgieva, S. (2019c). Human health problems and the classification of the most toxic pesticides. Proceedings of ADVED 2019 - 5th International Conference on Advances in Education and Social Sciences, 383 - 390.

Terziev, V., & Petkova-Georgieva, S. (2019d). Organo-phosphonate, organo-halogenated, cyanides and arsenic toxic impact on the human health care condition. Proceedings of ADVED 2019 - 5th International Conference on Advances in Education and Social Sciences, 426 - 431.

Terziev, V., & Petkova-Georgieva, S. (2019e). Human health prevention by detection and quantification of toxic chemical compounds. Proceedings of ADVED 2019 - 5th International Conference on Advances in Education and Social Sciences, 443 - 449.

Terziev, V., & Petkova-Georgieva, S. (2019f). Toxic chemical compounds detection for the society social health care prevention. Proceedings of ADVED 2019 - 5th International Conference on Advances in Education and Social Sciences, 432 - 442.

Terziev, V., & Petkova-Georgieva, S. (2019g). The level of decentralization impact on the Bulgarian social health care competitiveness. Proceedings of ADVED 2019 - 5th International Conference on Advances in Education and Social Sciences, 361 - 368.

Terziev, V., & Petkova-Georgieva, S. (2020d). Testing the cost assessment methods application at a hospital for the decision "make or buy". Proceedings of INTCESS 2020- 7th International Conference on Education and Social Sciences, 789-796.

Terziev, V., & Petkova-Georgieva, S. (2020e). Bulgarian health system cost assessment methods application for the decision "make or buy". Proceedings of INTCESS 2020- 7th International Conference on Education and Social Sciences, 797-801.

Terziev, V., Banabakova, V., & Georgiev, M. (2018a). Possibilities for Determining Customer's Profitability. Proceedings of INTCESS2018- 5th International Conference on Education and Social Sciences, 438-444.

Terziev, V., Banabakova, V., & Georgiev, M. (2018b). Customer service standards. Proceedings of INTCESS2018- 5th International Conference on Education and Social Sciences, 431-437.

Terziev, V., Bencheva, N., Stoeva, T., & Georgiev, M. (2020g). Developing social entrepreneurship in the EU: a cross-country analysis. Proceedings of INTCESS 2020- 7th International Conference on Education and Social Sciences, 746-753.

Terziev, V., Bogdanova, M., Kanev, D., Georgiev, M., & Simeonov, S. (2019). The social assistance system in Bulgaria. Proceedings of ADVED 2019 - 5th International Conference on Advances in Education and Social Sciences, 391-397. DOI: 10.2139/ssrn.3477129

Terziev, V., Georgiev, M., Simeonov, S., & Ivanov, I. (2021e). Knowledge in the context of strategic management of the military education system. 23rd RSEP International Economics, Finance & Business Conference, 136-141.

Terziev, V., Lyubcheva, M., & Georgiev, M. (2021b). Domestic and international challenges in higher education. *7 th ITEM Conference – "Innovation, Technology, Education and Management" and 67th International Scientific Conference on Economic and Social Development – Sveti Martin na Muri, 29-30 April, 2021, Economic and Social Development (Book of Proceedings),* 88-97

Terziev, V., Lyubcheva, M., & Georgiev, M. (2021b). Domestic and international challenges in higher education. *7 th ITEM Conference – "Innovation, Technology, Education and Management" and 67th International Scientific Conference on Economic and Social Development – Sveti Martin na Muri, 29-30 April,* 2021, *Economic and Social Development (Book of Proceedings),* 88-97.

Terziev, V., Lyubcheva, M., & Georgiev, M. (2021b). Domestic and international challenges in higher education. 7th ITEM Conference – "Innovation, Technology, Education and Management" and 67th International Scientific Conference on Economic and Social Development – Sveti Martin na Muri, 29-30 April, 2021, Economic and Social Development (Book of Proceedings), 88-97.

Terziev, V., Lyubcheva, M., & Georgiev, M. (2021c). The contemporary strategic challenges facing higher education. Proceedings of SOCIOINT 2021 8th International Conference on Education and Education of Social Sciences, 134-141.

Terziev, V., Lyubcheva, M., & Solovev, D. (2020a). The interaction: business-education- investment for development. Proceedings of INTCESS 2020- 7th International Conference on Education and Social Sciences, 865-869.

Terziev, V., Lyubcheva, M., Andreeva, O., & Georgiev, M. (2020a). Revolution in industry and evolution in education or development of intelligence. *63rd International Scientific Conference on Economic and Social Development – "Building Resilient Society" - Zagreb, 11-12 December, 2020, Economic and Social Development (Book of Proceedings),* 133-142.

Terziev, V., Lyubcheva, M., Andreeva, O., & Georgiev, M. (2020b). Revolution in industry and evolution in education or development of intelligence. *63rd International Scientific Conference on Economic and Social Development – "Building Resilient Society" - Zagreb, 11-12 December, 2020, Economic and Social Development (Book of Proceedings),* 133-142.

Terziev, V. K., Lyubcheva, M. I., Andreeva, O. V., & Simeonov, S. V. (2024). Creating an analytical model for the study of social entrepreneurship. *Economics & Society: Contemporary Models of Development*, 14(2), 91–112. DOI: 10.18334/ecsoc.14.2.121514

Terziev, V. K., Lyubcheva, M. I., & Georgiev, M. P. (2023b). Vocational education in Bulgaria: Professionalism, compliance and challenges. *Social Entrepreneurship and Corporate Social Responsibility*, 4(1), 41–58. DOI: 10.18334/social.4.1.116942

Terziev, V., & Georgiev, M. (2023). *Challenges to active social policies in Bulgaria, gabriell-e-lit.*

Terziev, V., Lyubcheva, M., & Georgiev, M. (2021c). The contemporary strategic challenges facing higher education. *Proceedings of SOCIOINT 2021 8th International Conference on Education and Education of Social Sciences 14-15 June,* 134-141.

Terziev, V., Lyubcheva, M., & Georgiev, M. (2021c). The contemporary strategic challenges facing higher education. *Proceedings of SOCIOINT 2021 8th International Conference on Education and Education of Social Sciences 14-15 June, 2021*, 134-141.

Terziev, V., Lyubcheva, M., & Mihailova, M. (2021a). The necessity of changes in the higher education in Bulgaria. *Proceedings of INTCESS 2021 8th International Conference on Education and Education of Social Sciences 18-19 January, 2021*, 646-657. DOI: 10.51508/intcess.202104

Terziev, V., Lyubcheva, M., & Solovev, D. (2020a). The interaction: business-education- investment for development. *Proceedings of INTCESS 2020- 7th International Conference on Education and Social Sciences 20-22 January, 2020 - DUBAI (UAE)*, 865-869.

The 7 Rs of Application Modernization: Your Strategic Roadmap to Digital Transformation. (2023). https://www.solix.com/bg/blog/learning/the-7rs-of-application-modernization-your-strategic-roadmap-to-digital-transformation/

The Banks Association of Türkiye. (2024a, Apr 14). Electronic Banking Terms: https://www.tbb.org.tr/terimler.asp

The Banks Association of Türkiye. (2024b, Apr 10). Digital Banking Statistics: https://www.tbb.org.tr/Content/Upload/istatistikiraporlar/ekler/4437/Dijital-Internet-Mobil_Bankacilik_Istatistikleri-Haziran_2024.pdf

Tienbergen, J. (1962). An Analysis of World Trade Flows. In Tienbergen, J. (Ed.), *Shaping the World Economy*. Twentieth Century Fund.

Tinbergen, J. (1942). Zur Theorie der Langfristigen Wirtschaftsentwicklung. *Weltwirtschaftliches Archiv*, 55, 541–549.

Tran. (2024). Strategic Management Process.

Trollman, H., & Colwill, J. (2021). The imperative of embedding sustainability in business: A model for transformational sustainable development. *Sustainable Development (Bradford)*, 29(5), 974–986. DOI: 10.1002/sd.2188

Tsai, W. Y., & Su, C. J. (2022). Digital Transformation of Business Model Innovation. *Frontiers in Psychology*, 13, 1017750. DOI: 10.3389/fpsyg.2022.1017750 PMID: 36389577

Tümsaş. (2024, Jan 5). https://tumsas.com.tr/en/about-us/index.htm

Türkiye Cumhuriyeti Ziraat Bankası. (2024, May 10). Ziraat Bank 2013 Sustainability Report: https://www.ziraatbank.com.tr/tr/Bankamiz-ZB/surdurulebilirlik/Documents/SurdurulebilirlikRaporu2013.pdf

Türkiye İşbank. (2024, Mar 5). www.isbank.com.tr

UASB. (2020). *Un acercamiento teórico a la economía digital*. Recuperado de https://revistas.uasb.edu.ec/index.php/eg/article/download/4116/3999/16300

UN Enviromental Programme. (2024). Retrieved from GOAL 11: Sustainable cities and communities: https://www.unep.org/topics/sustainable-development-goals/why-do-sustainable-development-goals-matter/goal-11

UNCTAD. (2022). World Investment Report 2022. https://unctad.org/publication/world-investment-report-2022

UNCTAD. (2023). Investment Trends Monitor (Issue 44, January 2023). https://unctad.org/system/files/official-document/diaeiainf2023d1_en.pdf

UNCTAD. (2023). World Investment Report 2023. Investing in Sustainable Energy for All.https://unctad.org/system/files/official-document/wir2023_en.pdf

University of York. (2024). What are business ethics, and why do they matter? https://online.york.ac.uk/what-are-business-ethics-and-why-do-they-matter/

US Department of State. (2024). Investment Climate Statements: Slovakia. https://www.state.gov/reports/2024-investment-climate-statements/slovakia

USFDA. (2000). "Cruelty Free"/"Not Tested on Animals". United States Food And Drug Administration. https://www.fda.gov/cosmetics/cosmetics-labeling-claims/cruelty-freenot-tested-animals

Vassilev, S. (2024). Media, media culture, communications: processes and transformations. Rhetoric and Communications, 59, 7-27.

Vial, G. (2019). Understanding Digital Transformation: A Review and a Research Agenda. *The Journal of Strategic Information Systems*, 28(2), 118–144. DOI: 10.1016/j.jsis.2019.01.003

Virtanen, I. (2011). Externalization of tacit knowledge implies a simplified theory of cognition. *Journal of Knowledge Management Practice*, 12(3), 139–145.

Vitari, C., & Raguseo, E. (2019). Big data analytics business value and firm performance: Linking with environmental context. *International Journal of Production Research*, 58(18), 5456–5476. DOI: 10.1080/00207543.2019.1660822

Von Kutzschenbach, M. (2017). "And then a miracle occurs ..." - Engaging the challenge of operationalizing theories of success in digital transformation. Systemics. *Cybernetics and Informatics*, 15(6), 101–105.

Vovchenko, N. G., Andreeva, O. V., Dmitrieva, V. D., Galazova, S. S., & Terziev, V. K. (2022). Modelling of Economic Clusters in the Russian Regions in the Context of Formation of the Industry 4.0. In Trifonov, P. V., & Charaeva, M. V. (Eds.), *Strategies and Trends in Organizational and Project Management. DITEM 2021. Lecture Notes in Networks and Systems* (Vol. 380). Springer. DOI: 10.1007/978-3-030-94245-8_91

Vovchenko, N. G., Andreeva, O. V., Dmitrieva, V. D., Kaptsova, V. S., & Terziev, V. K. (2023d). Technological, Economic, and Social Changes: The Role of End-to-End Technologies. In Makarenko, E. N., Vovchenko, N. G., & Tishchenko, E. N. (Eds.), *Technological Trends in the AI Economy. Smart Innovation, Systems and Technologies* (Vol. 625). Springer. DOI: 10.1007/978-981-19-7411-3_2

Walker, P. (2019). The Theory of the Firm. An overview of the economic mainstream.

Wang, X., & Qi, M. (2024). A Study of the Impact of Digital Transformation on the Risk Level of Commercial Banks. Proceedings of the 2024 3rd International Conference on Artificial Intelligence, Internet and Digital Economy (ICAID 2024). DOI: 10.2991/978-94-6463-490-7_29

What is digital transformation and what are its benefits. (2023). https://ditech.bg/tsifrovata-transformatsiya/

Williamson, O. (1964). *The Economics of Discretionary Behavior: Managerial Objectives in a Theory of the Firm*. Prentice-Hall.

Williamson, O. (1970). *Corporate Control and Business Behavior*. Prentice-Hall.

Williamson, O. E. (1981). The economics of organization: The transaction cost approach. *American Journal of Sociology*, 87(3), 548–577. DOI: 10.1086/227496

Wisskirchen, G., Biacabe, B. T., Bormann, U., Muntz, A., Niehaus, G., Soler, G. J., & von Brauchitsch, B. (2017). Artificial intelligence and robotics and their impact on the workplace. *IBA Global Employment Institute*, 11(5), 49–67.

Worldscience. (2023). Industrial Overcapacity and Duplicate Construction in China: Introduction. https://www.worldscience.com/doi/pdf/10.1142/9789813277281_0001.pdf

Wu, T. (2017). *The attention merchants: The epic scramble to get inside our heads*. Vintage.

Wu, X., Chong, H., Wang, G., & Li, S. (2018). The influence of social capitalism on construction safety behaviors: An exploratory megaproject case study. *Sustainability (Basel)*, 10(9), 3098. DOI: 10.3390/su10093098

Xie, B., Yang, C., Song, W., Song, L., & Wang, H. (2023). The impact of environmental regulation on capacity utilization of China's manufacturing industry: An empirical research based on the sector level. *Ecological Indicators*, 148, 110085. DOI: 10.1016/j.ecolind.2023.110085

Xie, D., Wei, W., & Li, Y. (2023). A General Theory of Digital Economy: The World after Turing. DOI: 10.2139/ssrn.4531884

Xu, X., & Zhao, M. (2020). Data capital and economic growth path. *Economic Research Journal*, 55(10), 38–54.

Yallop, A., & Seraphin, H. (2020). Big data and analytics in tourism and hospitality: Opportunities and risks. *Journal of Tourism Futures*, 6(3), 257–262. DOI: 10.1108/JTF-10-2019-0108

Yeow, A., Soh, C., & Hansen, R. (2018). Aligning with new digital strategy: A dynamic capabilities approach. *The Journal of Strategic Information Systems*, 27(1), 43–58. DOI: 10.1016/j.jsis.2017.09.001

Yoo, Y., Boland, R. J.Jr, Lyytinen, K., & Majchrzak, A. (2012). Organizing for innovation in the digitized world. *Organization Science*, 23(5), 1398–1408. DOI: 10.1287/orsc.1120.0771

Yuniarta, G., Purnamawati, I., & Suwena, K. (2023). The effect of using digital marketing platforms, optimizing potential assets on the inclusive and sustainable economy improvement. *International Journal of Organizational Behavior and Policy*, 2(1), 35–44. DOI: 10.9744/ijobp.2.1.35-44

Zaidan, E. (2015). Tourism shopping and new urban entertainment. *Journal of Vacation Marketing*, 22(1), 29–41. DOI: 10.1177/1356766715589426

Zaidan, E., & Abulibdeh, A. (2020). Master planning and the evolving urban model in the gulf cities: Principles, policies, and practices for the transition to sustainable urbanism. *Planning Practice and Research*, 36(2), 193–215. DOI: 10.1080/02697459.2020.1829278

Zammuto, R. F., Griffith, T. L., Majchrzak, A., Dougherty, D. J., & Faraj, S. (2007). Information technology and the changing fabric of organization. *Organization Science*, 18(5), 749–762. DOI: 10.1287/orsc.1070.0307

Zerrer, N., & Sept, A. (2020). Smart villagers as actors of digital social innovation in rural areas. *Urban Planning*, 5(4), 78–88. DOI: 10.17645/up.v5i4.3183

Zhang, C. (2021). An empirical study on the impact of digital economy development on the upgrading and optimization of industrial structure. *E3S Web of Conferences*, 275, 01046. DOI: 10.1051/e3sconf/202127501046

Zhang, X., Xu, Y. Y., & Ma, L. (2023b). Information Technology Investment and Digital Transformation: The Roles of Digital Transformation Strategy and Top Management. *Business Process Management Journal*, 29(2), 528–549. DOI: 10.1108/BPMJ-06-2022-0254

Zhang, Z. (2023). Digital operational strategies in the post-pandemic era for travel companies: A case study of ctrip. *Highlights in Business Economics and Management*, 23, 521–525. DOI: 10.54097/h0w3ar97

Zhuravleva, I.V. (2014c). Marketing technologies in creatng the image of Sevastopol tourist territory. Bulletn of Kemerovo State University, 2–7(62), 172–176.

Zohar, D., & Zohar, D. (2022). The Tao of Quantum Management. Zero Distance: Management in the Quantum Age, 71-80.

Zuboff, S. (2019). *The age of surveillance capitalism: The fight for a human future at the new frontier of power*. PublicAffairs.

About the Contributors

Meltem Okur Dinçsoy an Associate Professor in macroeconomics at Trakya University, Faculty of Economics and Administrative Sciences. She completed her undergraduate degree at Karadeniz Technical University/Türkiye, Faculty of Economics and Administrative Sciences, Department of Economics. She completed her masters and doctoral degree in Okayama University/Japan, Graduate School of Humanities and Social Sciences, Comparative Economics. In field of macroeconomics, she has many papers in journals, books, book chapters and conference papers in international meetings and experiences on book editing. She gives undergraduate and postgraduate lectures on her research subjects and proficiency. She is also an advisor of the student communities of Trakya Banking Research Society. In addition, she is a member of faculty board of directors.

Hamit Can studied for a BA in Computer Engineering, Nutrition and Dietetics, Business Administration and MA in Economics and PhD in Computer Science, Economics. His research interests include artificial intelligence, machine learning, data science, energy economics, economic growth, sports nutrition, clinical nutrition, phytotherapy. His paper on "The relationship between renewable energy consumption and economic growth: The case of Bulgaria" won the "Outstanding Paper Award" through the Emerald Publishing for International Journal of Energy Sector Management (IJESM) in 2020. In addition to his research, He serves as a referee for numerous professional Web of Science, Scopus indexed journals, including Environmental Science and Pollution Research, International Journal of Energy Sector Management, International Journal of Social Economics, World Journal of Science, Technology and Sustainable Development, Sustainability Accounting, Management and Policy Journal, Environmental Science and Pollution Research. He serves at the editorial board of CSR and Socially Responsible Investing Strategies in Transitioning and Emerging Economies, Three Seas Economic Journal. He has been cited over 130 times in scientific literature(h-index = 4). He also has internationally accredited certificates in these fields, including The British Dietetic Association (BDA), The Academy of Nutrition and Dietetics, Harvard University, Cambridge University, University of Oxford, Stanford University, Yale University, John Hopkins University, Case Western Reverse University, University of Copenhagen, Universite de Lausanne, University of Sydney, Universita Commerciale Luigi Bocconi, University of Colorado and San Diego, McMaster University, University of Minnesota, Emory University, University of Pennsylvania, Ludwig Maximilian Universitat Munchen, University of Edinburg, Illinois University, University of Toronto, Korea Advanced Institute of Science and Technology, University of Michigan, John Hopkins University, University of Florida.

* * *

Olga Valentinovna Andreeva is a PhD in Economics, Dean of the Accounting and Economics Faculty, Head of the Center for Strategic Research of the Socioeconomic Development of the South of Russia at the Rostov State University of Economics, Coordinator of the International Online Laboratory for Research of the Entrepreneurial Ecosystem; Associate Professor of the Finance Department; Public Representative of the Agency for Strategic Initiatives on Ecology and Climate. In 1996, she graduated from the Rostov State University of Economics with a degree in Finance and Credit. In 2002, she defended her PhD dissertation in the Dissertation Council of the Rostov State University of Economics on the topic: “Sources of Financing for Medical Services in Modern Russia”. In 2006, she received the academic title of Associate Professor. She has 28 years of teaching experience, and she has worked at the Finance Department since 1996. Dr. Andreeva's research interests include sustainable development, green economy and the ESG agenda, entrepreneurship (social, youth, technological). She is the author of over 200 scientific publications.

Enver Erdinç Dinçsoy is an Associate Professor at the Faculty of Applied Sciences at Trakya University. He completed his undergraduate degree at Karadeniz Technical University, Faculty of Economics and Administrative Sciences, Department of Business Administration. He also completed his master’s and doctoral degrees at the Okayama University/Japan, “Department of Natural Sciences and Technology”. In the field of economics, he has studied some research topics which are ‘development’, ‘banking and finance’, ‘income distribution’, ‘spatial analysis', and 'environmental economics and policies’. In this context, He has scientific articles published in various domestic and international scientific journals, books and book chapters, conferences, and seminars. He gives undergraduate and postgraduate courses within the scope of his research subjects and proficiency.

Michal Fabuš, PhD, is an associated professor of Management, obtained at Presov University and PhD. in International Economics Relations, obtained at University of Economics in Bratislava. Vice-rector for Foreign Affairs, Head of Department of Economics and Finance, Bratislava University of Economics and Management (BUEM). Special interest in International Economics Relations, International business, and Foreign Direct Investment.

Marin Georgiev is an Associate Professor from Georgi Rakovski Military Academy, Sofia, Bulgaria. Ph.D. in Organisation and Management at Vasil Levski National Military University, Veliko Tarnovo, Bulgaria. Assoc. Prof. Georgiev has over 200 scientific papers, articles, and reports in Bulgarian, Russian, and English published in scientific journals and proceedings of international conferences, 2 monographs in Bulgarian, and 1 textbook. There are more than 40 publications in the referenced systems of Web of Science and Scopus. His research interests are in the areas of Economics, Education, and National security.

Seda Karagoz Zeren is a seasoned academic and researcher with a multifaceted background in mathematics, business, and tourism. She holds three bachelor's degrees in mathematics, business administration, and tourism and hospitality management, along with dual master's degrees in business administration and applied mathematics. She earned her Ph.D. in Business Administration, completing the first doctoral dissertation in Türkiye focused on applying blockchain technology within the tourism sector. With over a decade of academic experience, Dr. Karagoz Zeren served as a faculty member at Trakya University, Türkiye, from 2013 to 2023. She has recently been invited as a Visiting Postdoctoral Research Scholar at the University of Massachusetts Amherst in the United States. Dr. Karagoz Zeren has served as a researcher and project leader on numerous national and international initiatives, notably including EU-funded projects and TUBITAK-supported studies within Türkiye. Her research portfolio includes more than 30 national and international academic publications with expertise spanning blockchain technology, tourism, sustainability, mathematics, accounting, and finance.

Zhivo Petrov is Associate professor in the Defence Advanced Research Institute Rakovski National Defence College-Sofia. He received his Masters degree in "Radio and Television Engineering" in 1994 from Bulgarian Air Force Academy "Georgi Benkovski" and Ph.D. degree in "Radiolocation and radionavigation" in 2011. He is the author of one monograph and more than 7 0 articles, of which 28 are Scopus and Web of Science. His research interests are in the field of radiolocation, navigation and avionics.

Ninel Seniuk, PhD, is an Associate Professor of International Political Economy, obtained at NRU HSE University and PhD in Economics obtained at MGIMO University. Highly qualified researcher at Bratislava University of Economics and Management (BUEM). Researching Chinese Foreign Direct Investment in the EU: drivers and determinants. Special interest in International Business, International Economic Relations, International Relations, International Political Economy, Global Political Economy, Foreign Direct Investment, Global Value Chains, Emerging Markets and BRICS+ countries, EU and Visegrad Economies (V4).

Simeon Simeonov is a Ph.D. in Organisation and Management at Vasil Levski National Military University, Veliko Tarnovo, Bulgaria. Simeon Simeonov has over 40 scientific papers, articles, and reports in Bulgarian, Russian, and English published in scientific journals and proceedings of international conferences. There are more than 20 publications in the referenced systems of Web of Science and Scopus. His research interests are in the areas of Economics, Education, and Medicine.

Venelin Terziev is a Professor from Angel Kanchev Rousse University – Bulgaria, Vasil Levski National Military University, Veliko Tarnovo, Bulgaria, and University of Telecommunications and Post, Sofia, Bulgaria. D.Sc. in Economics – "Organization and management in the sphere of immaterial production (defence and national security)" at the Vasil Levski National Military University – Veliko Tarnovo, Bulgaria; D.Sc. in Economics – "Finance, currency, credit, and insurance (social security)" at Dimitar Tzenov Academy of Economics – Svishtov, Bulgaria; D.Sc. in Social Activities – "Organization and management of social activities" at Burgas Free University – Burgas, Bulgaria; Ph.D. in Political economy at Chernorisets Hrabar Varna Free University – Bulgaria. Full Member of the Russian Academy of Natural History, Moscow, Russia. Prof. Terziev has over 2000 scientific papers, articles, and reports in Bulgarian, Russian, English, and French published in scientific journals and proceedings of international conferences; 40 monographs in English and Russian; 4 monographs in Bulgarian and 4 textbooks and handbooks.

Omar Vargas-González is professor, research assistant and former Head of Computer Systems Department at Tecnológico Nacional de México Campus Ciudad Guzmán, professor at Telematic Engineering at Centro Universitario del Sur Universidad de Guadalajara with a master degree in Computer Systems. Has been trained in Innovation and Multidisciplinary Entrepreneurship at Arizona State University (2018) and a Generation of Ecosystems of Innovation, Entrepreneurship and Sustainability for Jalisco course by Harvard University T.H. Chan School of Health. At present conduct research on diverse fields such as Entrepreneurship,

Economy, Statistics, Mathematics and Information and Computer Sciences. Has collaborated in the publication of many scientific articles and conducted diverse Innovation and Technological Development projects.

Elizabeth Yoneva holds a Ph.D. degree in Political Science. She is Associate Professor in the International Relations Department at the Faculty of International Economics and Politics, University of National and World Economy, Sofia (Bulgaria). Her teaching activity and research interests include energy security, European integration and regional cooperation in the Black Sea zone and Central Asia.She is a member of the editorial board of the "Bulgarian Journal of International Economics and Politics" and of the scientific board of "The Scientific Bulletin" of Fan S. Noli University, Albania.

Index

T

V

www.ingramcontent.com/pod-product-compliance
Lightning Source LLC
LaVergne TN
LVHW080343011026
849161LV00009B/2167
9798369394359